Shojo Beat

Yurara

Volume 4

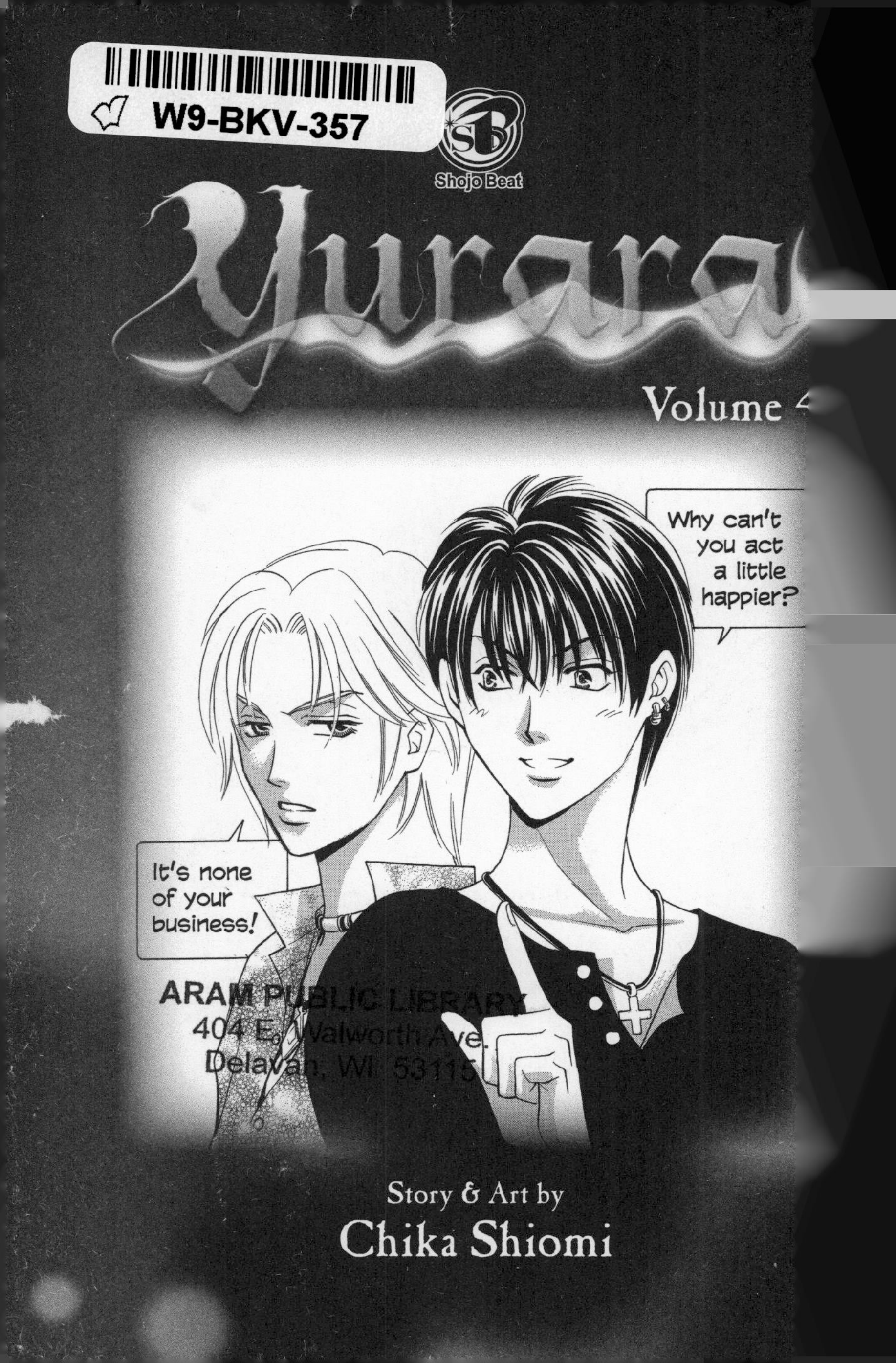
Why can't you act a little happier?
It's none of your business!

Story & Art by
Chika Shiomi

Contents

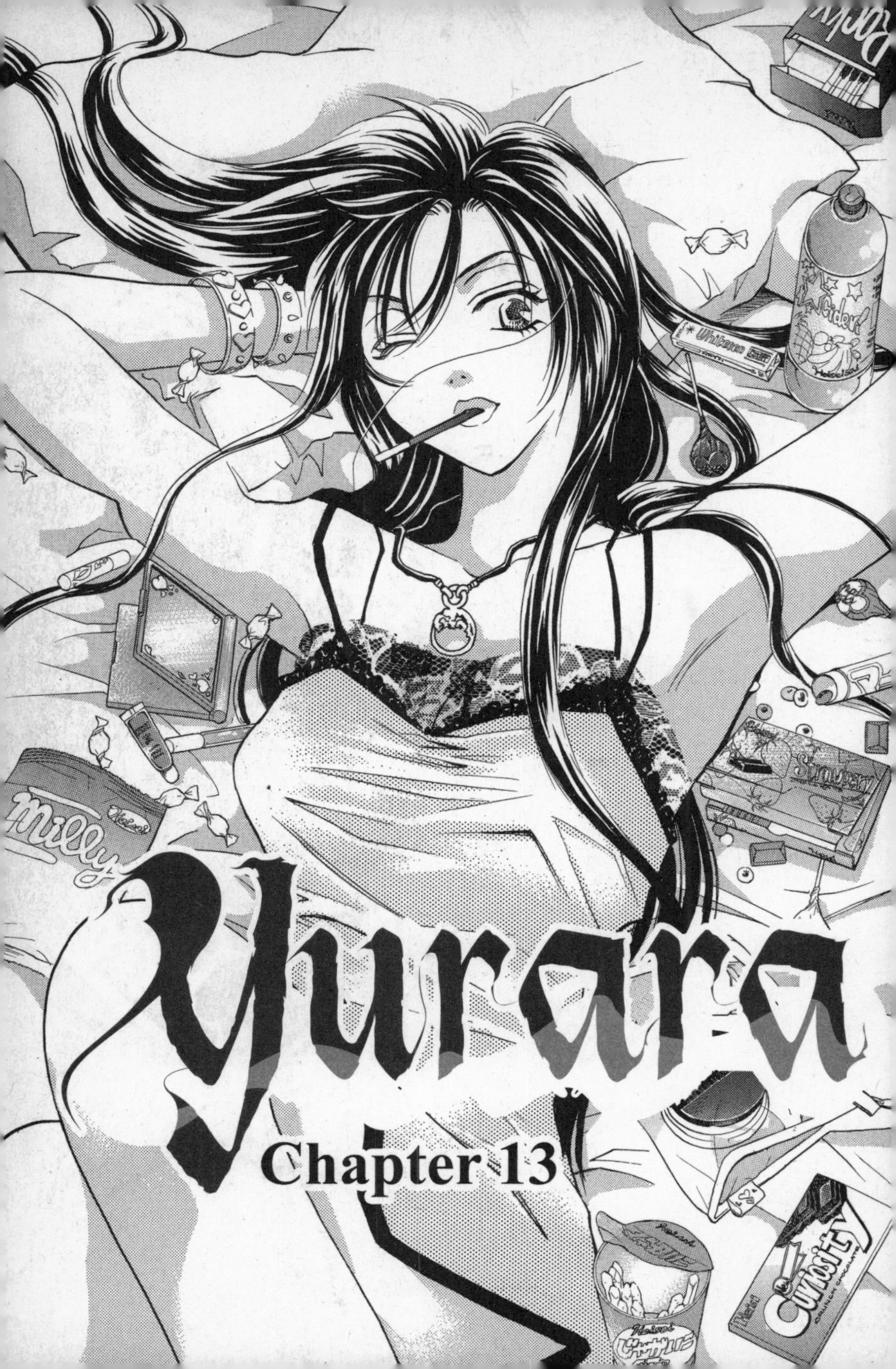
Yurara
Chapter 13
Milly
Curiosity

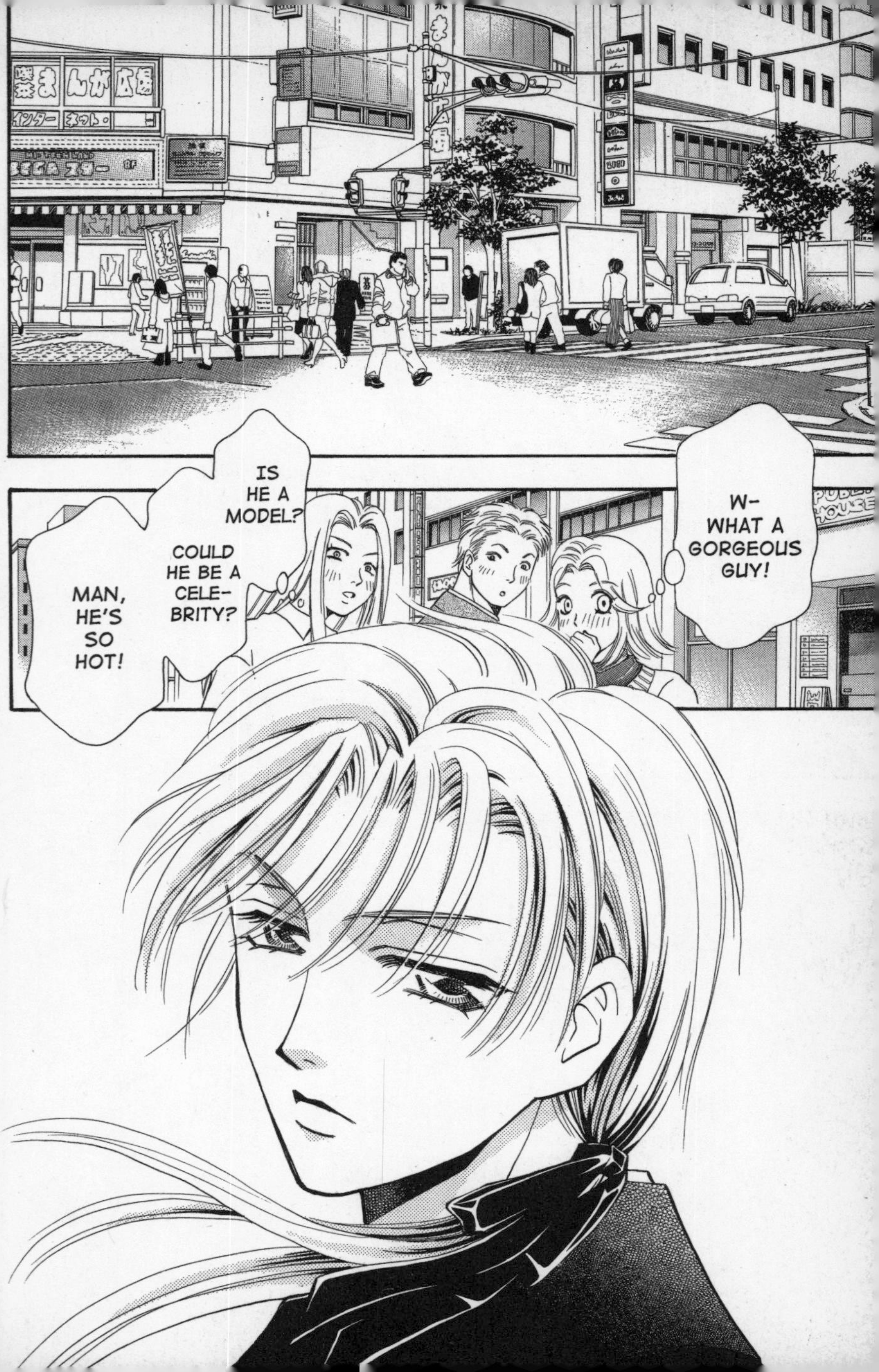
W- WHAT A GORGEOUS GUY!
IS HE A MODEL?
COULD HE BE A CELE-BRITY?
MAN, HE'S SO HOT!

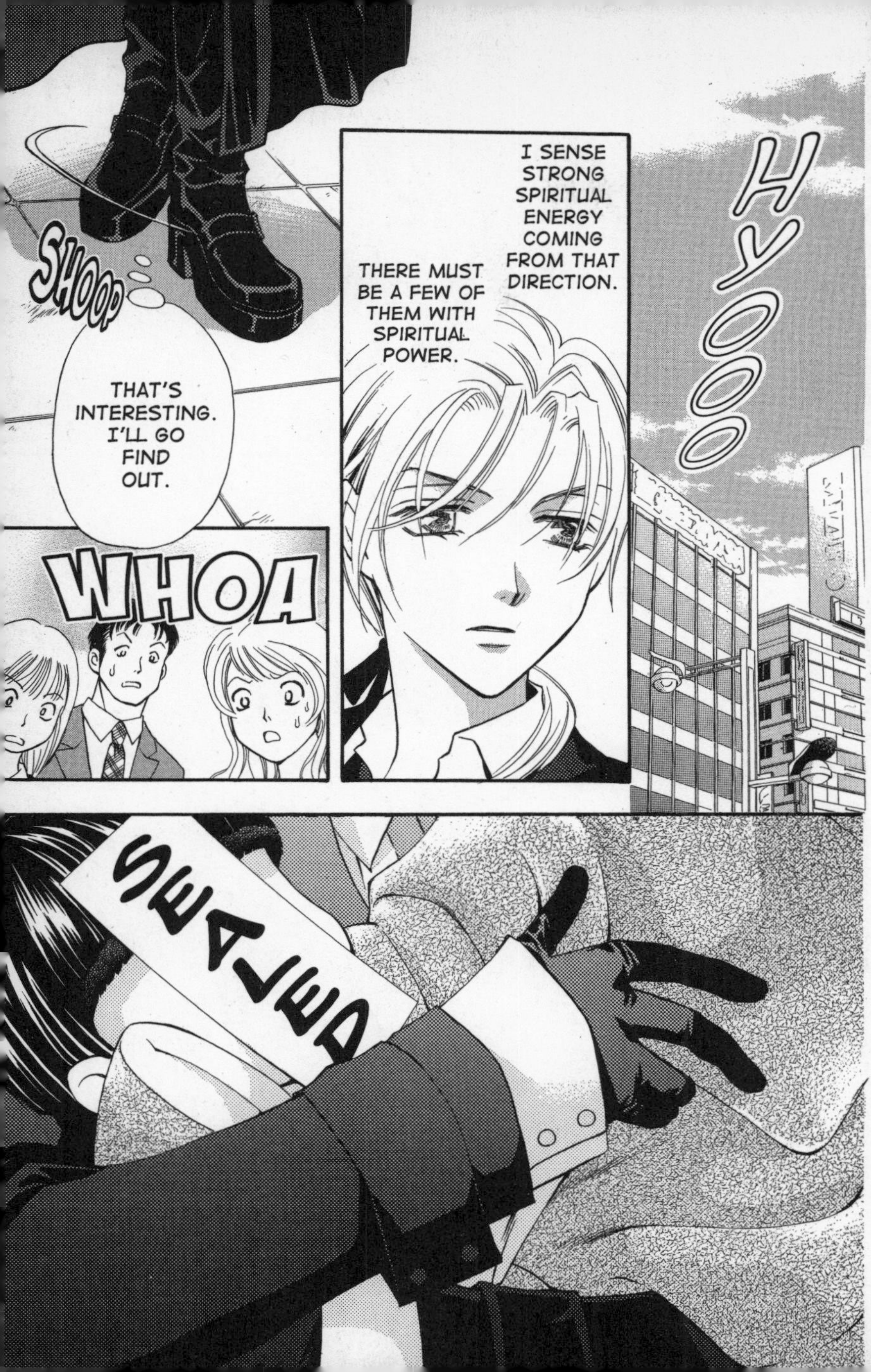
HYOOOO
I SENSE STRONG SPIRITUAL ENERGY COMING FROM THAT DIRECTION.
THERE MUST BE A FEW OF THEM WITH SPIRITUAL POWER.
SHOOP
THAT'S INTERESTING. I'LL GO FIND OUT.
WHOA
SEALED

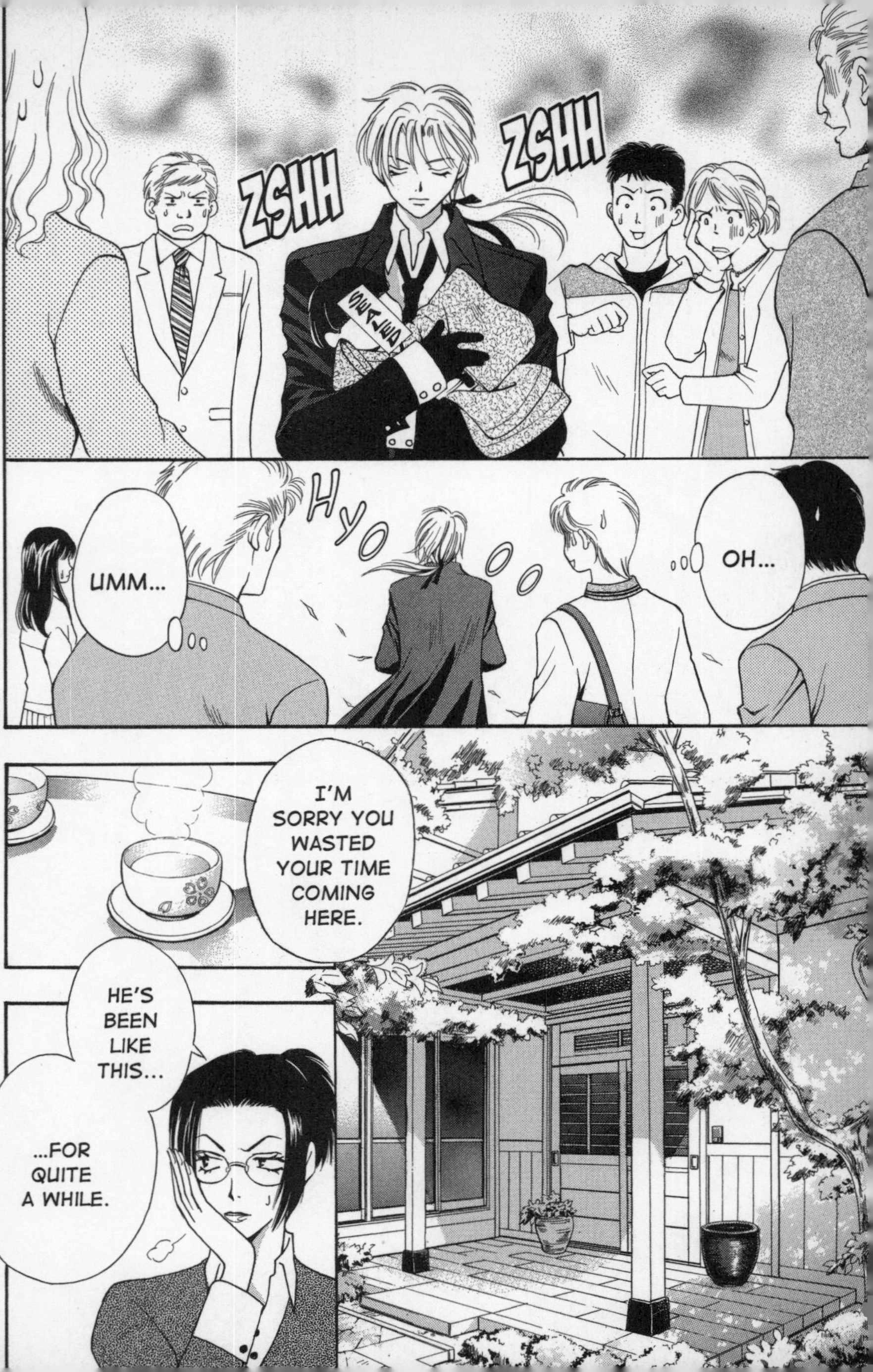
ZSHH
ZSHH
OH...
HYOOOO
UMM...
I'M SORRY YOU WASTED YOUR TIME COMING HERE.
HE'S BEEN LIKE THIS...
...FOR QUITE A WHILE.

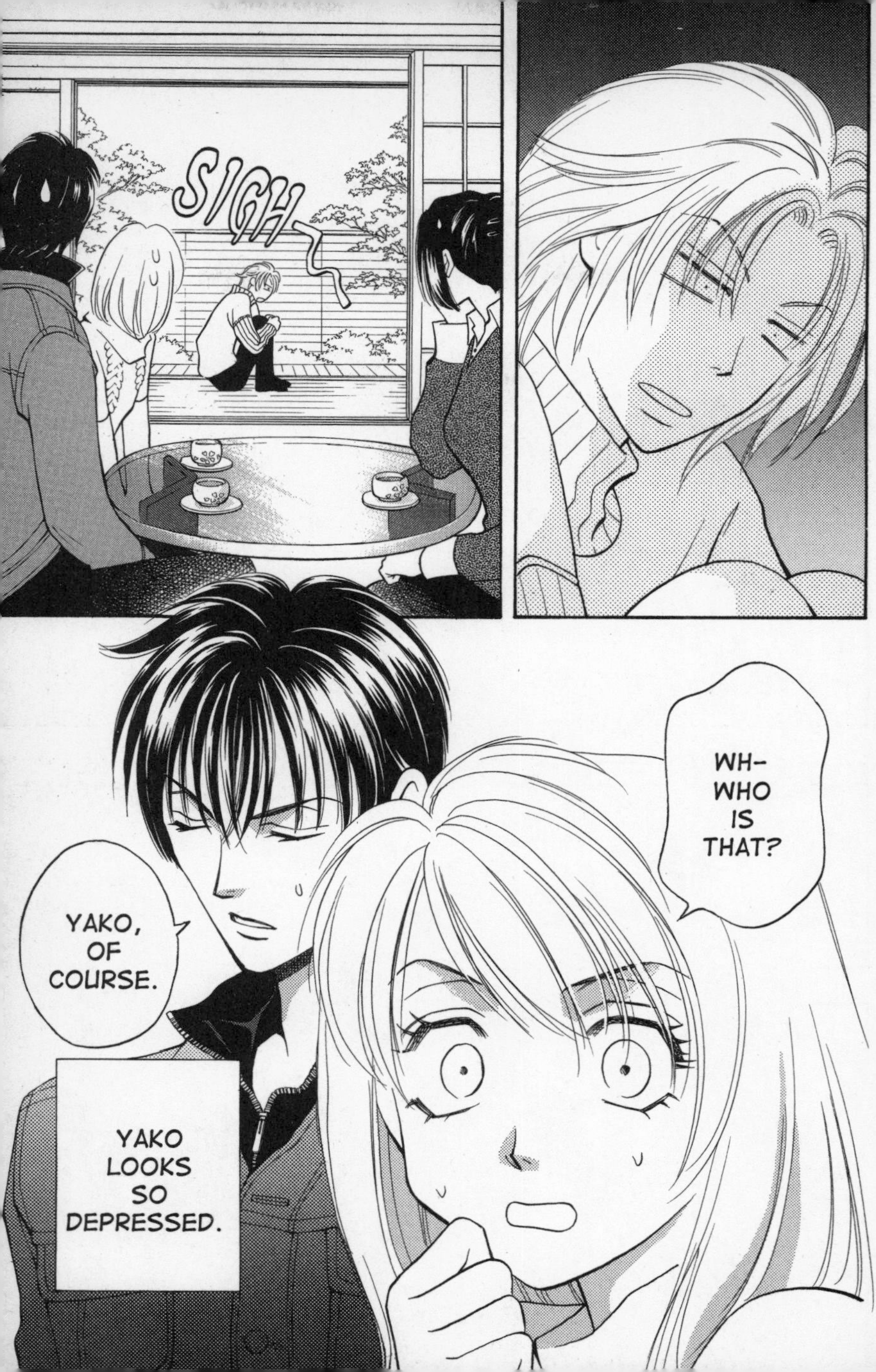
SIGH
WH- WHO IS THAT?
YAKO, OF COURSE.
YAKO LOOKS SO DEPRESSED.

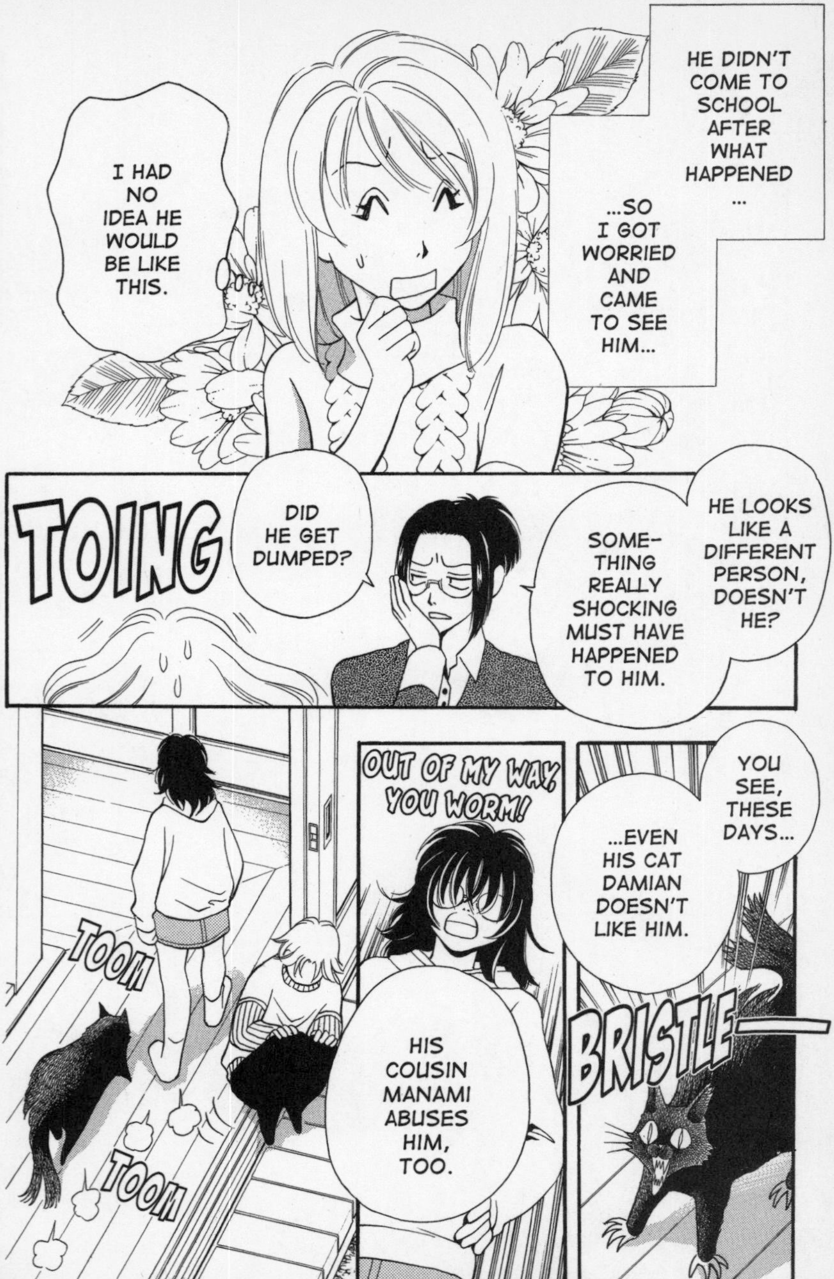
HE DIDN'T COME TO SCHOOL AFTER WHAT HAPPENED ...
...SO I GOT WORRIED AND CAME TO SEE HIM...
I HAD NO IDEA HE WOULD BE LIKE THIS.
HE LOOKS LIKE A DIFFERENT PERSON, DOESN'T HE?
SOME-THING REALLY SHOCKING MUST HAVE HAPPENED TO HIM.
DID HE GET DUMPED?
TOING
YOU SEE, THESE DAYS...
...EVEN HIS CAT DAMIAN DOESN'T LIKE HIM.
BRISTLE—
OUT OF MY WAY, YOU WORM!
HIS COUSIN MANAMI ABUSES HIM, TOO.
TOOM
TOOM

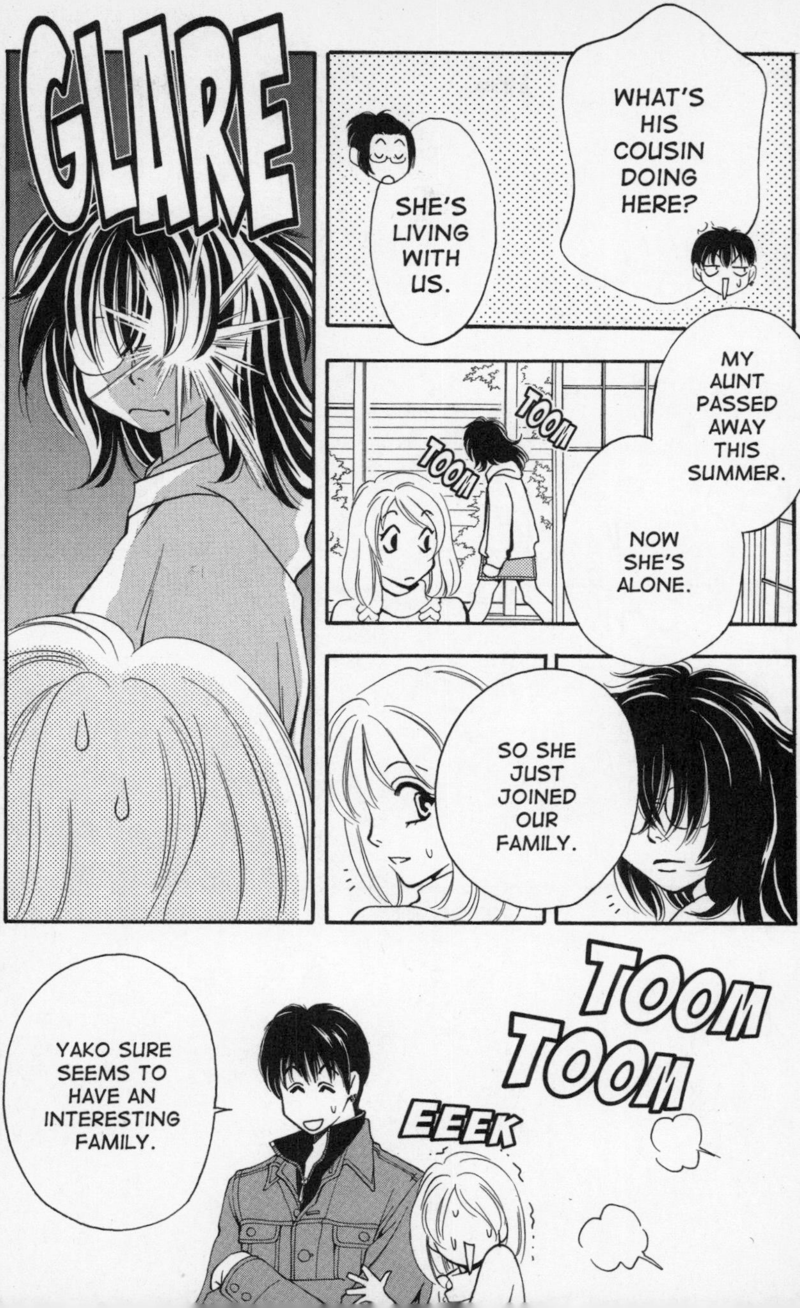
WHAT'S HIS COUSIN DOING HERE?
SHE'S LIVING WITH US.
MY AUNT PASSED AWAY THIS SUMMER.
TOOM
TOOM
NOW SHE'S ALONE.
SO SHE JUST JOINED OUR FAMILY.
GLARE
TOOM TOOM
EEEK
YAKO SURE SEEMS TO HAVE AN INTERESTING FAMILY.

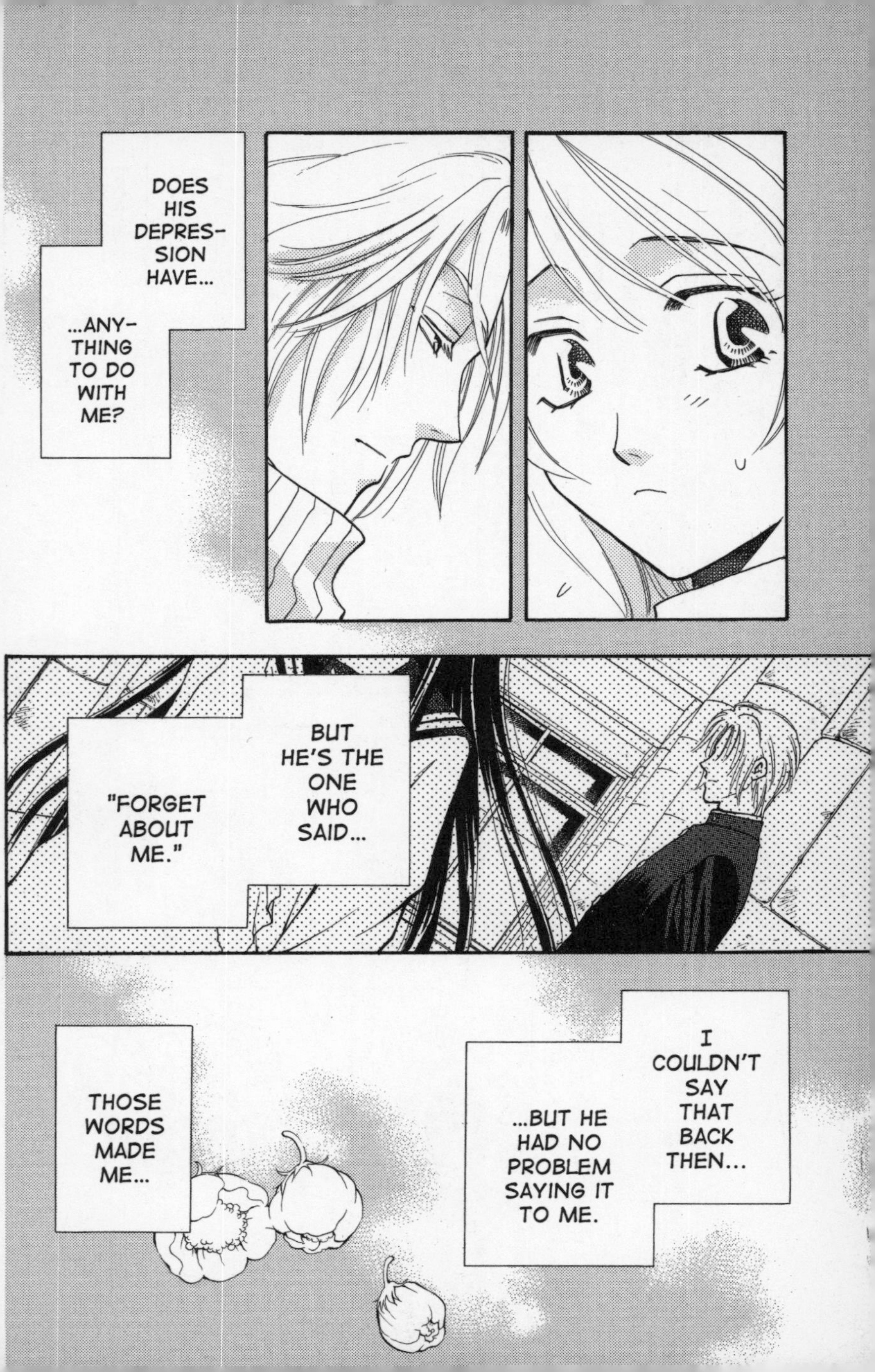
DOES HIS DEPRES-SION HAVE...
...ANY-THING TO DO WITH ME?
BUT HE'S THE ONE WHO SAID...
"FORGET ABOUT ME."
I COULDN'T SAY THAT BACK THEN...
...BUT HE HAD NO PROBLEM SAYING IT TO ME.
THOSE WORDS MADE ME...

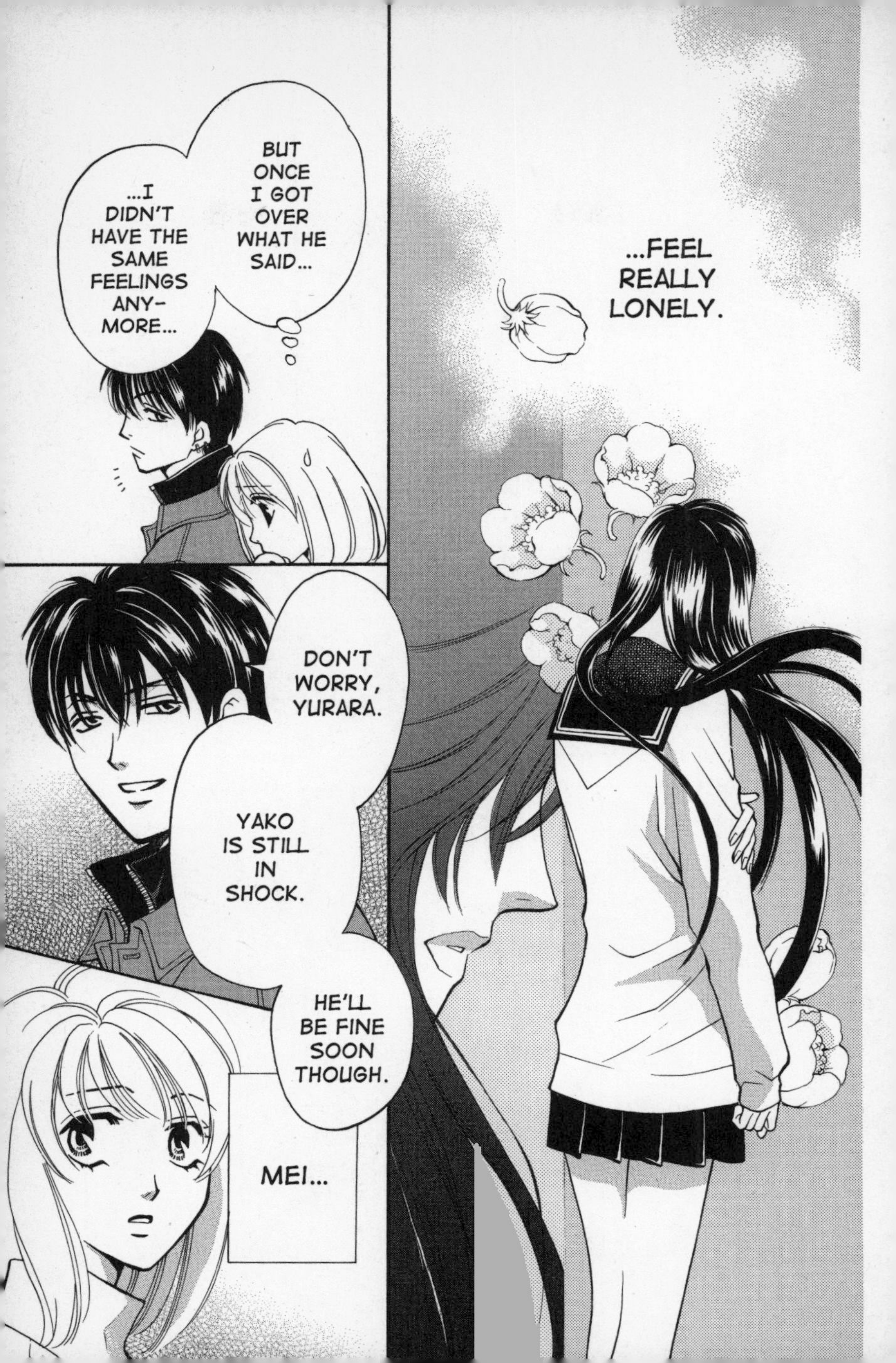
...FEEL REALLY LONELY.
BUT ONCE I GOT OVER WHAT HE SAID...
...I DIDN'T HAVE THE SAME FEELINGS ANYMORE...
DON'T WORRY, YURARA.
YAKO IS STILL IN SHOCK.
HE'LL BE FINE SOON THOUGH.
MEI...

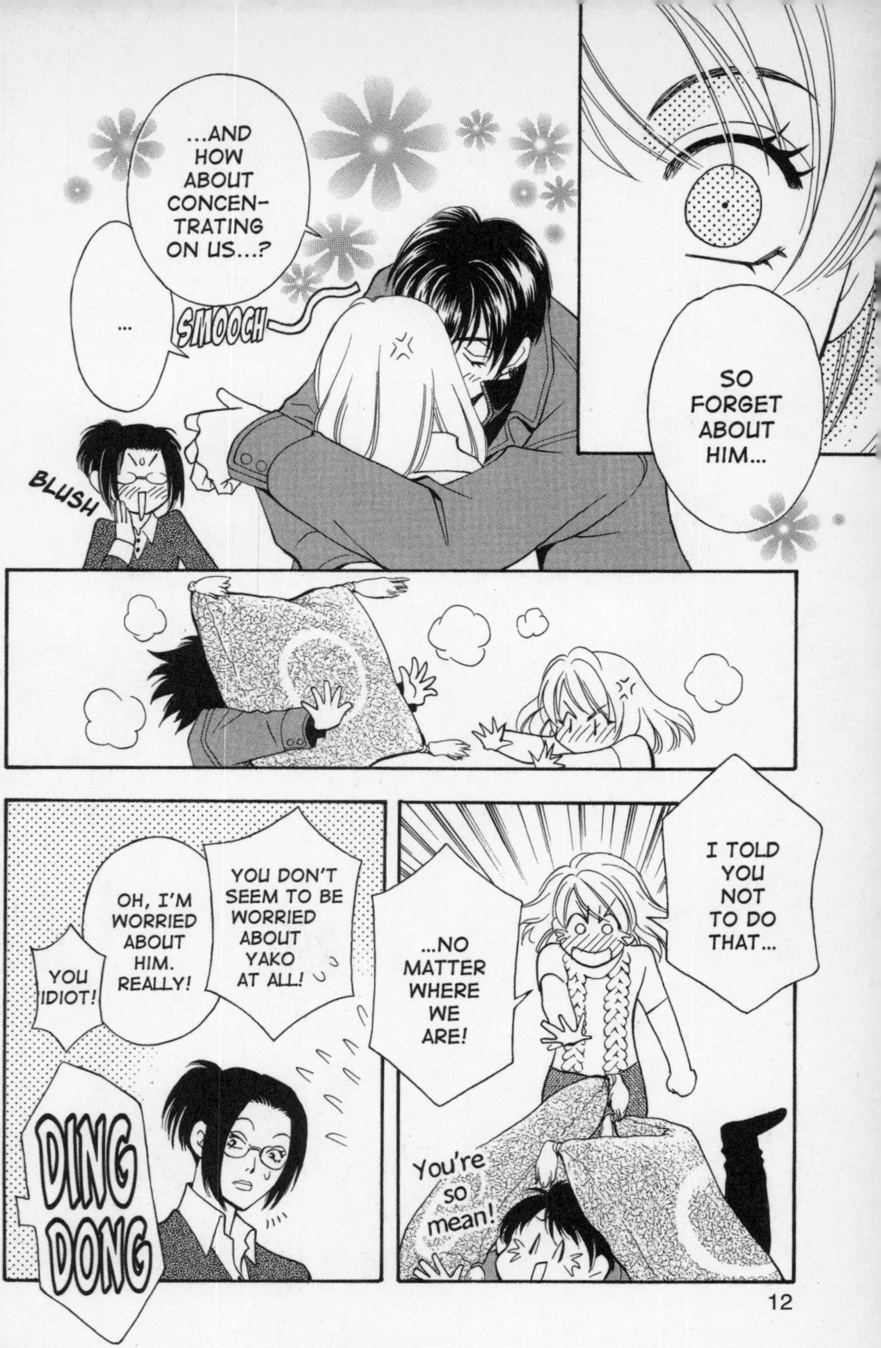
SO FORGET ABOUT HIM...
...AND HOW ABOUT CONCENTRATING ON US...?
SMOOCH
...
BLUSH
I TOLD YOU NOT TO DO THAT...
...NO MATTER WHERE WE ARE!
You're so mean!
YOU DON'T SEEM TO BE WORRIED ABOUT YAKO AT ALL!
OH, I'M WORRIED ABOUT HIM. REALLY!
YOU IDIOT!
DING DONG

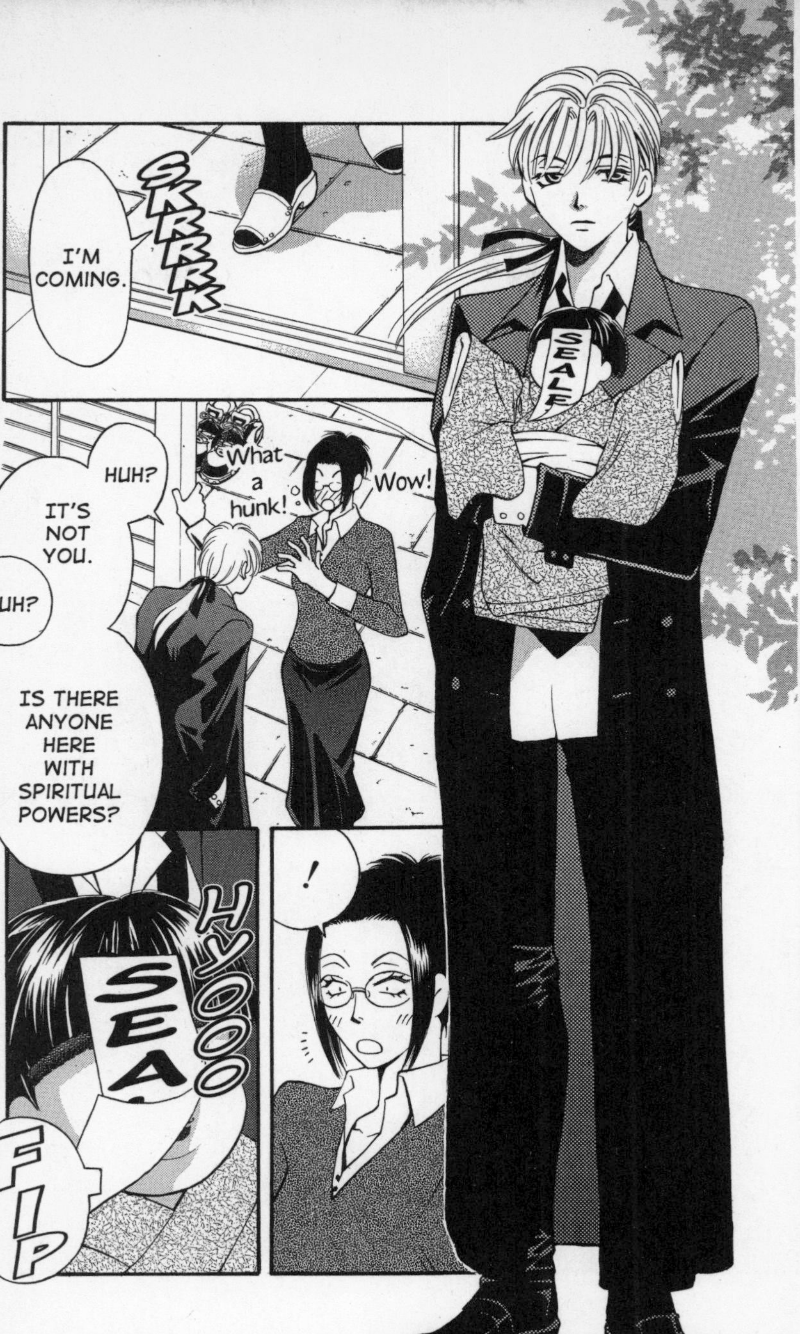
SEALF
SKRRRK
I'M COMING.
Wow!
What a hunk!
HUH? IT'S NOT YOU.
HUH?
IS THERE ANYONE HERE WITH SPIRITUAL POWERS?
!
HYOOOO
SEA
FIP

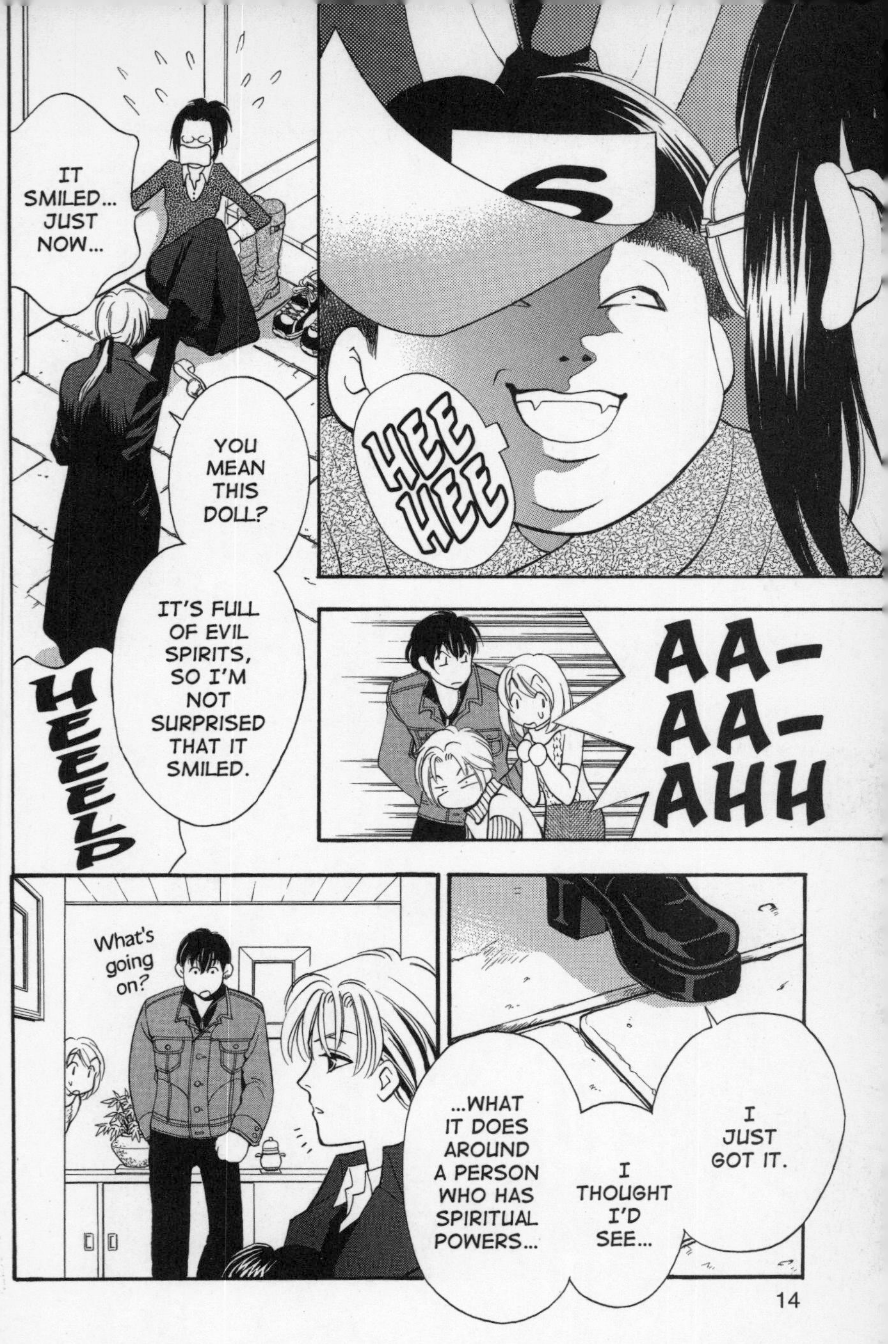
HEE HEE
AA-AA-AHH
IT SMILED... JUST NOW...
YOU MEAN THIS DOLL?
IT'S FULL OF EVIL SPIRITS, SO I'M NOT SURPRISED THAT IT SMILED.
HEEELP
I JUST GOT IT.
I THOUGHT I'D SEE...
...WHAT IT DOES AROUND A PERSON WHO HAS SPIRITUAL POWERS...
What's going on?

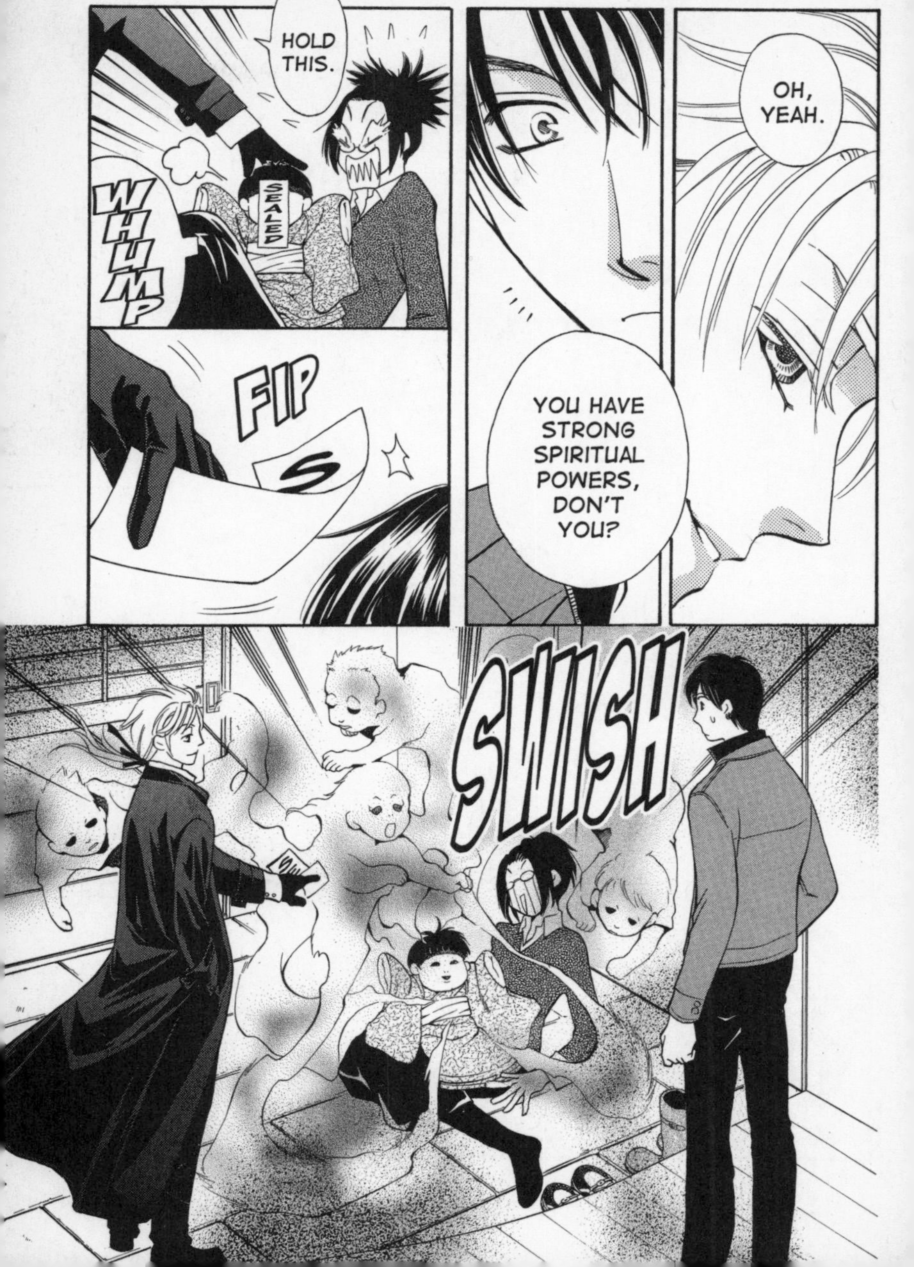
OH, YEAH.
YOU HAVE STRONG SPIRITUAL POWERS, DON'T YOU?
HOLD THIS.
SEALED
WHUMP
FIP
S
SWISH

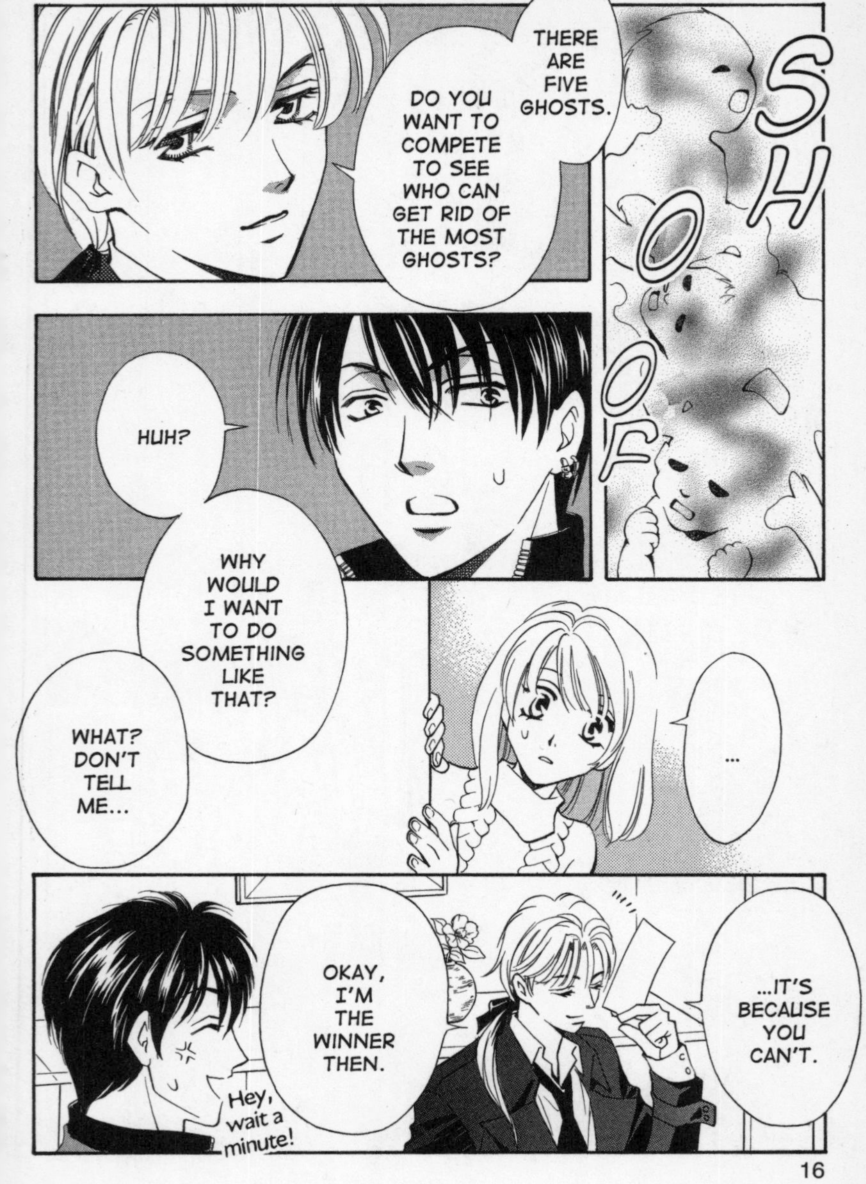
SHOOOF
THERE ARE FIVE GHOSTS.
DO YOU WANT TO COMPETE TO SEE WHO CAN GET RID OF THE MOST GHOSTS?
HUH?
WHY WOULD I WANT TO DO SOMETHING LIKE THAT?
...
WHAT? DON'T TELL ME...
...IT'S BECAUSE YOU CAN'T.
OKAY, I'M THE WINNER THEN.
Hey, wait a minute!

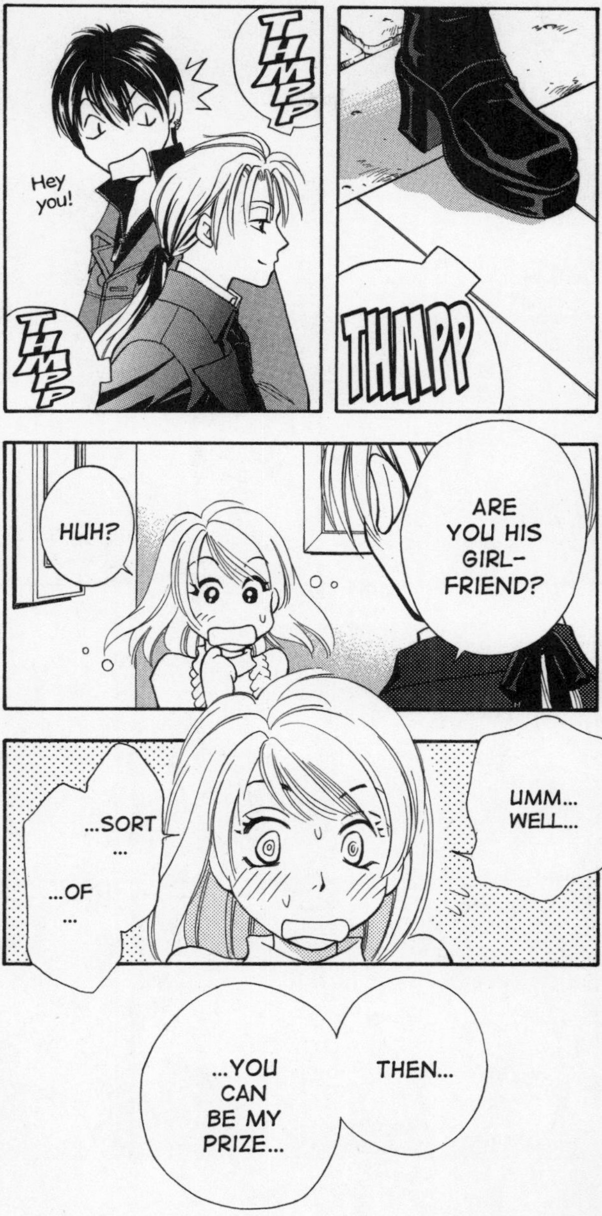
THMPP
THMPP
Hey you!
THMPP
ARE YOU HIS GIRL-FRIEND?
HUH?
UMM... WELL...
...SORT ...
...OF ...
THEN...
...YOU CAN BE MY PRIZE...

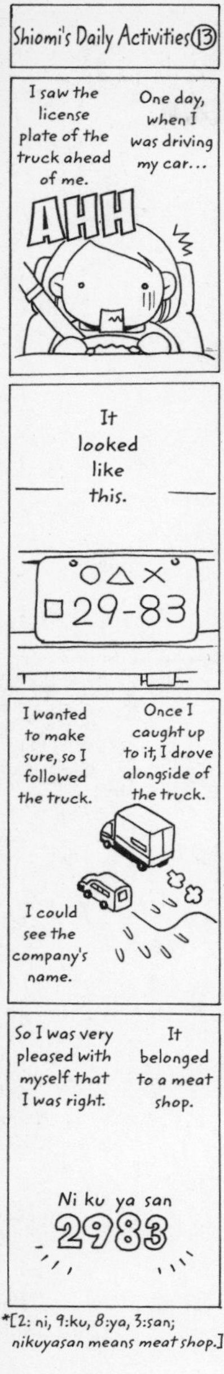
Shiomi's Daily Activities ⑬
One day, when I was driving my car...
I saw the license plate of the truck ahead of me.
AHH
It looked like this.
○△×
□29-83
Once I caught up to it, I drove alongside of the truck.
I wanted to make sure, so I followed the truck.
I could see the company's name.
It belonged to a meat shop.
So I was very pleased with myself that I was right.
Ni ku ya san
2983

*[2: ni, 9:ku, 8:ya, 3:san; nikuyasan means meat shop.]

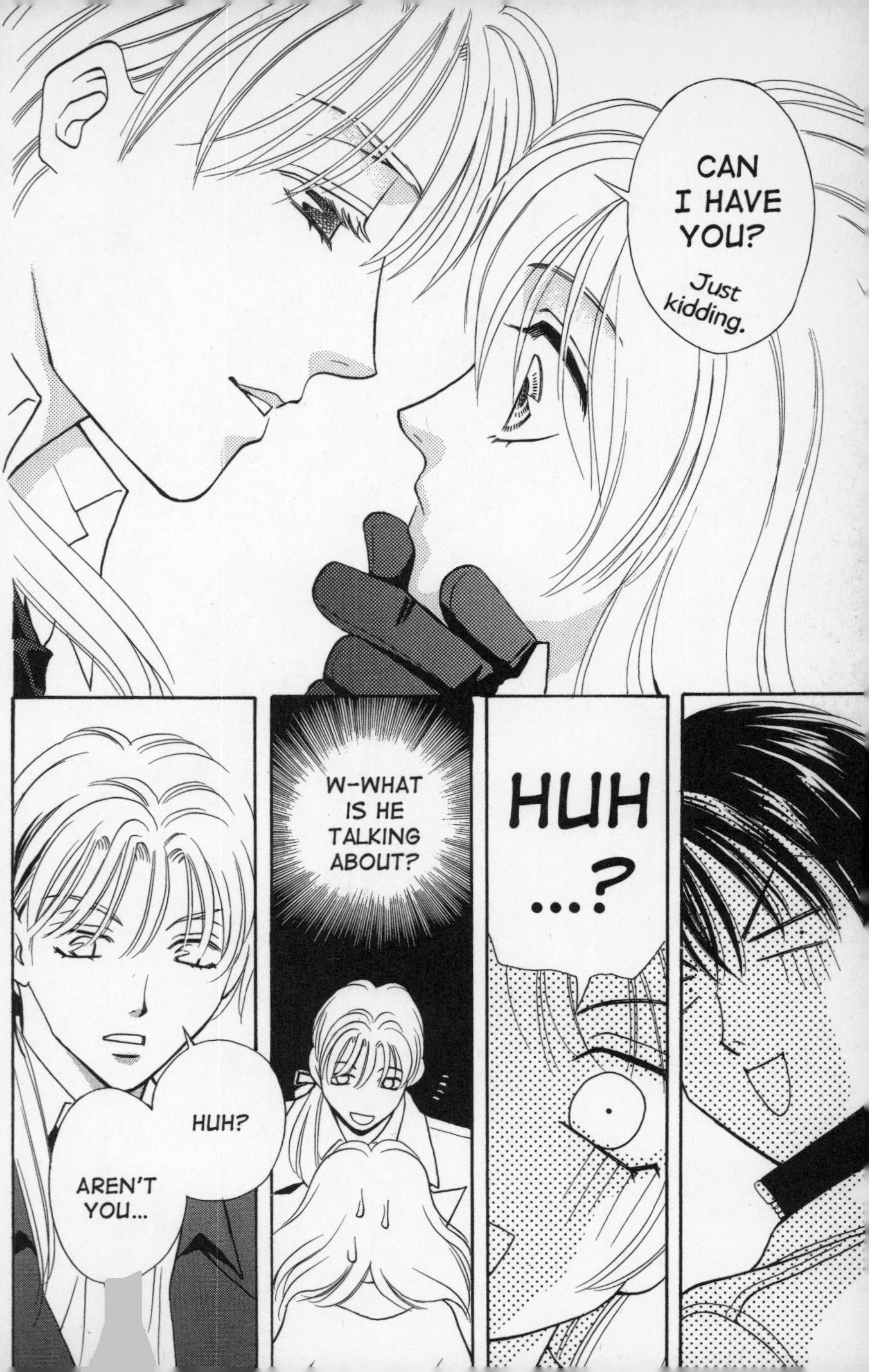
CAN I HAVE YOU?
Just kidding.
HUH ...?
W-WHAT IS HE TALKING ABOUT?
HUH?
AREN'T YOU...

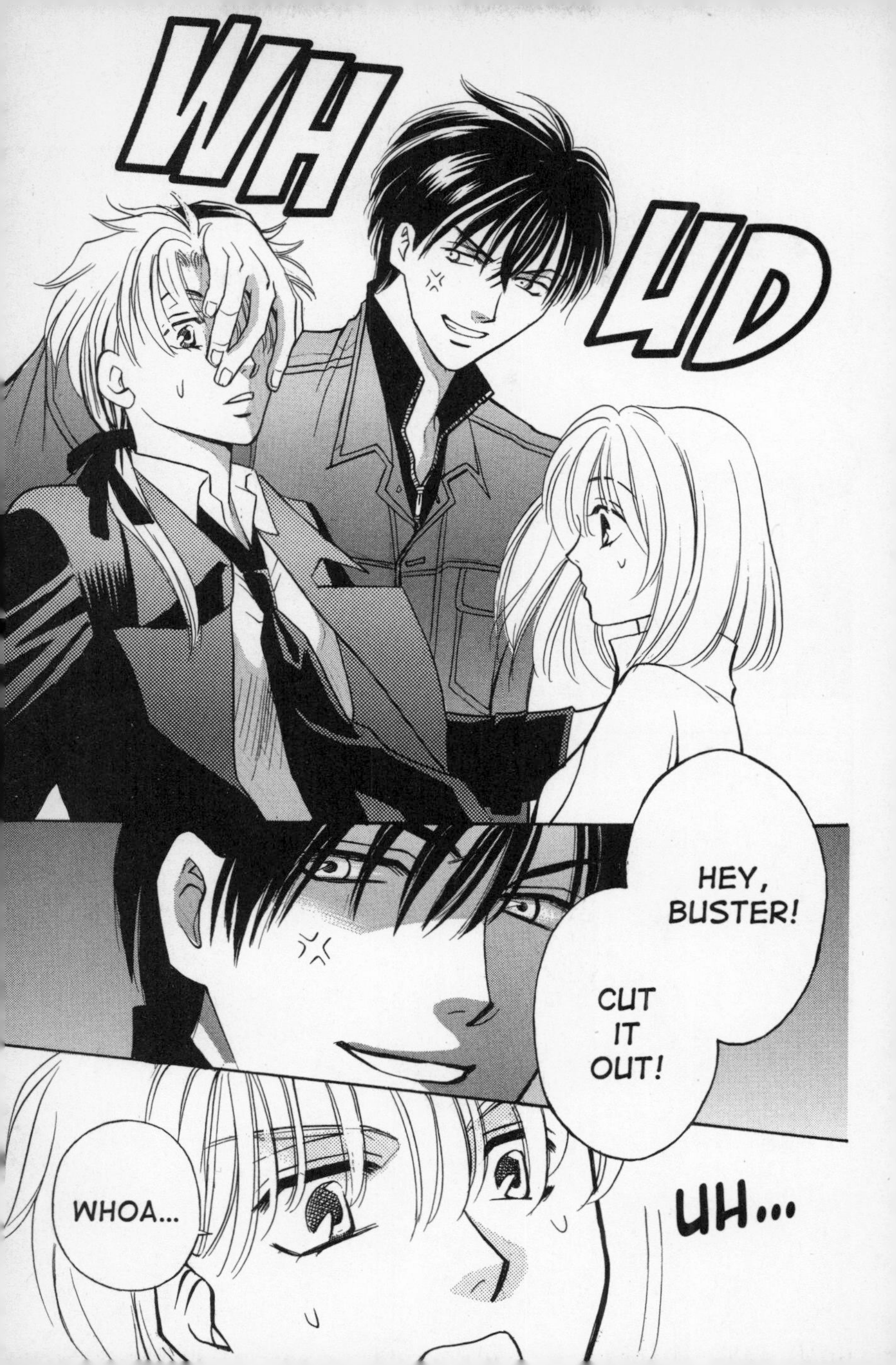
WHUD
HEY, BUSTER!
CUT IT OUT!
UH...
WHOA...

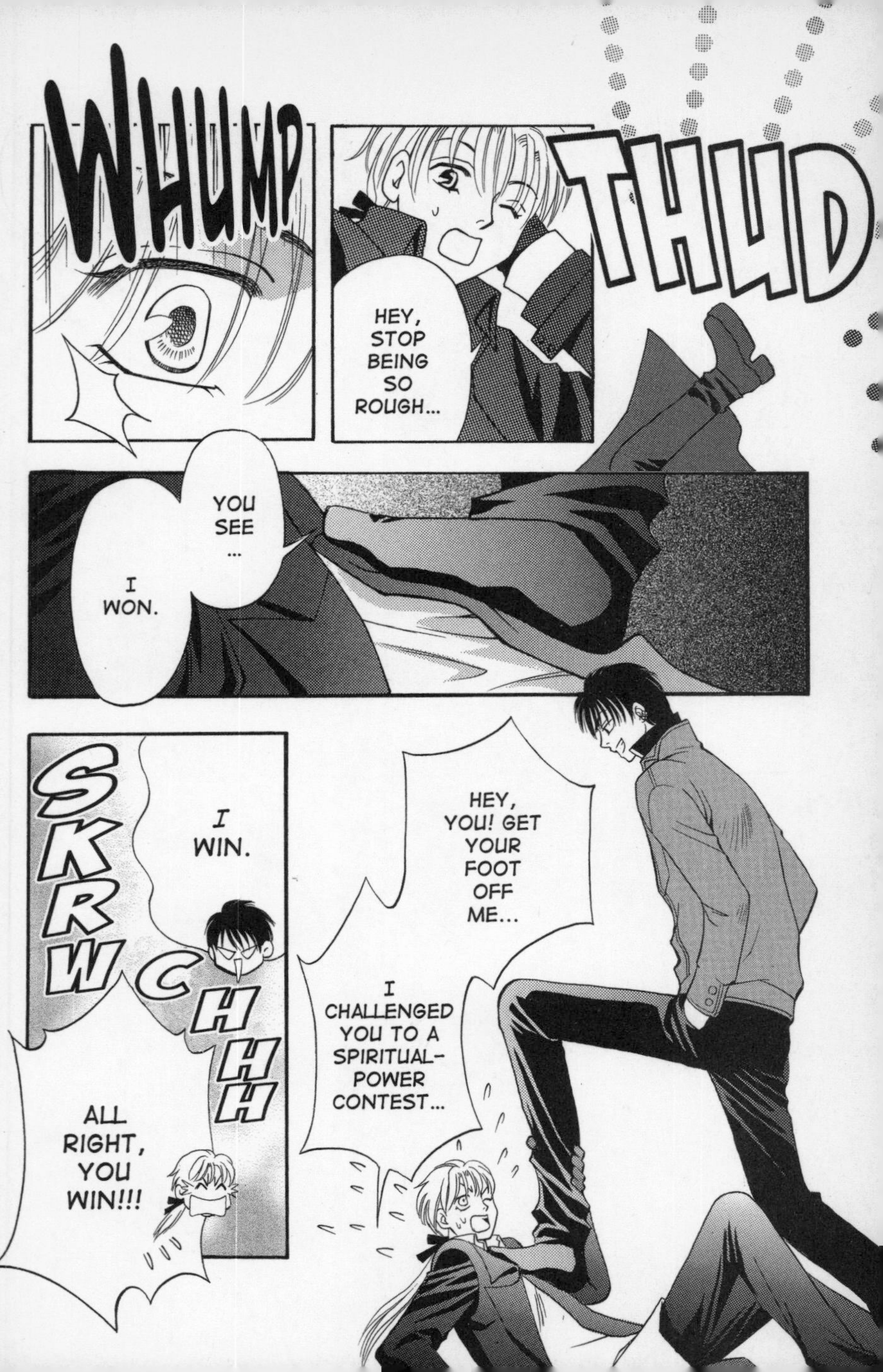
THUD
HEY, STOP BEING SO ROUGH...
WHUMP
YOU SEE... I WON.
HEY, YOU! GET YOUR FOOT OFF ME...
I CHALLENGED YOU TO A SPIRITUAL-POWER CONTEST...
I WIN.
SKRWCHHH
ALL RIGHT, YOU WIN!!!

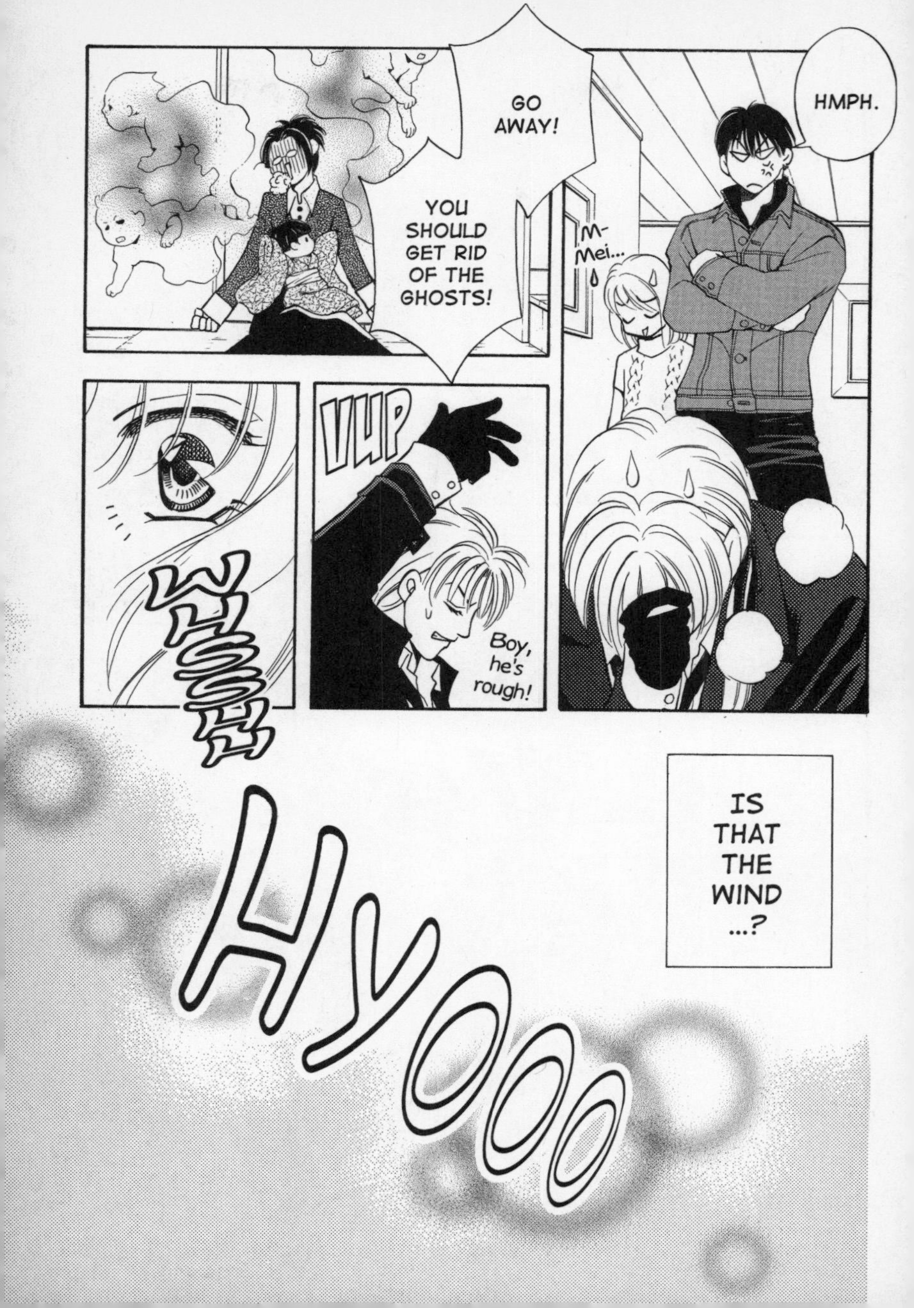
HMPH.
M-Mei...
GO AWAY!
YOU SHOULD GET RID OF THE GHOSTS!
VUP
Boy, he's rough!
WHSSHH
IS THAT THE WIND ...?
HYOOO

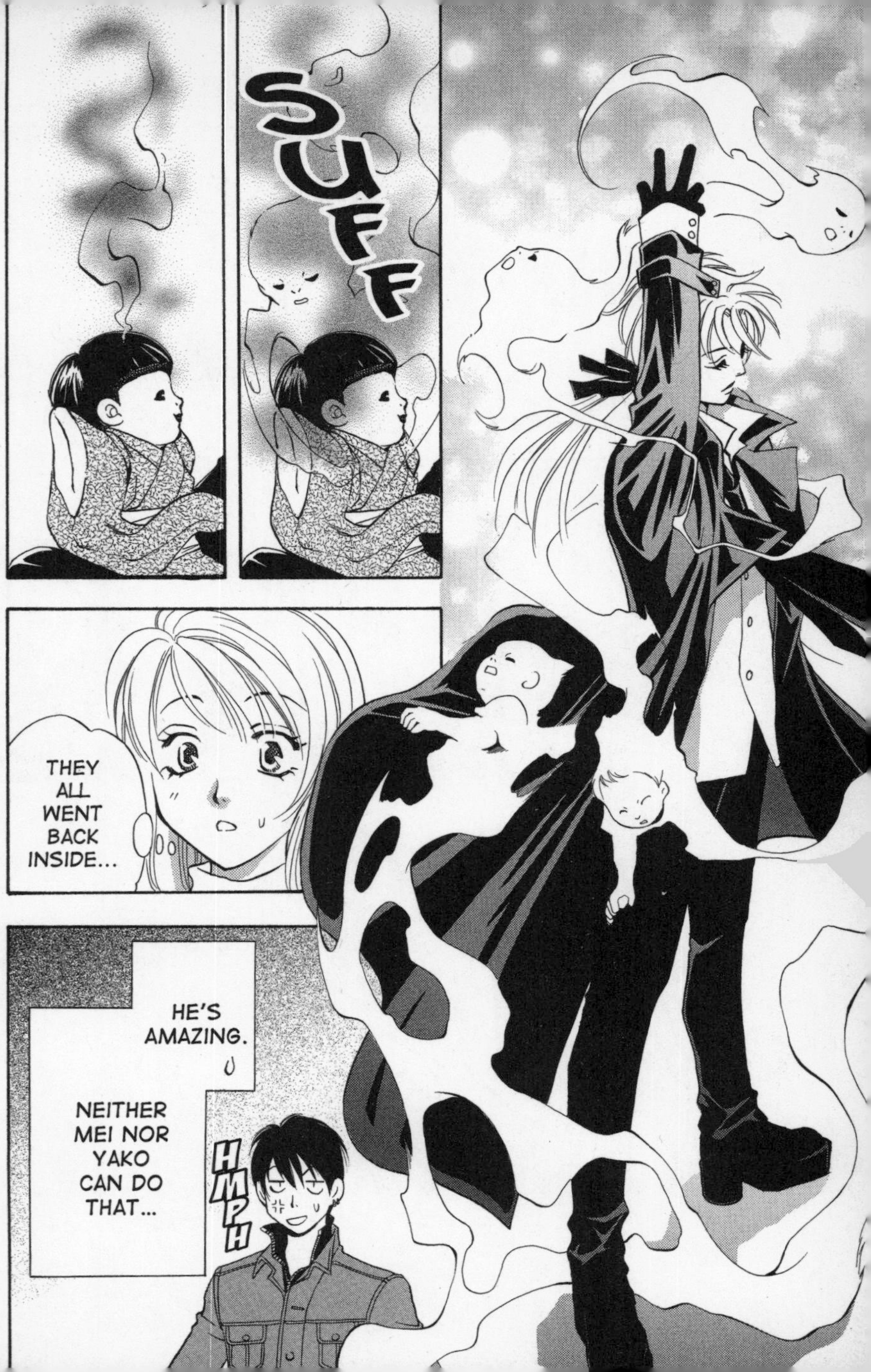
SUFF
THEY ALL WENT BACK INSIDE...
HE'S AMAZING.
HMPH
NEITHER MEI NOR YAKO CAN DO THAT...

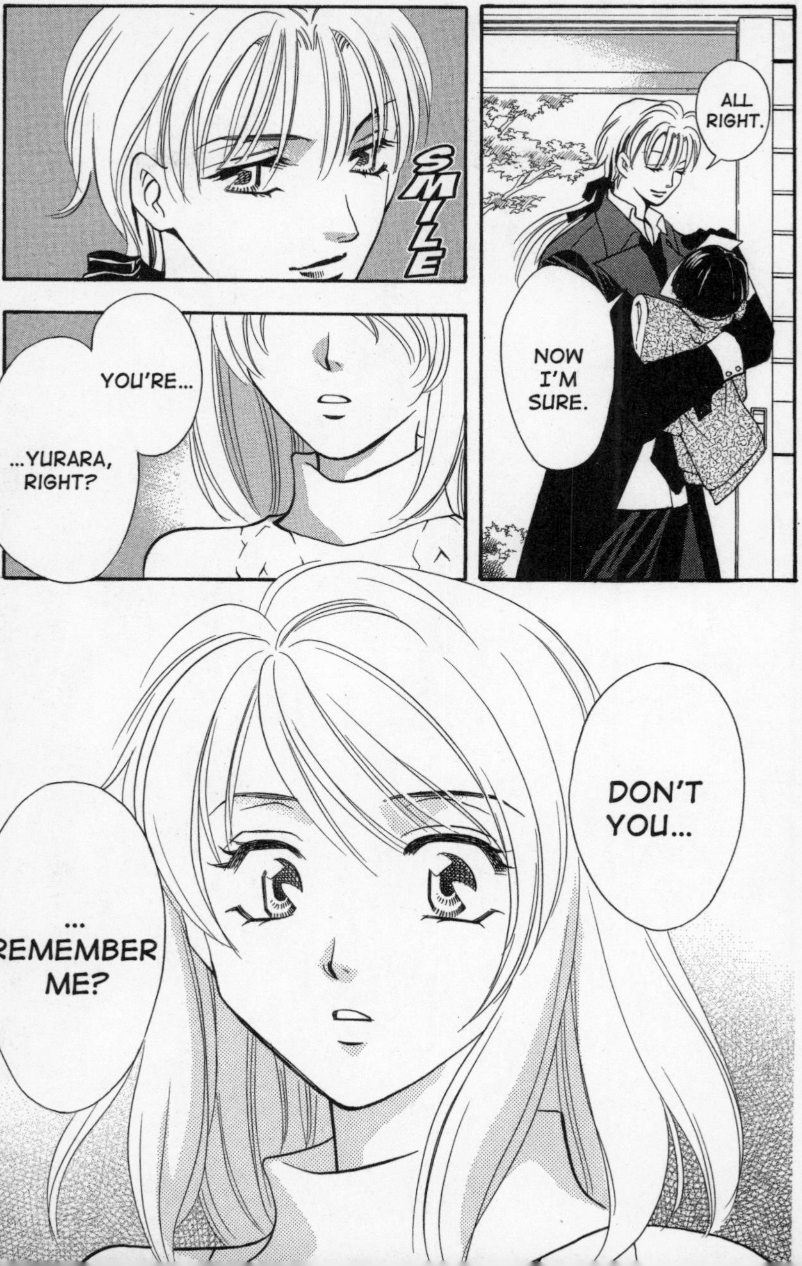
ALL RIGHT.
NOW I'M SURE.
SMILE
YOU'RE...
...YURARA, RIGHT?
DON'T YOU...
...REMEMBER ME?

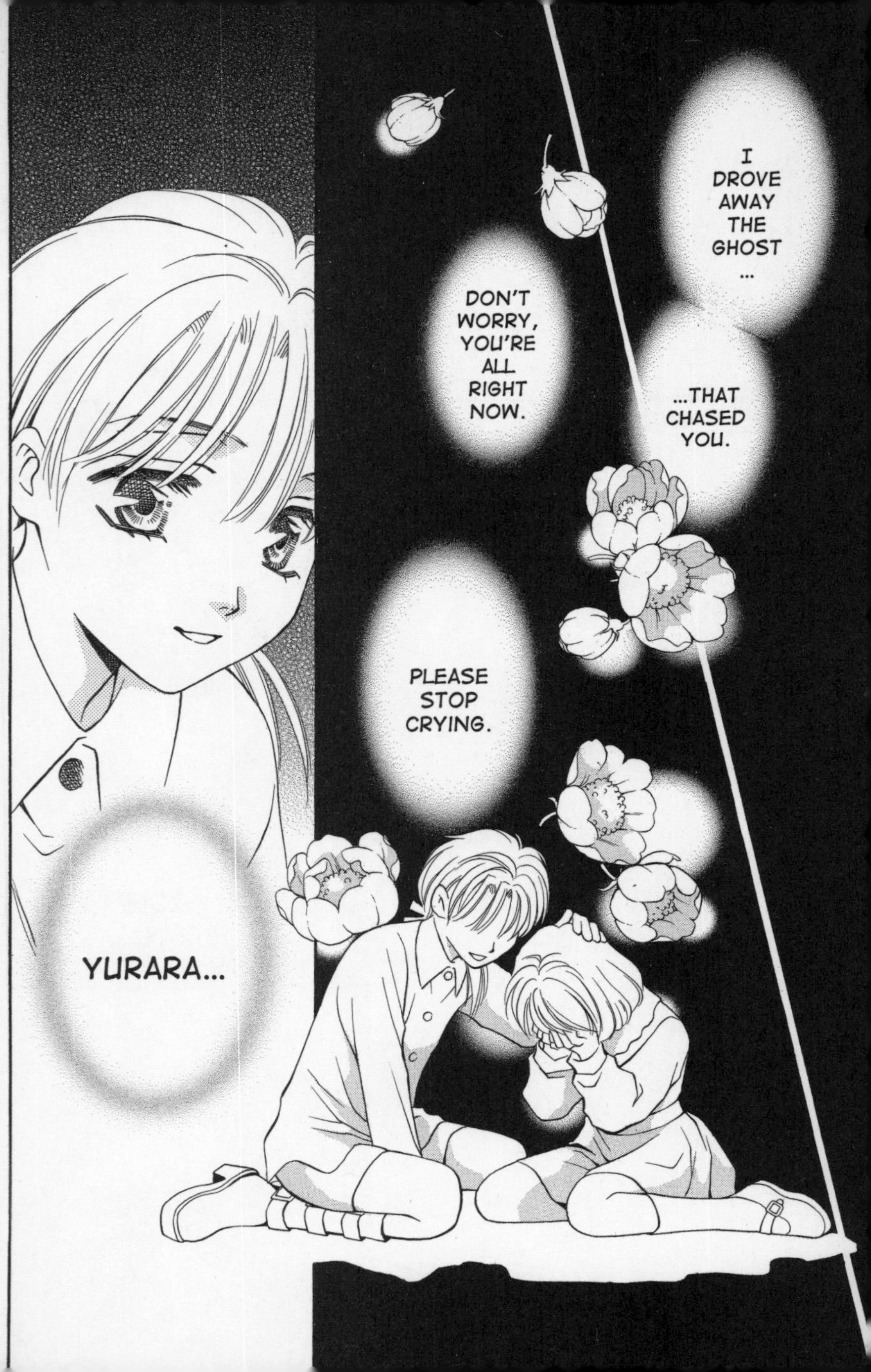
I DROVE AWAY THE GHOST ...
...THAT CHASED YOU.
DON'T WORRY, YOU'RE ALL RIGHT NOW.
PLEASE STOP CRYING.
YURARA...

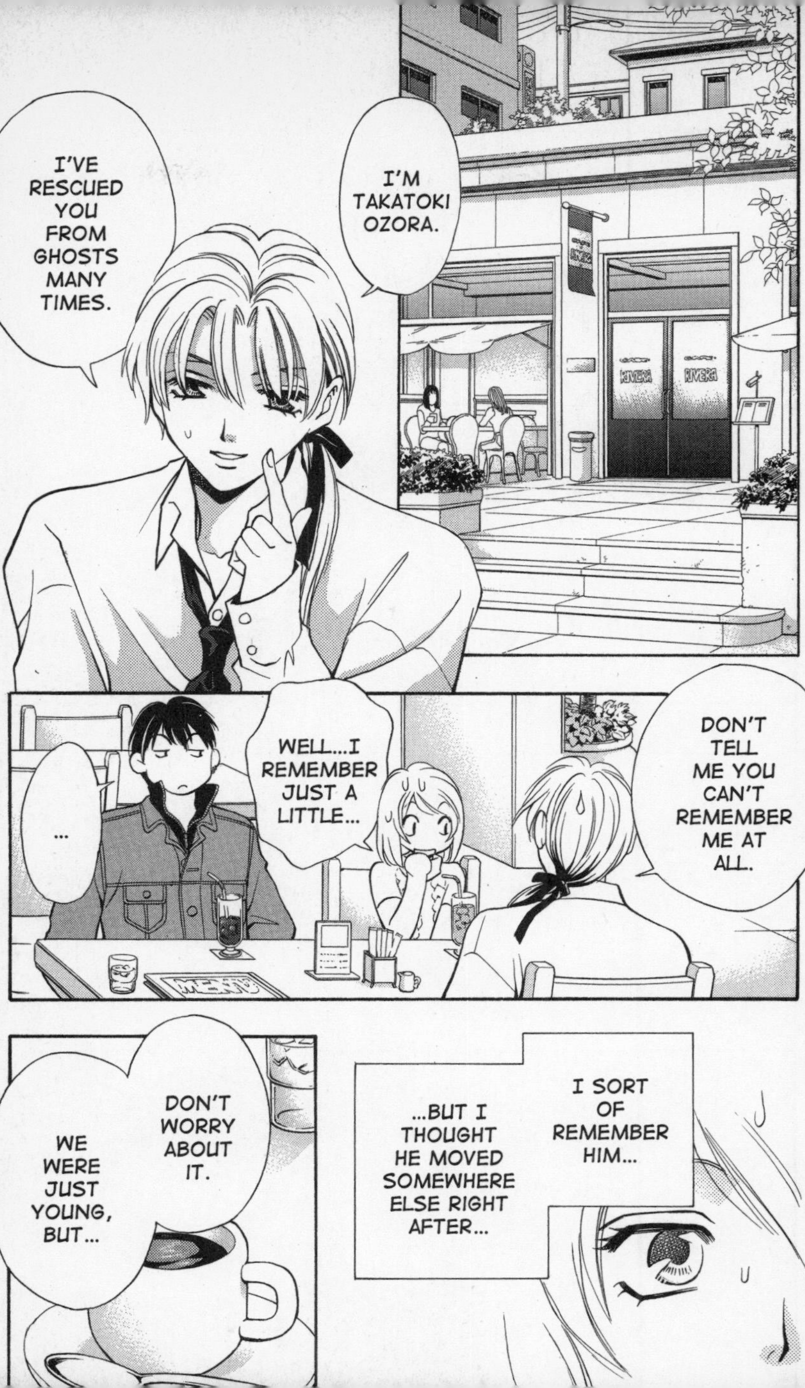
I'M TAKATOKI OZORA.
I'VE RESCUED YOU FROM GHOSTS MANY TIMES.
DON'T TELL ME YOU CAN'T REMEMBER ME AT ALL.
WELL...I REMEMBER JUST A LITTLE...
...
I SORT OF REMEMBER HIM...
...BUT I THOUGHT HE MOVED SOMEWHERE ELSE RIGHT AFTER...
DON'T WORRY ABOUT IT.
WE WERE JUST YOUNG, BUT...

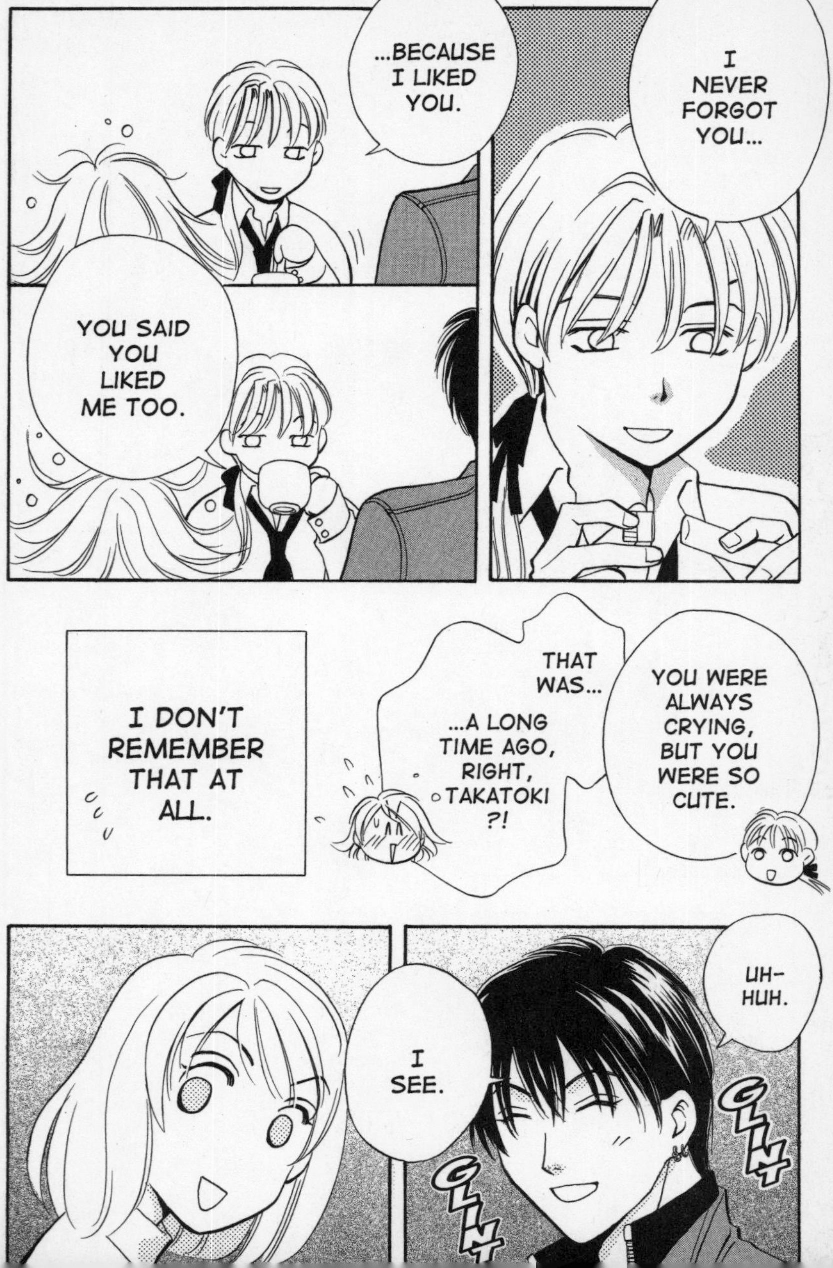
I NEVER FORGOT YOU...
...BECAUSE I LIKED YOU.
YOU SAID YOU LIKED ME TOO.
YOU WERE ALWAYS CRYING, BUT YOU WERE SO CUTE.
THAT WAS...
...A LONG TIME AGO, RIGHT, TAKATOKI?!
I DON'T REMEMBER THAT AT ALL.
UH-HUH.
I SEE.
GLINT
GLINT

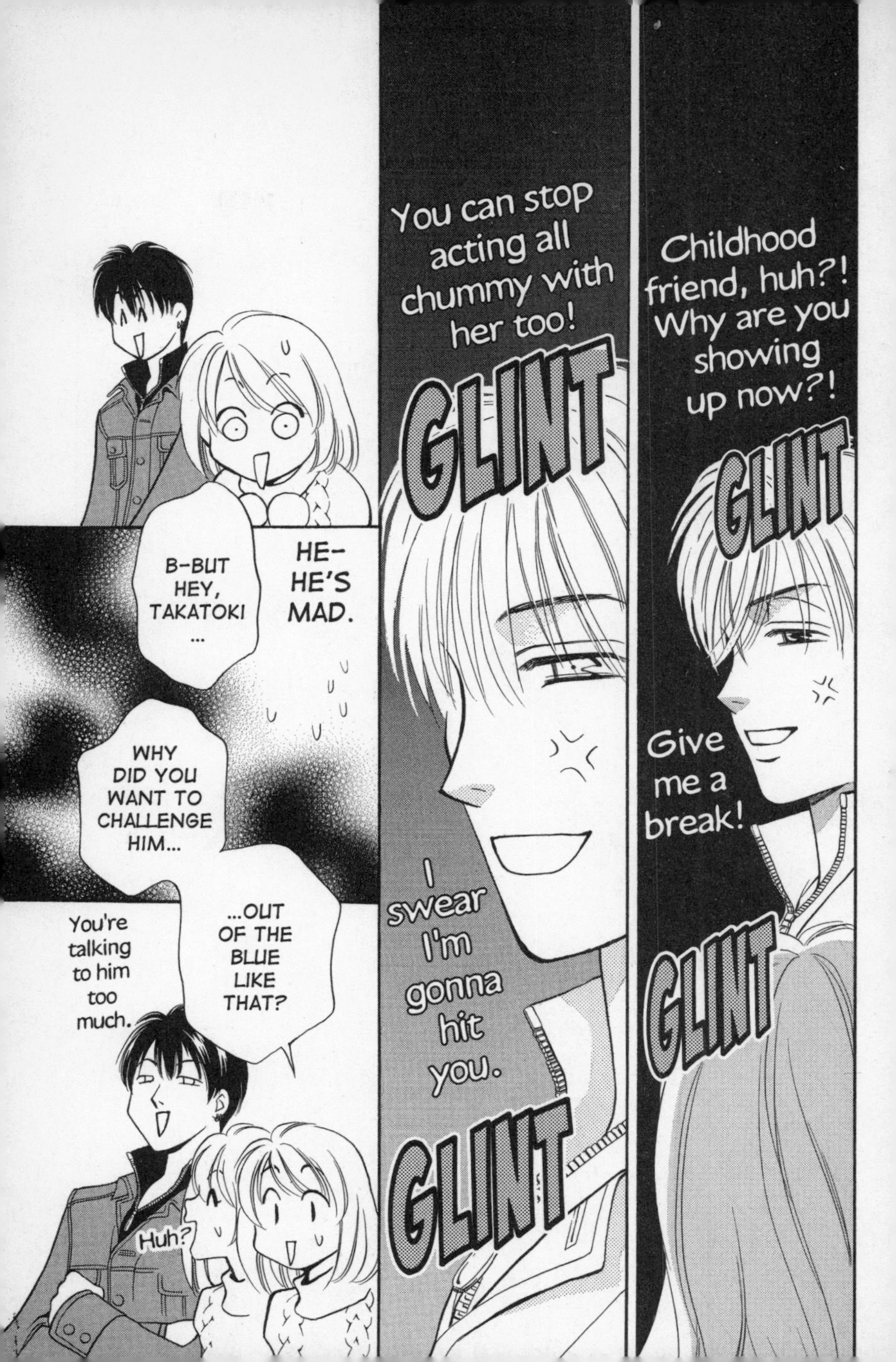
Childhood friend, huh?! Why are you showing up now?!
GLINT
Give me a break!
GLINT
You can stop acting all chummy with her too!
GLINT
I swear I'm gonna hit you.
GLINT
HE-HE'S MAD.
B-BUT HEY, TAKATOKI ...
WHY DID YOU WANT TO CHALLENGE HIM...
...OUT OF THE BLUE LIKE THAT?
You're talking to him too much.
Huh?

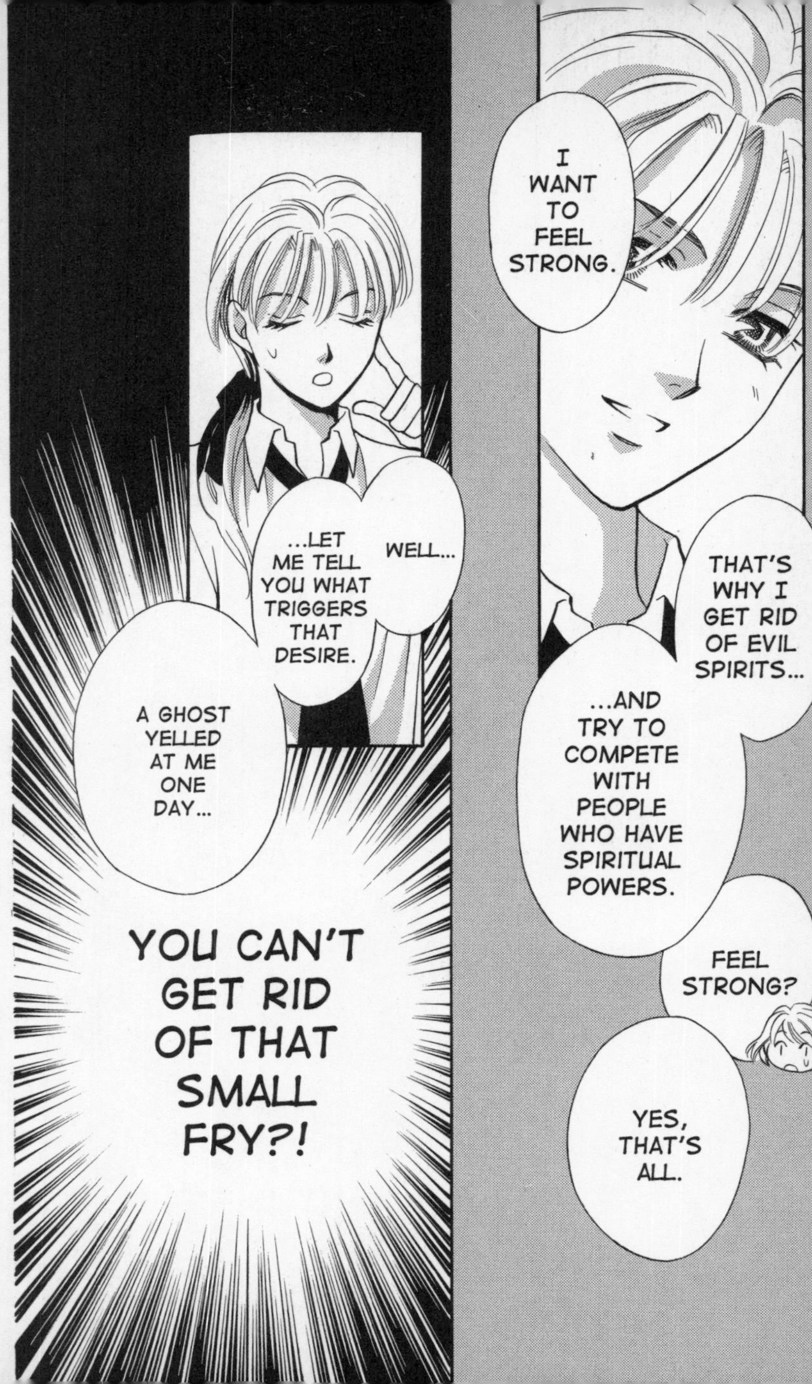
I WANT TO FEEL STRONG.
THAT'S WHY I GET RID OF EVIL SPIRITS...
...AND TRY TO COMPETE WITH PEOPLE WHO HAVE SPIRITUAL POWERS.
FEEL STRONG?
YES, THAT'S ALL.
WELL...
...LET ME TELL YOU WHAT TRIGGERS THAT DESIRE.
A GHOST YELLED AT ME ONE DAY...
YOU CAN'T GET RID OF THAT SMALL FRY?!

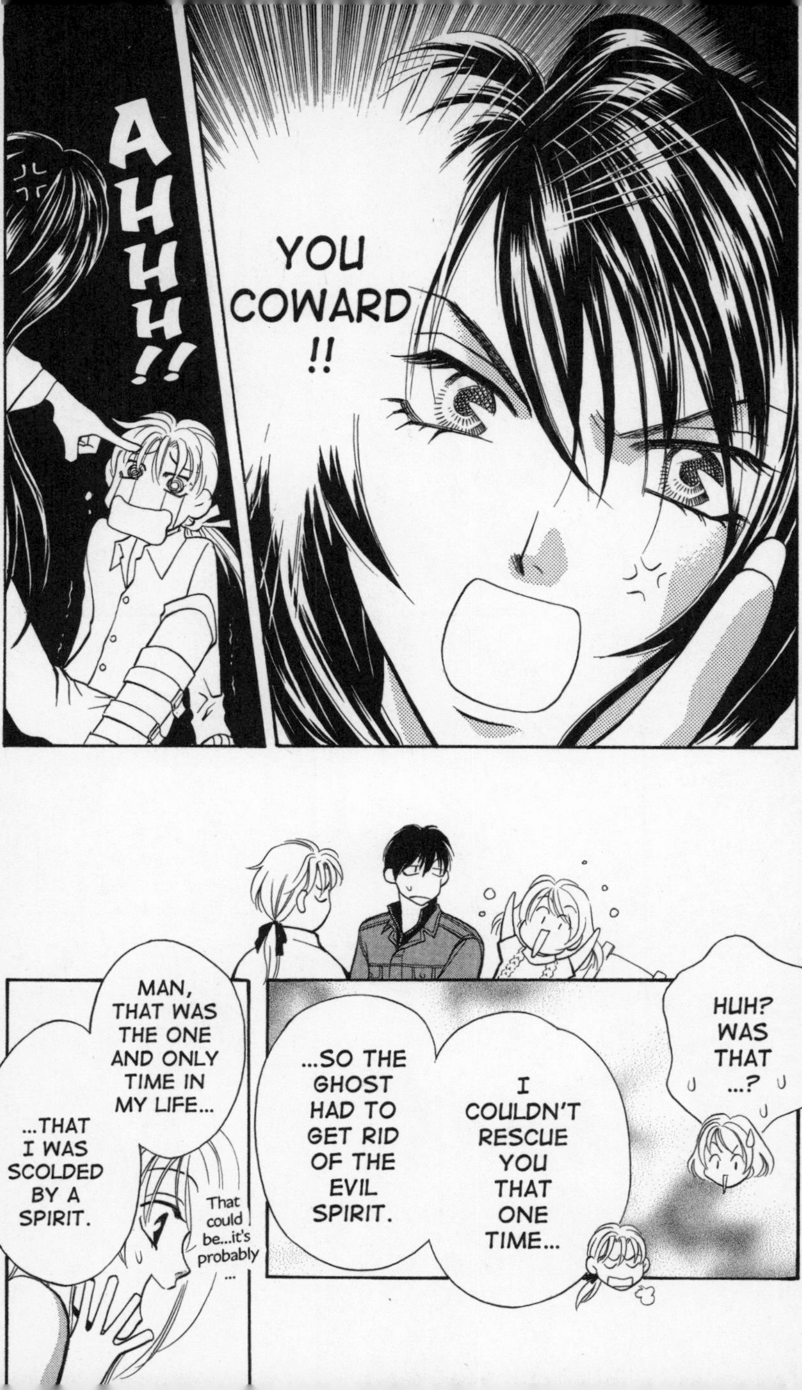
YOU COWARD !!
AHHH!!
HUH? WAS THAT ...?
I COULDN'T RESCUE YOU THAT ONE TIME...
...SO THE GHOST HAD TO GET RID OF THE EVIL SPIRIT.
MAN, THAT WAS THE ONE AND ONLY TIME IN MY LIFE...
...THAT I WAS SCOLDED BY A SPIRIT.
That could be...it's probably ...

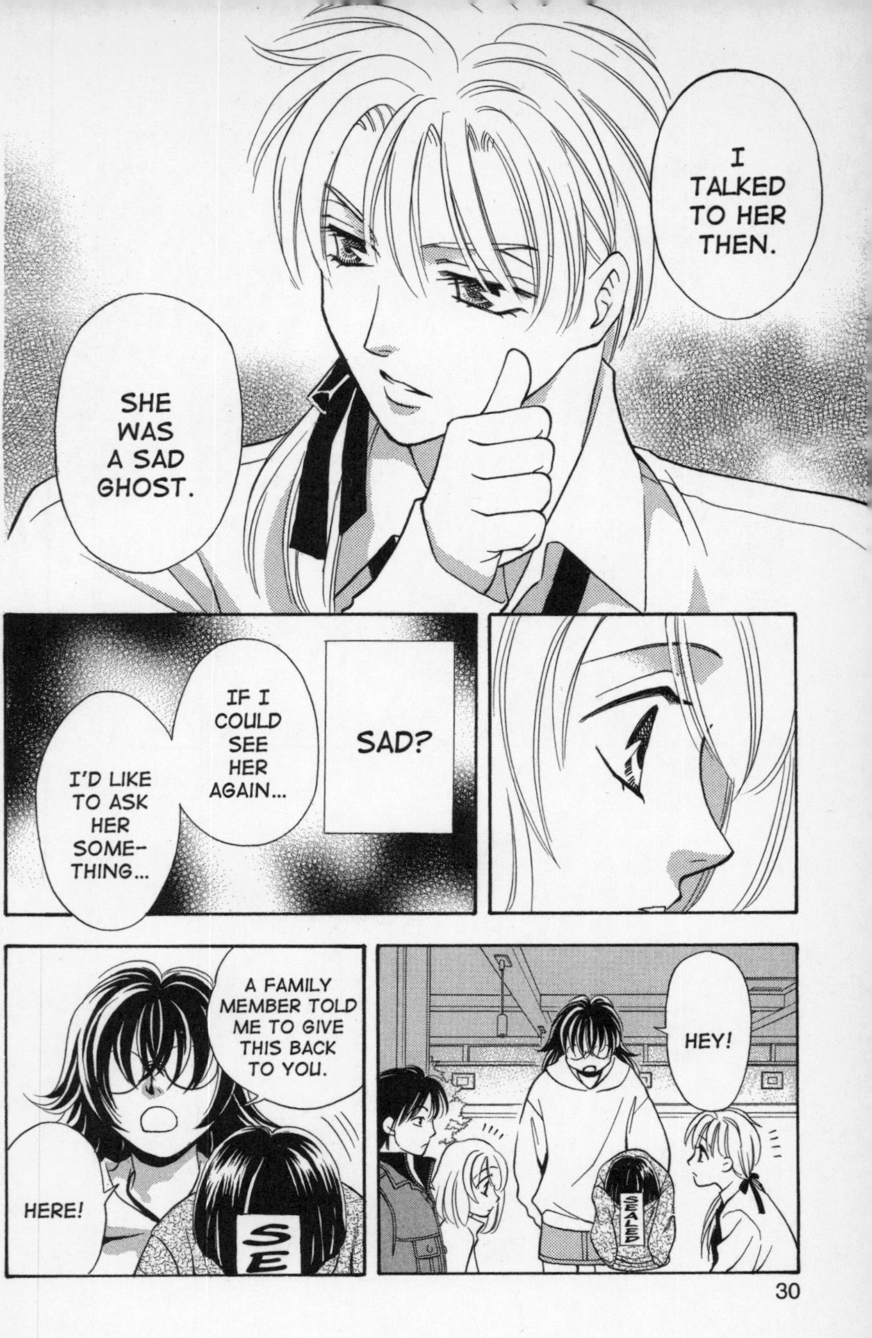
I TALKED TO HER THEN.
SHE WAS A SAD GHOST.
SAD?
IF I COULD SEE HER AGAIN...
I'D LIKE TO ASK HER SOMETHING...
HEY!
SEALED
A FAMILY MEMBER TOLD ME TO GIVE THIS BACK TO YOU.
HERE!
SE

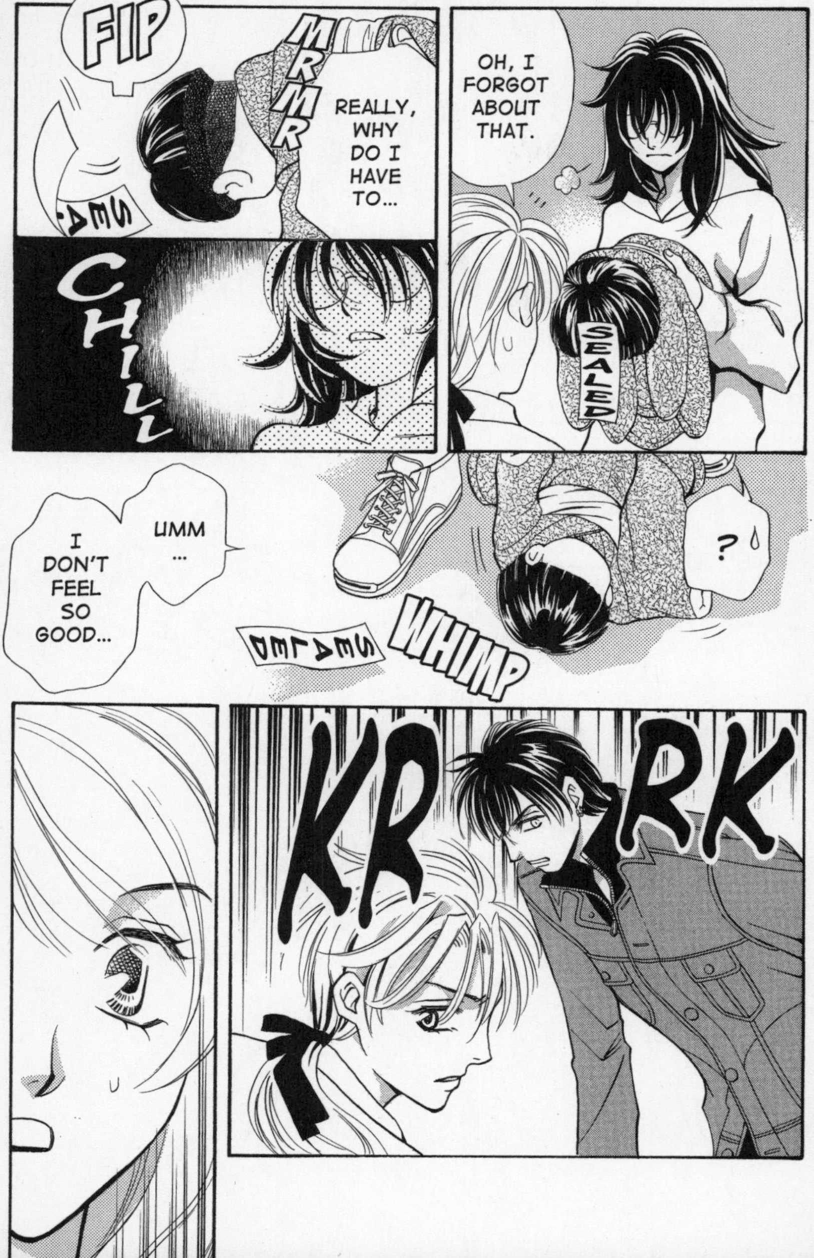
OH, I FORGOT ABOUT THAT.
SEALED
REALLY, WHY DO I HAVE TO...
MRMR
FIP
SEA.
CHILL
?
WHIMP
SEALED
UMM ...
I DON'T FEEL SO GOOD...
KR RK

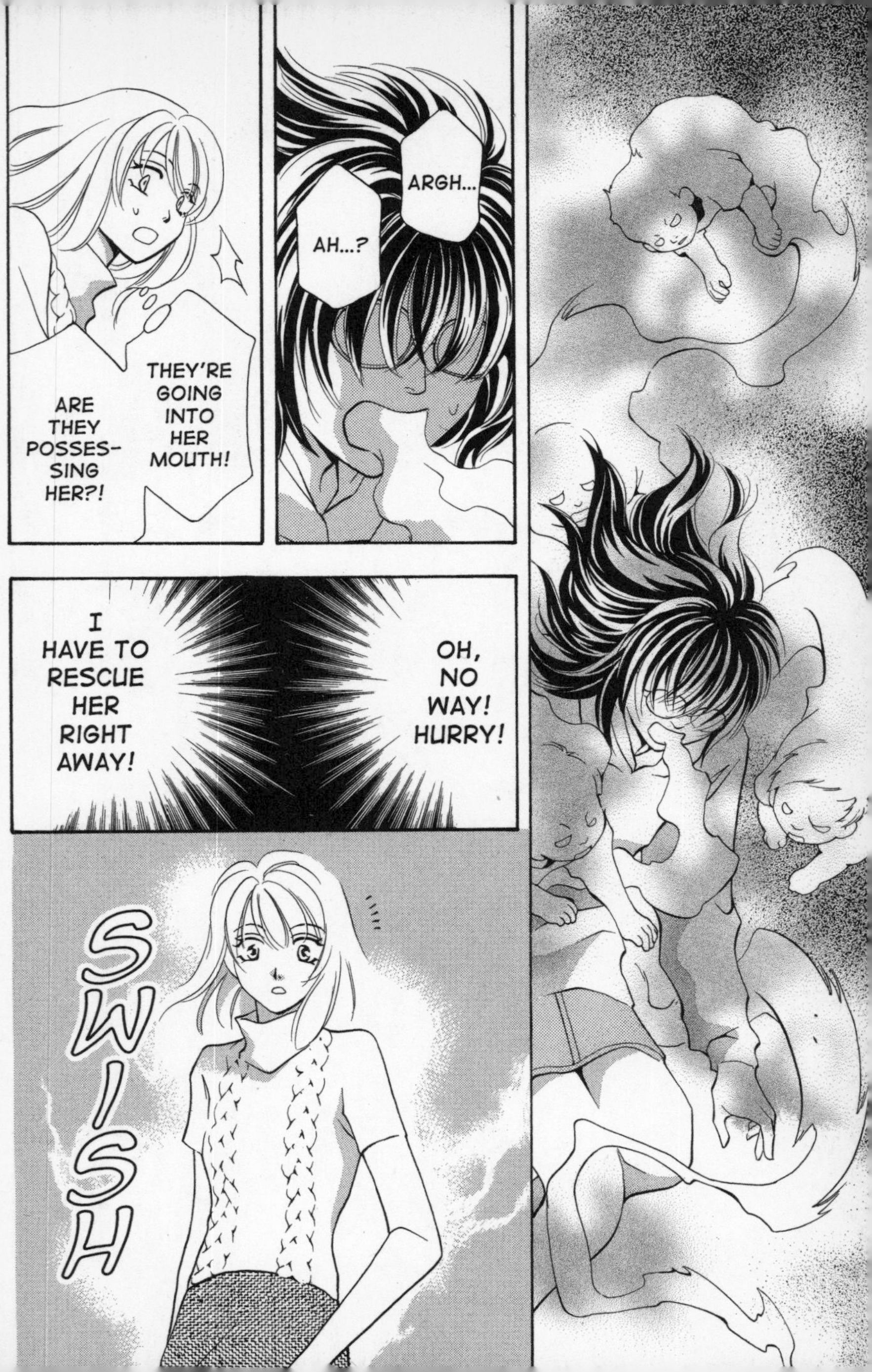
ARGH...
AH...?
THEY'RE GOING INTO HER MOUTH!
ARE THEY POSSES-SING HER?!
OH, NO WAY! HURRY!
I HAVE TO RESCUE HER RIGHT AWAY!
SWISH

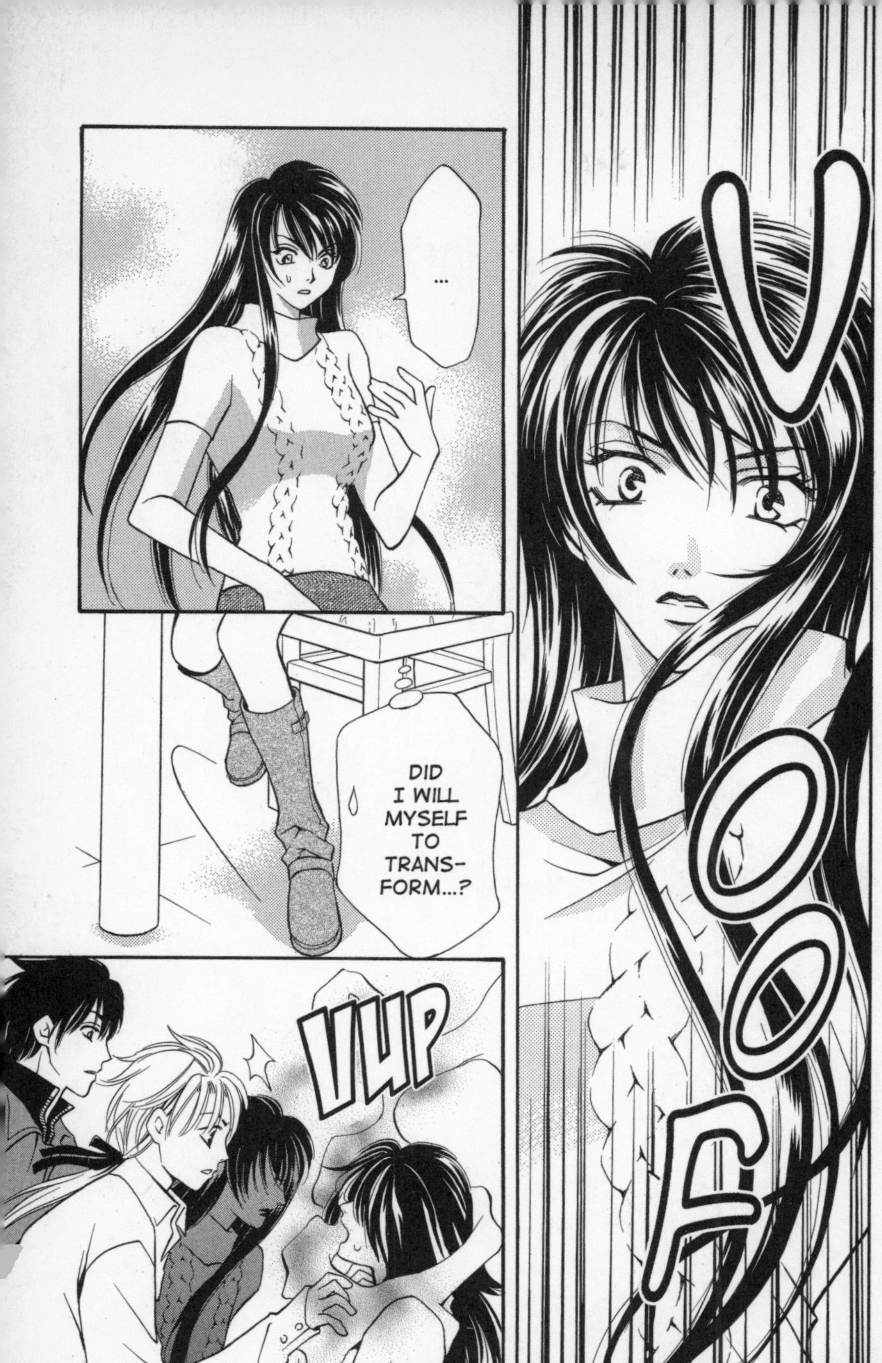
VOOF
...
DID I WILL MYSELF TO TRANS-FORM...?
VUP

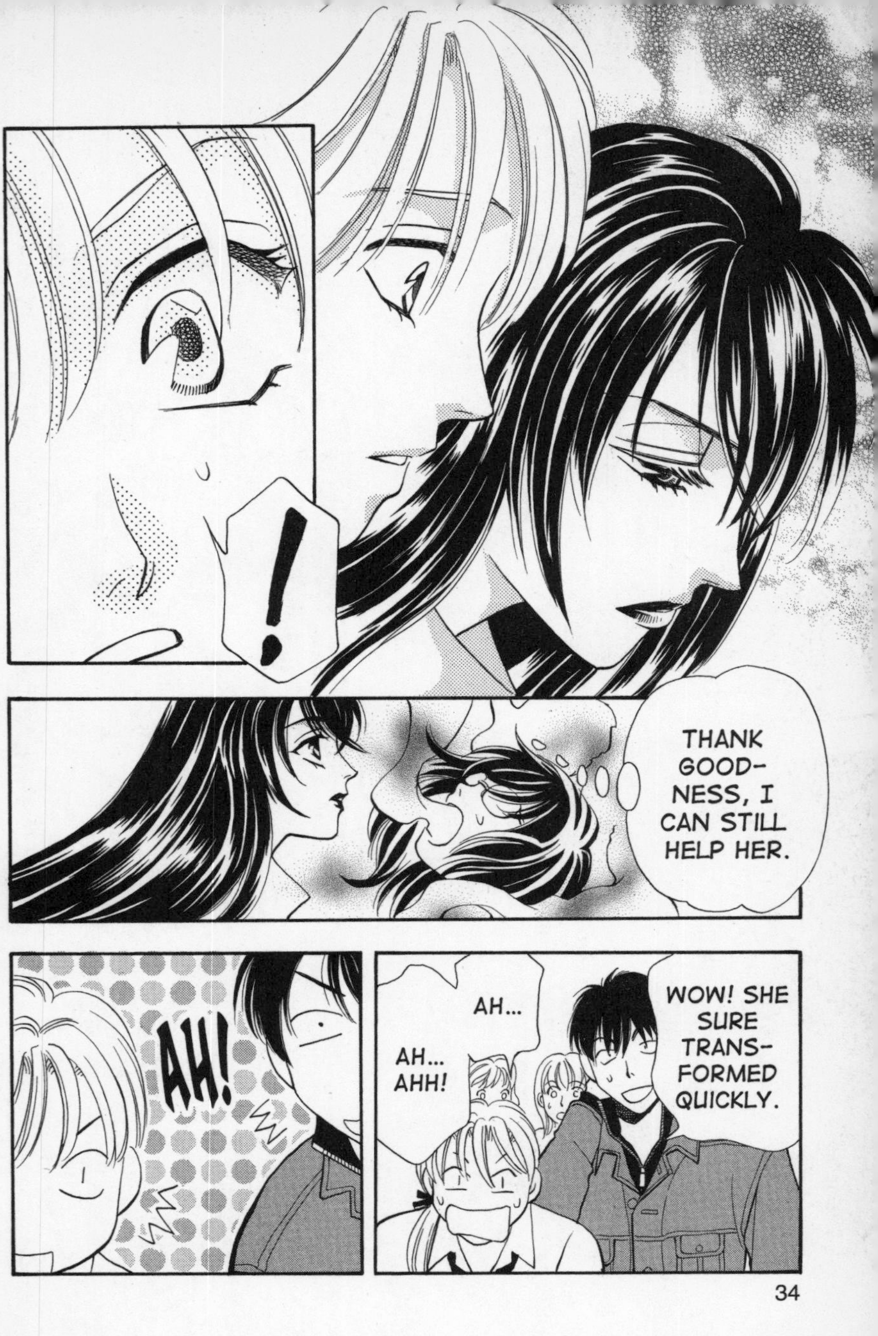
!
THANK GOODNESS, I CAN STILL HELP HER.
WOW! SHE SURE TRANSFORMED QUICKLY.
AH...
AH... AHH!
AH!

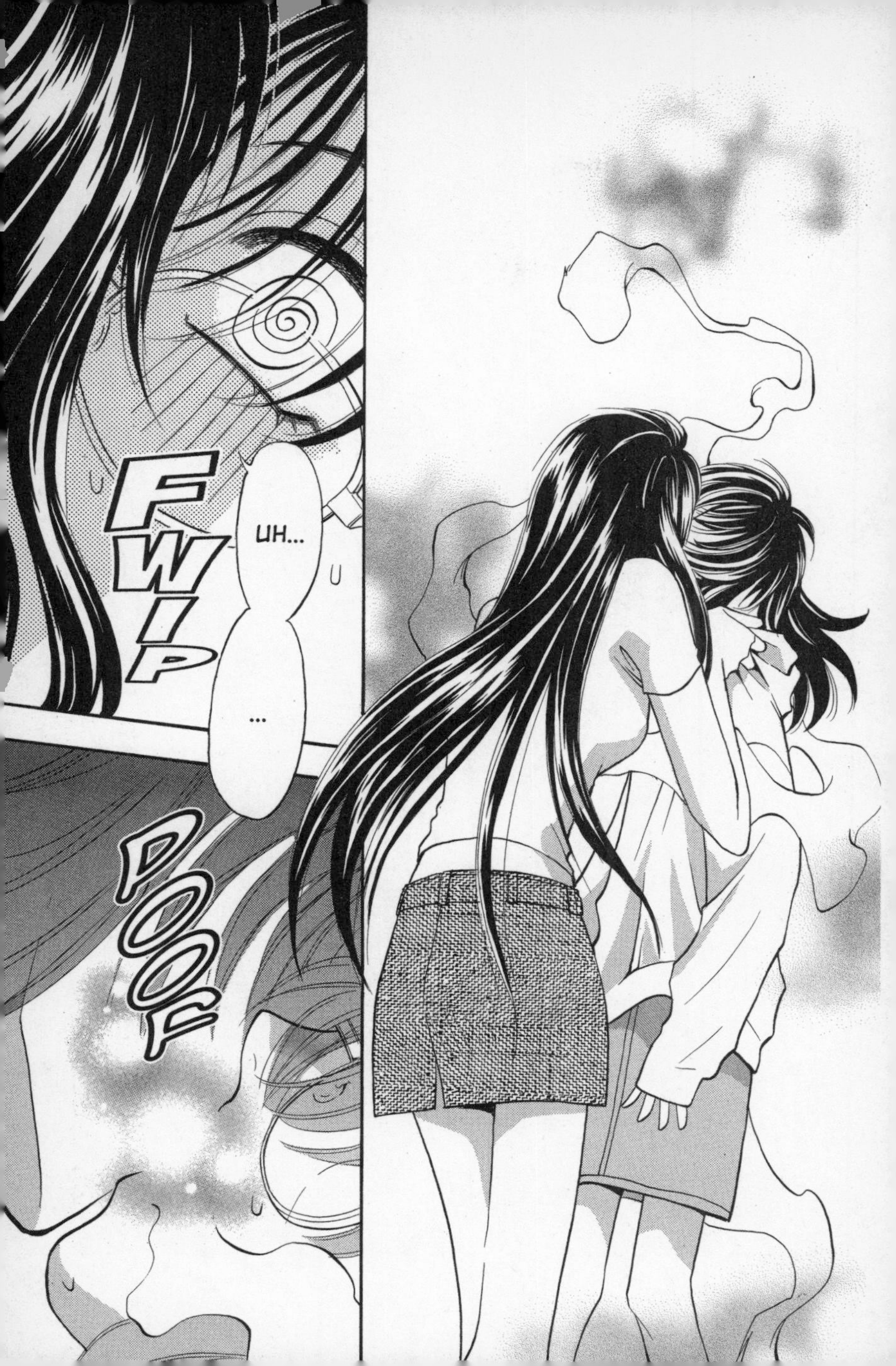
FWIP
UH...
...
POOF

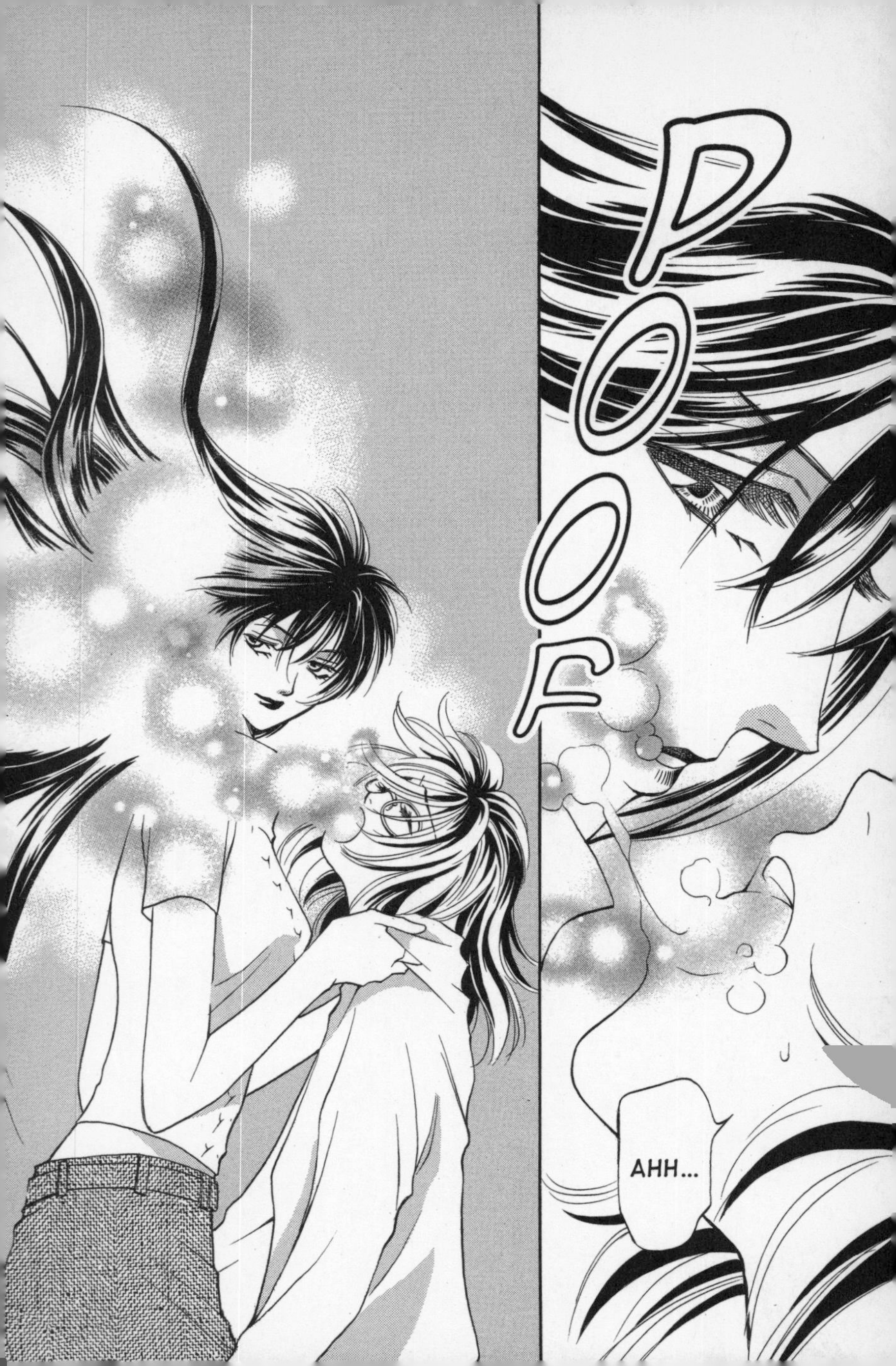
POOOF
AHH...

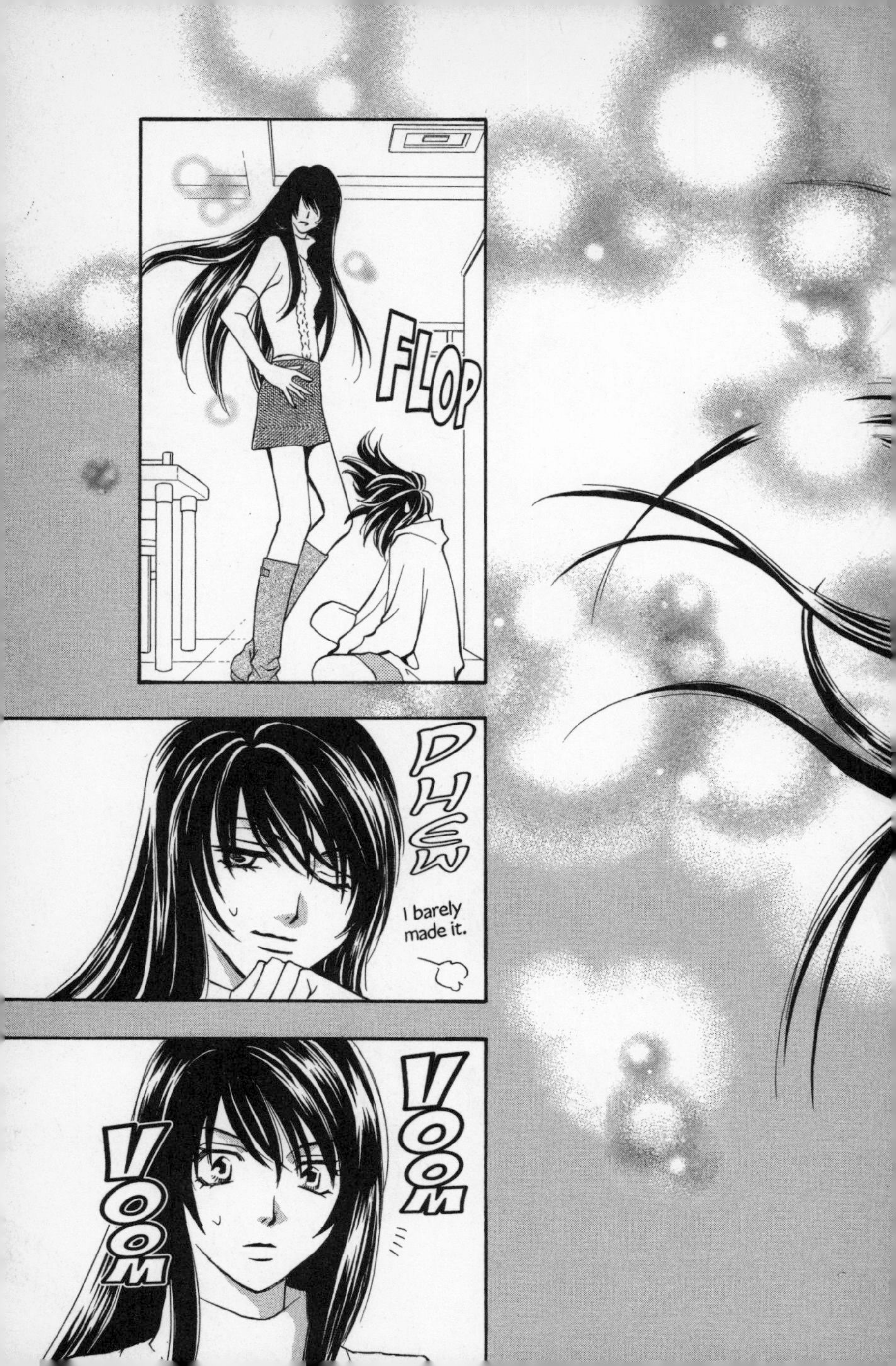
FLOP
PHEW
I barely made it.
VOOM
VOOM

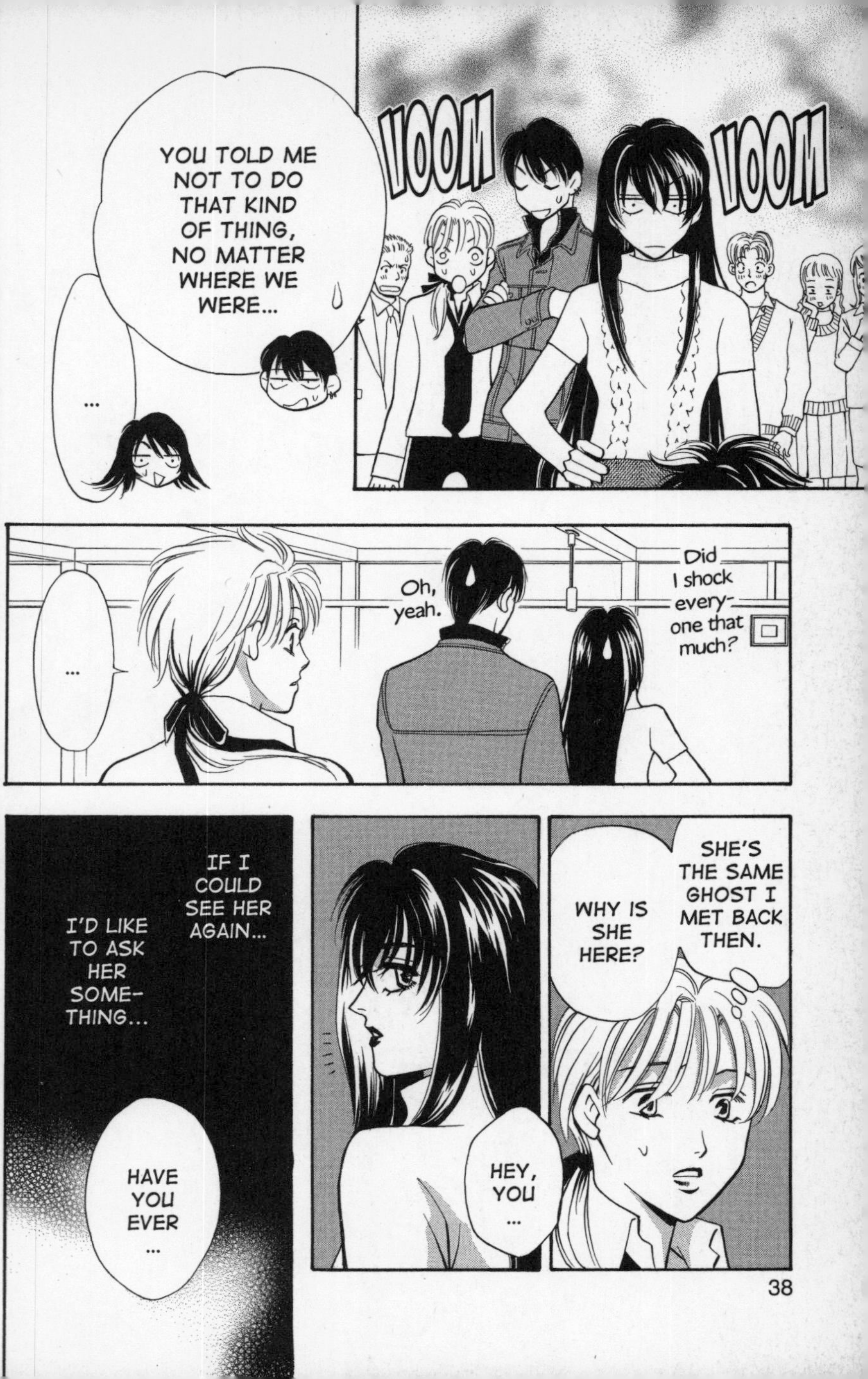
VOOM
VOOM
YOU TOLD ME NOT TO DO THAT KIND OF THING, NO MATTER WHERE WE WERE...
...
Did I shock every-one that much?
Oh, yeah.
...
SHE'S THE SAME GHOST I MET BACK THEN.
WHY IS SHE HERE?
HEY, YOU ...
IF I COULD SEE HER AGAIN...
I'D LIKE TO ASK HER SOME-THING...
HAVE YOU EVER ...

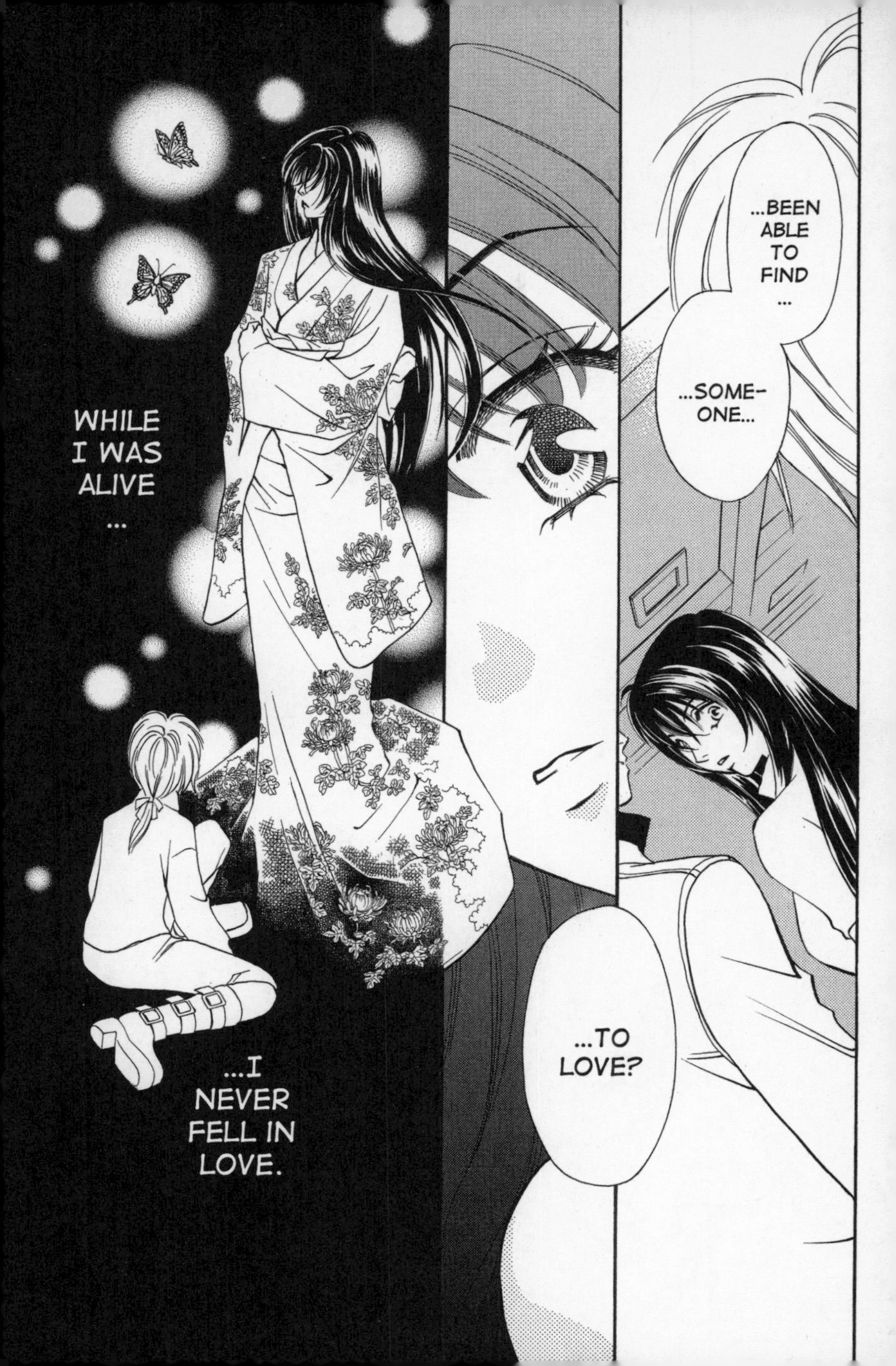
...BEEN ABLE TO FIND ...
...SOME-ONE...
...TO LOVE?
WHILE I WAS ALIVE ...
...I NEVER FELL IN LOVE.

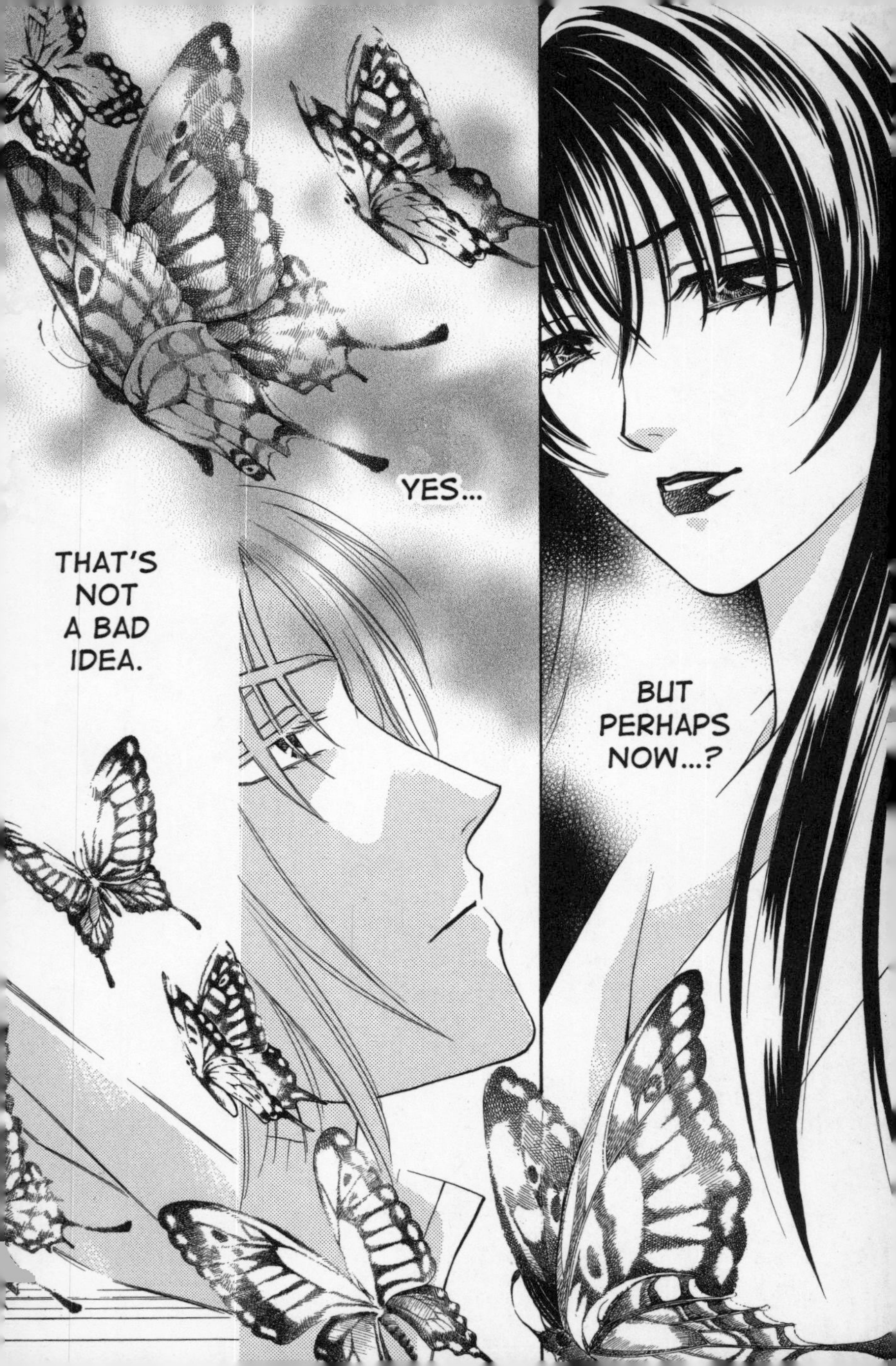
BUT PERHAPS NOW...?
YES...
THAT'S NOT A BAD IDEA.

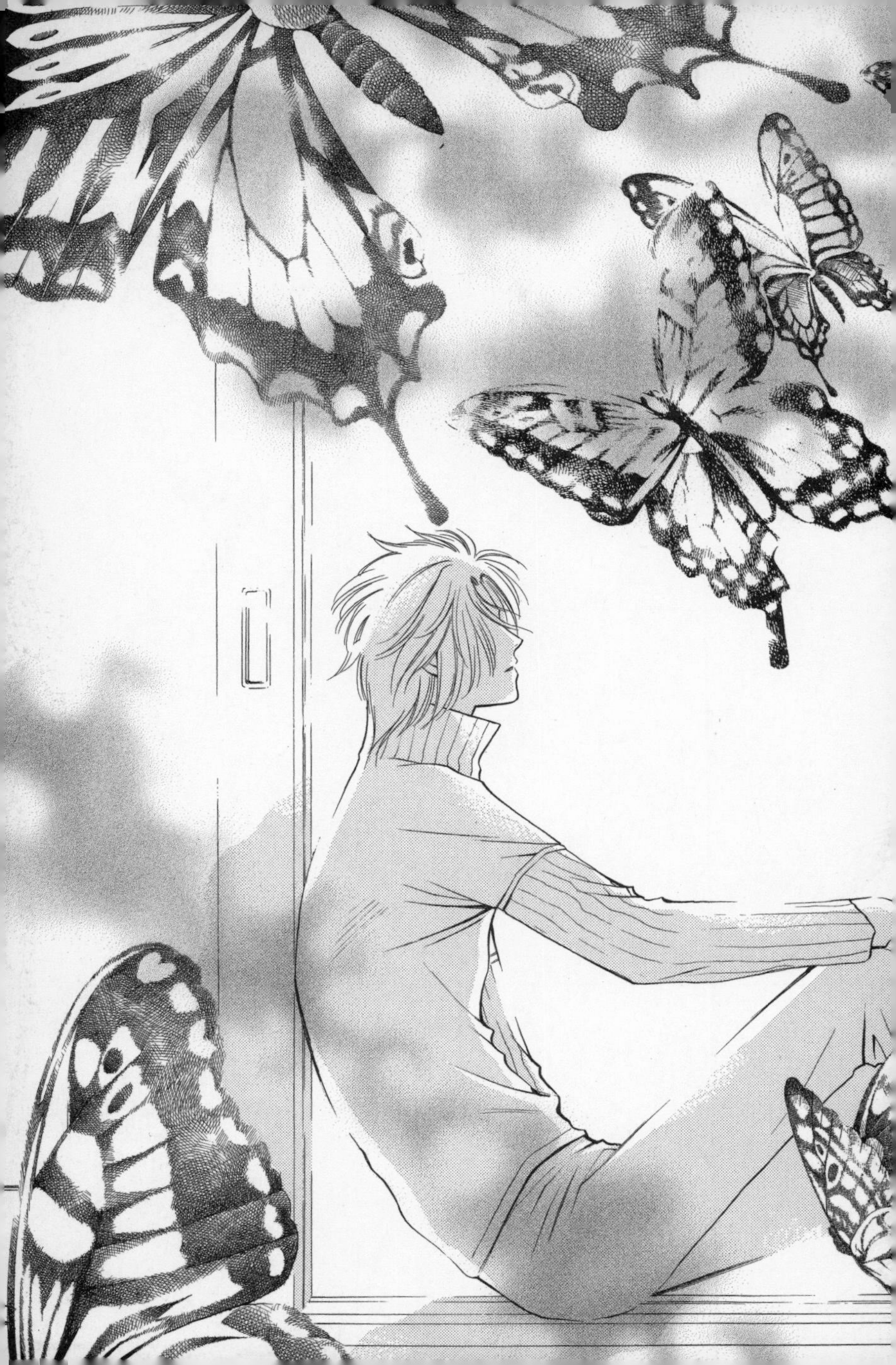

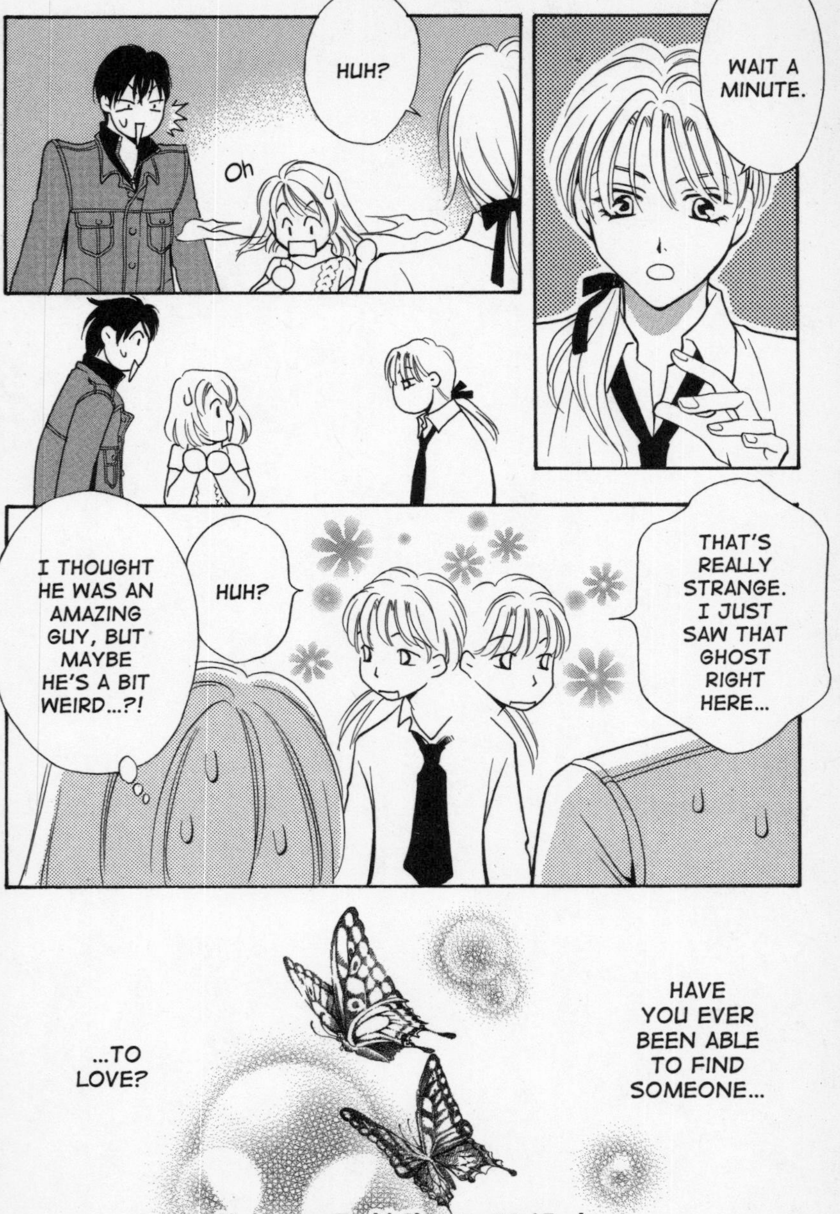
WAIT A MINUTE.
HUH?
Oh
THAT'S REALLY STRANGE. I JUST SAW THAT GHOST RIGHT HERE...
HUH?
I THOUGHT HE WAS AN AMAZING GUY, BUT MAYBE HE'S A BIT WEIRD...?!
HAVE YOU EVER BEEN ABLE TO FIND SOMEONE...
...TO LOVE?

***Yurara no Tsuki* Chapter 13 / End**

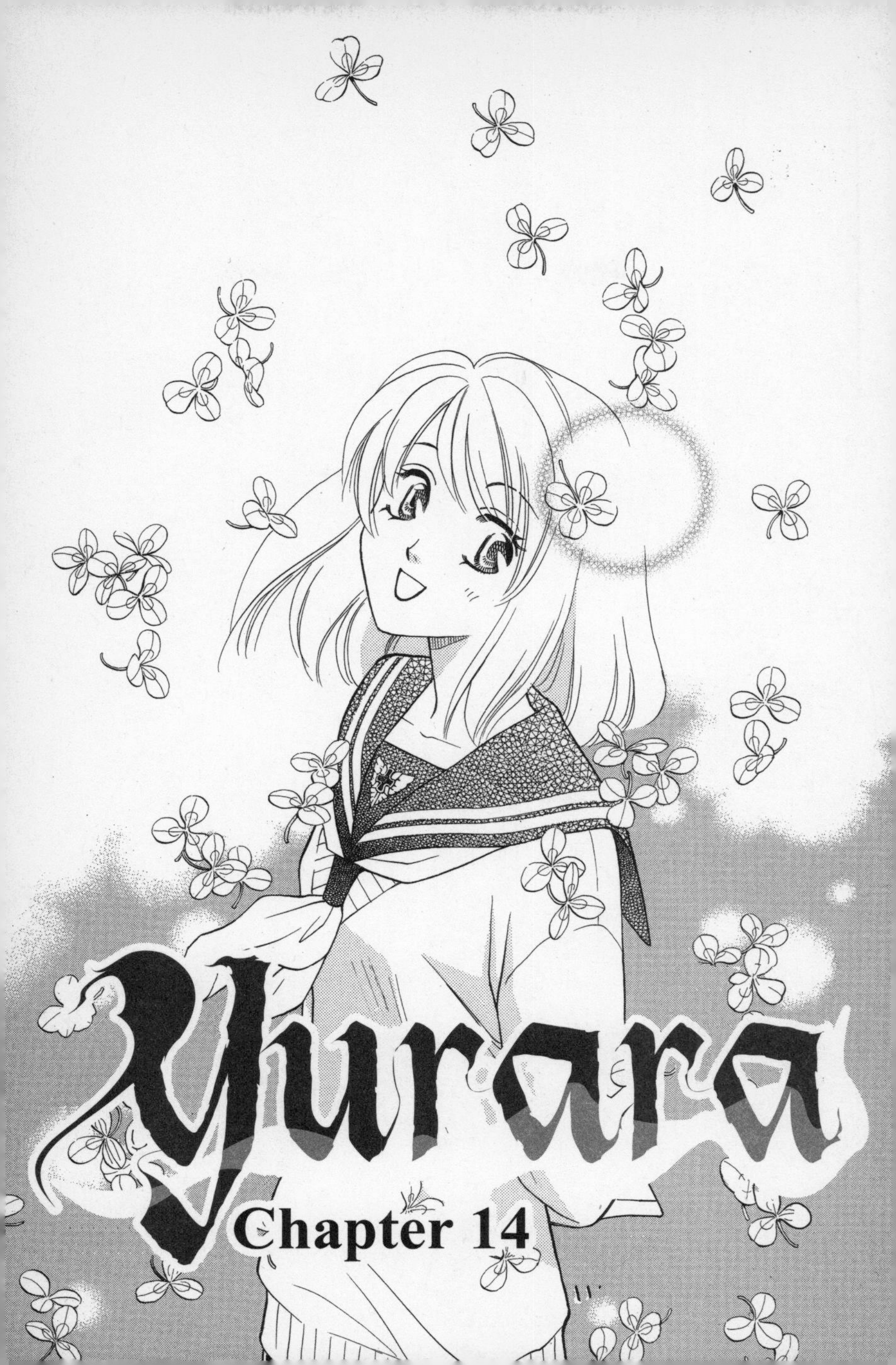
Yurara
Chapter 14

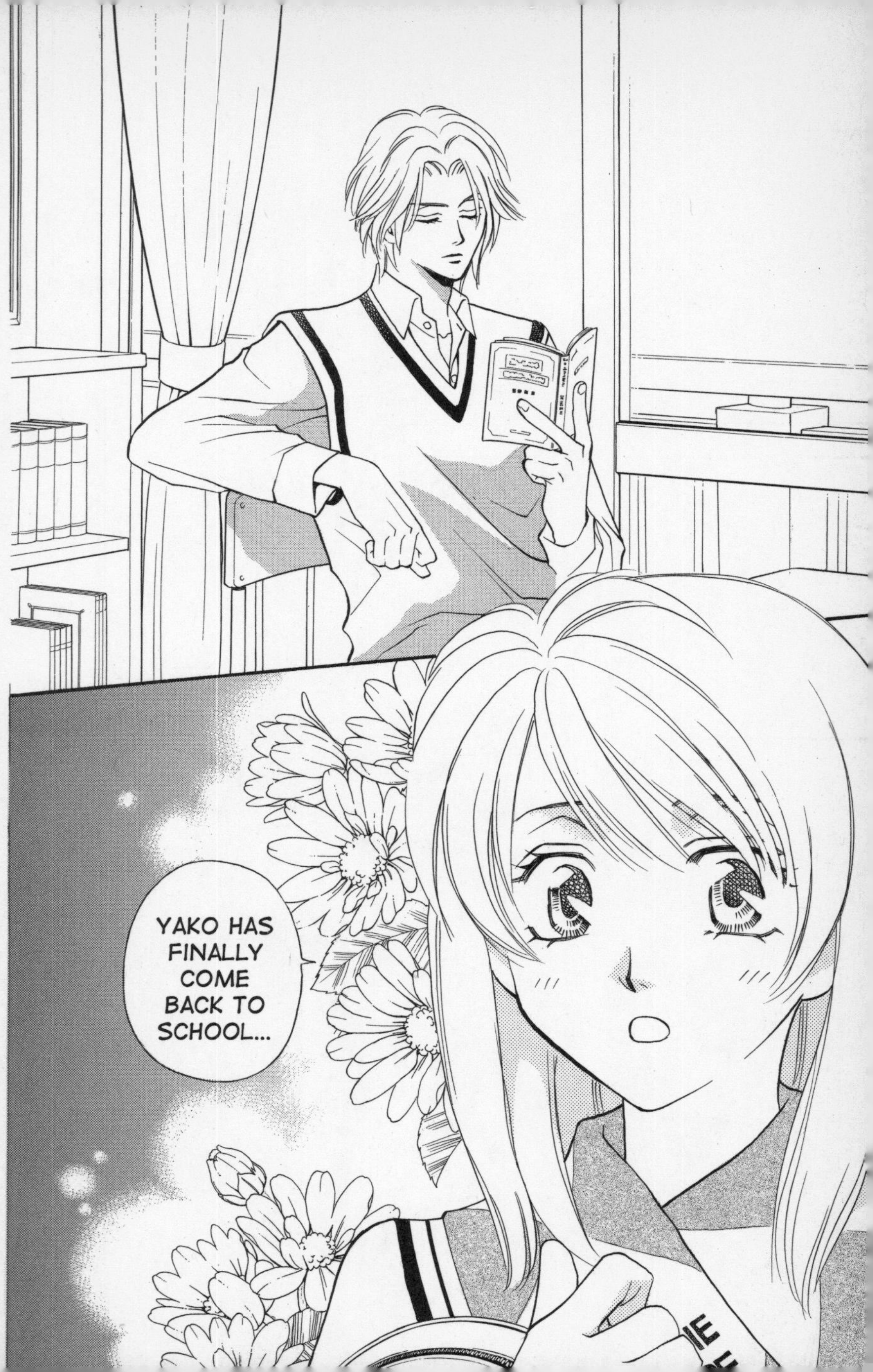
YAKO HAS FINALLY COME BACK TO SCHOOL...

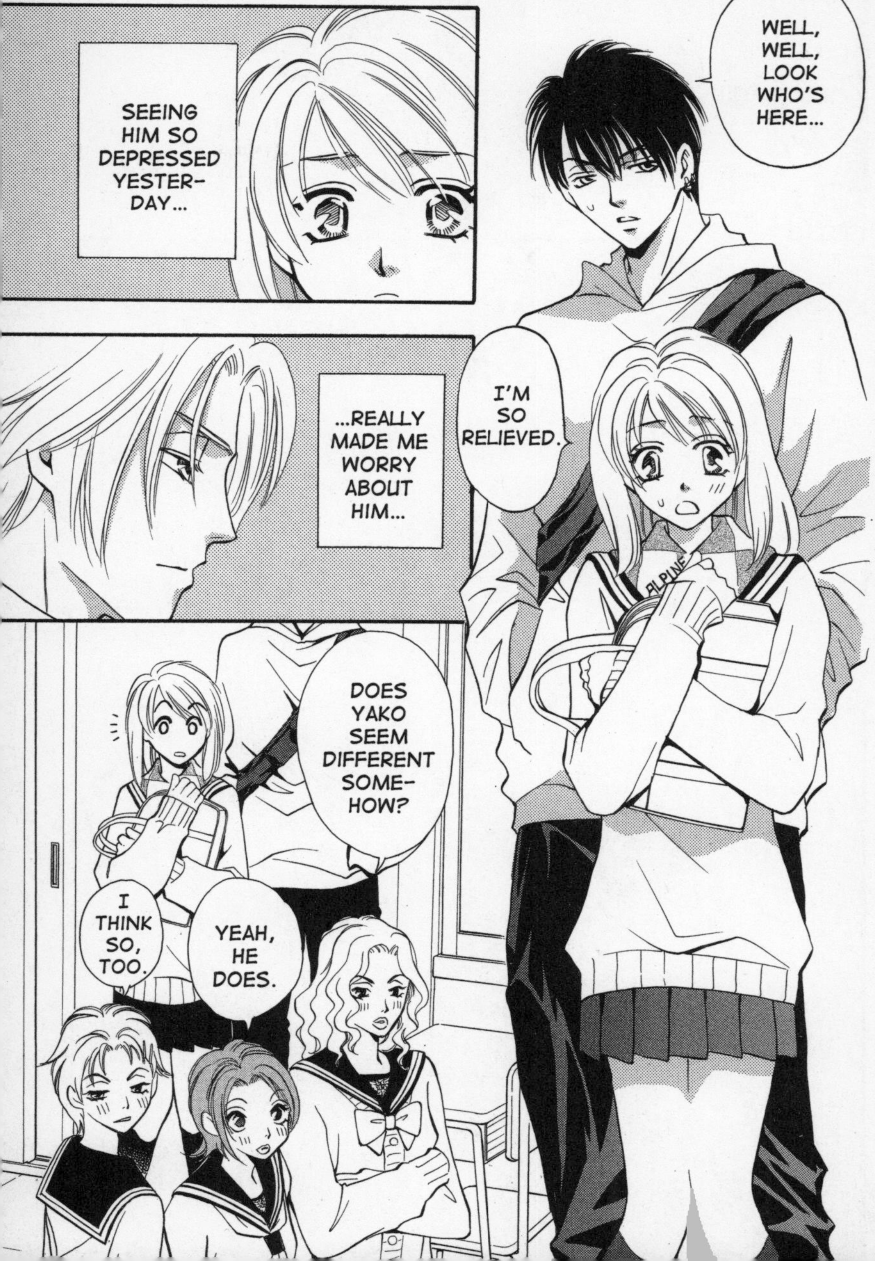
WELL, WELL, LOOK WHO'S HERE...
I'M SO RELIEVED.
SEEING HIM SO DEPRESSED YESTER-DAY...
...REALLY MADE ME WORRY ABOUT HIM...
DOES YAKO SEEM DIFFERENT SOME-HOW?
YEAH, HE DOES.
I THINK SO, TOO.

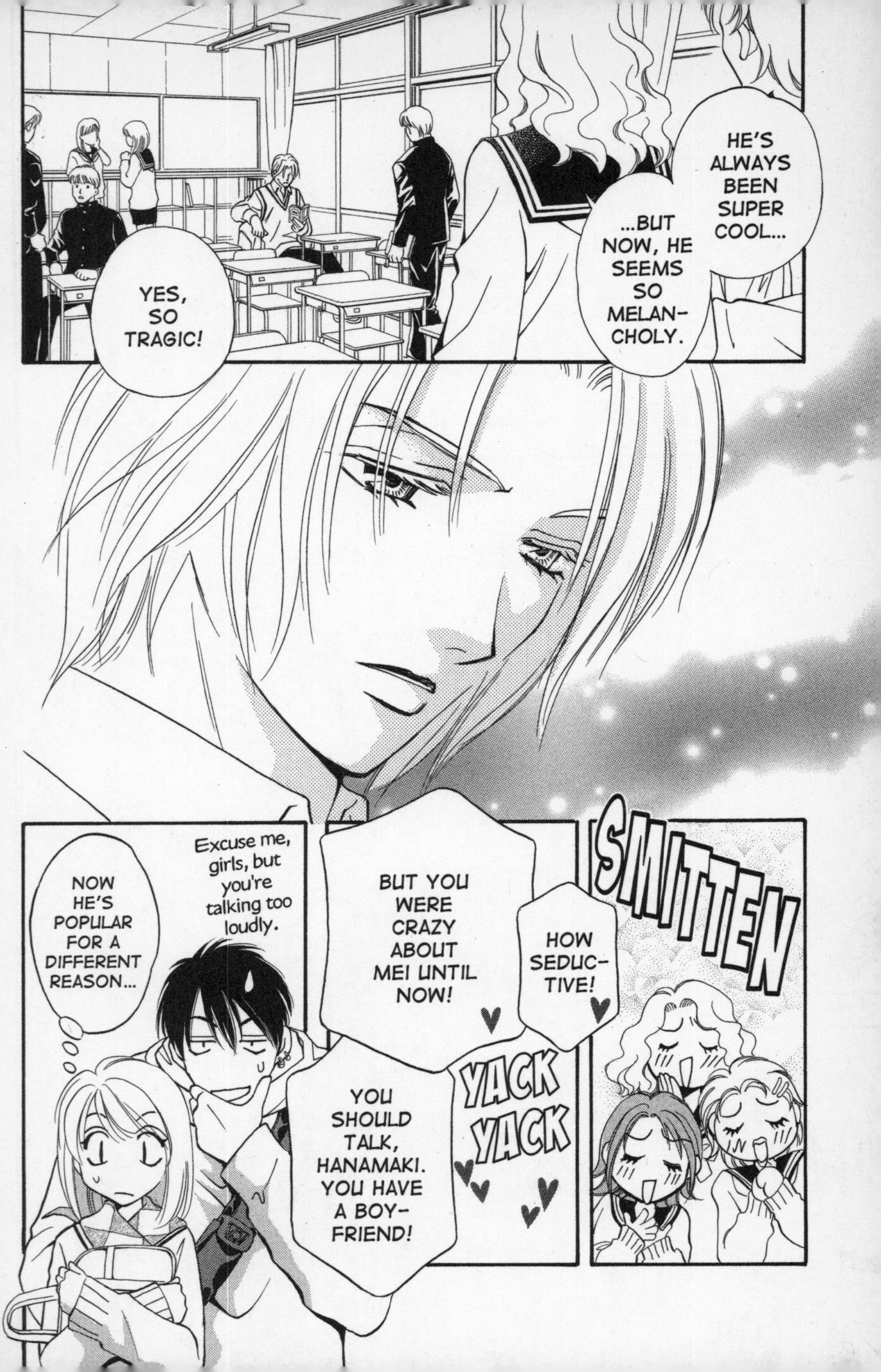
HE'S ALWAYS BEEN SUPER COOL...
...BUT NOW, HE SEEMS SO MELAN-CHOLY.
YES, SO TRAGIC!
SMITTEN
HOW SEDUC-TIVE!
BUT YOU WERE CRAZY ABOUT MEI UNTIL NOW!
YACK YACK
YOU SHOULD TALK, HANAMAKI. YOU HAVE A BOY-FRIEND!
Excuse me, girls, but you're talking too loudly.
NOW HE'S POPULAR FOR A DIFFERENT REASON...

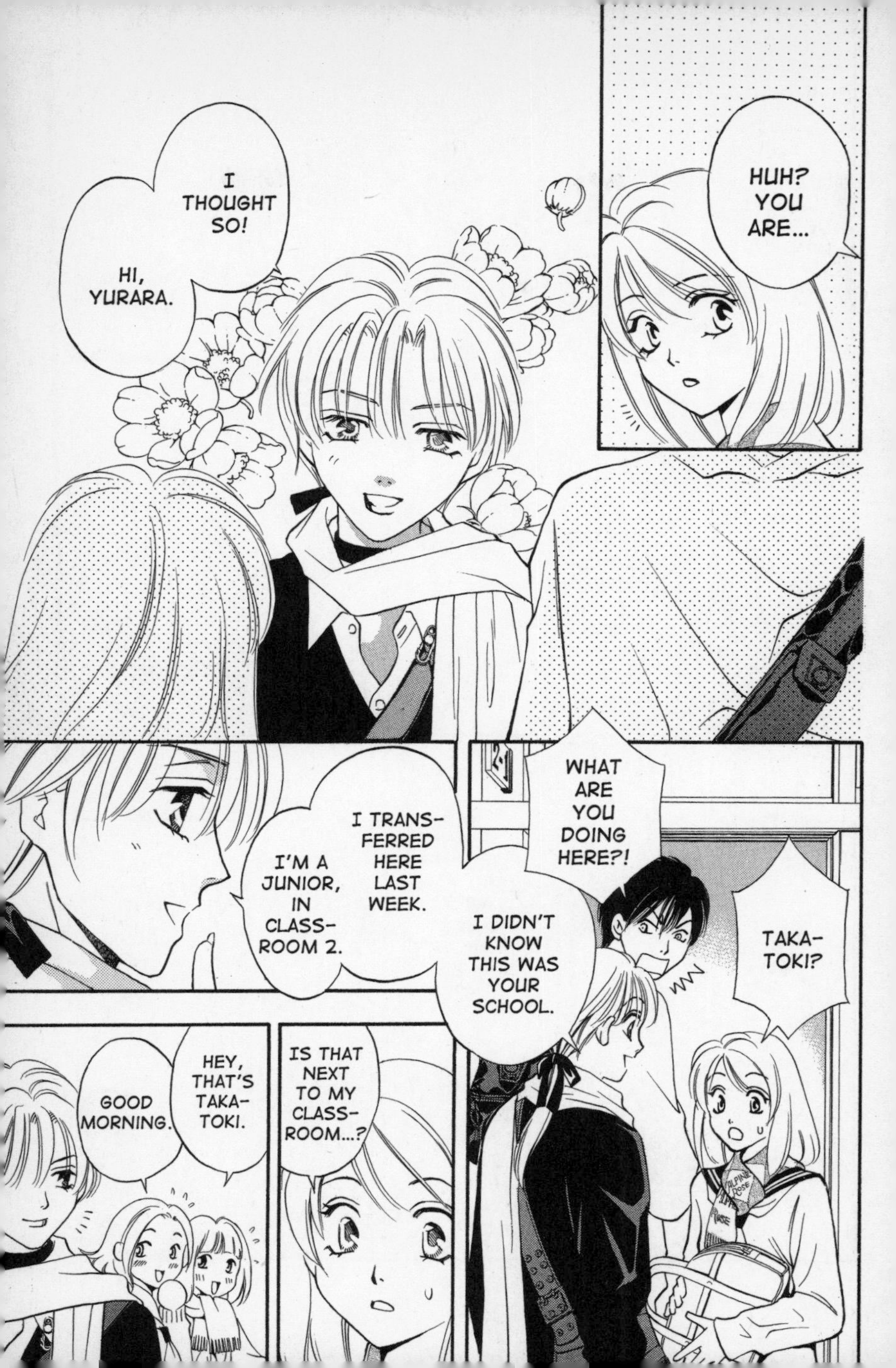
HUH? YOU ARE...
I THOUGHT SO!
HI, YURARA.
WHAT ARE YOU DOING HERE?!
TAKA-TOKI?
I DIDN'T KNOW THIS WAS YOUR SCHOOL.
I TRANS-FERRED HERE LAST WEEK.
I'M A JUNIOR, IN CLASS-ROOM 2.
IS THAT NEXT TO MY CLASS-ROOM...?
HEY, THAT'S TAKA-TOKI.
GOOD MORNING.

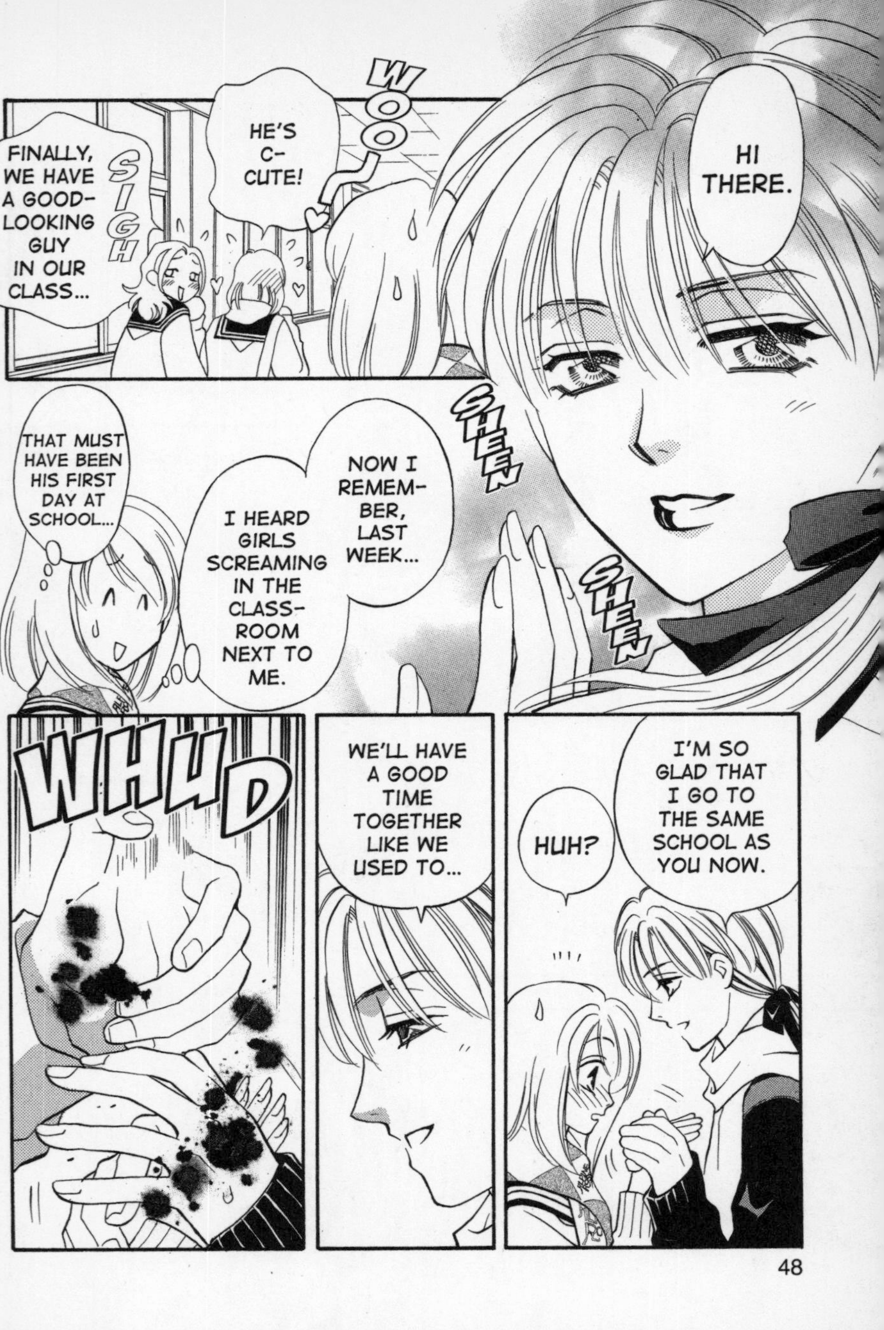
HI THERE.
WOOO
HE'S C-CUTE!
SIGH
FINALLY, WE HAVE A GOOD-LOOKING GUY IN OUR CLASS...
SHEEN
SHEEN
NOW I REMEMBER, LAST WEEK...
I HEARD GIRLS SCREAMING IN THE CLASSROOM NEXT TO ME.
THAT MUST HAVE BEEN HIS FIRST DAY AT SCHOOL...
I'M SO GLAD THAT I GO TO THE SAME SCHOOL AS YOU NOW.
HUH?
WE'LL HAVE A GOOD TIME TOGETHER LIKE WE USED TO...
WHUD

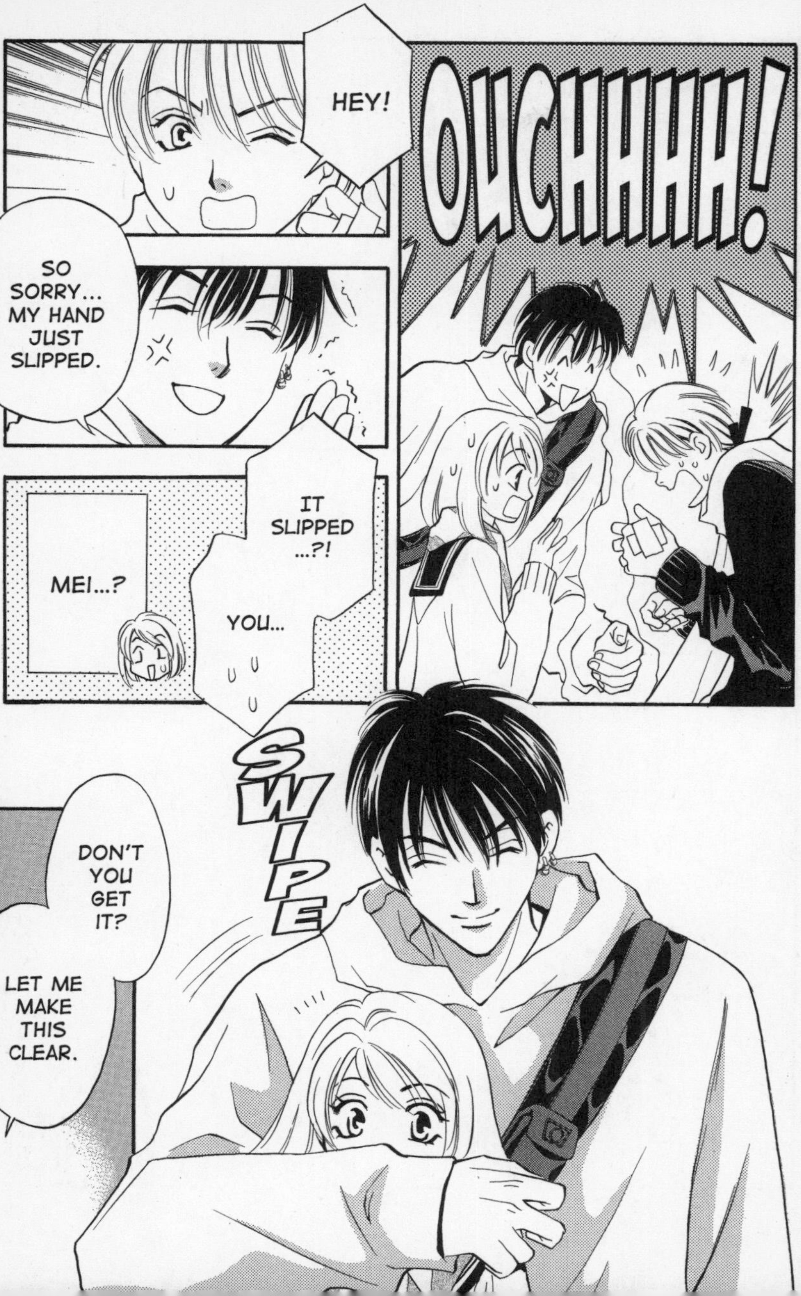
OUCHHHH!
HEY!
SO SORRY... MY HAND JUST SLIPPED.
IT SLIPPED ...?!
YOU...
MEI...?
SWIPE
DON'T YOU GET IT?
LET ME MAKE THIS CLEAR.

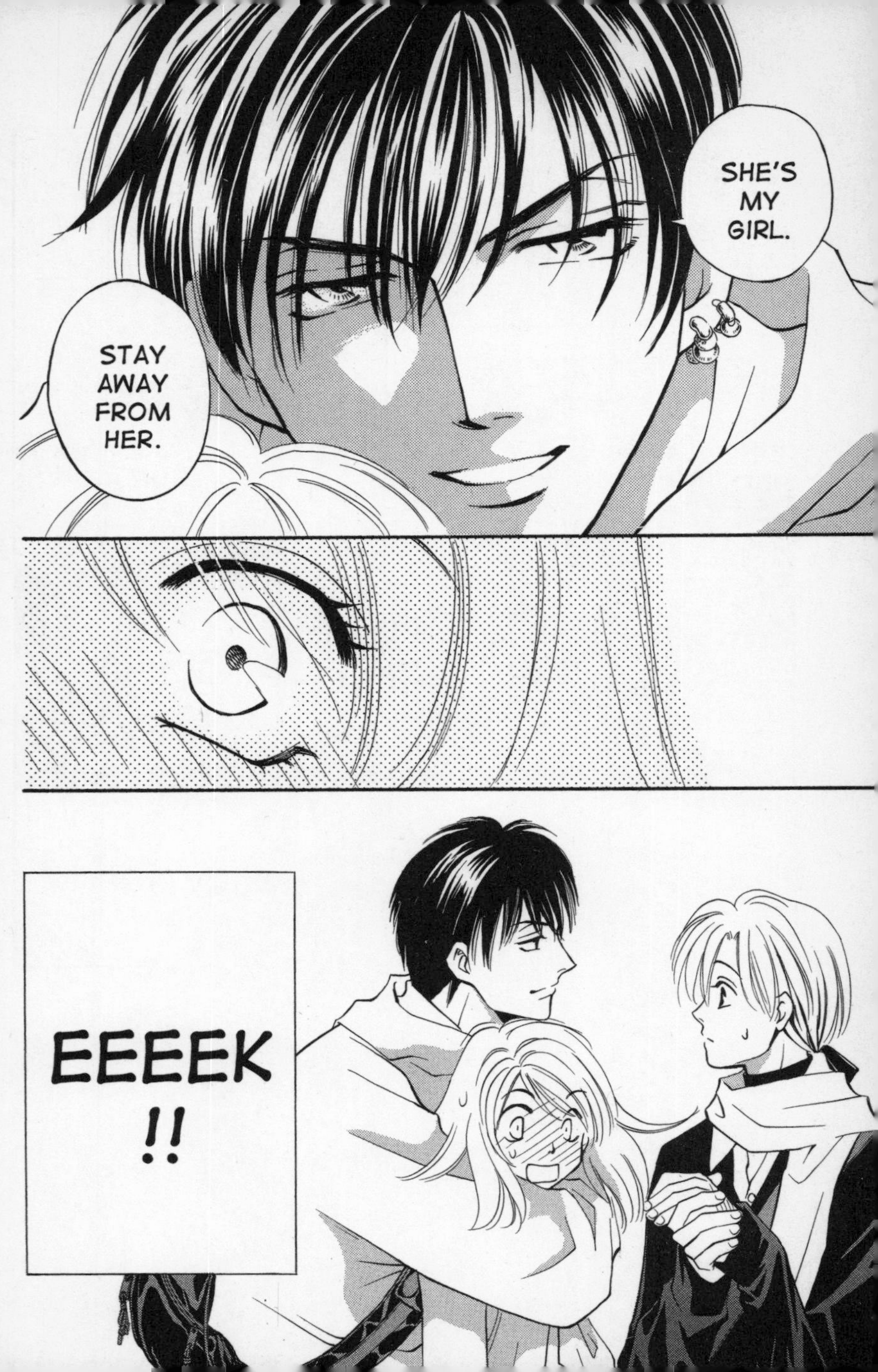
SHE'S MY GIRL.
STAY AWAY FROM HER.
EEEEK !!

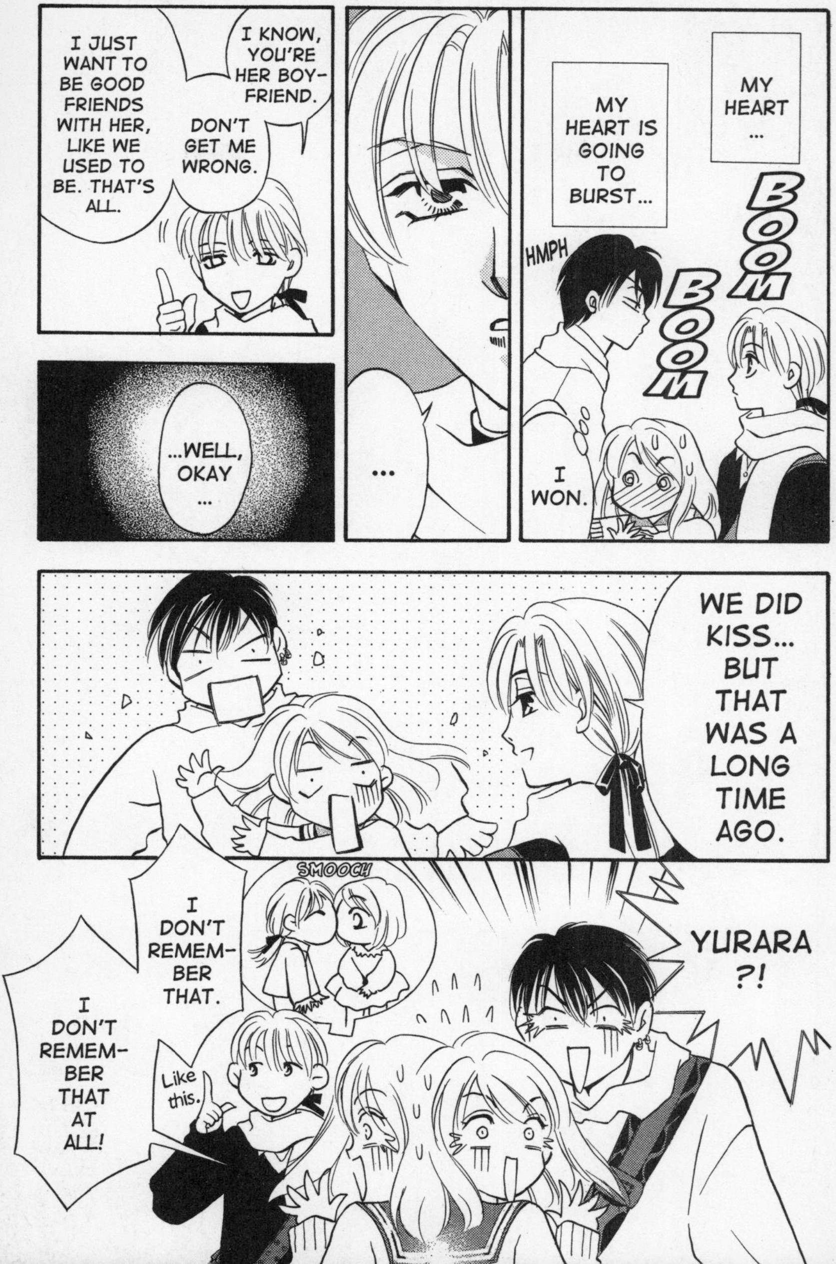
MY HEART ...
BOOM
MY HEART IS GOING TO BURST...
BOOM
HMPH
I WON.
...
I KNOW, YOU'RE HER BOY-FRIEND.
DON'T GET ME WRONG.
I JUST WANT TO BE GOOD FRIENDS WITH HER, LIKE WE USED TO BE. THAT'S ALL.
...WELL, OKAY ...
WE DID KISS... BUT THAT WAS A LONG TIME AGO.
YURARA ?!
SMOOCH
I DON'T REMEM-BER THAT.
I DON'T REMEM-BER THAT AT ALL!
Like this.

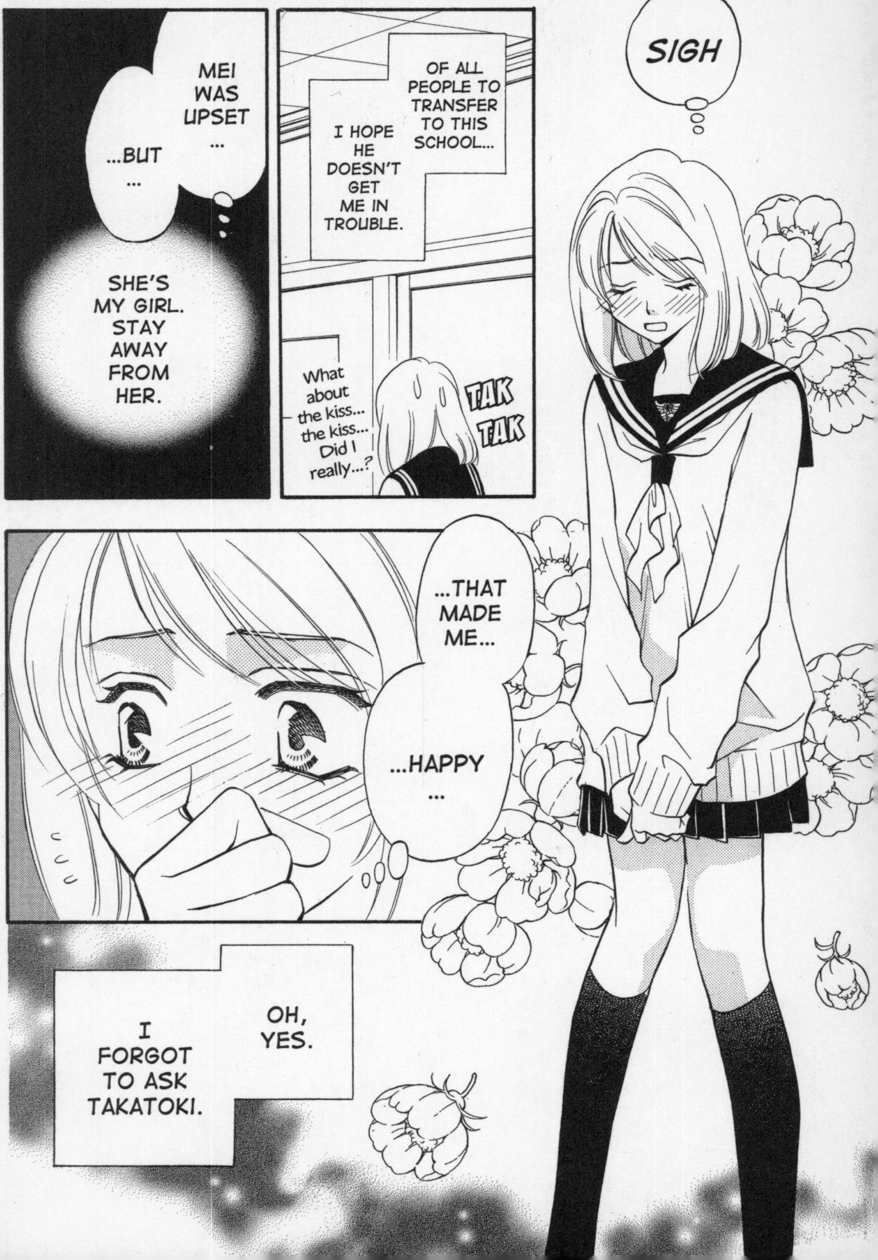
SIGH
OF ALL PEOPLE TO TRANSFER TO THIS SCHOOL...
I HOPE HE DOESN'T GET ME IN TROUBLE.
What about the kiss... the kiss... Did I really...?
TAK TAK
MEI WAS UPSET ...
...BUT ...
SHE'S MY GIRL. STAY AWAY FROM HER.
...THAT MADE ME...
...HAPPY ...
OH, YES.
I FORGOT TO ASK TAKATOKI.

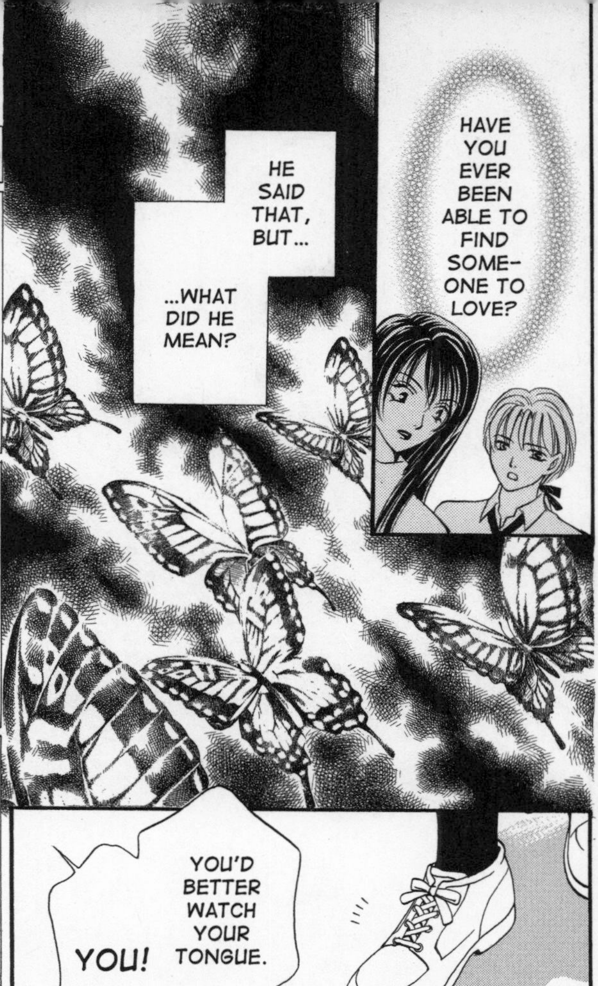
HAVE YOU EVER BEEN ABLE TO FIND SOME-ONE TO LOVE?
HE SAID THAT, BUT...
...WHAT DID HE MEAN?

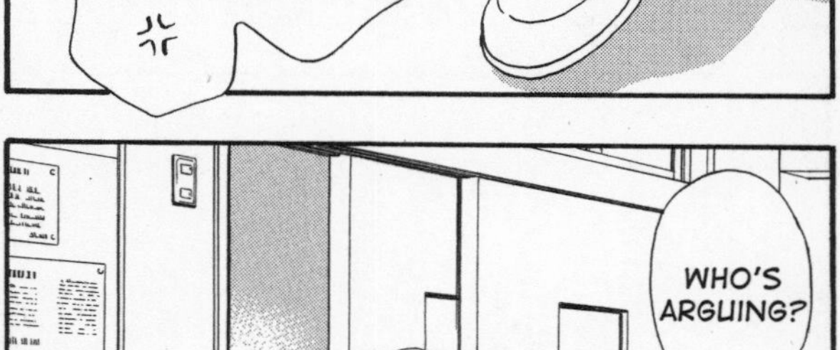
YOU'D BETTER WATCH YOUR TONGUE.
YOU!

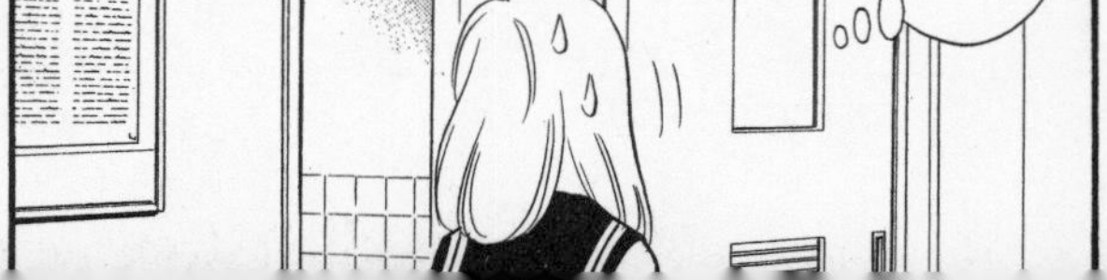
WHO'S ARGUING?

Shiomi's Daily Activities ⑭

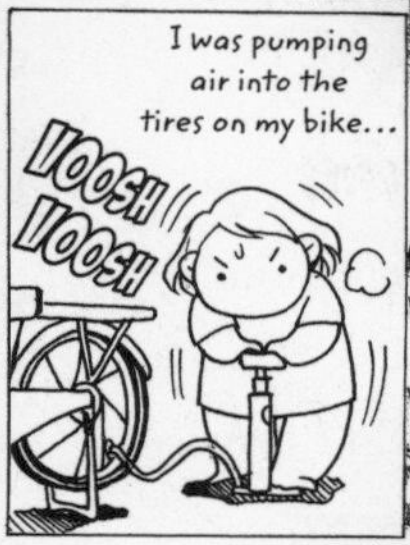
I was pumping air into the tires on my bike...
VOOSH VOOSH

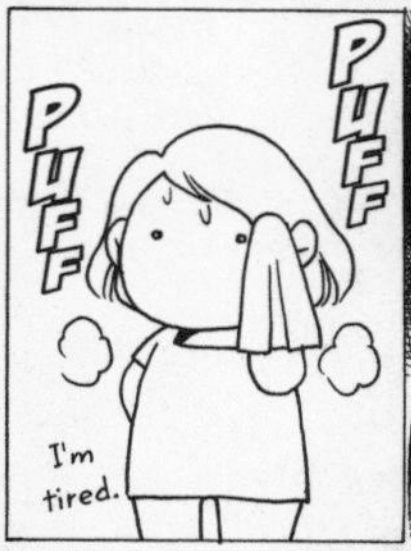
PUFF
PUFF
I'm tired.

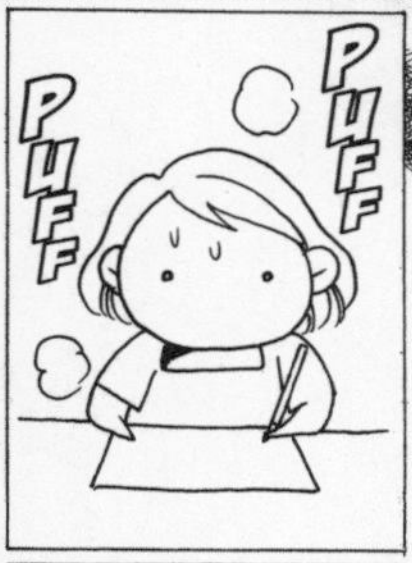
PUFF
PUFF

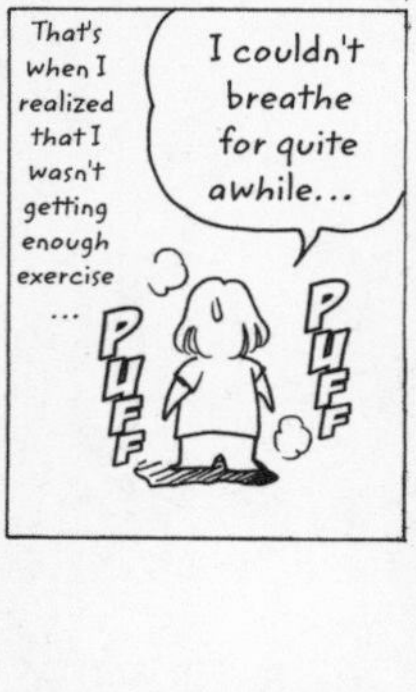
That's when I realized that I wasn't getting enough exercise...
I couldn't breathe for quite awhile...
PUFF
PUFF

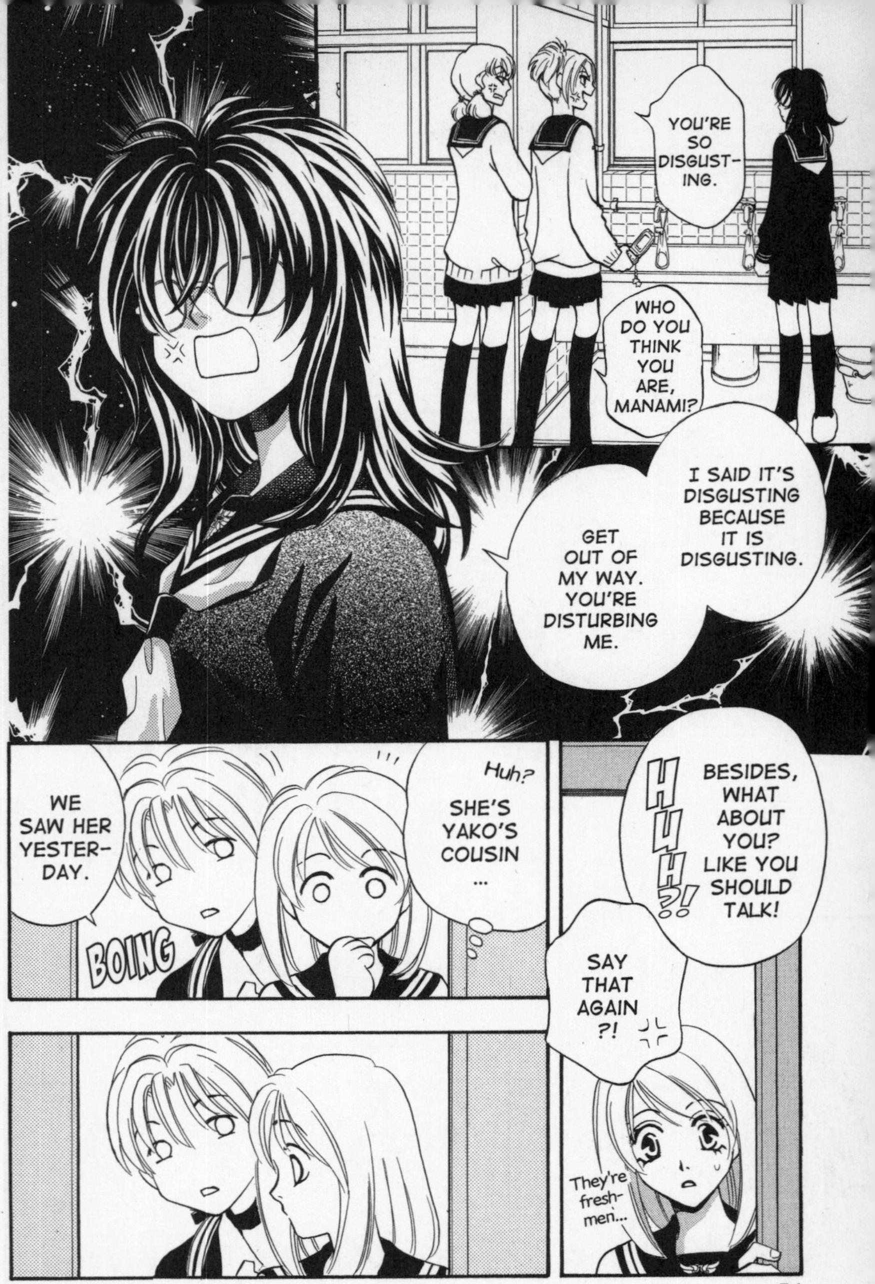
YOU'RE SO DISGUSTING.
WHO DO YOU THINK YOU ARE, MANAMI?
I SAID IT'S DISGUSTING BECAUSE IT IS DISGUSTING.
GET OUT OF MY WAY. YOU'RE DISTURBING ME.
HUHH?!
BESIDES, WHAT ABOUT YOU? LIKE YOU SHOULD TALK!
SAY THAT AGAIN?!
They're freshmen...
Huh?
SHE'S YAKO'S COUSIN...
WE SAW HER YESTERDAY.
BOING

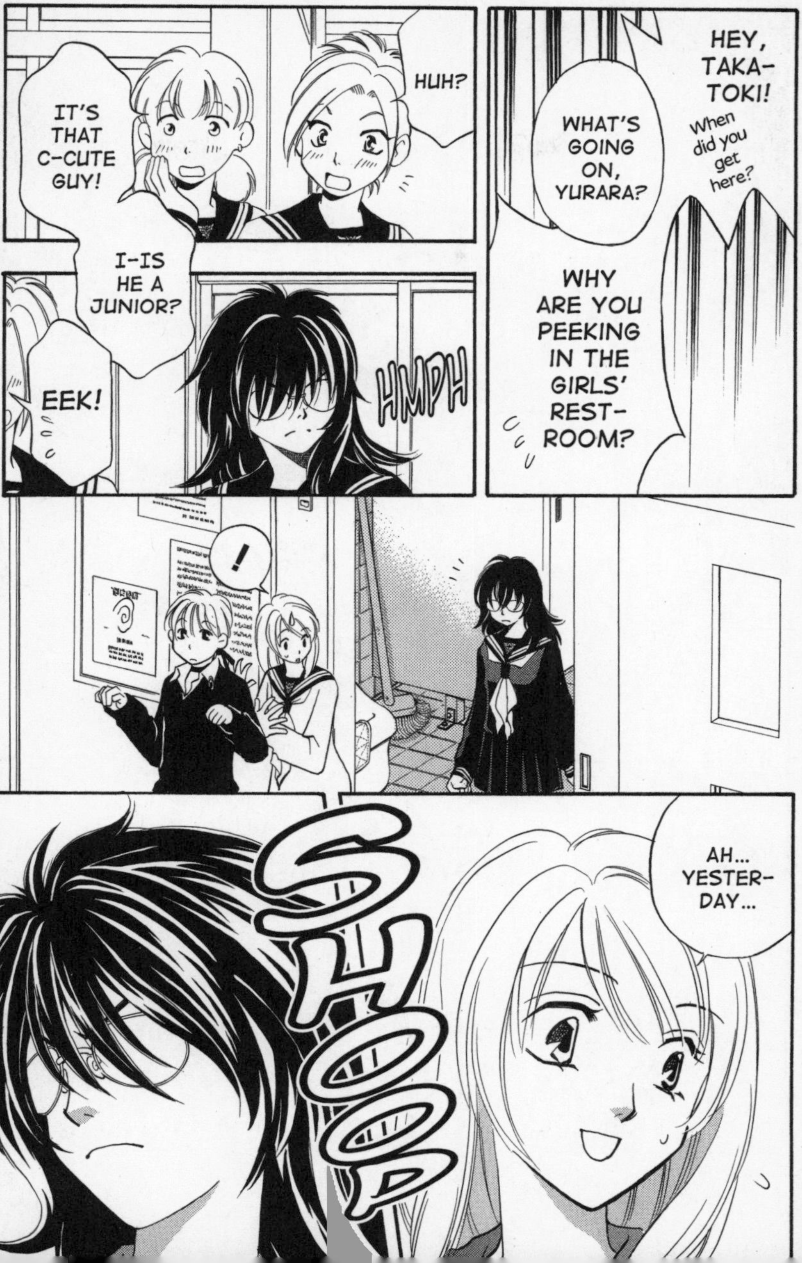

HEY, TAKA-TOKI!
When did you get here?
WHAT'S GOING ON, YURARA?
WHY ARE YOU PEEKING IN THE GIRLS' REST-ROOM?
HUH?
IT'S THAT C-CUTE GUY!
I-IS HE A JUNIOR?
HMPH
EEK!
!
AH... YESTER-DAY...
SHOOP

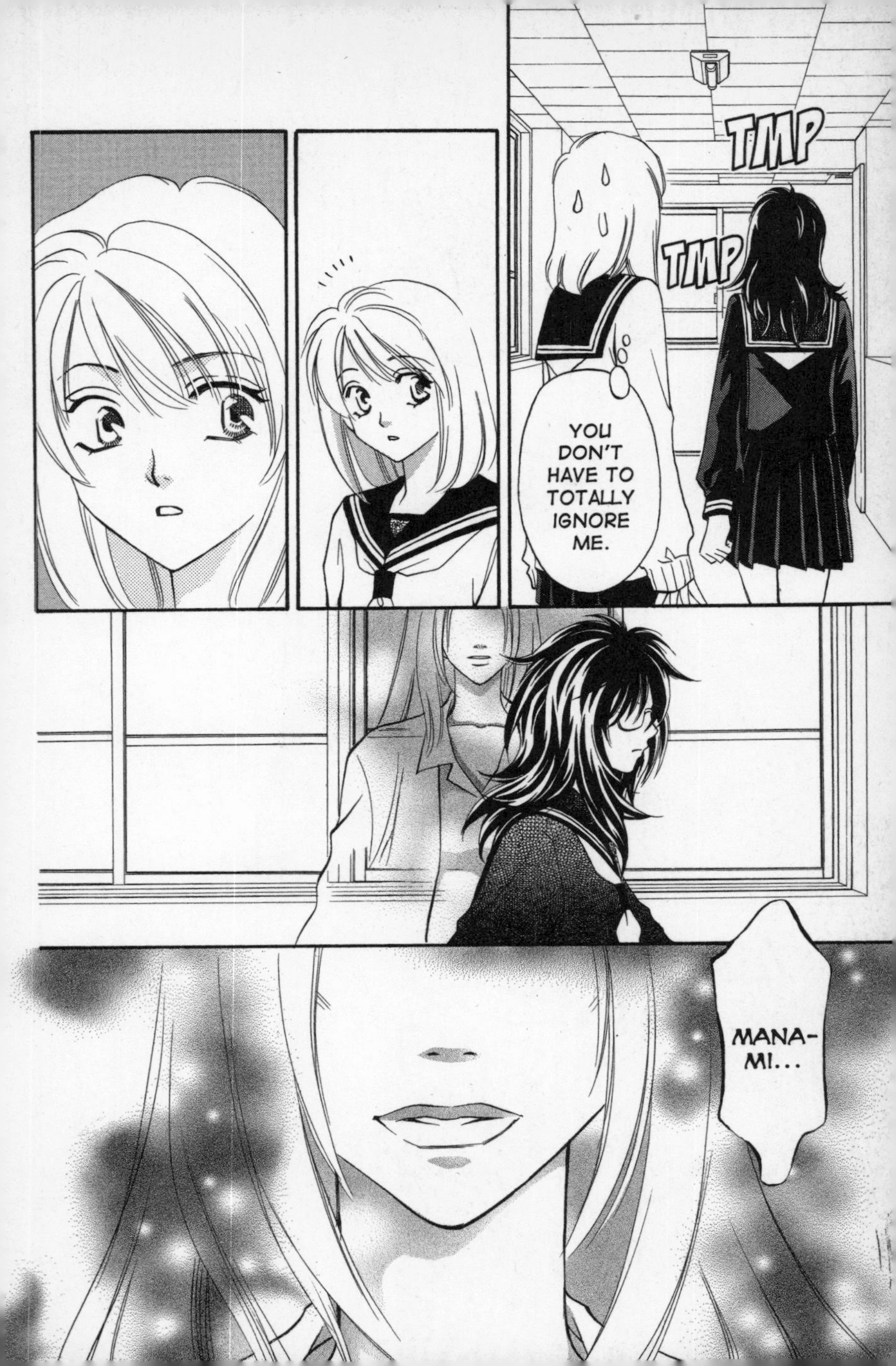
TMP
TMP
YOU DON'T HAVE TO TOTALLY IGNORE ME.
MANA-MI...

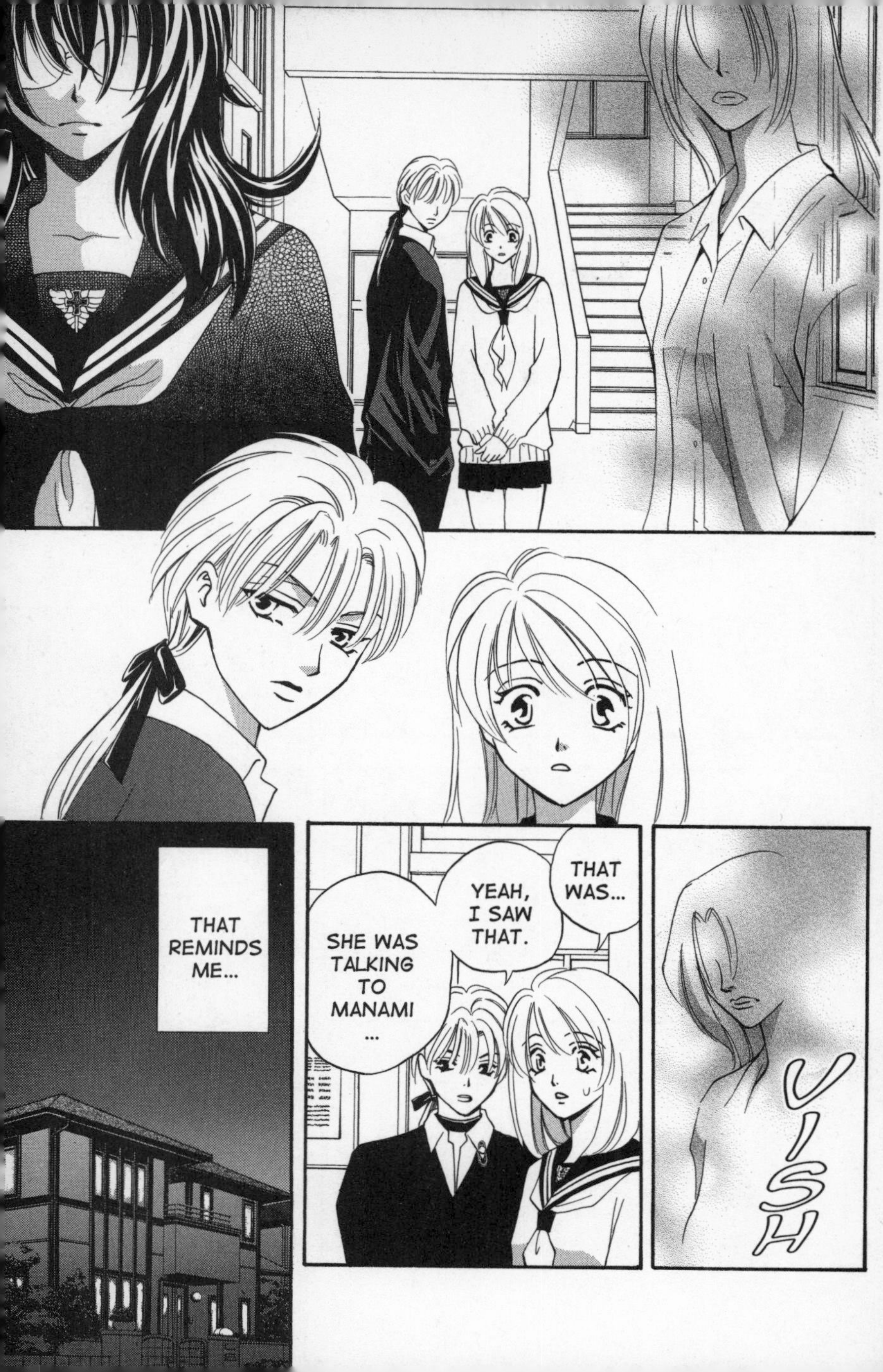
VISH
THAT WAS...
YEAH, I SAW THAT.
SHE WAS TALKING TO MANAMI ...
THAT REMINDS ME...

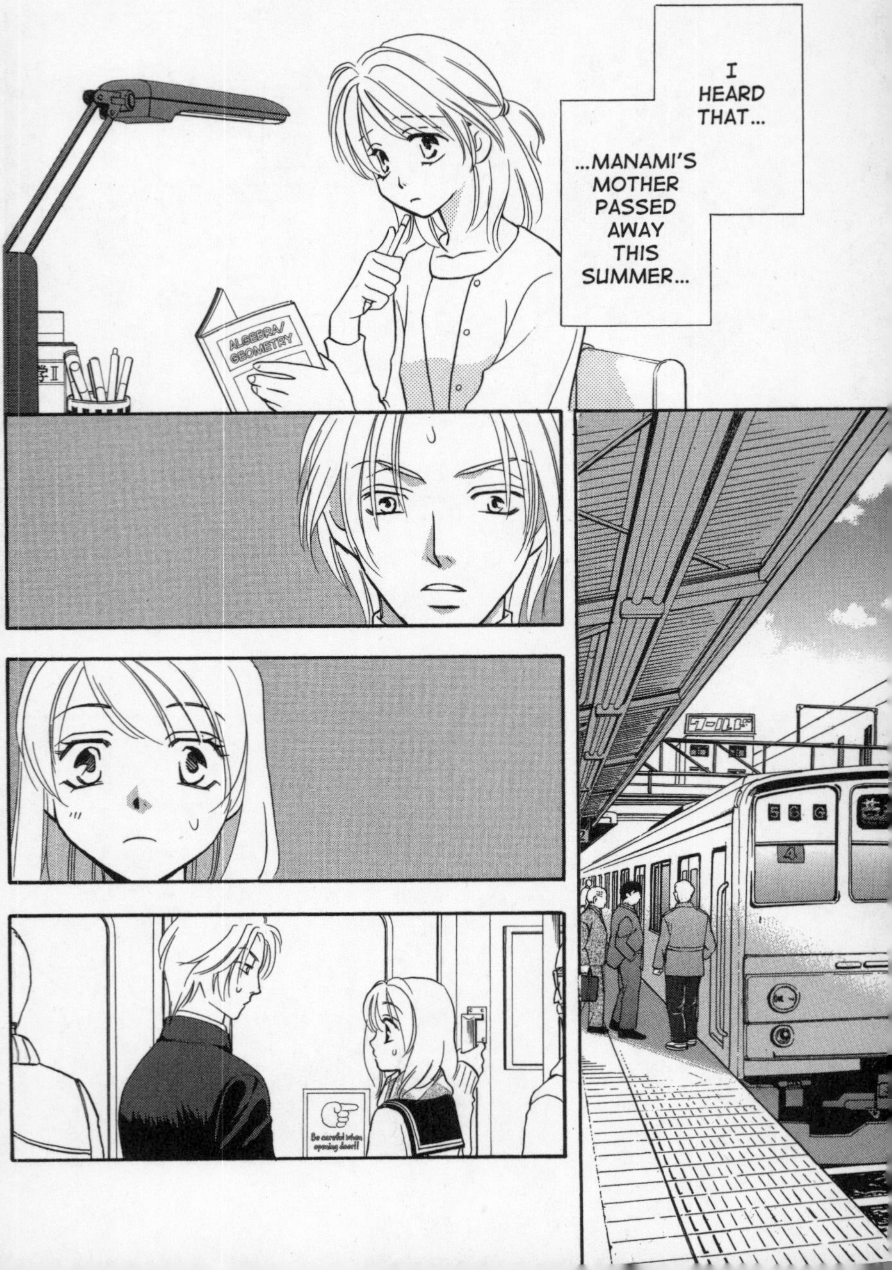
I HEARD THAT...
...MANAMI'S MOTHER PASSED AWAY THIS SUMMER...
ALGEBRA/ GEOMETRY
Be careful when opening door!!

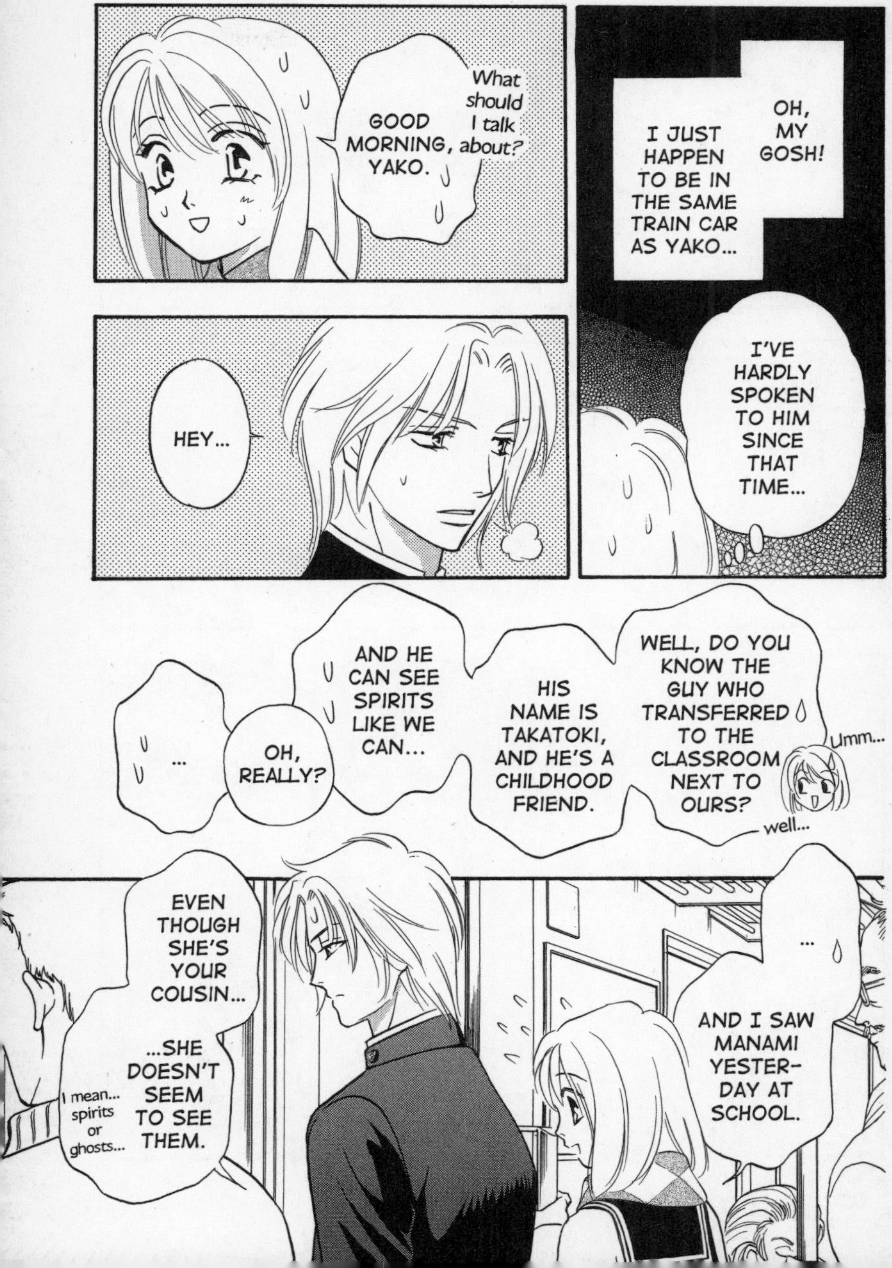
OH, MY GOSH!
I JUST HAPPEN TO BE IN THE SAME TRAIN CAR AS YAKO...
I'VE HARDLY SPOKEN TO HIM SINCE THAT TIME...
What should I talk about?
GOOD MORNING, YAKO.
HEY...
Umm... well...
WELL, DO YOU KNOW THE GUY WHO TRANSFERRED TO THE CLASSROOM NEXT TO OURS?
HIS NAME IS TAKATOKI, AND HE'S A CHILDHOOD FRIEND.
AND HE CAN SEE SPIRITS LIKE WE CAN...
OH, REALLY?
...
...
AND I SAW MANAMI YESTER-DAY AT SCHOOL.
EVEN THOUGH SHE'S YOUR COUSIN...
...SHE DOESN'T SEEM TO SEE THEM.
I mean... spirits or ghosts...

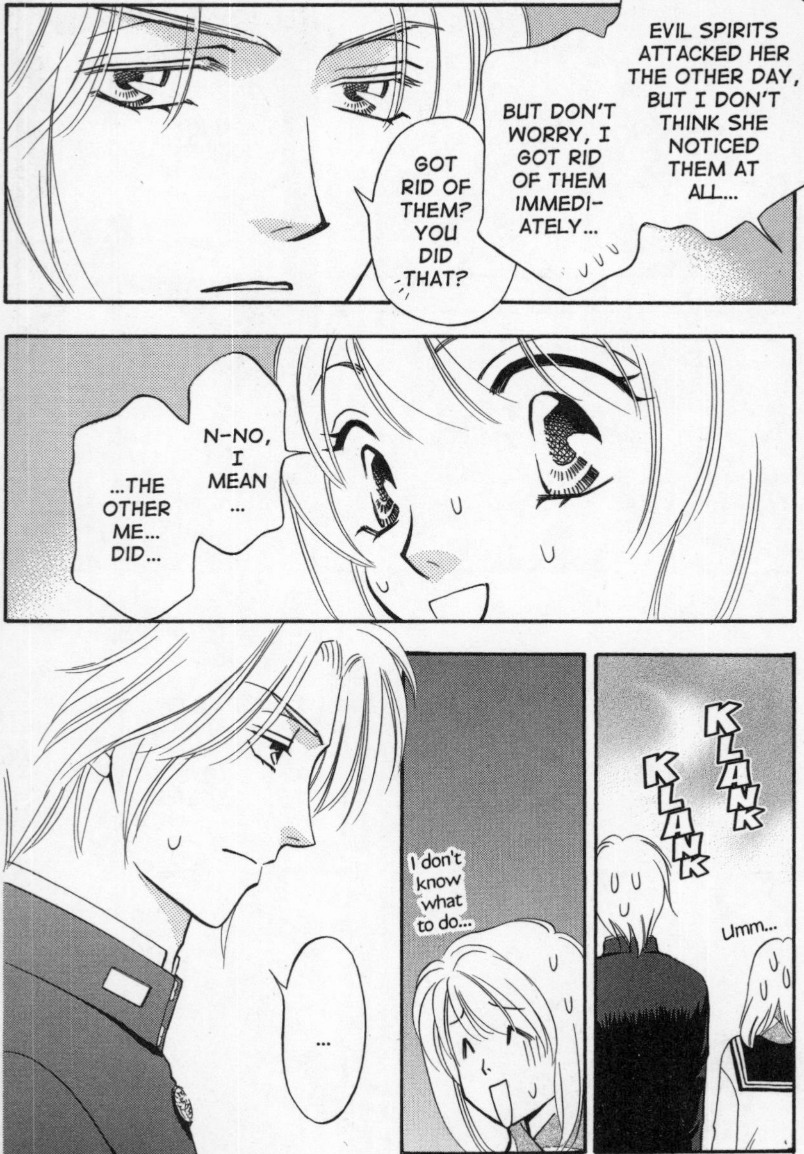
EVIL SPIRITS ATTACKED HER THE OTHER DAY, BUT I DON'T THINK SHE NOTICED THEM AT ALL...
BUT DON'T WORRY, I GOT RID OF THEM IMMEDI-ATELY...
GOT RID OF THEM? YOU DID THAT?
N-NO, I MEAN ...
...THE OTHER ME... DID...
KLANK
KLANK
Umm...
I don't know what to do...
...

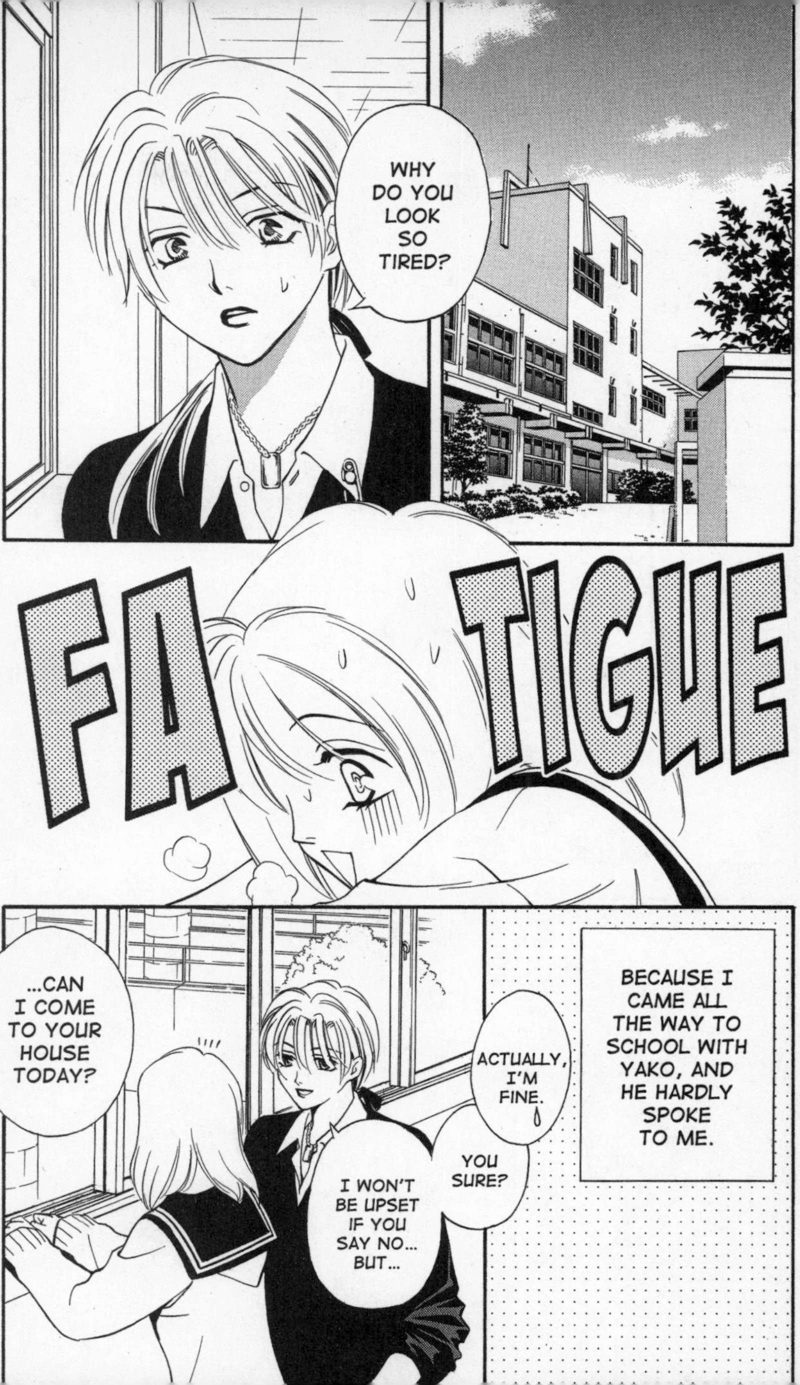
WHY DO YOU LOOK SO TIRED?
FATIGUE
BECAUSE I CAME ALL THE WAY TO SCHOOL WITH YAKO, AND HE HARDLY SPOKE TO ME.
ACTUALLY, I'M FINE.
YOU SURE?
I WON'T BE UPSET IF YOU SAY NO... BUT...
...CAN I COME TO YOUR HOUSE TODAY?

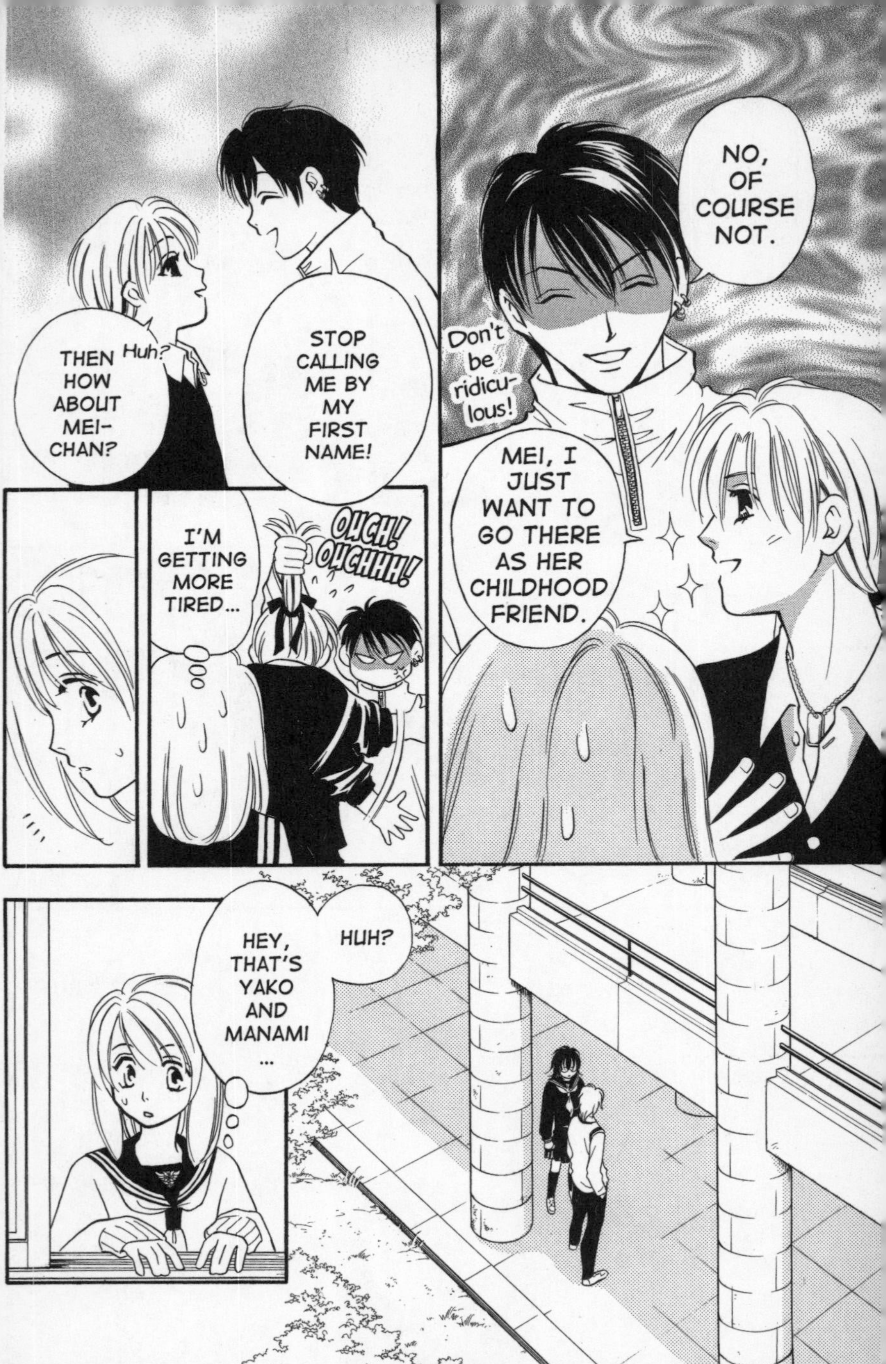
NO, OF COURSE NOT.
Don't be ridiculous!
MEI, I JUST WANT TO GO THERE AS HER CHILDHOOD FRIEND.
STOP CALLING ME BY MY FIRST NAME!
THEN HOW ABOUT MEI-CHAN?
Huh?
I'M GETTING MORE TIRED...
OUCH! OUCHHH!
HUH?
HEY, THAT'S YAKO AND MANAMI ...

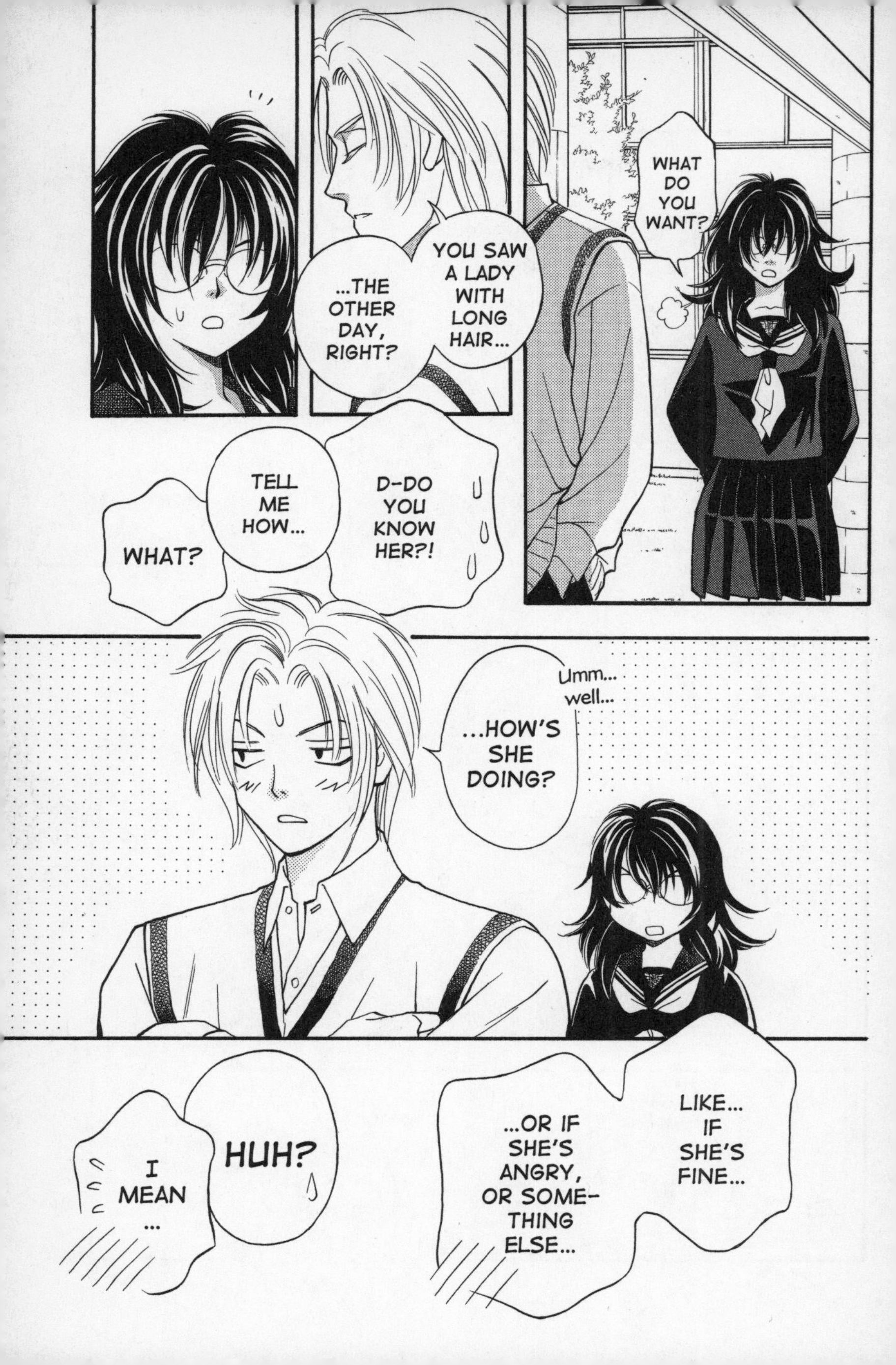
WHAT DO YOU WANT?
YOU SAW A LADY WITH LONG HAIR...
...THE OTHER DAY, RIGHT?
D-DO YOU KNOW HER?!
TELL ME HOW...
WHAT?
Umm... well...
...HOW'S SHE DOING?
LIKE... IF SHE'S FINE...
...OR IF SHE'S ANGRY, OR SOME-THING ELSE...
HUH?
I MEAN ...

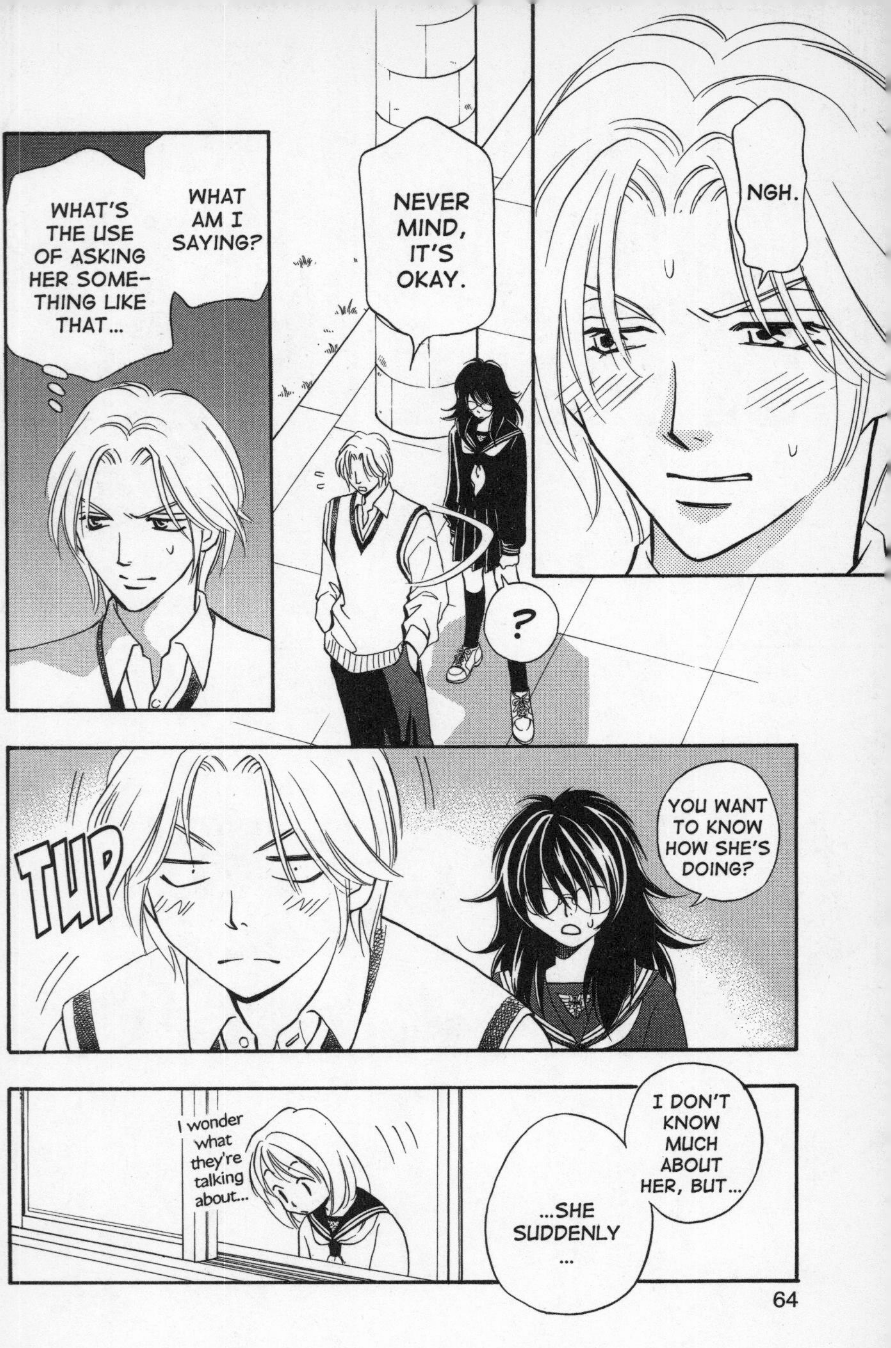
NGH.
NEVER MIND, IT'S OKAY.
?
WHAT AM I SAYING?
WHAT'S THE USE OF ASKING HER SOME-THING LIKE THAT...
YOU WANT TO KNOW HOW SHE'S DOING?
TUP
I DON'T KNOW MUCH ABOUT HER, BUT...
...SHE SUDDENLY ...
I wonder what they're talking about...

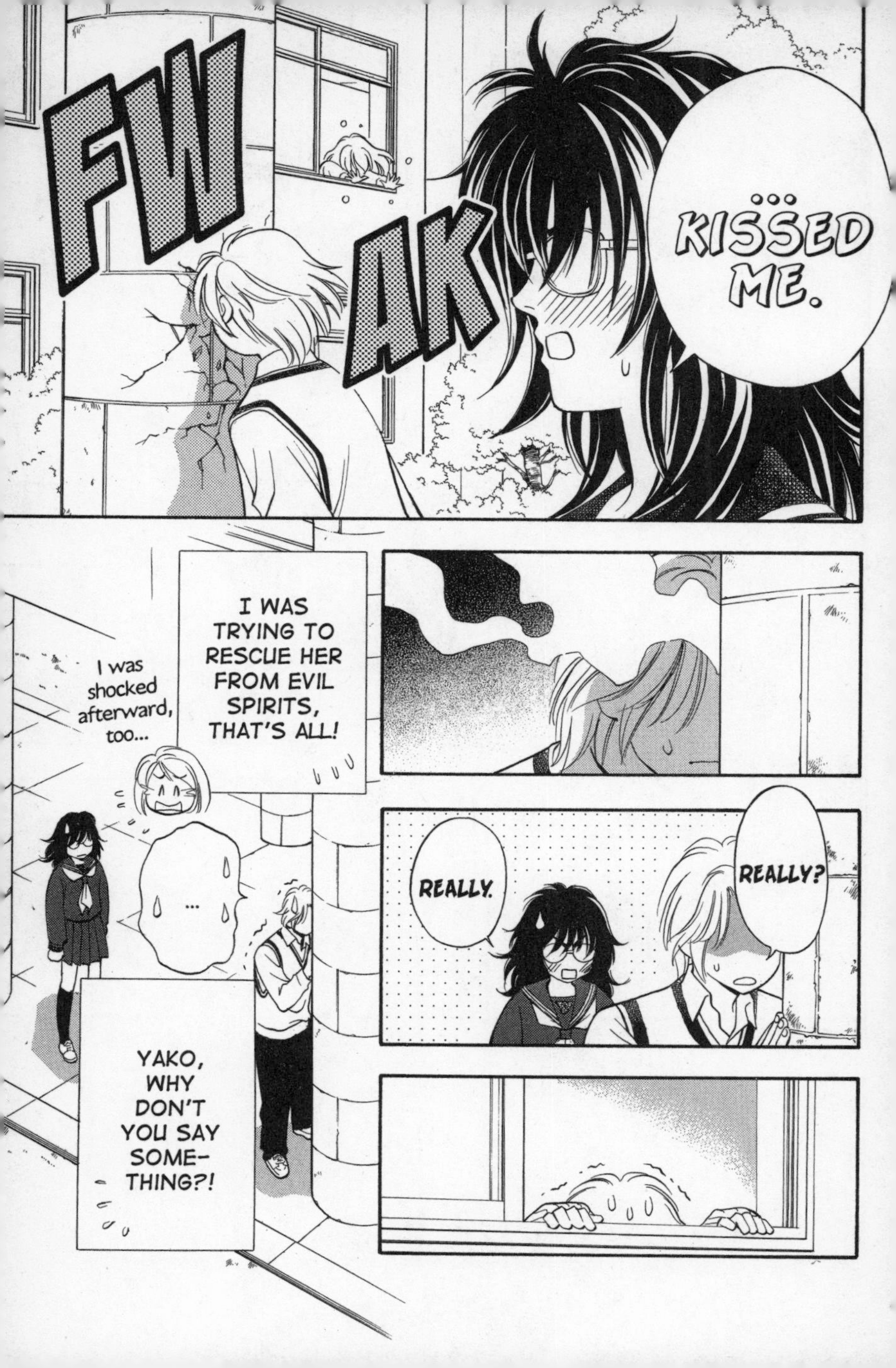
...KISSED ME.
FWAK
REALLY?
REALLY.
I WAS TRYING TO RESCUE HER FROM EVIL SPIRITS, THAT'S ALL!
I was shocked afterward, too...
...
YAKO, WHY DON'T YOU SAY SOME-THING?!

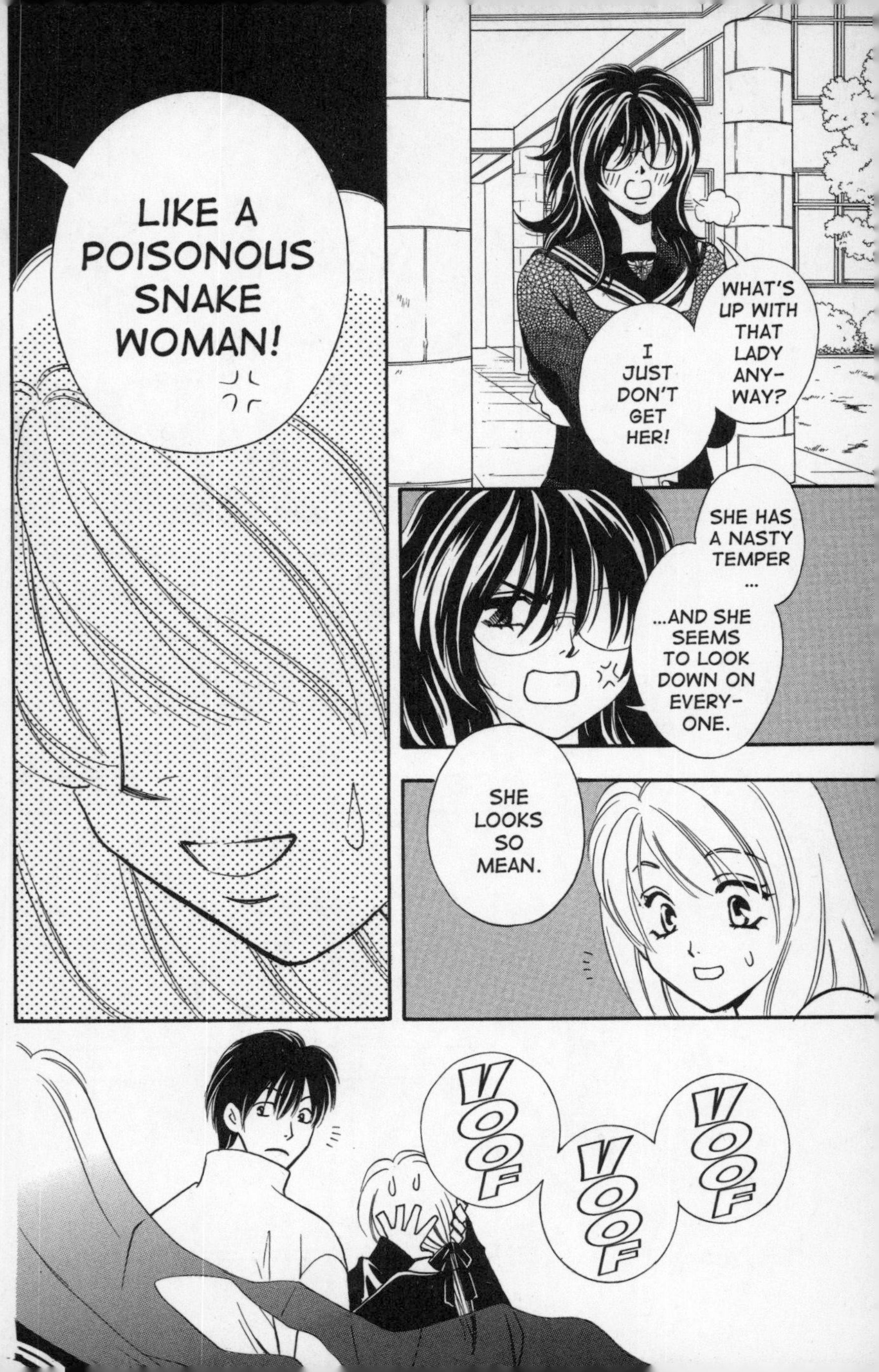
WHAT'S UP WITH THAT LADY ANY-WAY?
I JUST DON'T GET HER!
SHE HAS A NASTY TEMPER ...
...AND SHE SEEMS TO LOOK DOWN ON EVERY-ONE.
SHE LOOKS SO MEAN.
LIKE A POISONOUS SNAKE WOMAN!
VOOF
VOOF
VOOF

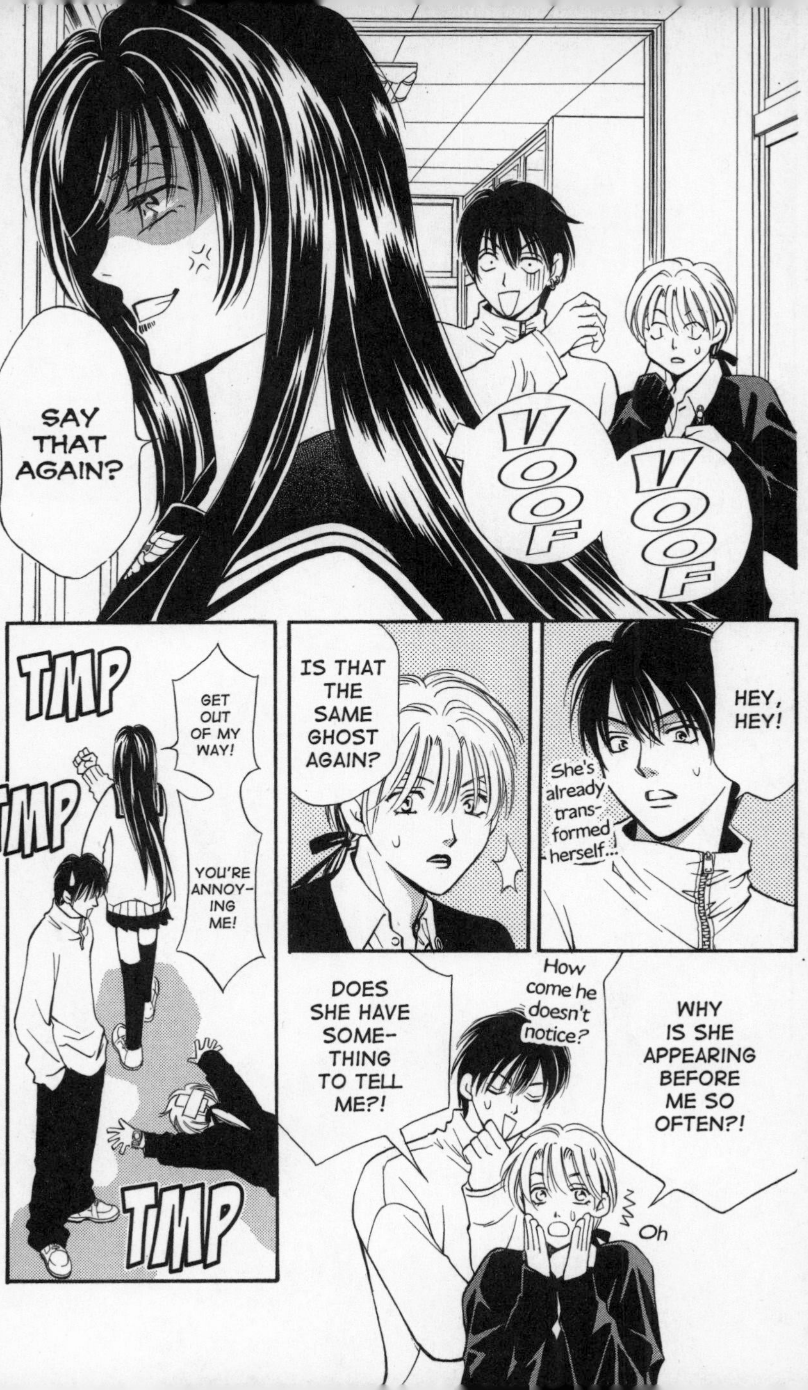
VOOF
VOOF
SAY THAT AGAIN?
HEY, HEY!
She's already transformed herself...
IS THAT THE SAME GHOST AGAIN?
WHY IS SHE APPEARING BEFORE ME SO OFTEN?!
Oh
How come he doesn't notice?
DOES SHE HAVE SOMETHING TO TELL ME?!
TMP
GET OUT OF MY WAY!
YOU'RE ANNOYING ME!
TMP
TMP

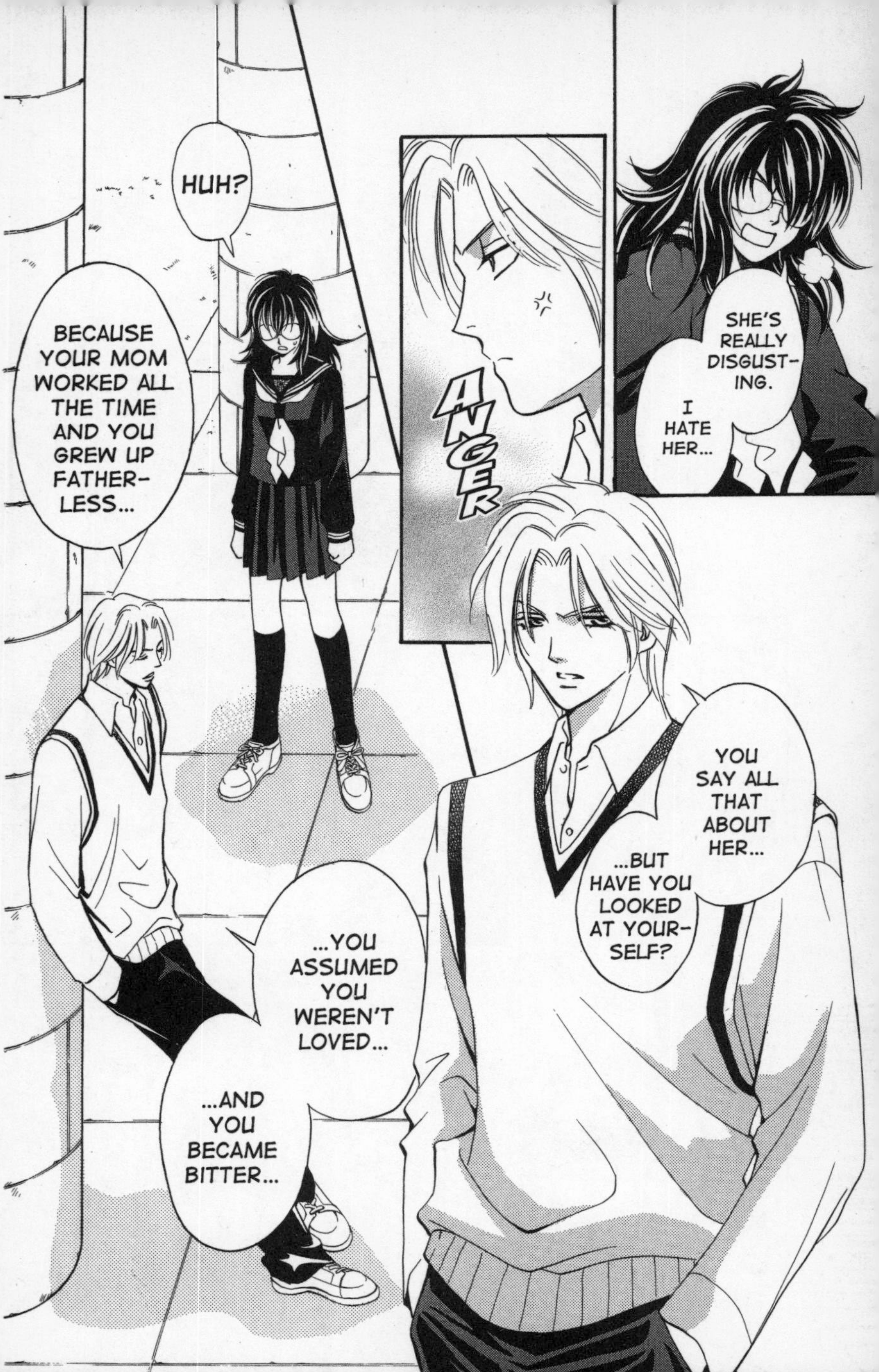
SHE'S REALLY DISGUSTING.
I HATE HER...
ANGER
YOU SAY ALL THAT ABOUT HER...
...BUT HAVE YOU LOOKED AT YOURSELF?
HUH?
BECAUSE YOUR MOM WORKED ALL THE TIME AND YOU GREW UP FATHERLESS...
...YOU ASSUMED YOU WEREN'T LOVED...
...AND YOU BECAME BITTER...

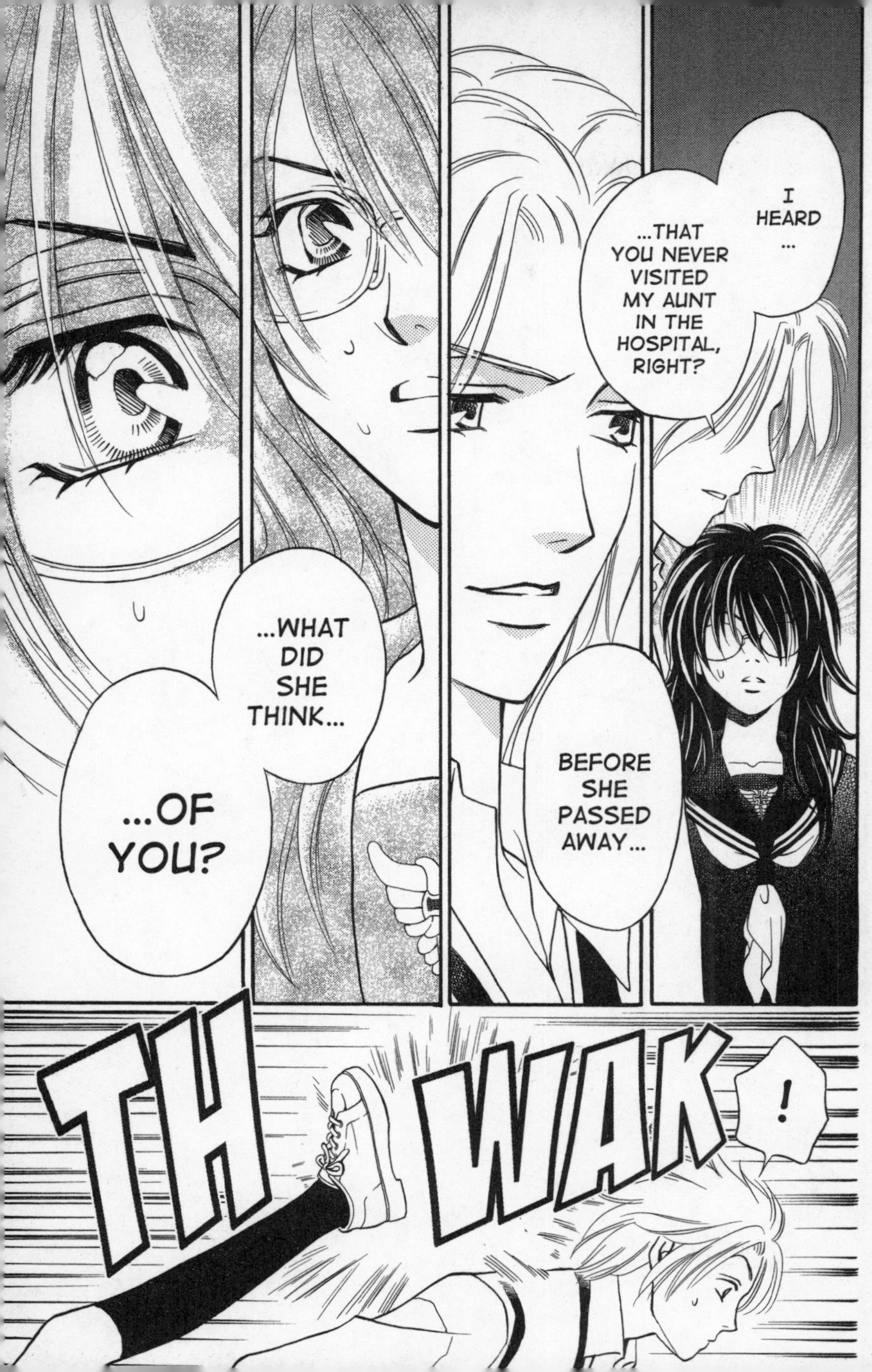
I HEARD ...
...THAT YOU NEVER VISITED MY AUNT IN THE HOSPITAL, RIGHT?
BEFORE SHE PASSED AWAY...
...WHAT DID SHE THINK...
...OF YOU?
THWAK
!

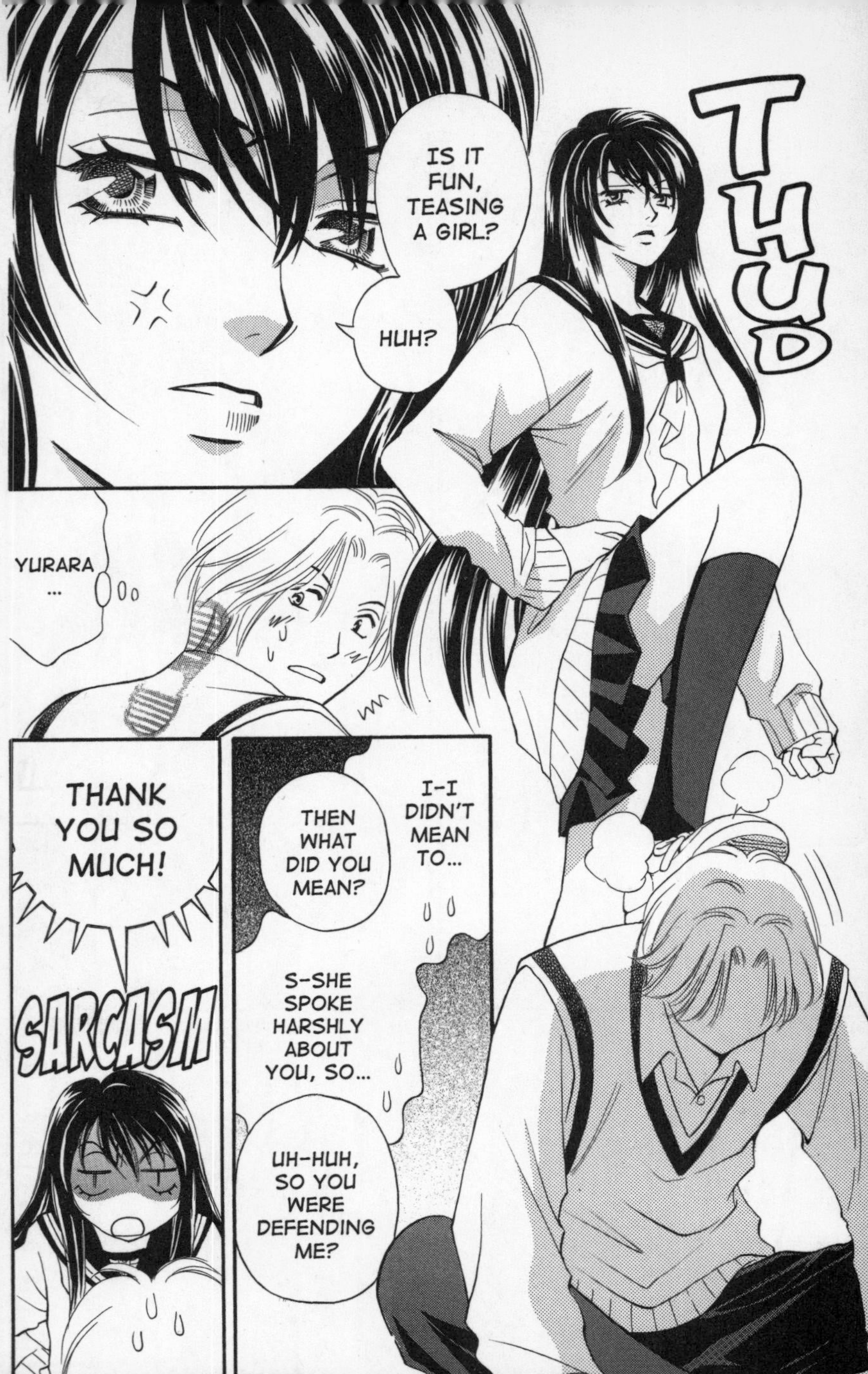
THUD
IS IT FUN, TEASING A GIRL?
HUH?
YURARA ...
I-I DIDN'T MEAN TO...
THEN WHAT DID YOU MEAN?
S-SHE SPOKE HARSHLY ABOUT YOU, SO...
UH-HUH, SO YOU WERE DEFENDING ME?
THANK YOU SO MUCH!
SARCASM

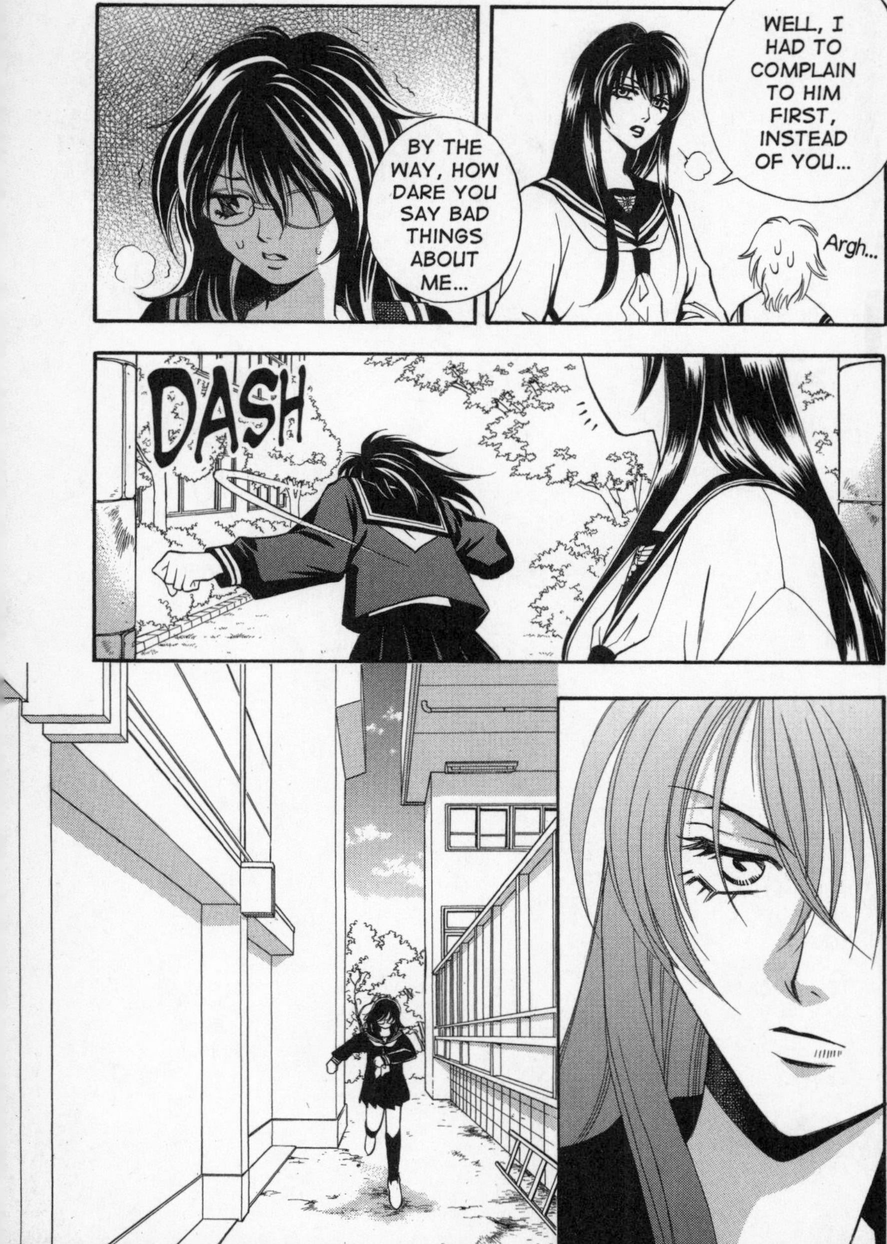
WELL, I HAD TO COMPLAIN TO HIM FIRST, INSTEAD OF YOU...
Argh...
BY THE WAY, HOW DARE YOU SAY BAD THINGS ABOUT ME...
DASH

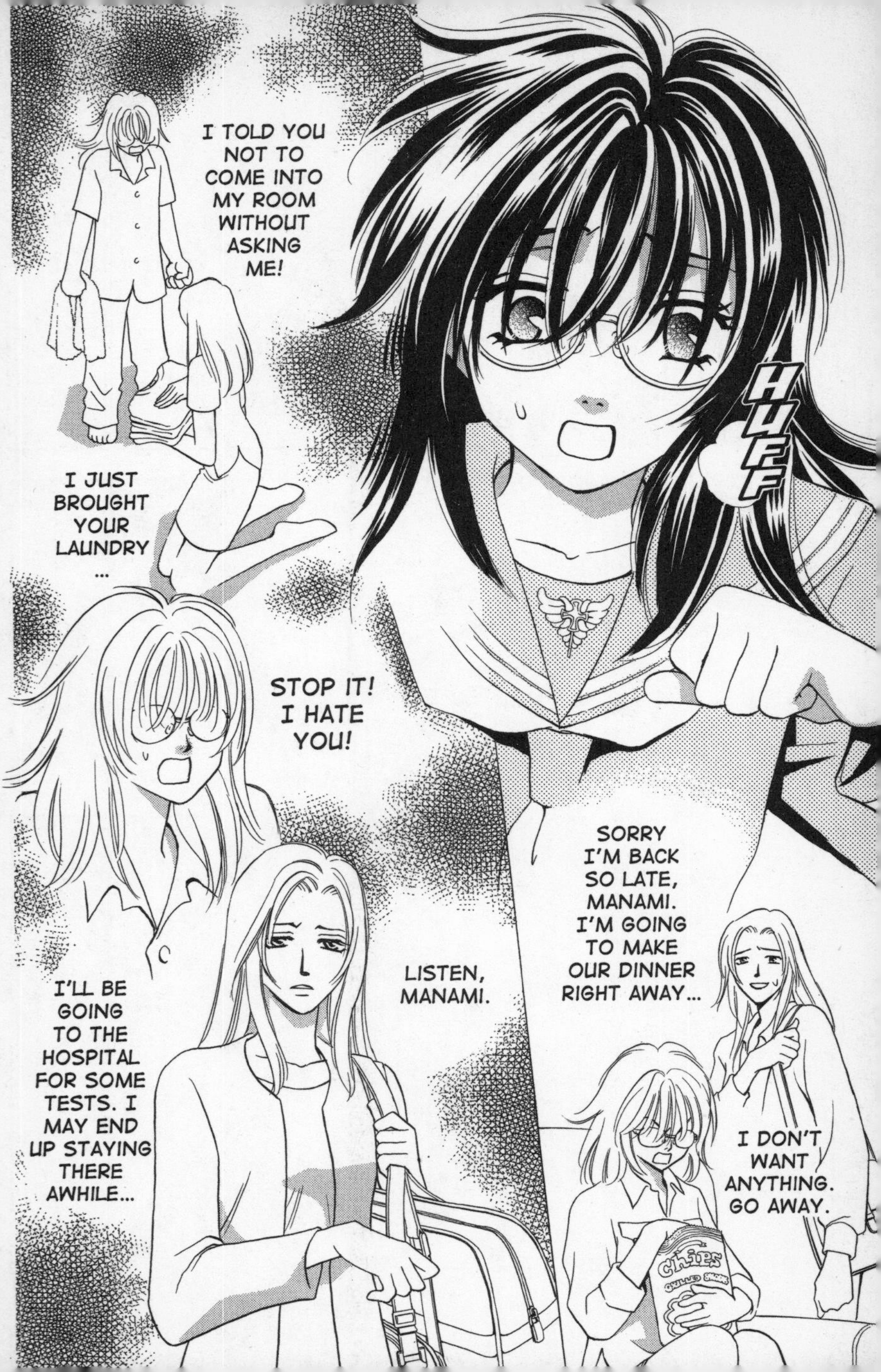
HUFF
I TOLD YOU NOT TO COME INTO MY ROOM WITHOUT ASKING ME!
I JUST BROUGHT YOUR LAUNDRY ...
STOP IT! I HATE YOU!
SORRY I'M BACK SO LATE, MANAMI. I'M GOING TO MAKE OUR DINNER RIGHT AWAY...
I DON'T WANT ANYTHING. GO AWAY.
Chips
LISTEN, MANAMI.
I'LL BE GOING TO THE HOSPITAL FOR SOME TESTS. I MAY END UP STAYING THERE AWHILE...

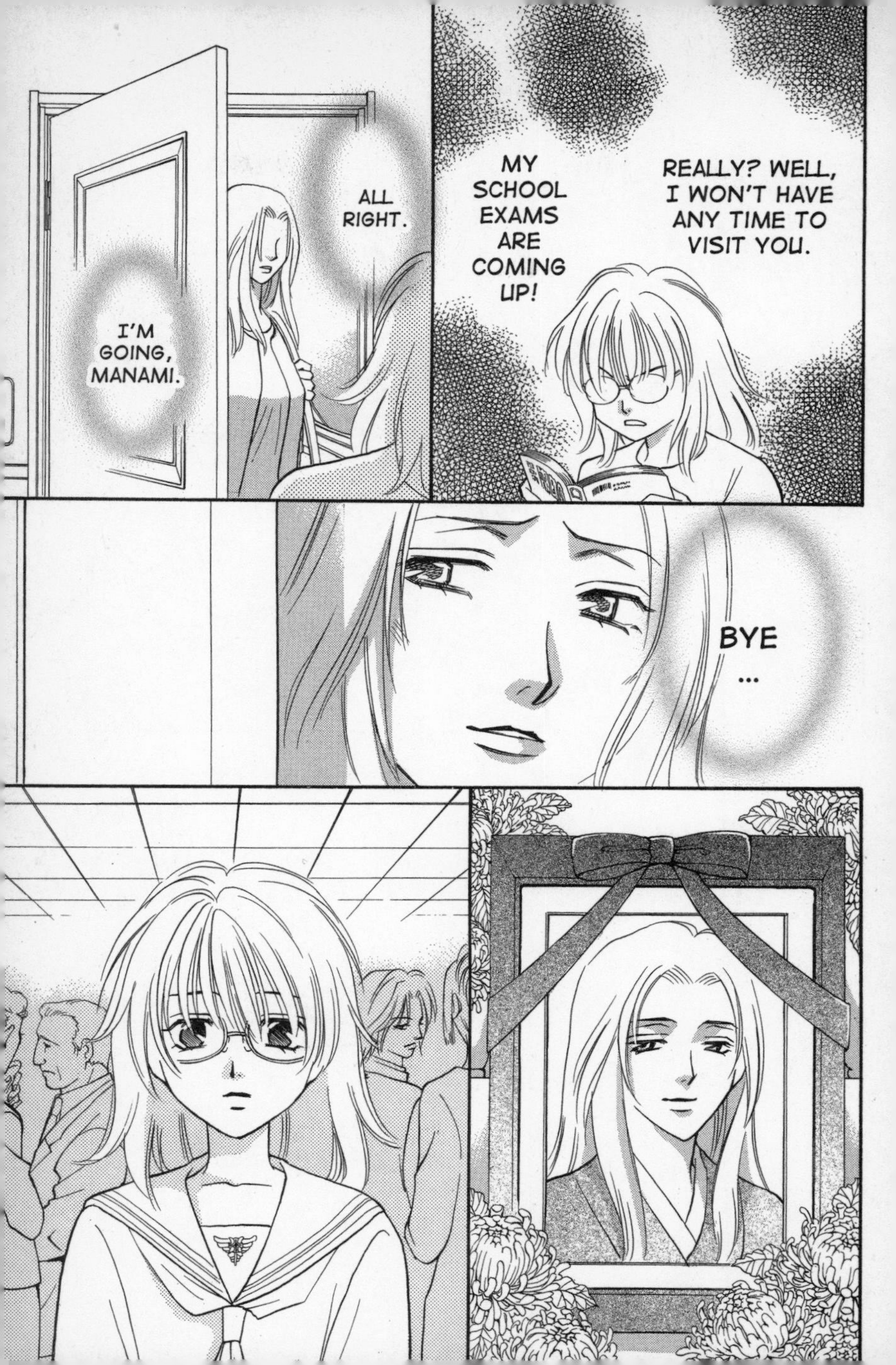
REALLY? WELL, I WON'T HAVE ANY TIME TO VISIT YOU.
MY SCHOOL EXAMS ARE COMING UP!
ALL RIGHT.
I'M GOING, MANAMI.
BYE ...

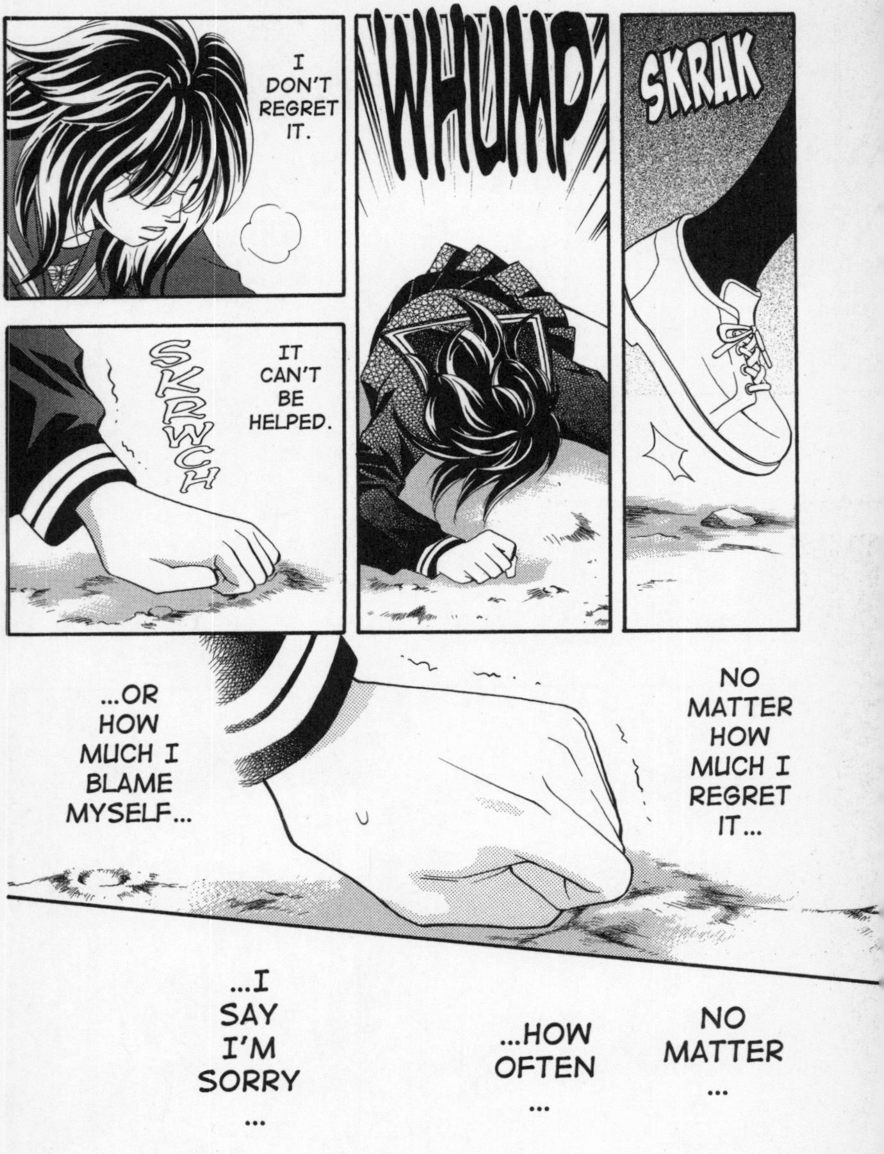
SKRAK
WHUMP
I DON'T REGRET IT.
IT CAN'T BE HELPED.
SKRWCH
NO MATTER HOW MUCH I REGRET IT...
...OR HOW MUCH I BLAME MYSELF...
NO MATTER ...
...HOW OFTEN ...
...I SAY I'M SORRY ...

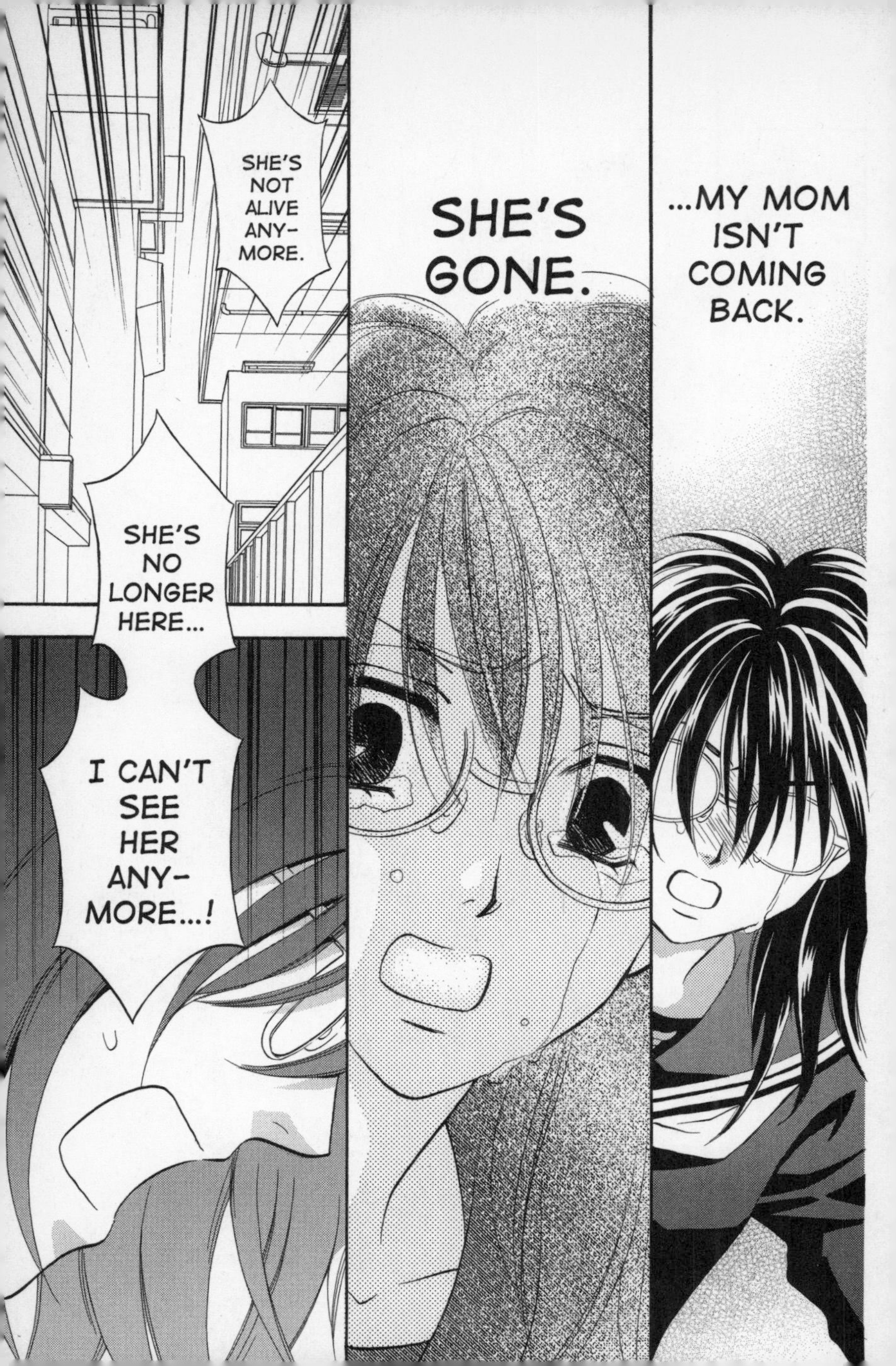
...MY MOM ISN'T COMING BACK.
SHE'S GONE.
SHE'S NOT ALIVE ANY-MORE.
SHE'S NO LONGER HERE...
I CAN'T SEE HER ANY-MORE...!

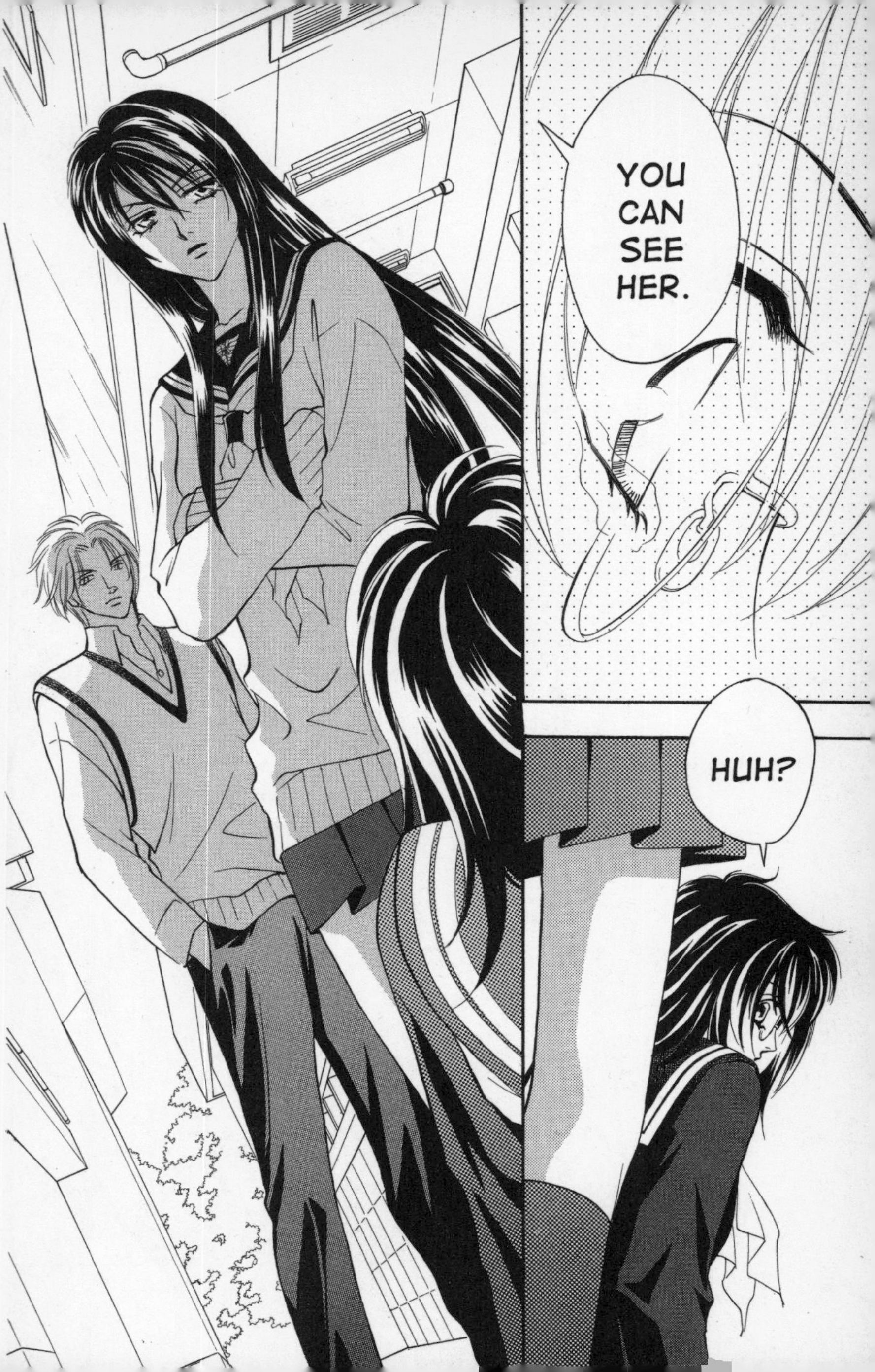
YOU CAN SEE HER.
HUH?

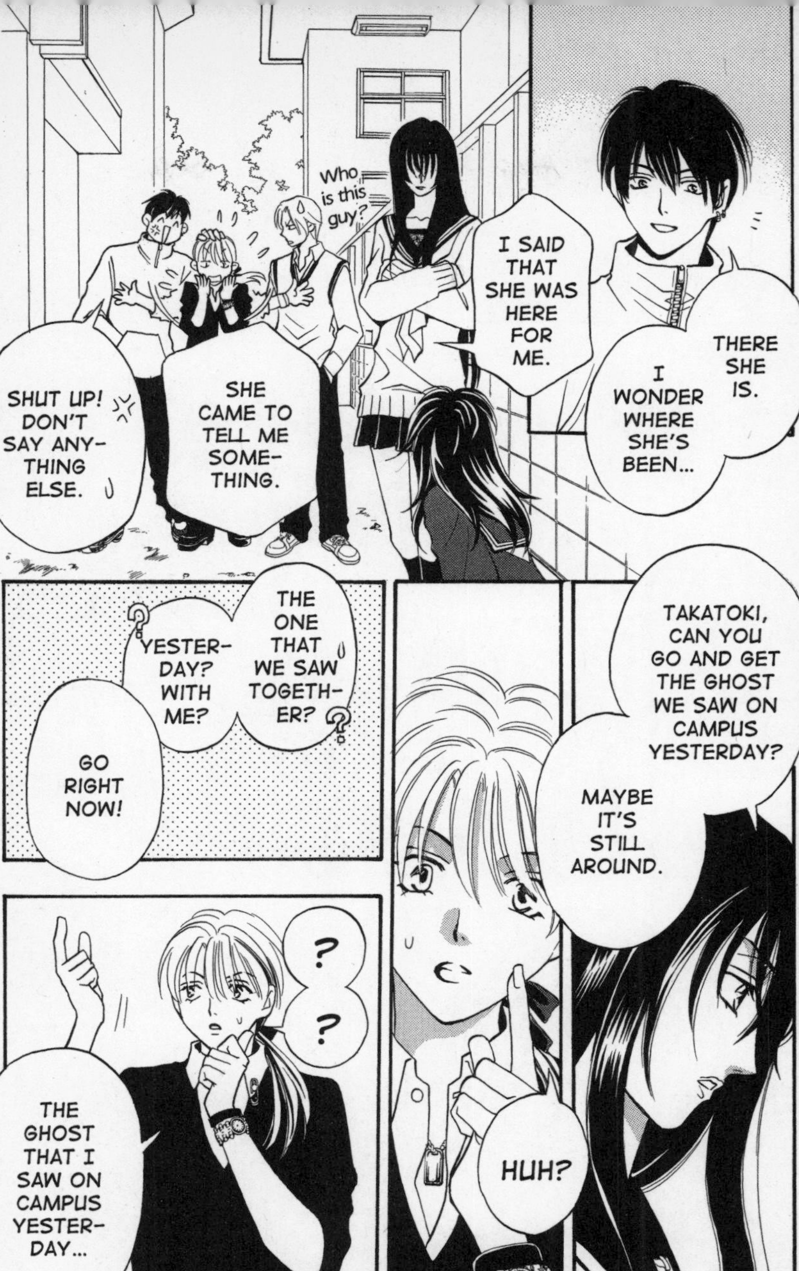
THERE SHE IS.
I WONDER WHERE SHE'S BEEN...
I SAID THAT SHE WAS HERE FOR ME.
Who is this guy?
SHE CAME TO TELL ME SOMETHING.
SHUT UP! DON'T SAY ANY-THING ELSE.
TAKATOKI, CAN YOU GO AND GET THE GHOST WE SAW ON CAMPUS YESTERDAY?
MAYBE IT'S STILL AROUND.
HUH?
THE ONE THAT WE SAW TOGETH-ER?
YESTER-DAY? WITH ME?
GO RIGHT NOW!
? ?
THE GHOST THAT I SAW ON CAMPUS YESTER-DAY...

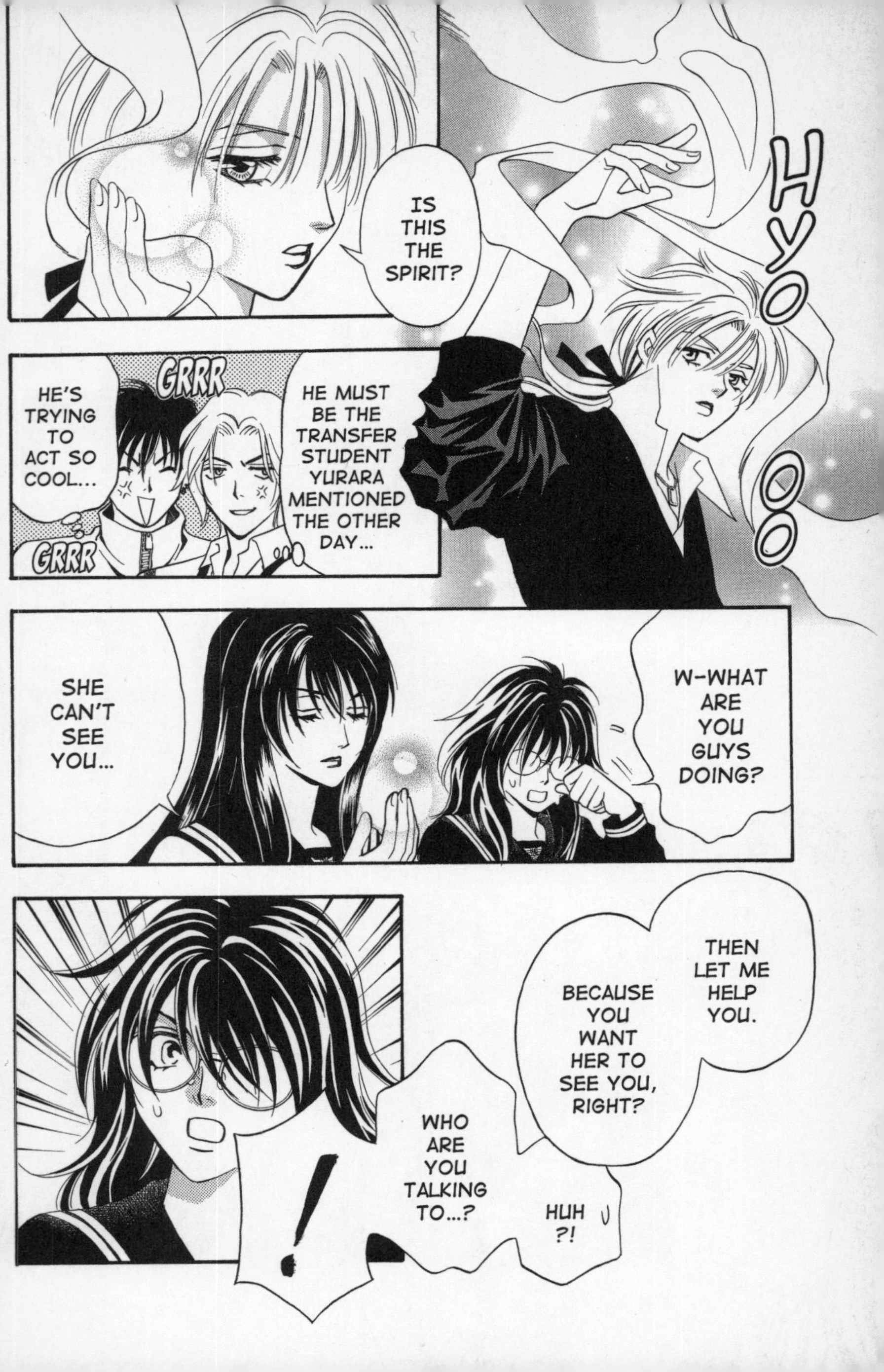
HYOOO
IS THIS THE SPIRIT?
HE MUST BE THE TRANSFER STUDENT YURARA MENTIONED THE OTHER DAY...
GRRR
HE'S TRYING TO ACT SO COOL...
GRRR
W-WHAT ARE YOU GUYS DOING?
SHE CAN'T SEE YOU...
THEN LET ME HELP YOU.
BECAUSE YOU WANT HER TO SEE YOU, RIGHT?
HUH ?!
WHO ARE YOU TALKING TO...?
!

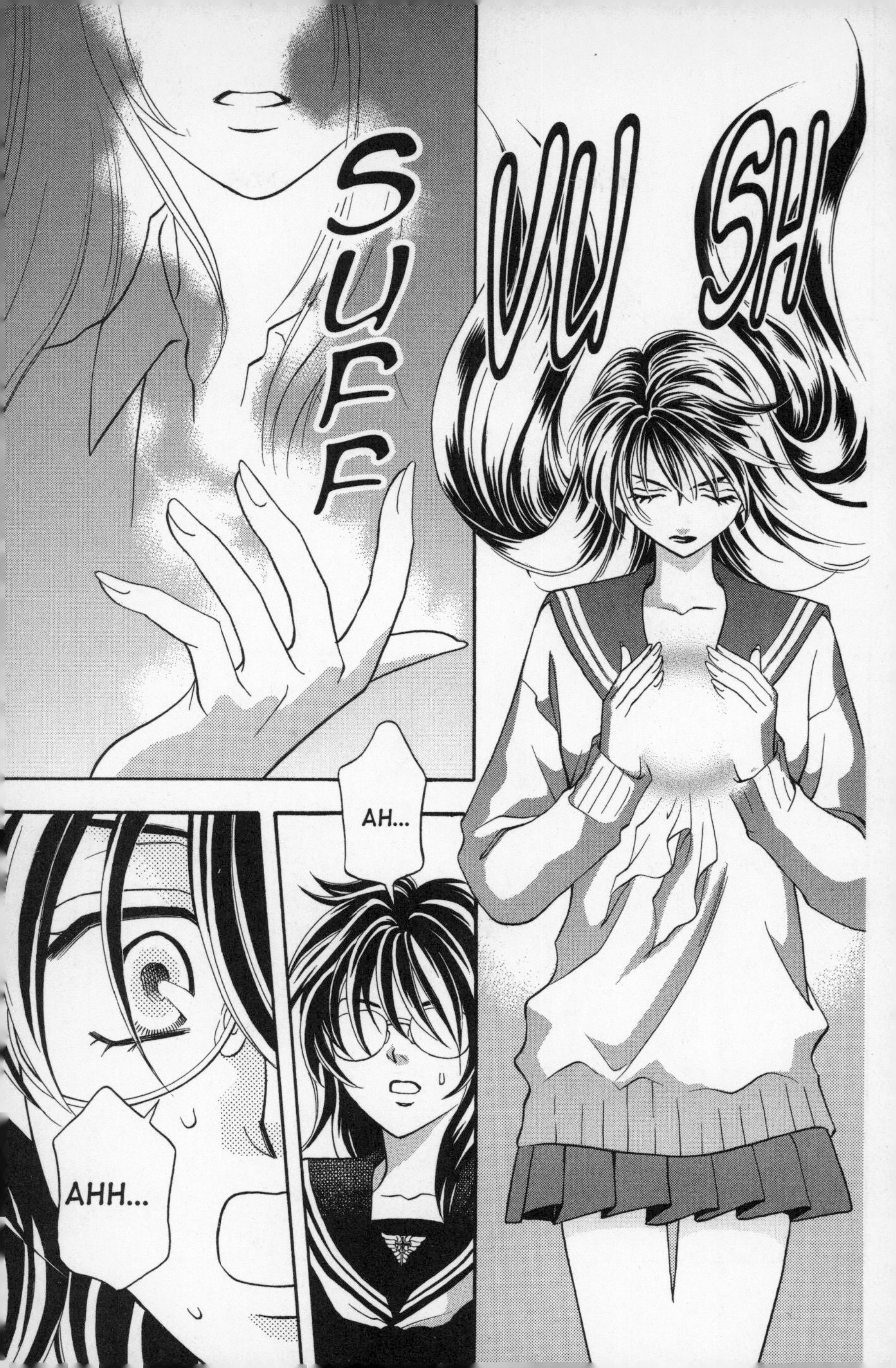
VUSH
SUFF
AH...
AHH...

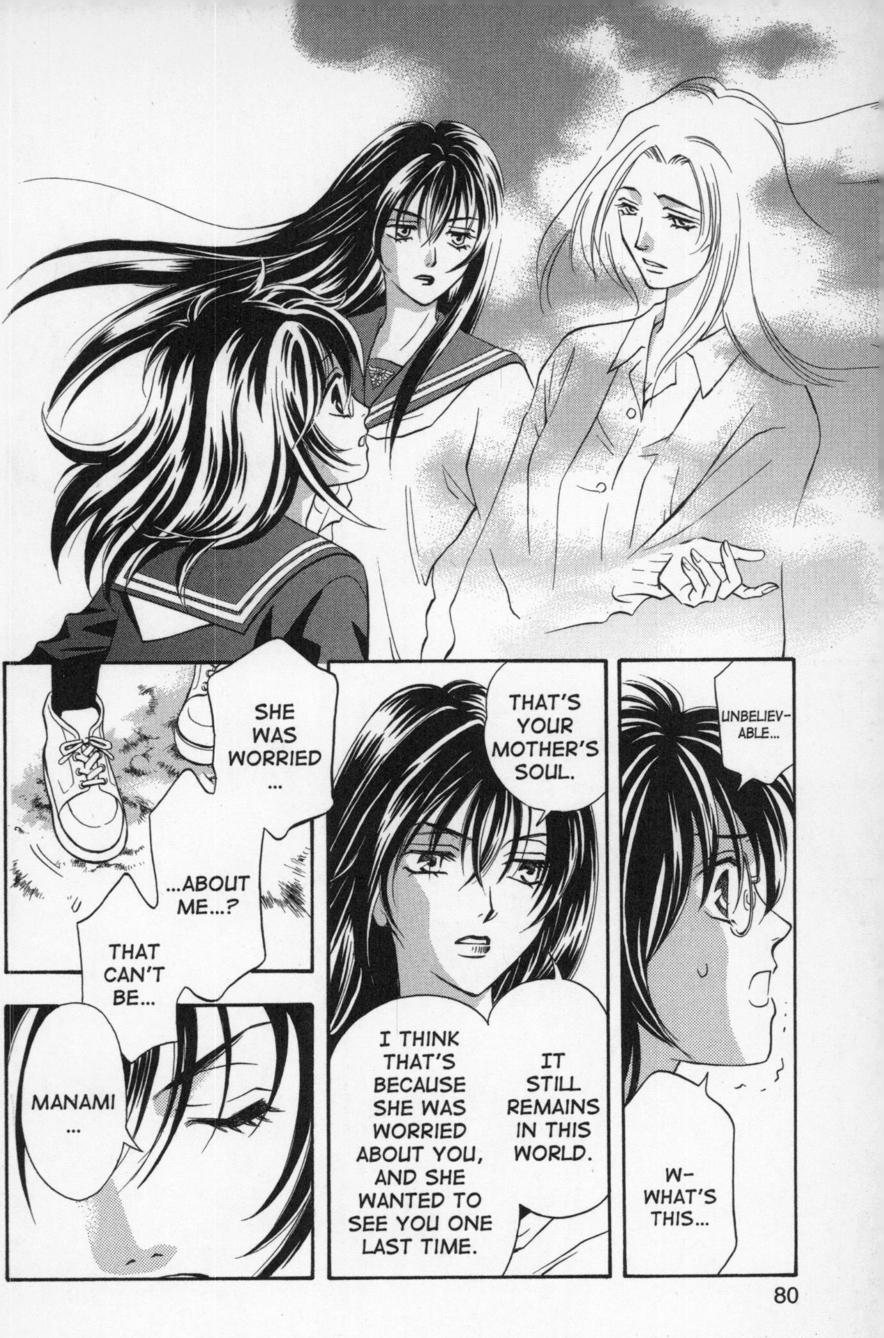
UNBELIEVABLE...
W-WHAT'S THIS...
THAT'S YOUR MOTHER'S SOUL.
IT STILL REMAINS IN THIS WORLD.
I THINK THAT'S BECAUSE SHE WAS WORRIED ABOUT YOU, AND SHE WANTED TO SEE YOU ONE LAST TIME.
SHE WAS WORRIED ...
...ABOUT ME...?
THAT CAN'T BE...
MANAMI ...

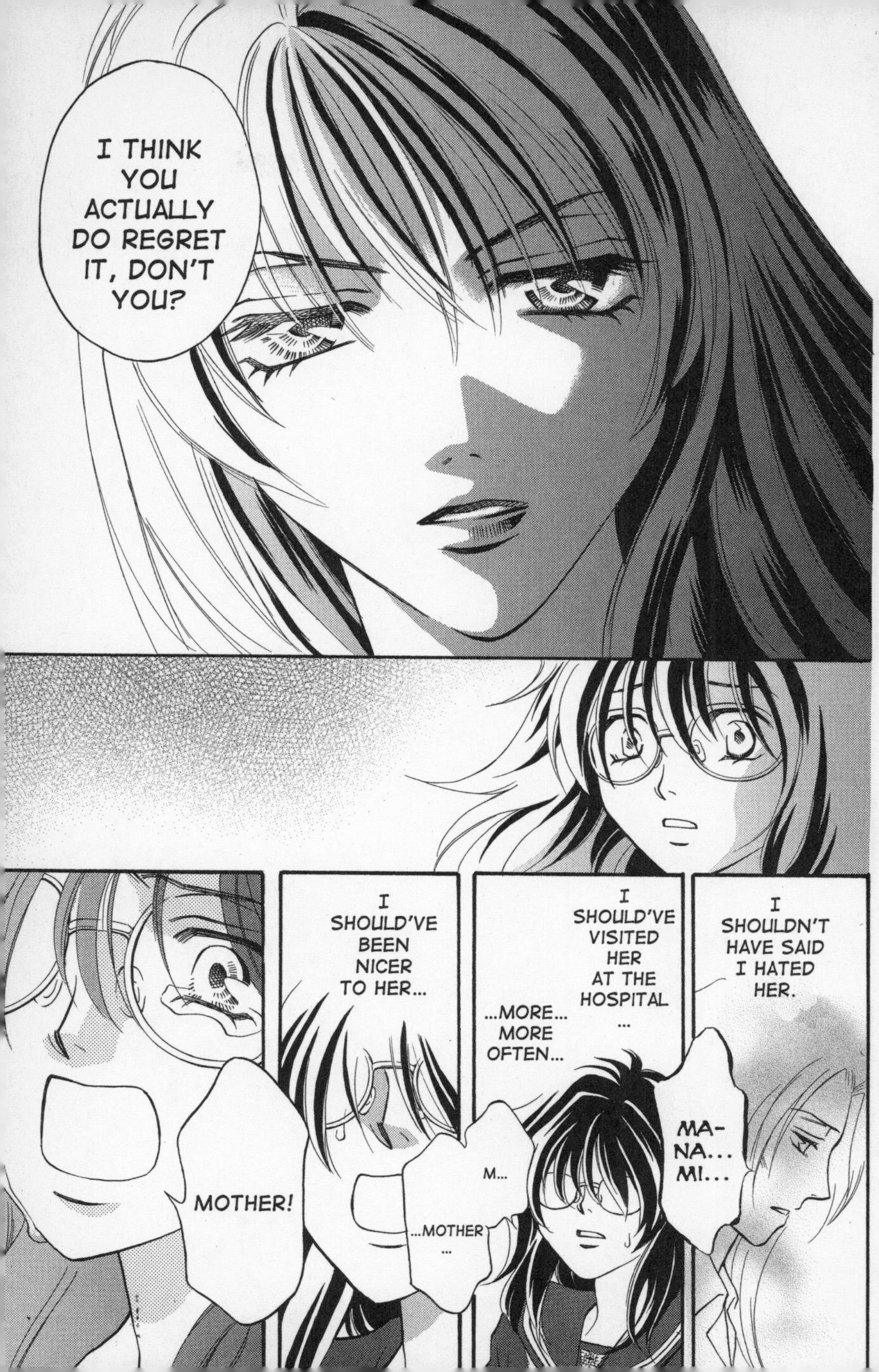
I THINK YOU ACTUALLY DO REGRET IT, DON'T YOU?
I SHOULDN'T HAVE SAID I HATED HER.
MA-NA... MI...
I SHOULD'VE VISITED HER AT THE HOSPITAL ...
...MORE... MORE OFTEN...
M...
...MOTHER ...
I SHOULD'VE BEEN NICER TO HER...
MOTHER!

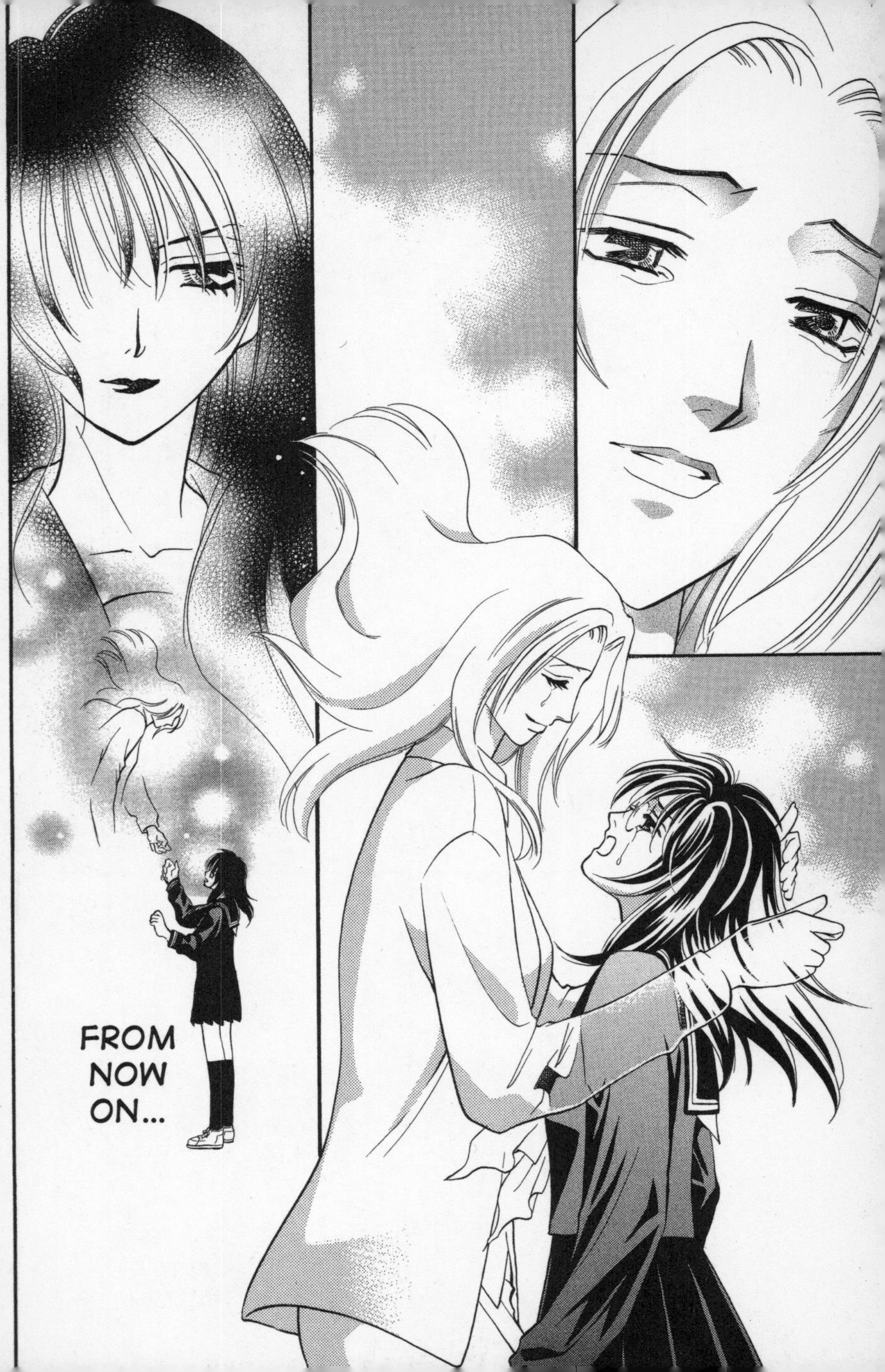
FROM NOW ON...

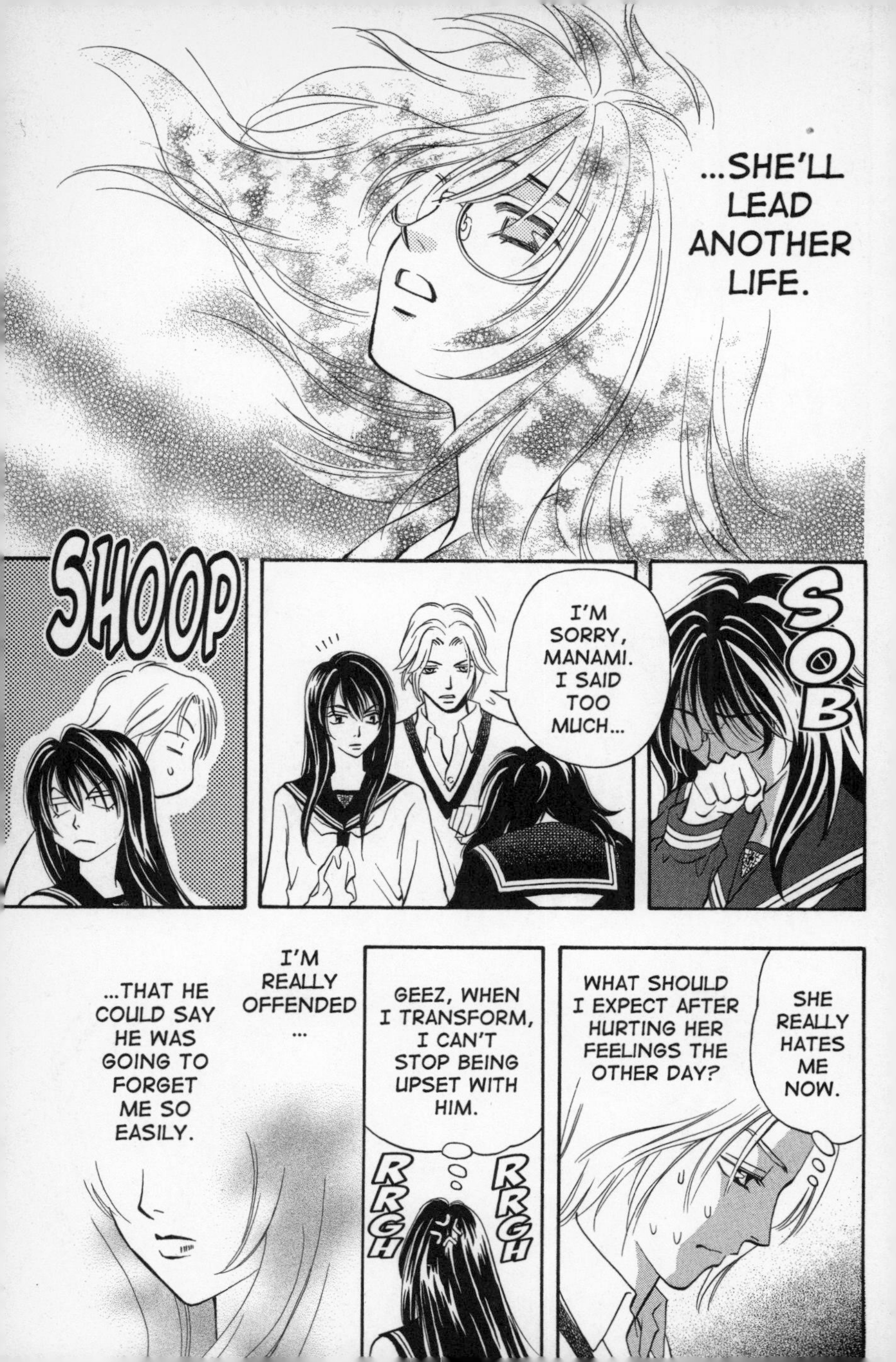
...SHE'LL LEAD ANOTHER LIFE.
SOB
I'M SORRY, MANAMI. I SAID TOO MUCH...
SHOOP
SHE REALLY HATES ME NOW.
WHAT SHOULD I EXPECT AFTER HURTING HER FEELINGS THE OTHER DAY?
GEEZ, WHEN I TRANSFORM, I CAN'T STOP BEING UPSET WITH HIM.
RRGH
RRGH
I'M REALLY OFFENDED ...
...THAT HE COULD SAY HE WAS GOING TO FORGET ME SO EASILY.

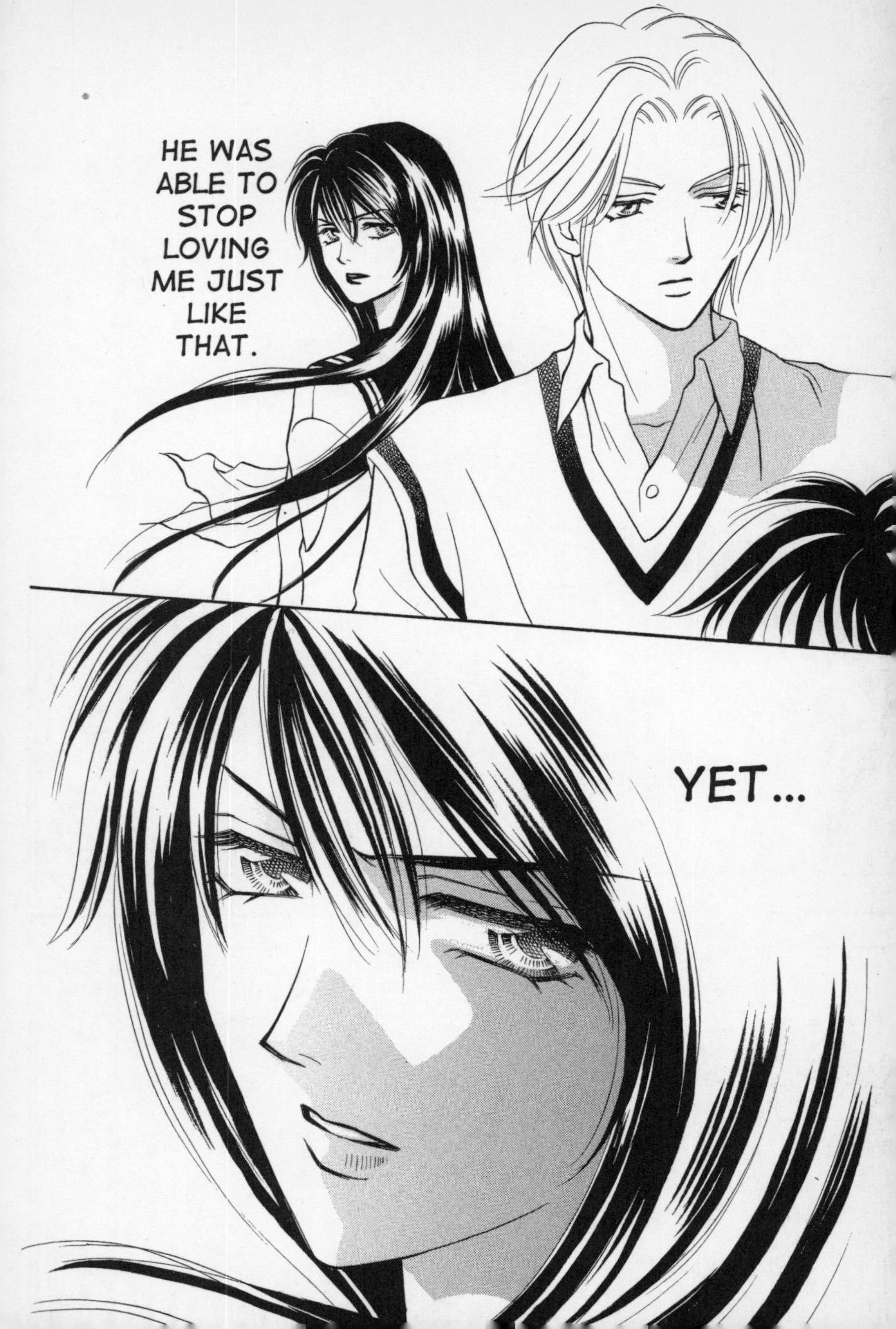
HE WAS ABLE TO STOP LOVING ME JUST LIKE THAT.
YET...

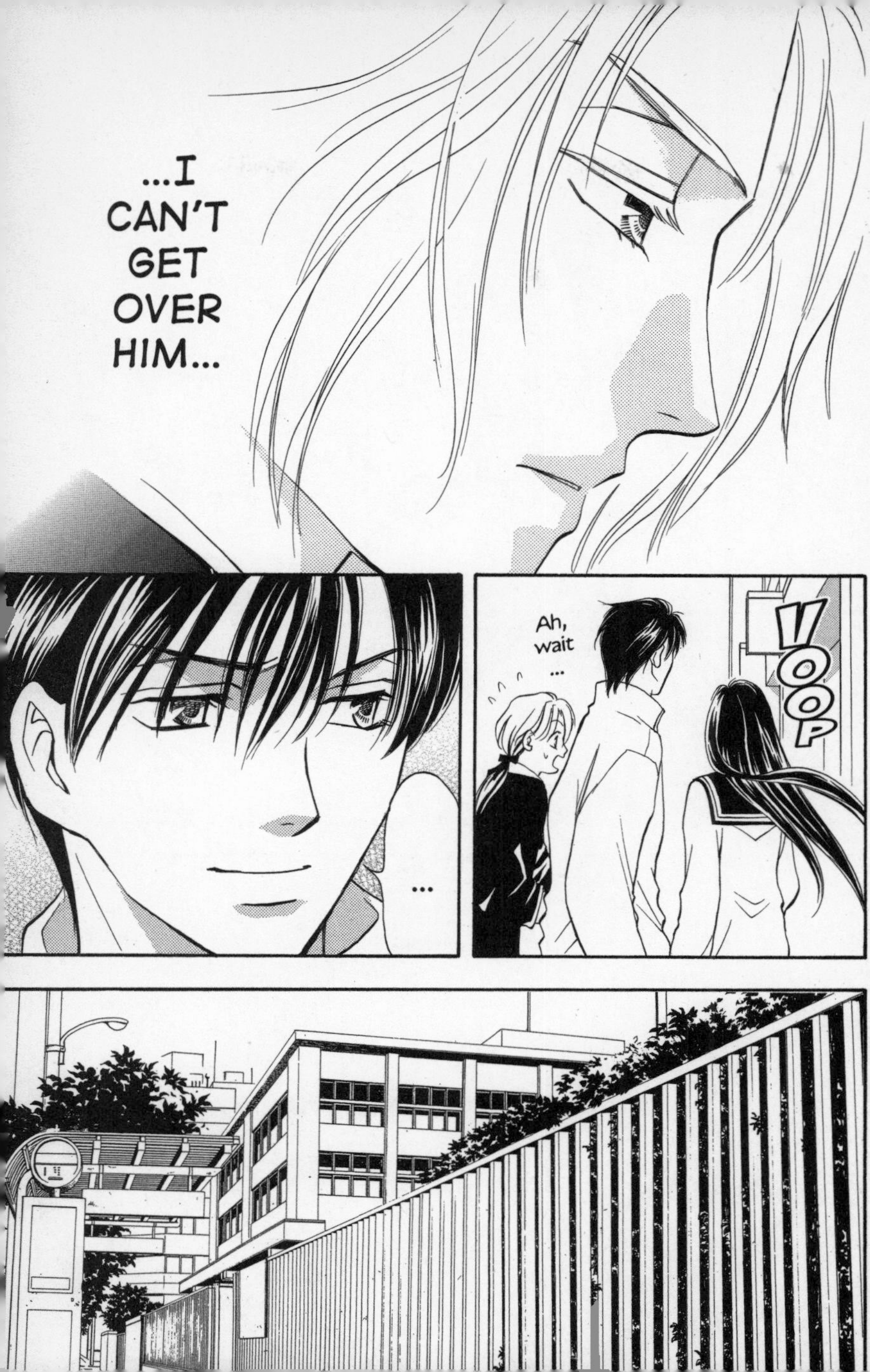
...I CAN'T GET OVER HIM...
Ah, wait ...
VOOP
...

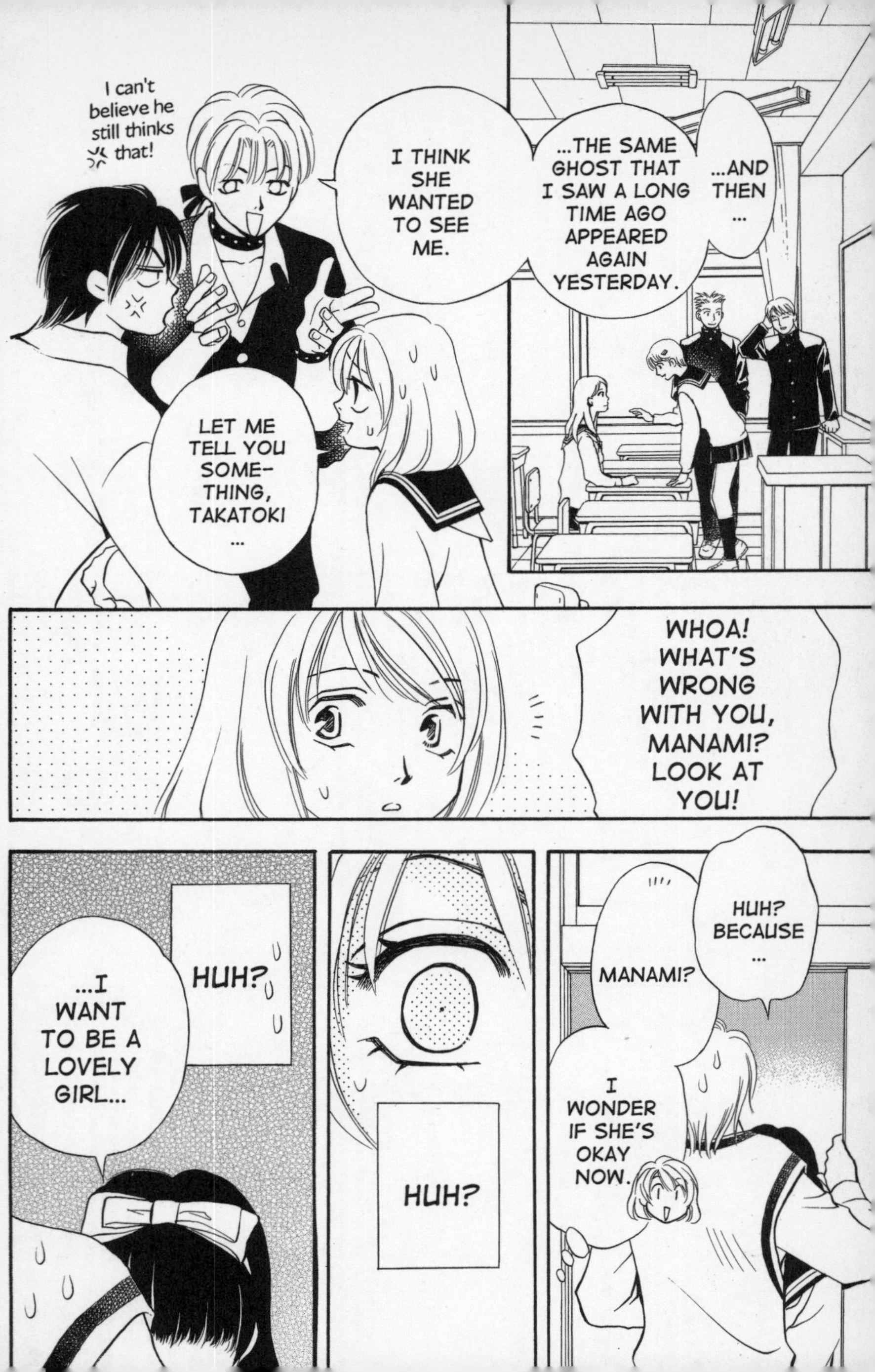
...AND THEN ...
...THE SAME GHOST THAT I SAW A LONG TIME AGO APPEARED AGAIN YESTERDAY.
I THINK SHE WANTED TO SEE ME.
I can't believe he still thinks that!
LET ME TELL YOU SOMETHING, TAKATOKI ...
WHOA! WHAT'S WRONG WITH YOU, MANAMI? LOOK AT YOU!
HUH? BECAUSE ...
MANAMI?
I WONDER IF SHE'S OKAY NOW.
HUH?
HUH?
...I WANT TO BE A LOVELY GIRL...

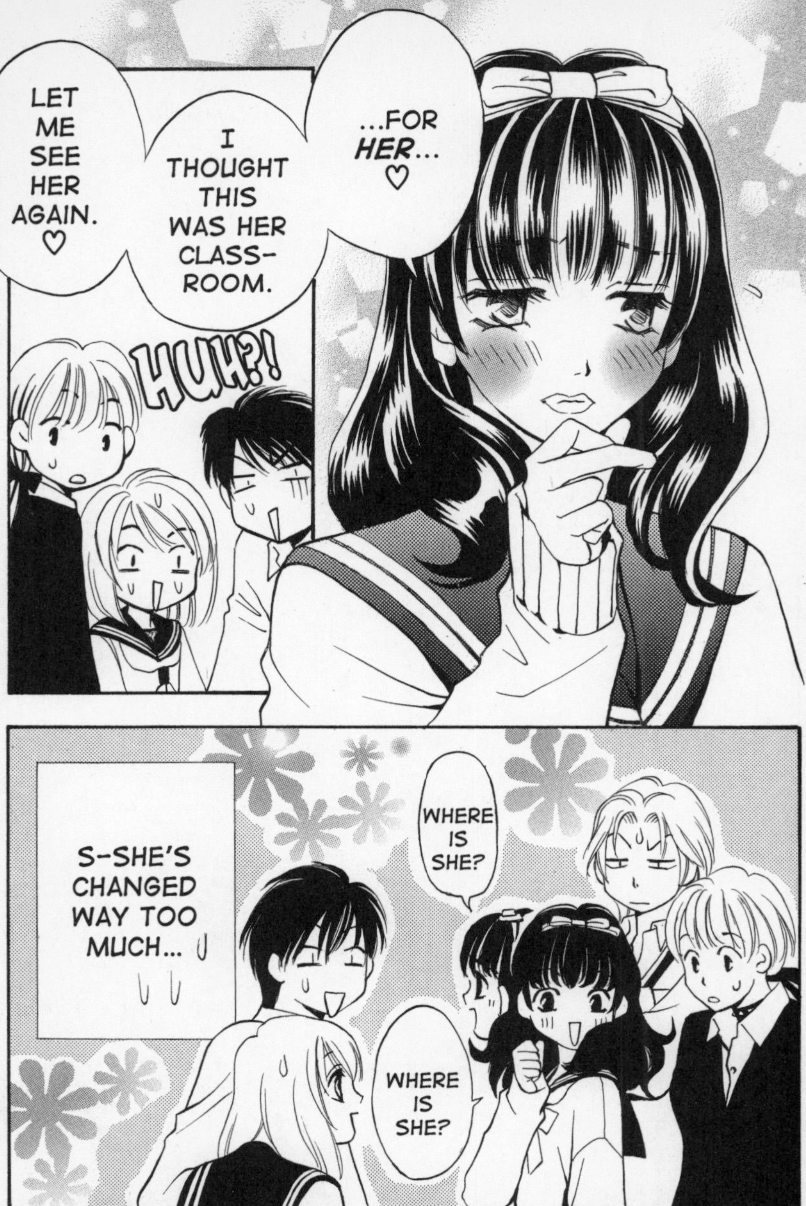
...FOR HER... ♡
I THOUGHT THIS WAS HER CLASSROOM.
LET ME SEE HER AGAIN. ♡
HUH?!
WHERE IS SHE?
WHERE IS SHE?
S-SHE'S CHANGED WAY TOO MUCH...

Yurara no Tsuki Chapter 14 / End

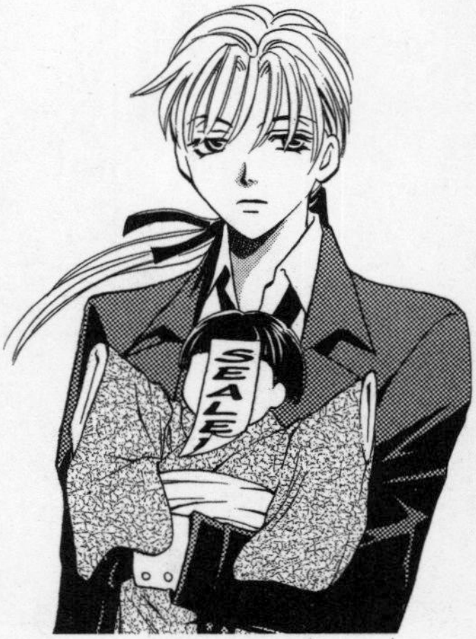
SEALED

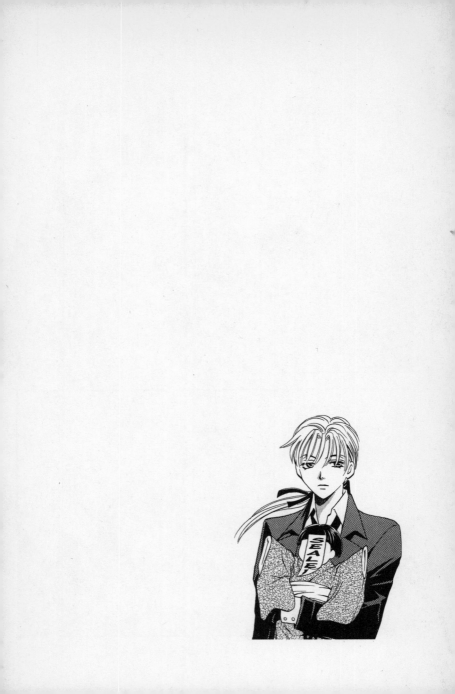

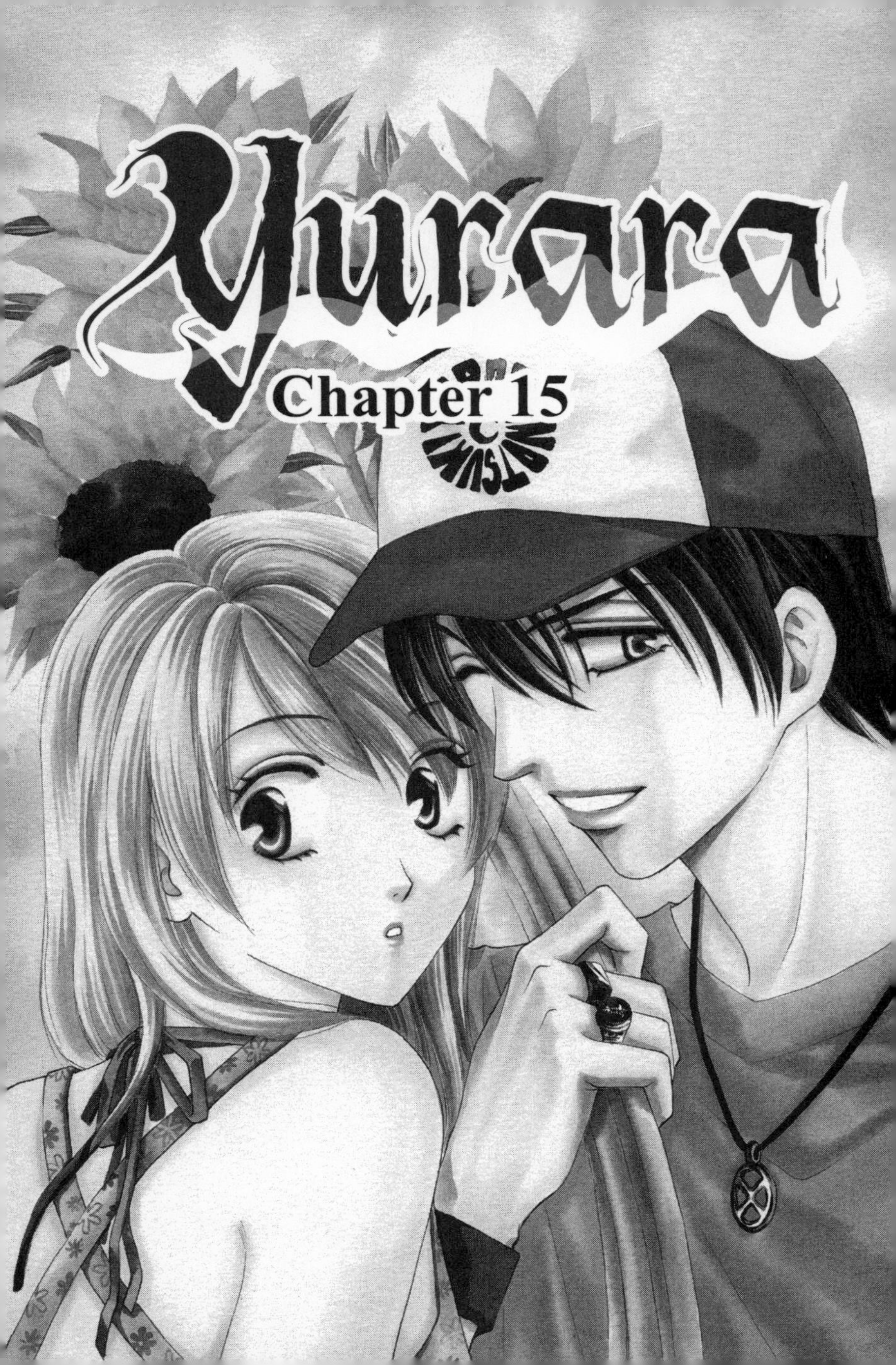
Yurara
Chapter 15

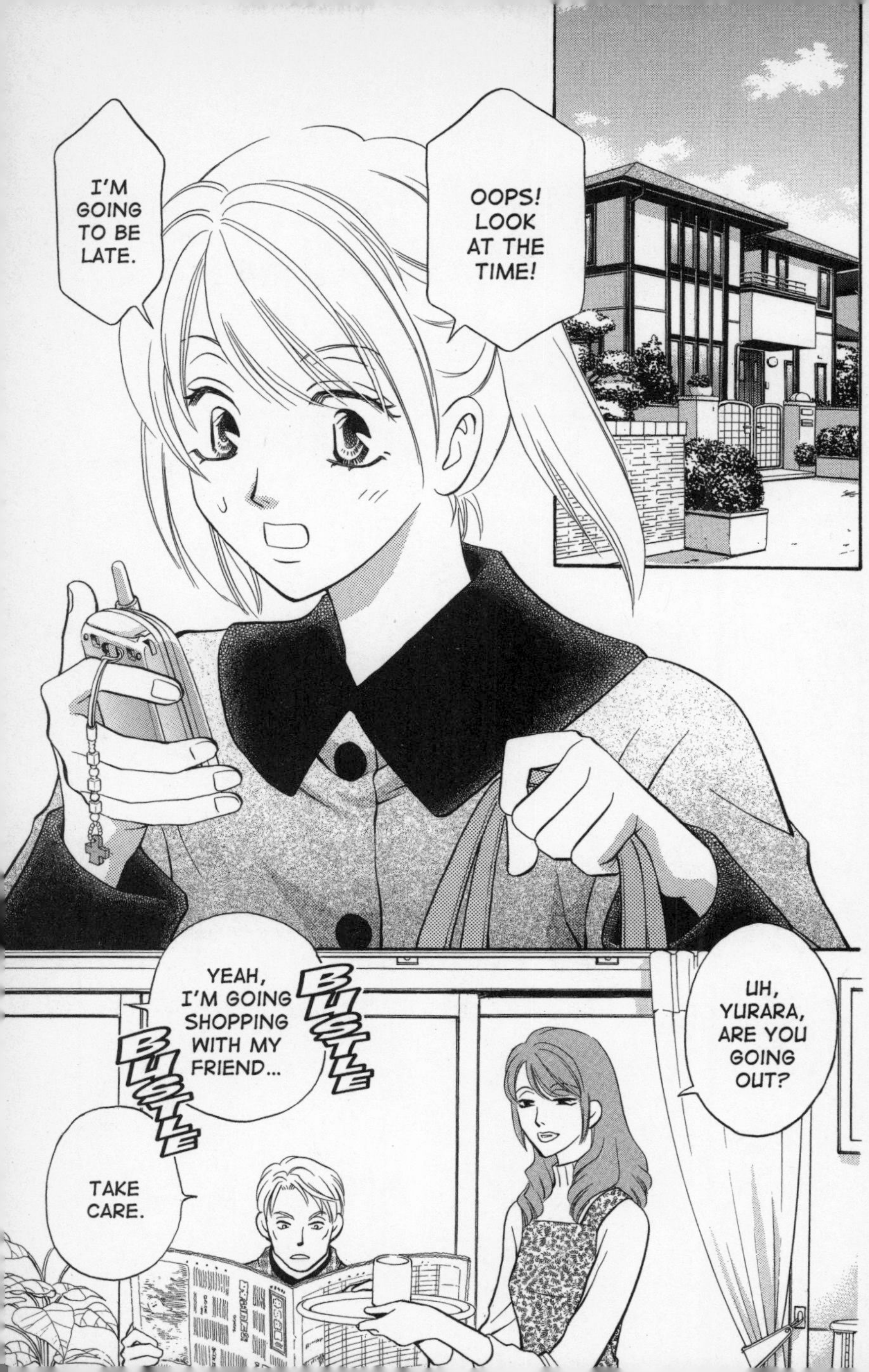
OOPS! LOOK AT THE TIME!
I'M GOING TO BE LATE.
UH, YURARA, ARE YOU GOING OUT?
BUSTLE
YEAH, I'M GOING SHOPPING WITH MY FRIEND...
BUSTLE
TAKE CARE.

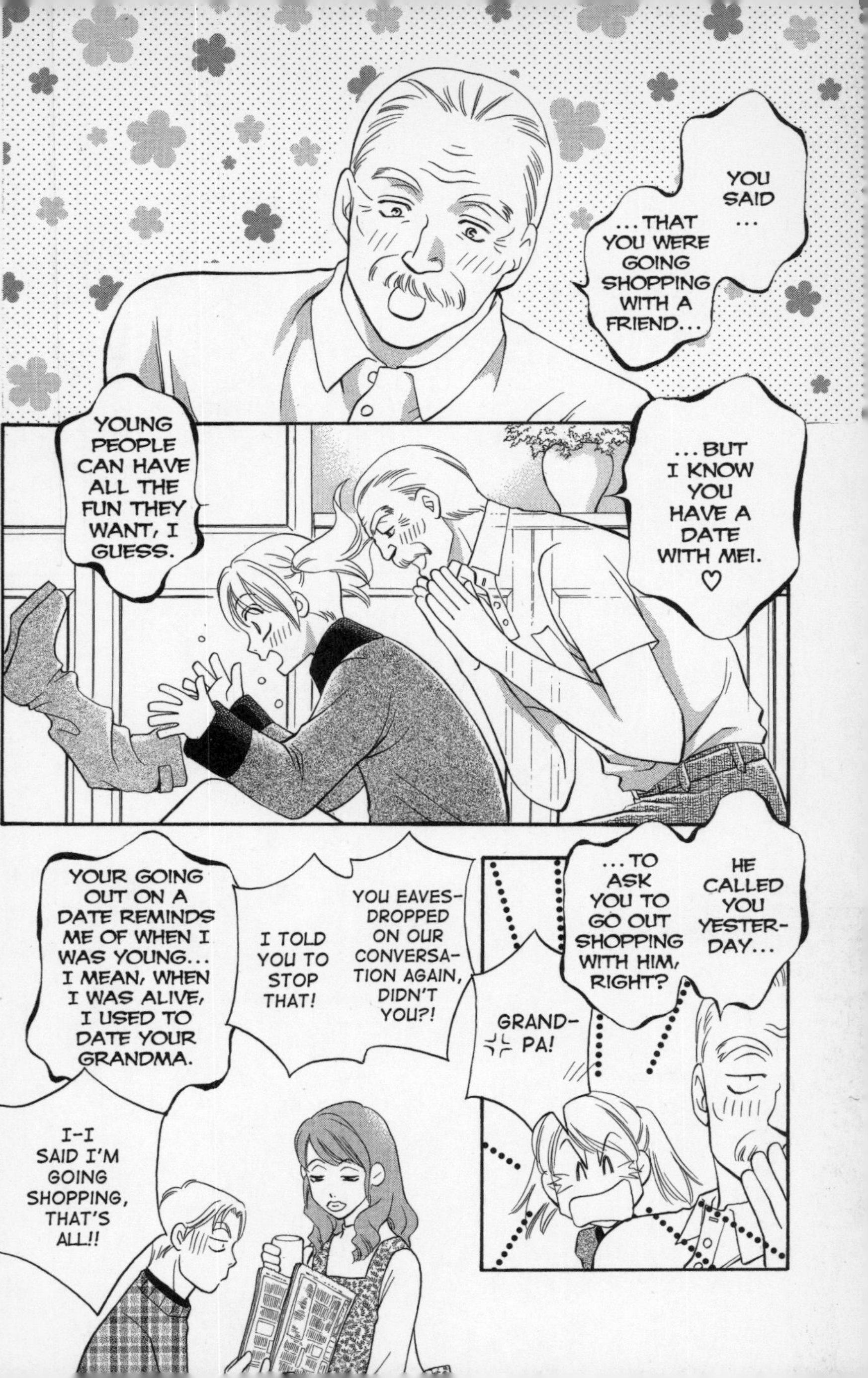
YOU SAID ...
...THAT YOU WERE GOING SHOPPING WITH A FRIEND...
...BUT I KNOW YOU HAVE A DATE WITH MEI. ♡
YOUNG PEOPLE CAN HAVE ALL THE FUN THEY WANT, I GUESS.
HE CALLED YOU YESTER-DAY...
...TO ASK YOU TO GO OUT SHOPPING WITH HIM, RIGHT?
GRAND-PA!
YOU EAVES-DROPPED ON OUR CONVERSA-TION AGAIN, DIDN'T YOU?!
I TOLD YOU TO STOP THAT!
YOUR GOING OUT ON A DATE REMINDS ME OF WHEN I WAS YOUNG... I MEAN, WHEN I WAS ALIVE, I USED TO DATE YOUR GRANDMA.
I-I SAID I'M GOING SHOPPING, THAT'S ALL!!

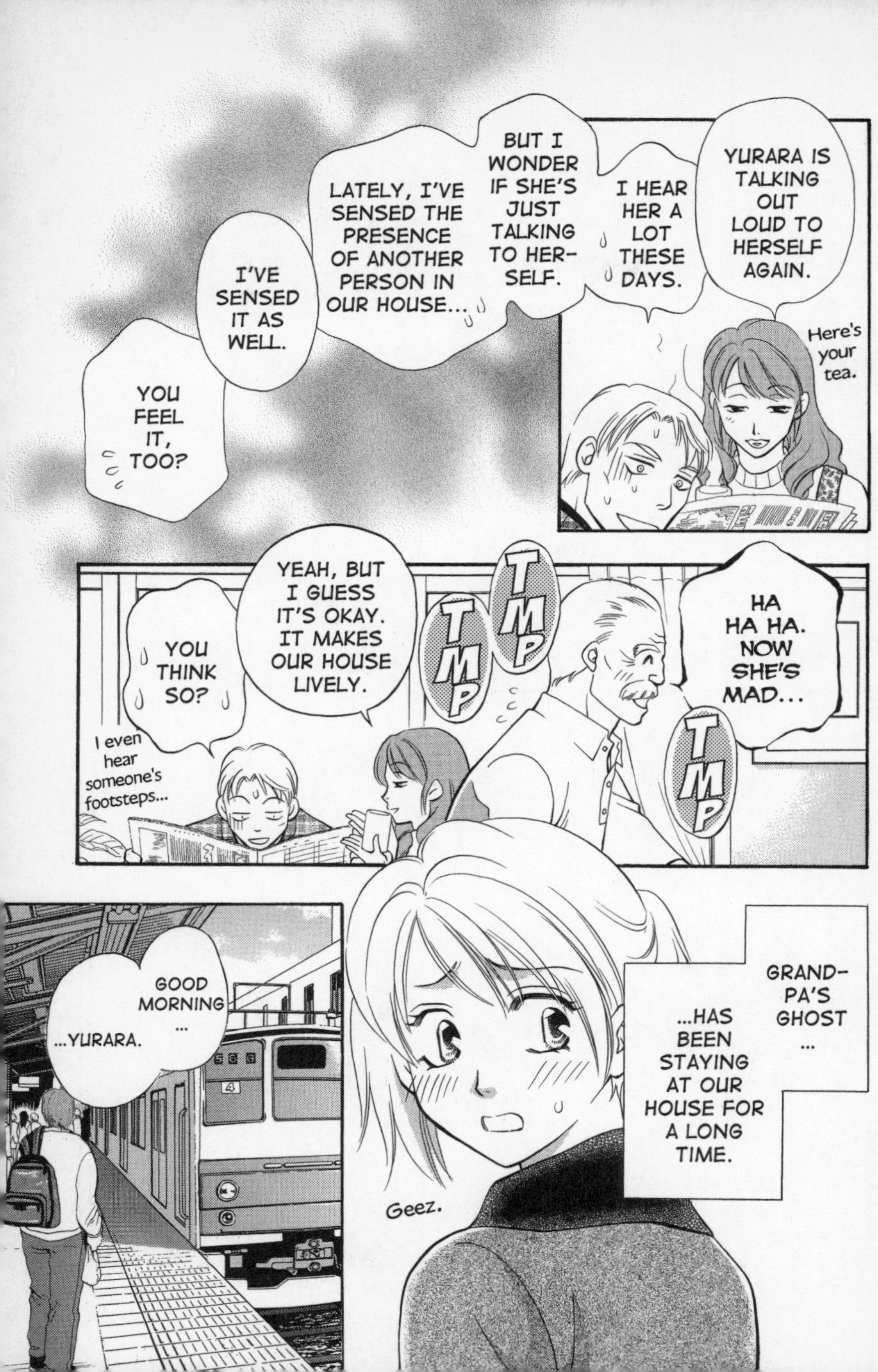
YURARA IS TALKING OUT LOUD TO HERSELF AGAIN.
Here's your tea.
I HEAR HER A LOT THESE DAYS.
BUT I WONDER IF SHE'S JUST TALKING TO HER-SELF.
LATELY, I'VE SENSED THE PRESENCE OF ANOTHER PERSON IN OUR HOUSE...
I'VE SENSED IT AS WELL.
YOU FEEL IT, TOO?
HA HA HA. NOW SHE'S MAD...
TMP
TMP
TMP
TMP
YEAH, BUT I GUESS IT'S OKAY. IT MAKES OUR HOUSE LIVELY.
YOU THINK SO?
I even hear someone's footsteps...
GRAND-PA'S GHOST ...
...HAS BEEN STAYING AT OUR HOUSE FOR A LONG TIME.
Geez.
GOOD MORNING ...
...YURARA.

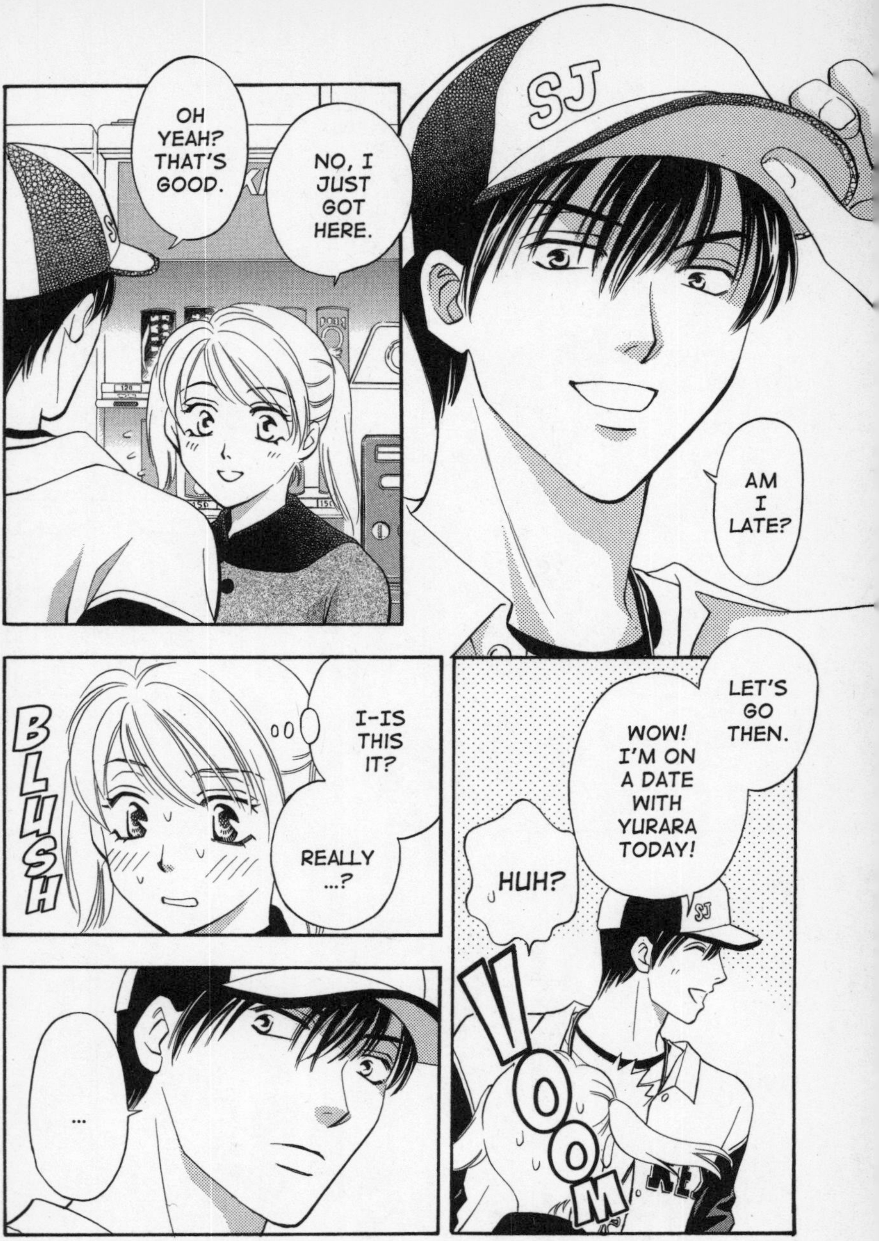
AM I LATE?
NO, I JUST GOT HERE.
OH YEAH? THAT'S GOOD.
LET'S GO THEN.
WOW! I'M ON A DATE WITH YURARA TODAY!
HUH?
VOOM
I-IS THIS IT?
REALLY ...?
BLUSH
...

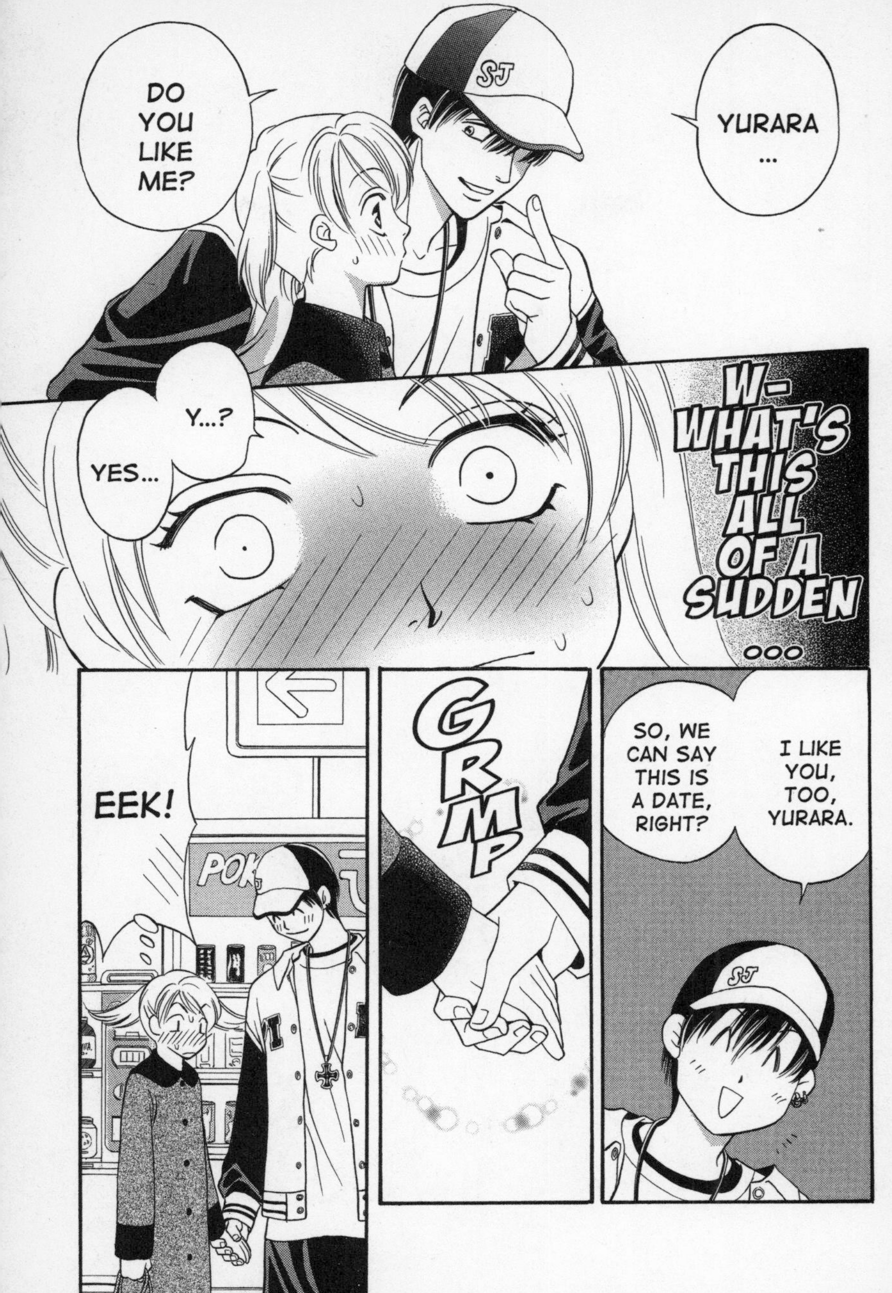
YURARA ...
DO YOU LIKE ME?
W-WHAT'S THIS ALL OF A SUDDEN ...
Y...?
YES...
I LIKE YOU, TOO, YURARA.
SO, WE CAN SAY THIS IS A DATE, RIGHT?
GRMP
EEK!

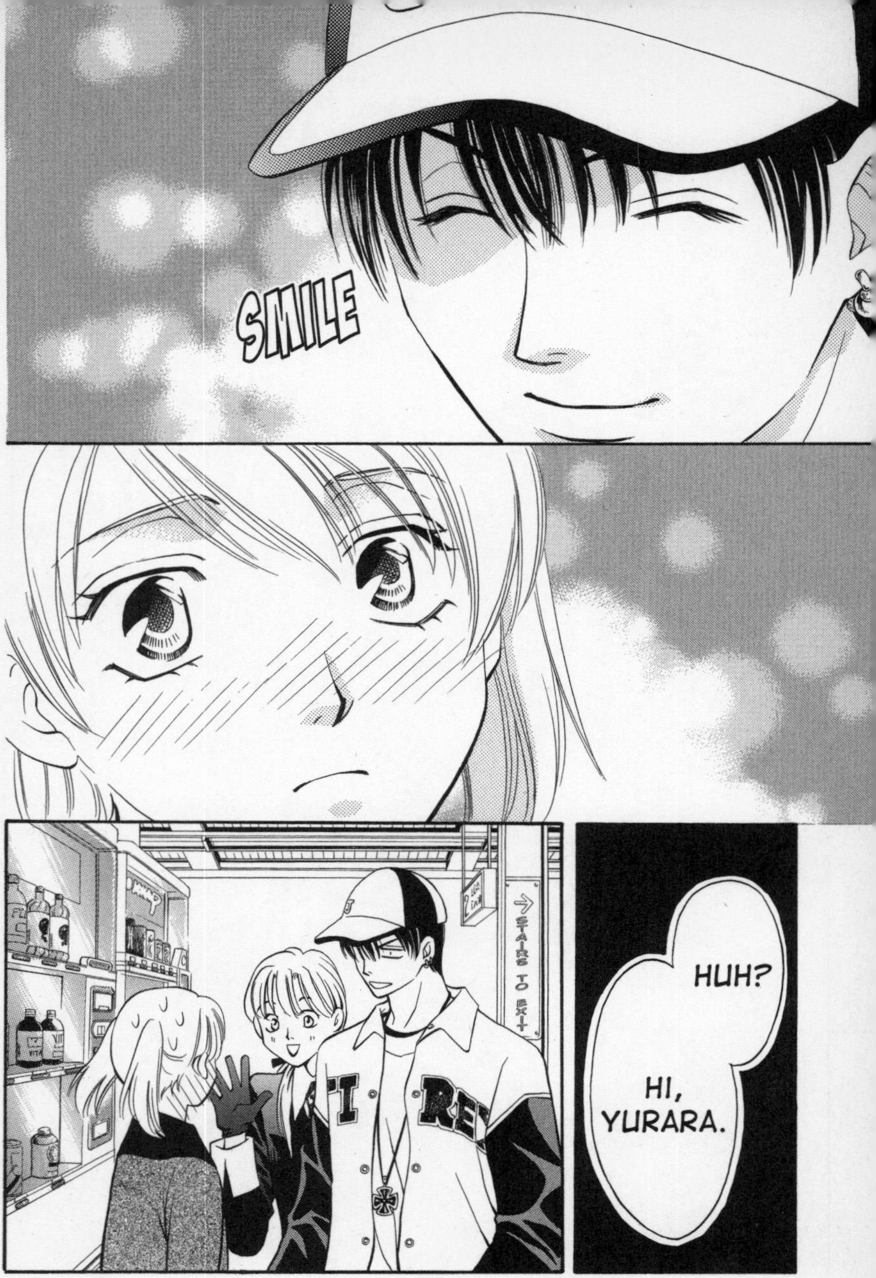
SMILE
HUH?
HI, YURARA.
STAIRS TO EXIT

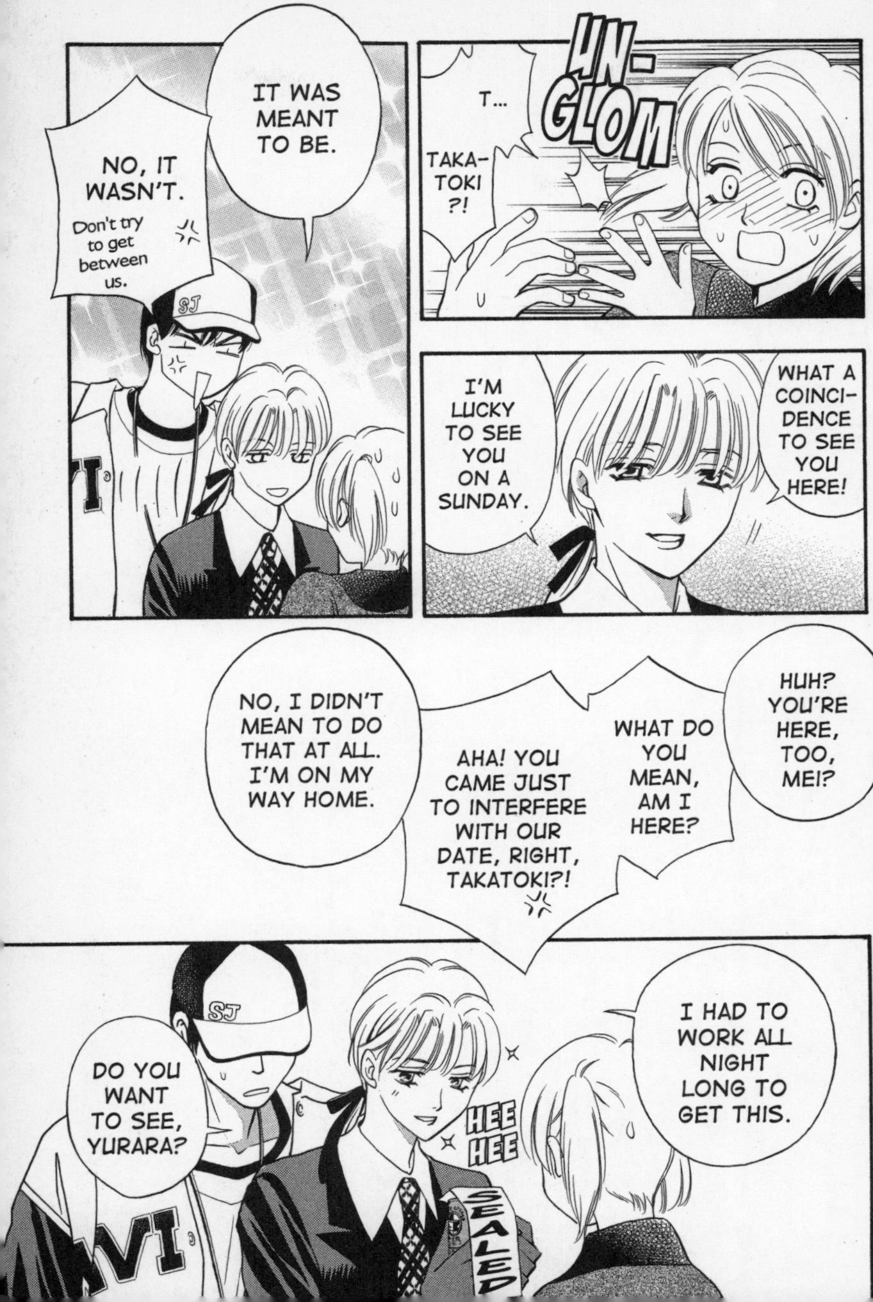
T...
TAKA-TOKI?!
UN-GLOM
WHAT A COINCI-DENCE TO SEE YOU HERE!
I'M LUCKY TO SEE YOU ON A SUNDAY.
IT WAS MEANT TO BE.
NO, IT WASN'T.
Don't try to get between us.
HUH? YOU'RE HERE, TOO, MEI?
WHAT DO YOU MEAN, AM I HERE?
AHA! YOU CAME JUST TO INTERFERE WITH OUR DATE, RIGHT, TAKATOKI!?!
NO, I DIDN'T MEAN TO DO THAT AT ALL. I'M ON MY WAY HOME.
I HAD TO WORK ALL NIGHT LONG TO GET THIS.
HEE HEE
SEALED
DO YOU WANT TO SEE, YURARA?
SJ
SJ

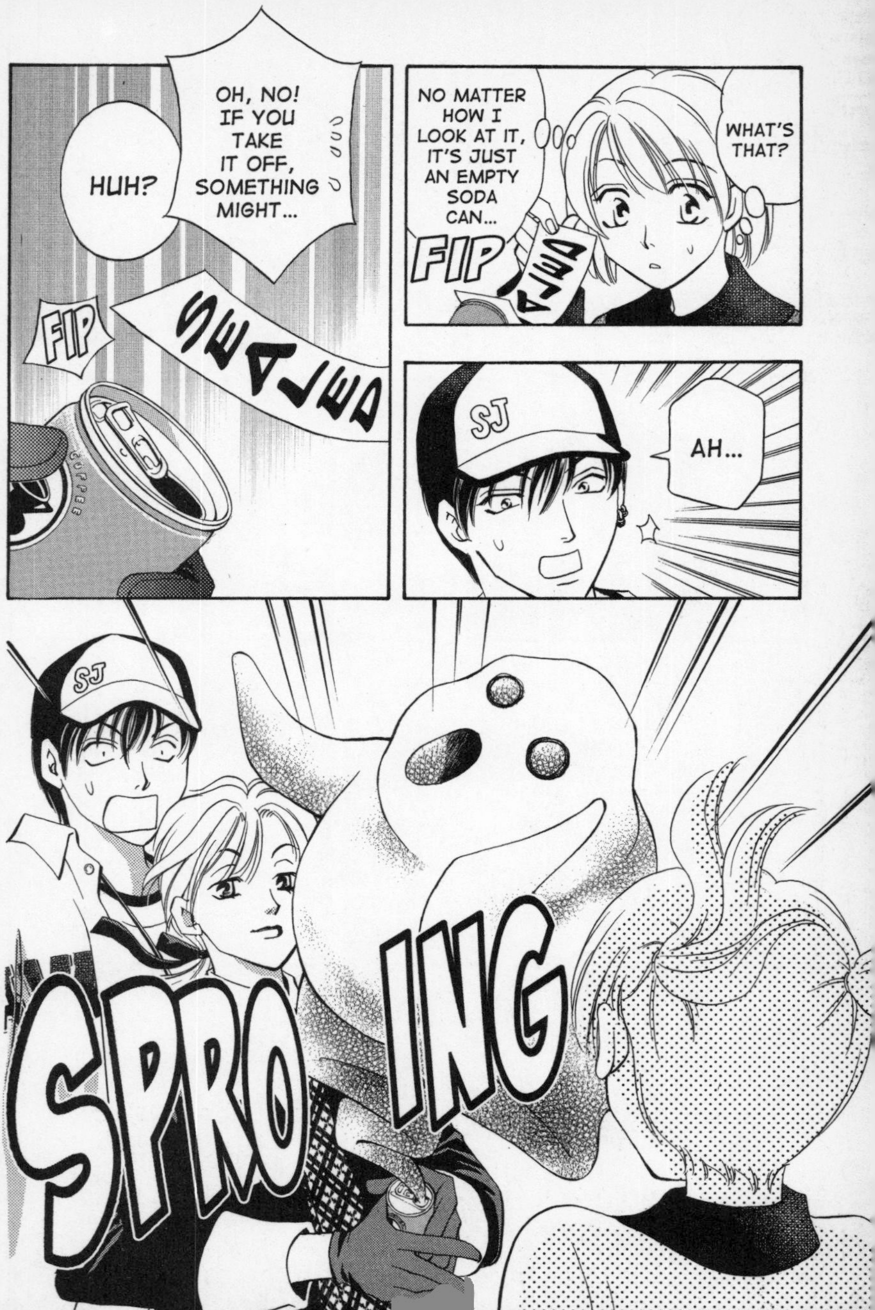
WHAT'S THAT?
NO MATTER HOW I LOOK AT IT, IT'S JUST AN EMPTY SODA CAN...
FIP
AH...
OH, NO! IF YOU TAKE IT OFF, SOMETHING MIGHT...
HUH?
FIP
SEALED
SPRO ING

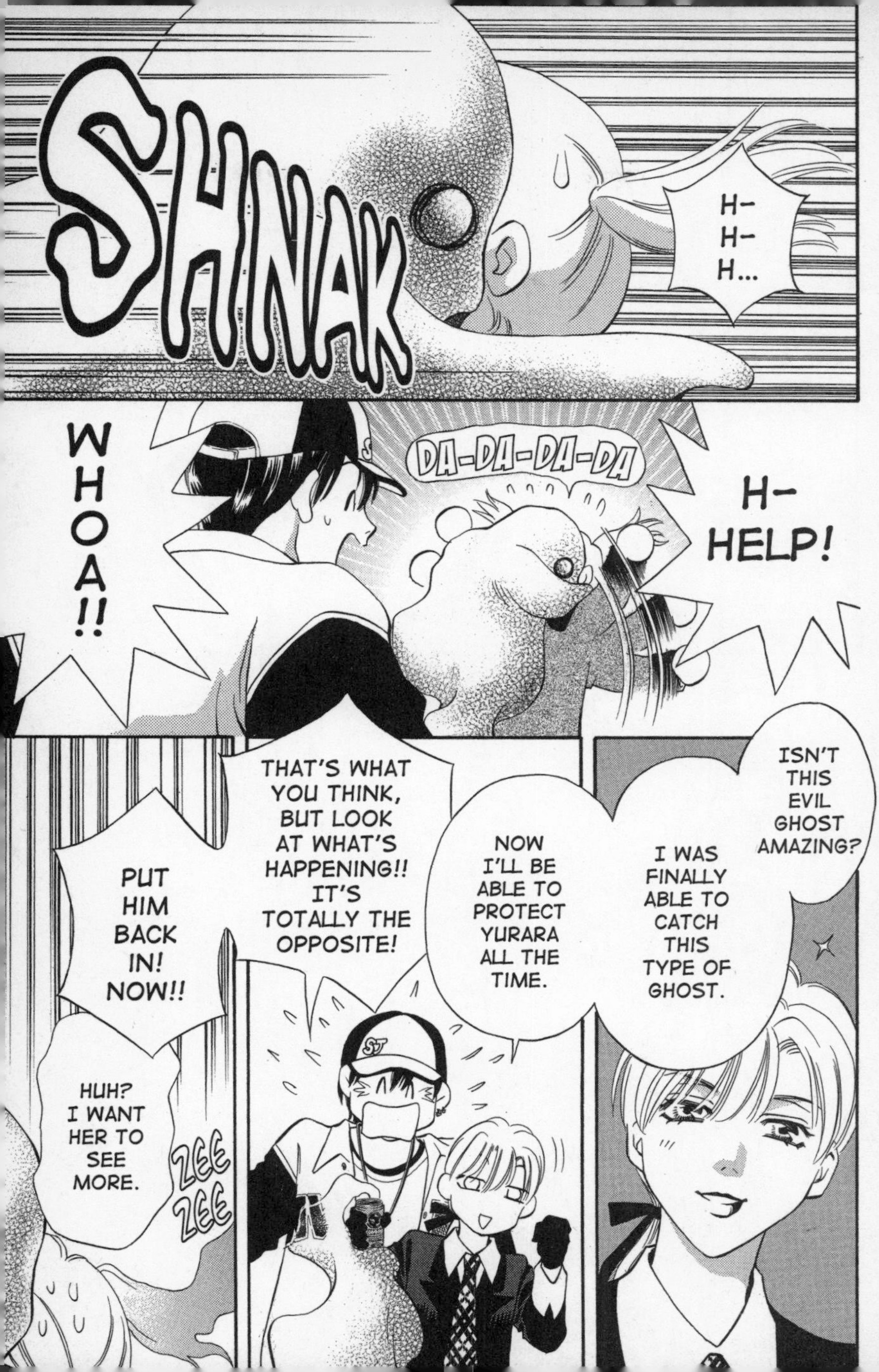
SHNAK
H- H- H...
H- HELP!
DA-DA-DA-DA
WHOA!!
ISN'T THIS EVIL GHOST AMAZING?
I WAS FINALLY ABLE TO CATCH THIS TYPE OF GHOST.
NOW I'LL BE ABLE TO PROTECT YURARA ALL THE TIME.
THAT'S WHAT YOU THINK, BUT LOOK AT WHAT'S HAPPENING!! IT'S TOTALLY THE OPPOSITE!
PUT HIM BACK IN! NOW!!
HUH? I WANT HER TO SEE MORE.
ZEE ZEE

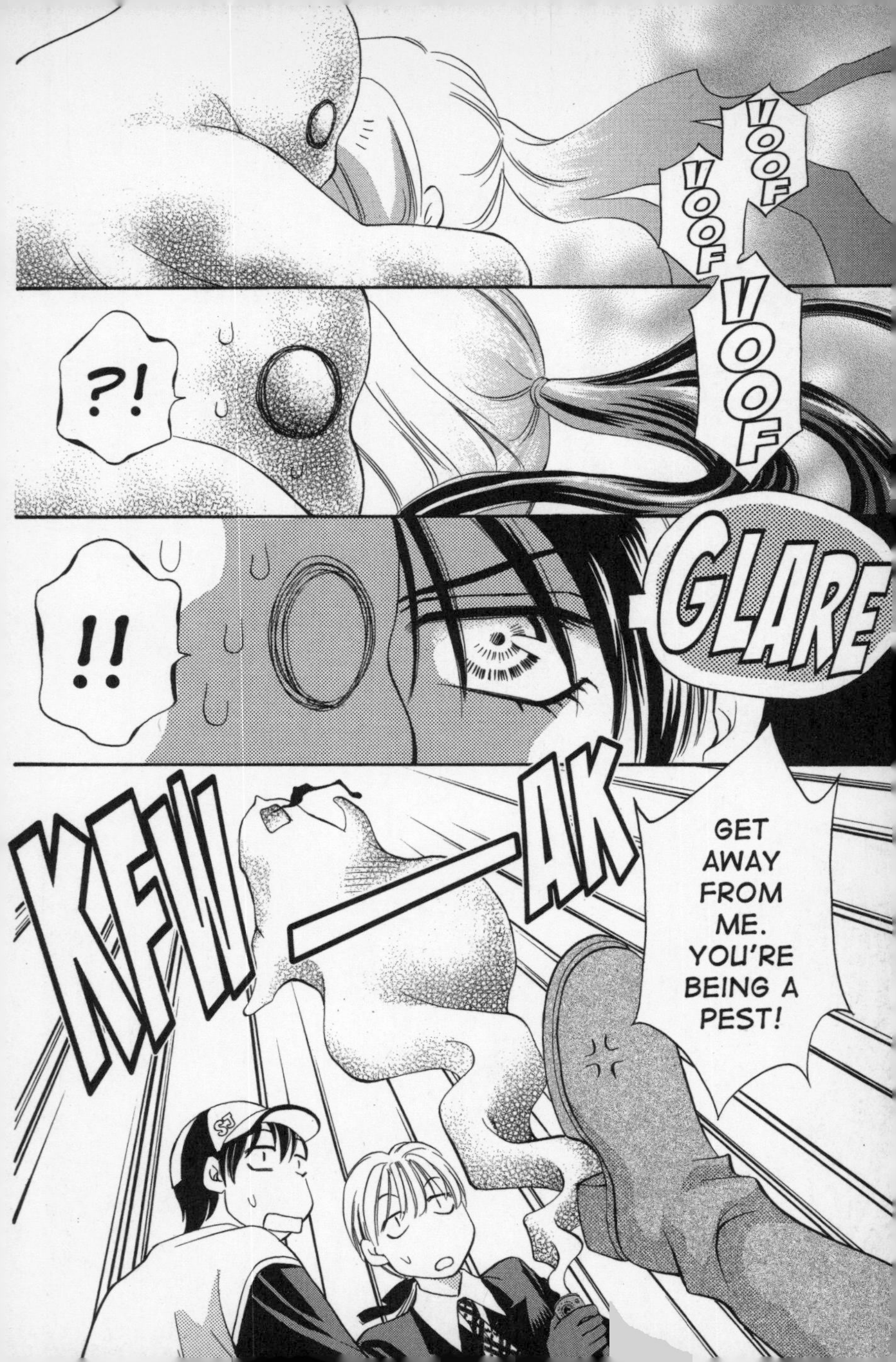
VOOF
VOOF
VOOF
?!
GLARE
!!
GET AWAY FROM ME. YOU'RE BEING A PEST!
KEW—AK

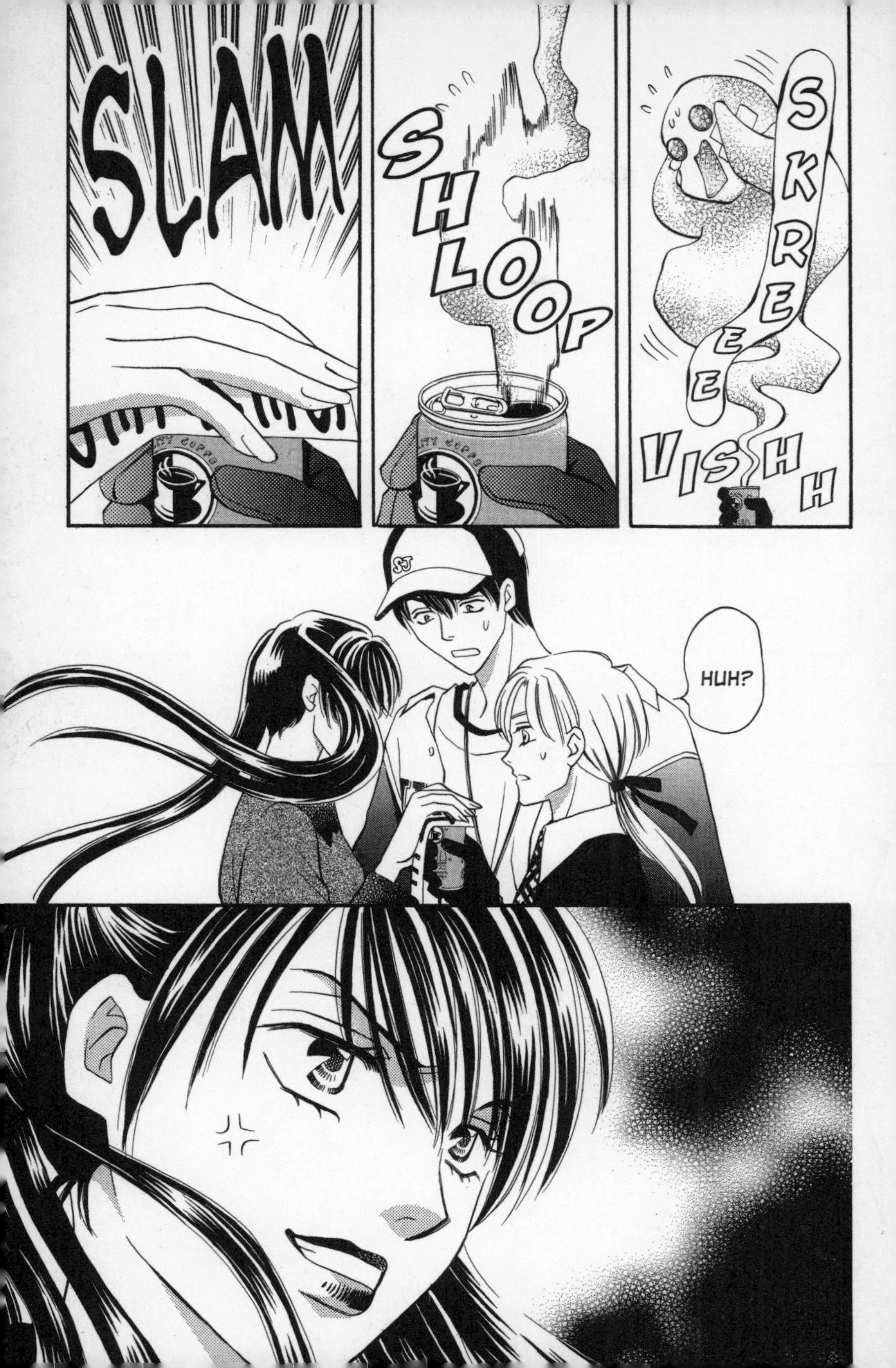
SKREEEE
VISHHH
SHLOOP
SLAM
HUH?

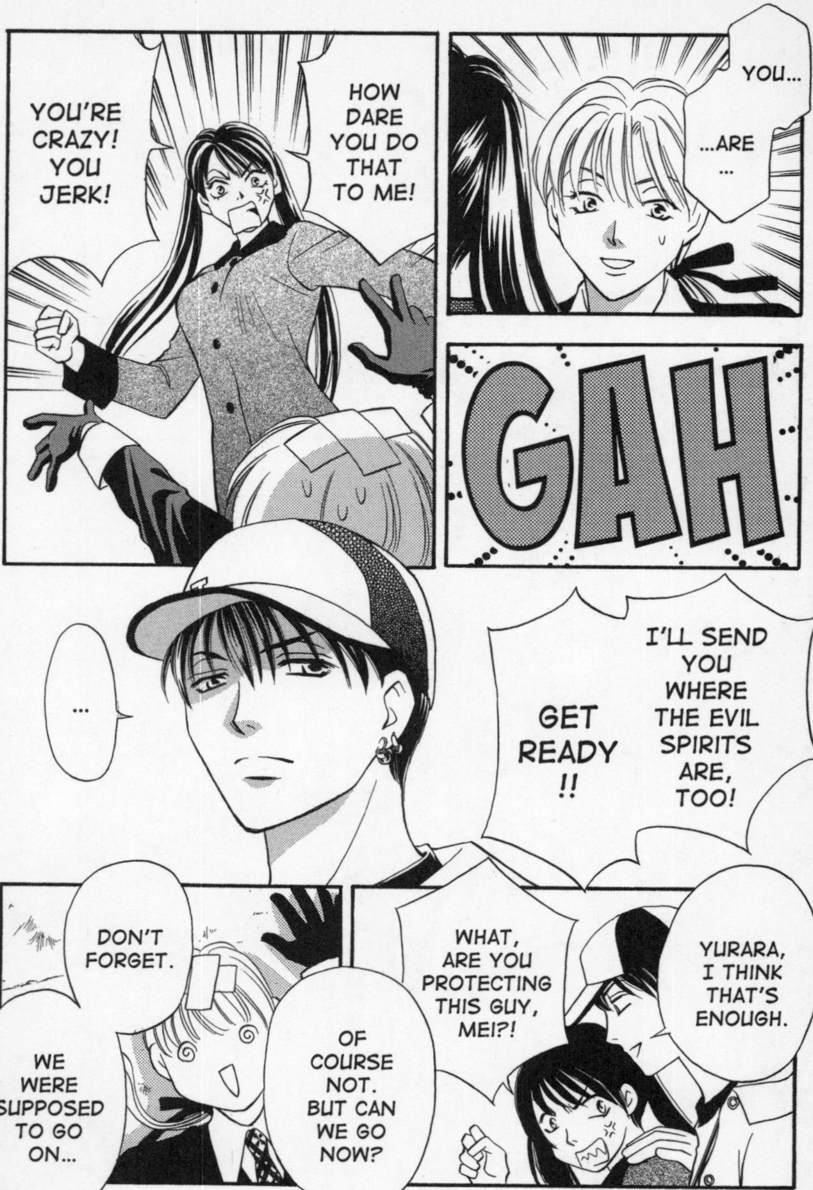
YOU...
...ARE ...
GAH
HOW DARE YOU DO THAT TO ME!
YOU'RE CRAZY! YOU JERK!
I'LL SEND YOU WHERE THE EVIL SPIRITS ARE, TOO!
GET READY !!
...
YURARA, I THINK THAT'S ENOUGH.
WHAT, ARE YOU PROTECTING THIS GUY, MEI?!
OF COURSE NOT. BUT CAN WE GO NOW?
DON'T FORGET.
WE WERE SUPPOSED TO GO ON...

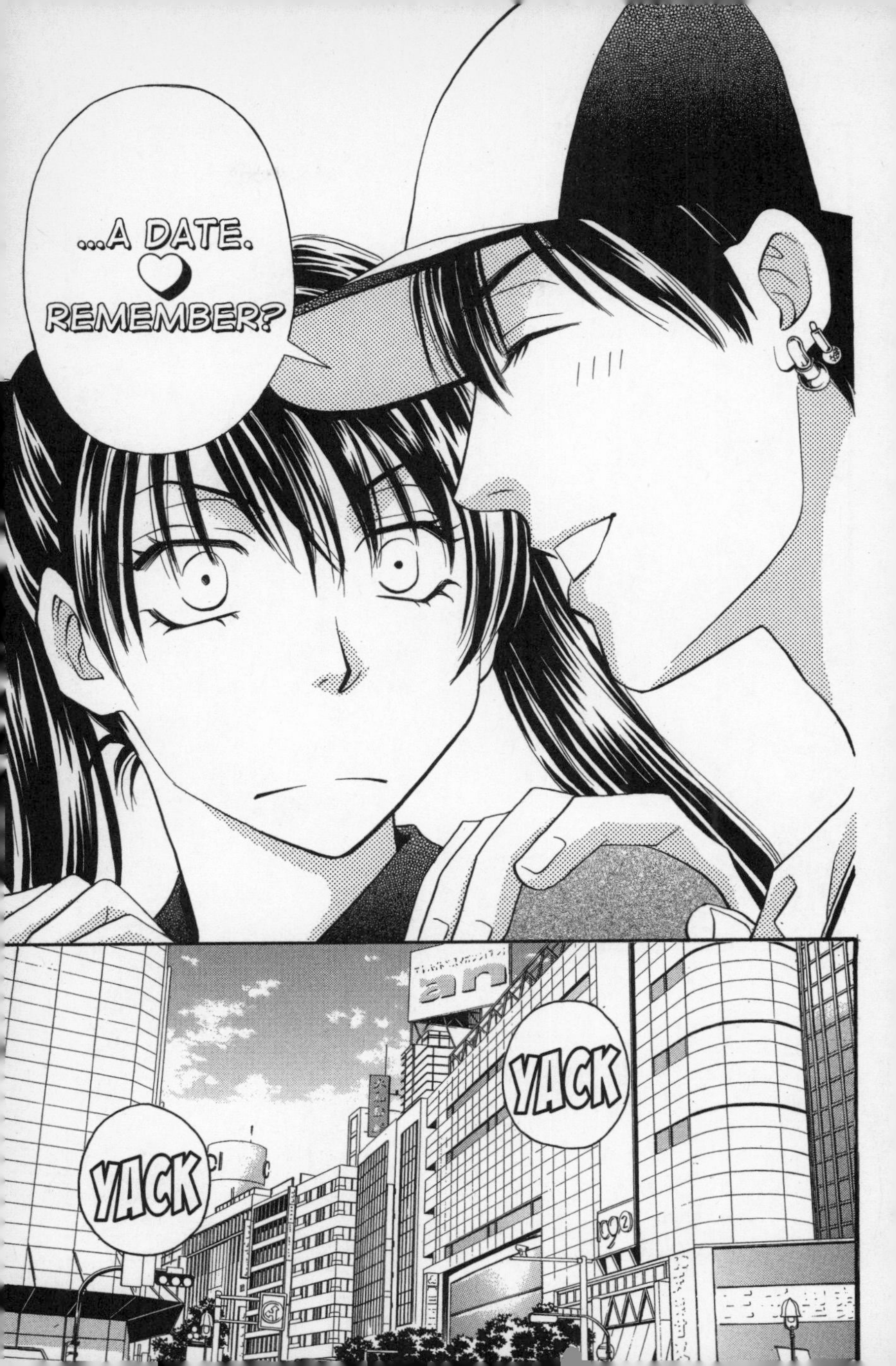
...A DATE. ♥ REMEMBER?
YACK
YACK

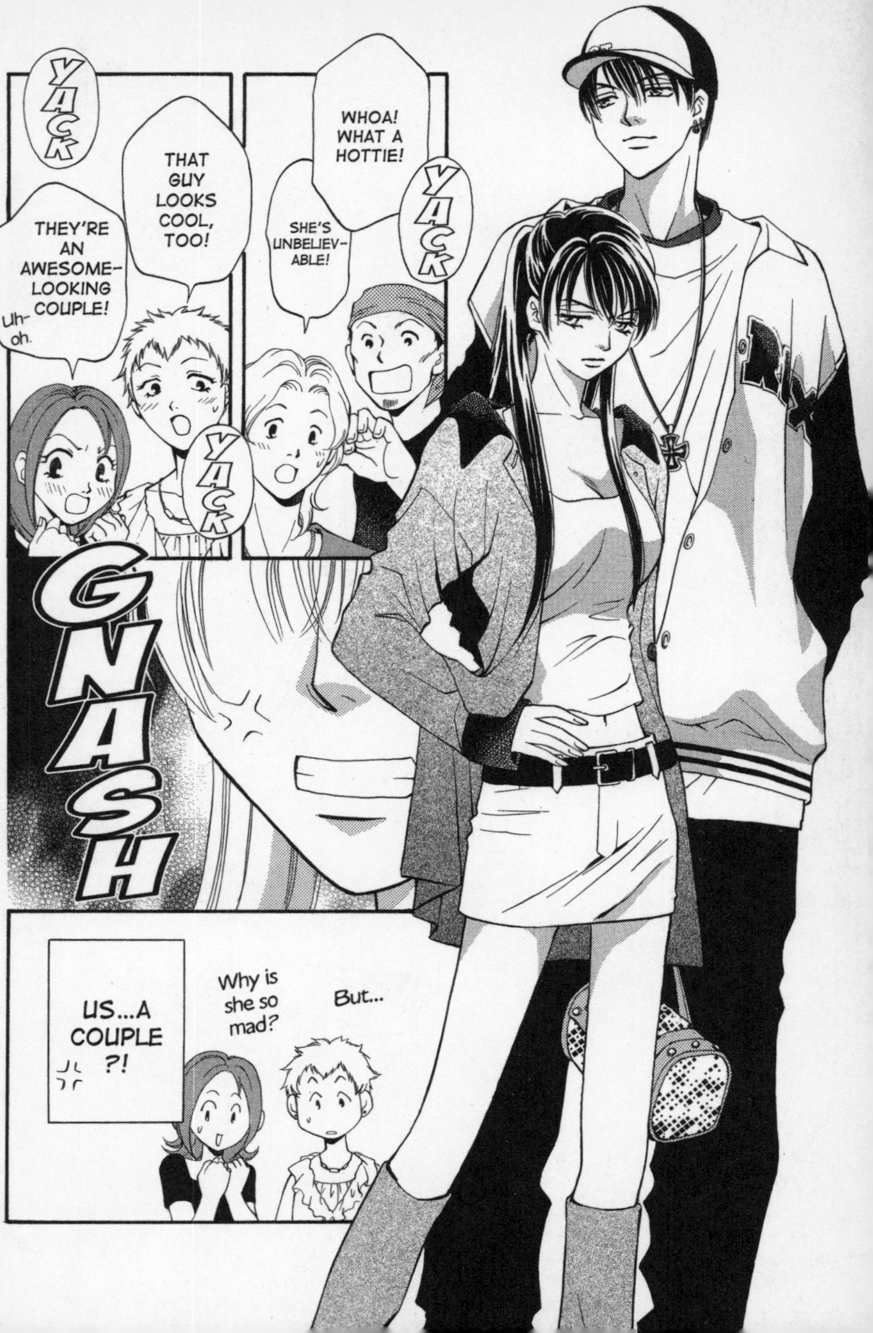
WHOA! WHAT A HOTTIE!
YACK
SHE'S UNBELIEVABLE!
YACK
THAT GUY LOOKS COOL, TOO!
YACK
THEY'RE AN AWESOME-LOOKING COUPLE!
Uh-oh.
GNASH
But...
Why is she so mad?
US...A COUPLE?!

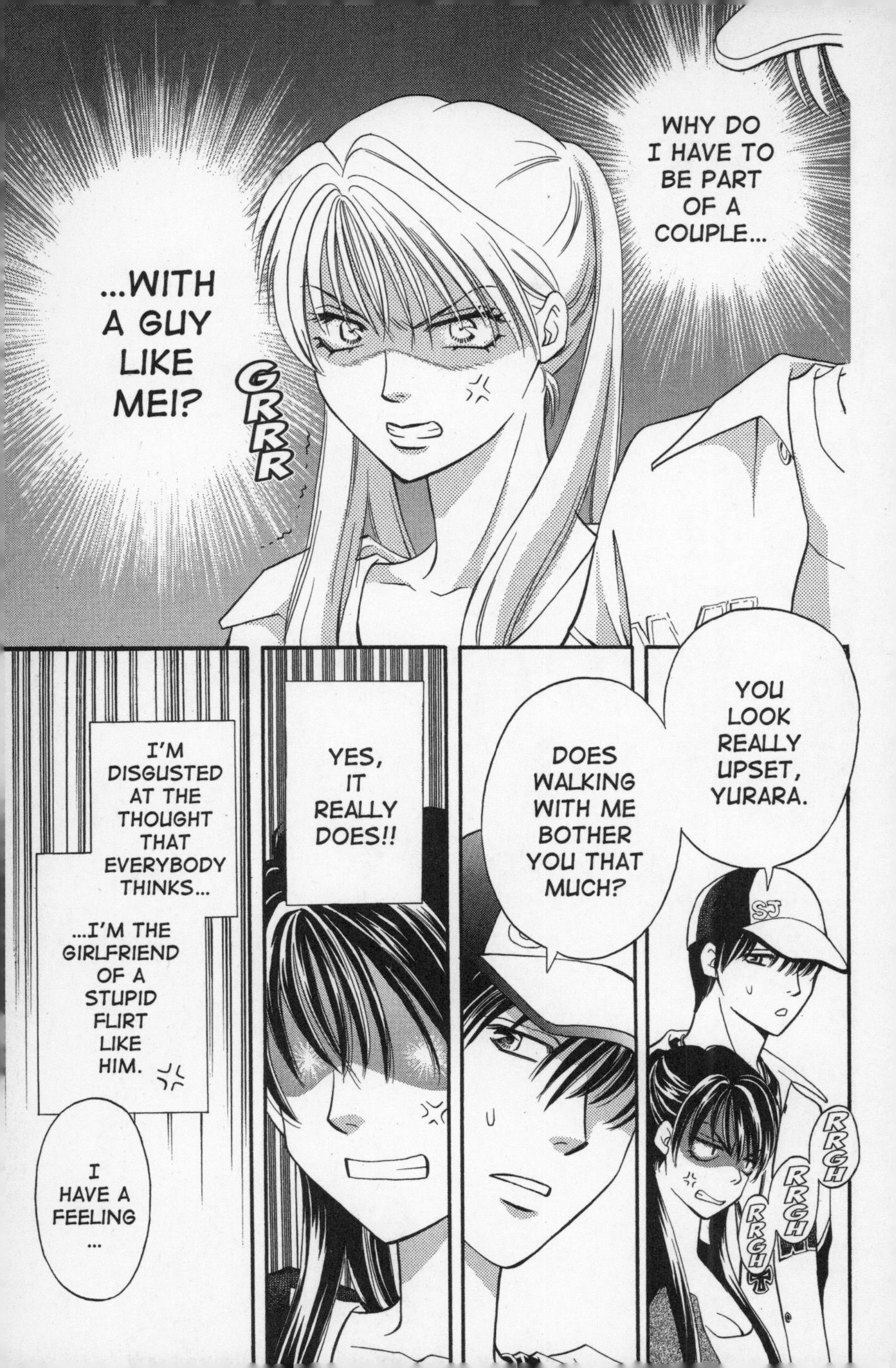
WHY DO I HAVE TO BE PART OF A COUPLE...
...WITH A GUY LIKE MEI?
GRRR
YOU LOOK REALLY UPSET, YURARA.
RRGH
RRGH
RRGH
DOES WALKING WITH ME BOTHER YOU THAT MUCH?
YES, IT REALLY DOES!!
I'M DISGUSTED AT THE THOUGHT THAT EVERYBODY THINKS...
...I'M THE GIRLFRIEND OF A STUPID FLIRT LIKE HIM.
I HAVE A FEELING ...

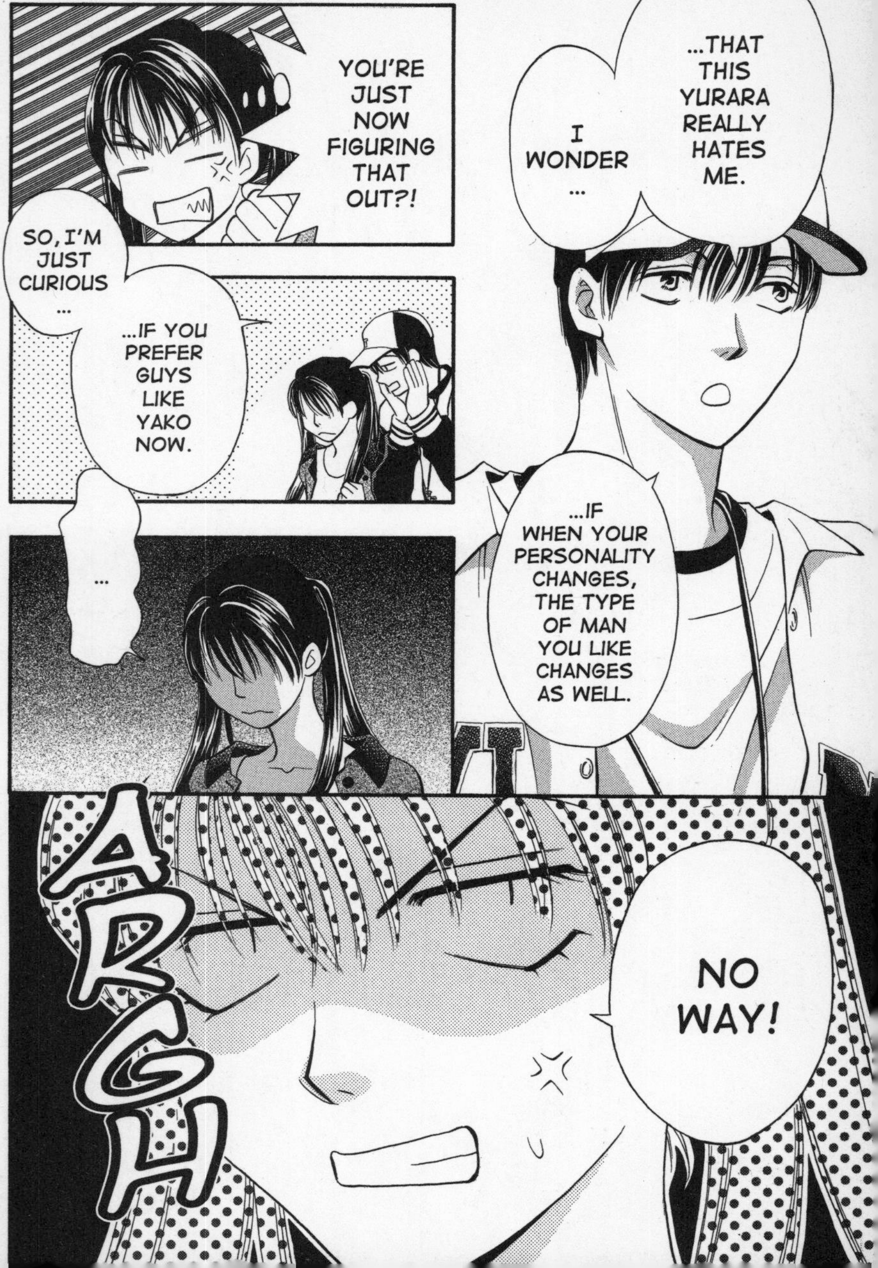
I WONDER...
...THAT THIS YURARA REALLY HATES ME.
YOU'RE JUST NOW FIGURING THAT OUT?!
SO, I'M JUST CURIOUS...
...IF WHEN YOUR PERSONALITY CHANGES, THE TYPE OF MAN YOU LIKE CHANGES AS WELL.
...IF YOU PREFER GUYS LIKE YAKO NOW.
...
NO WAY!
ARGH

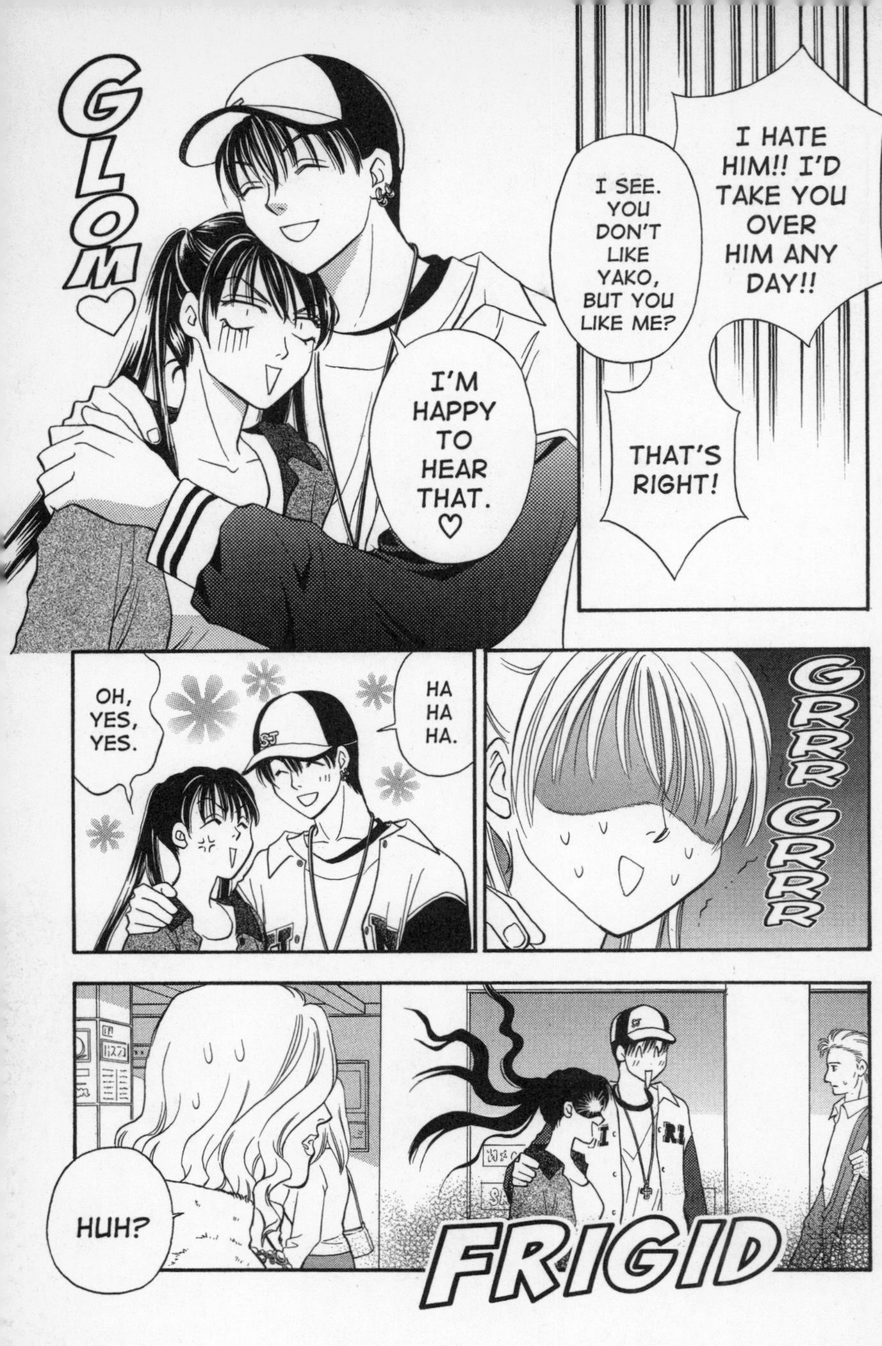

I HATE HIM!! I'D TAKE YOU OVER HIM ANY DAY!!
I SEE. YOU DON'T LIKE YAKO, BUT YOU LIKE ME?
THAT'S RIGHT!
I'M HAPPY TO HEAR THAT. ♡
GLOM ♡
GRRR GRRR
HA HA HA.
OH, YES, YES.
FRIGID
HUH?

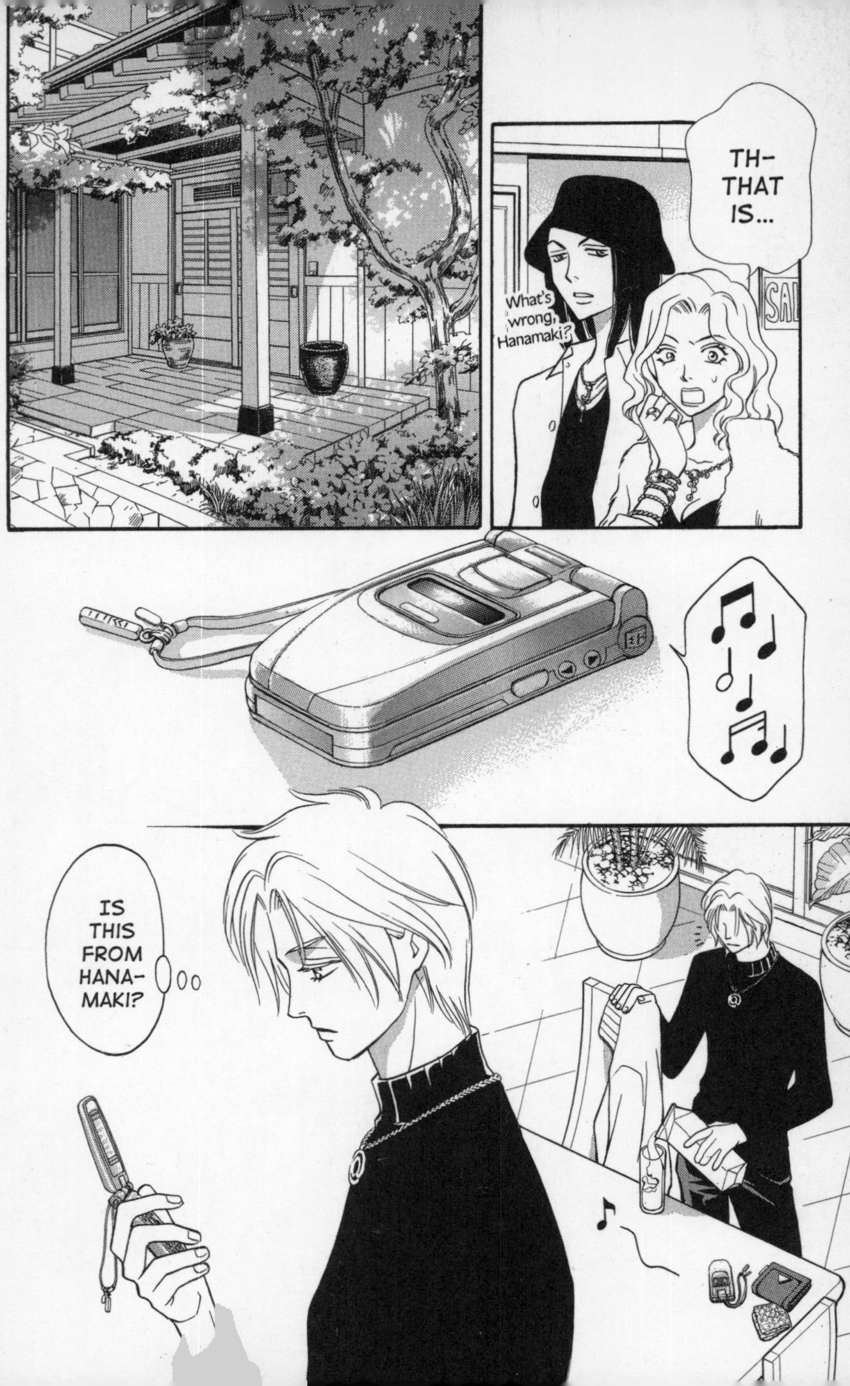
TH-THAT IS...
What's wrong, Hanamaki?
IS THIS FROM HANA-MAKI?

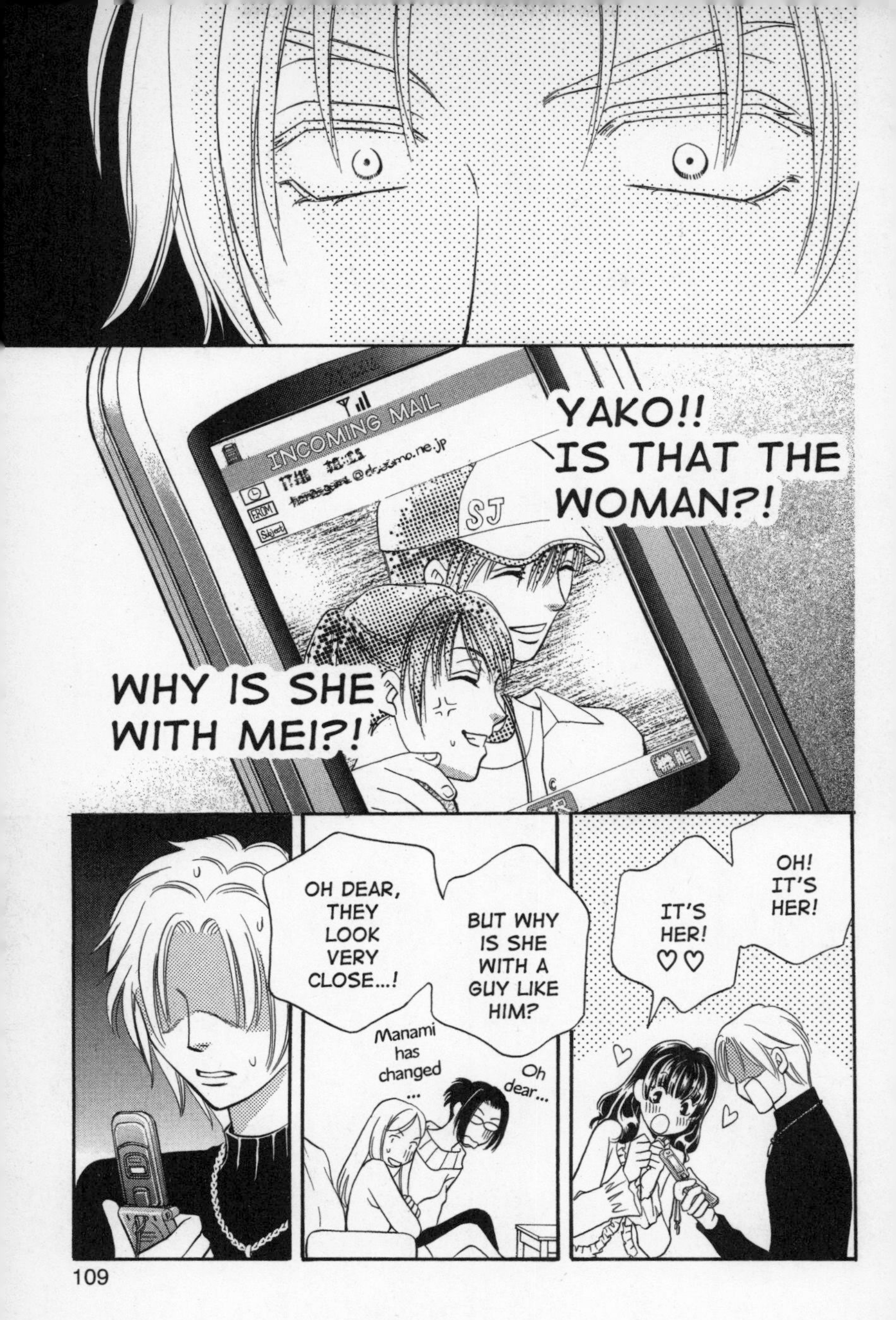
INCOMING MAIL
YAKO!! IS THAT THE WOMAN?!
WHY IS SHE WITH MEI?!
OH! IT'S HER!
IT'S HER! ♡♡
OH DEAR, THEY LOOK VERY CLOSE...!
BUT WHY IS SHE WITH A GUY LIKE HIM?
Oh dear...
Manami has changed ...

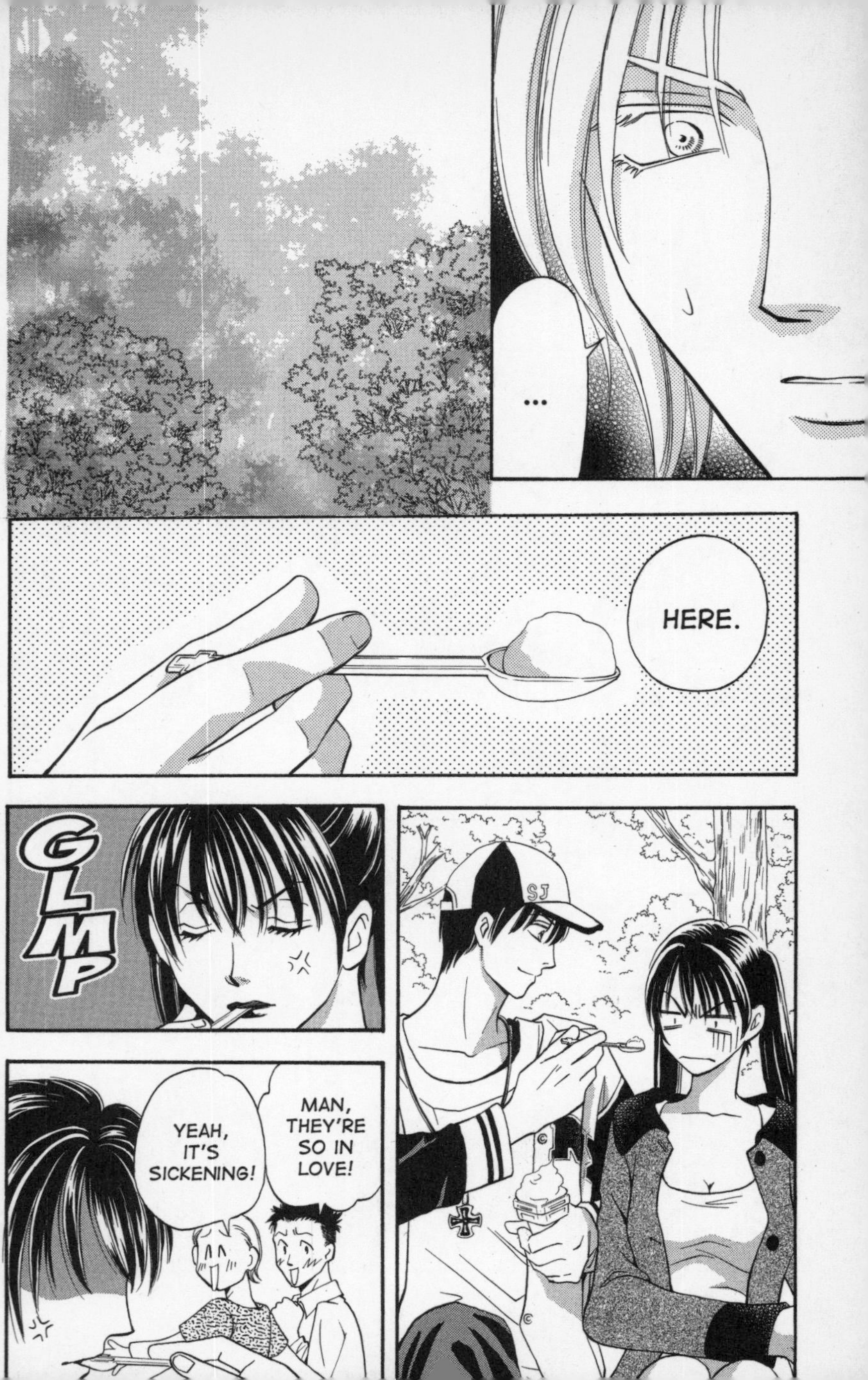
...
HERE.
GLMP
MAN, THEY'RE SO IN LOVE!
YEAH, IT'S SICKENING!

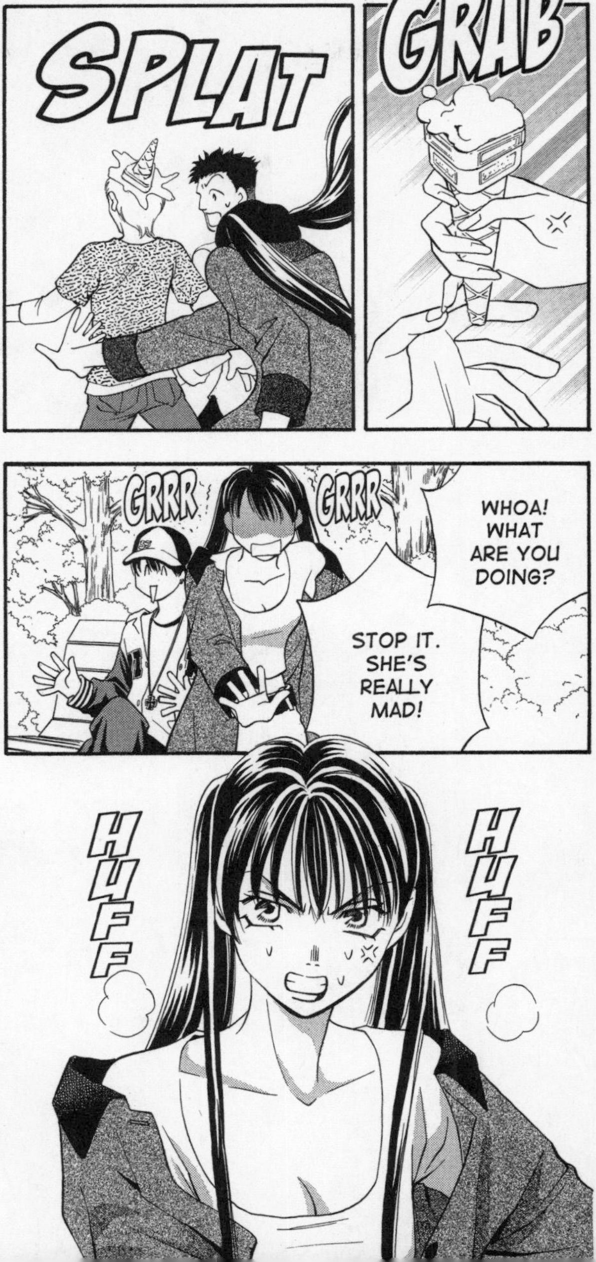
GRAB
SPLAT
GRRR
GRRR
WHOA! WHAT ARE YOU DOING?
STOP IT. SHE'S REALLY MAD!
HUFF
HUFF

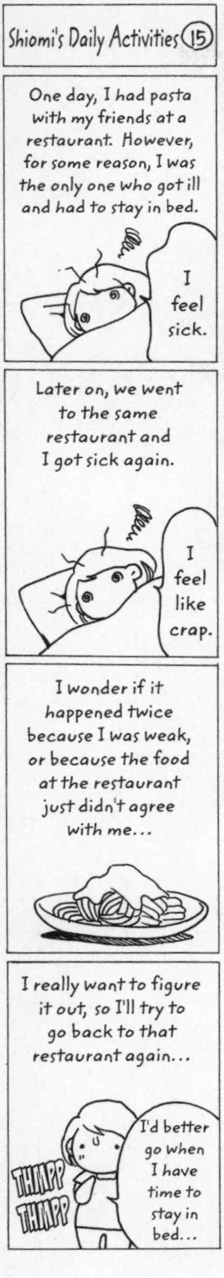
Shiomi's Daily Activities 15
One day, I had pasta with my friends at a restaurant. However, for some reason, I was the only one who got ill and had to stay in bed.
I feel sick.
Later on, we went to the same restaurant and I got sick again.
I feel like crap.
I wonder if it happened twice because I was weak, or because the food at the restaurant just didn't agree with me...
I really want to figure it out, so I'll try to go back to that restaurant again...
I'd better go when I have time to stay in bed...
THMPP THMPP

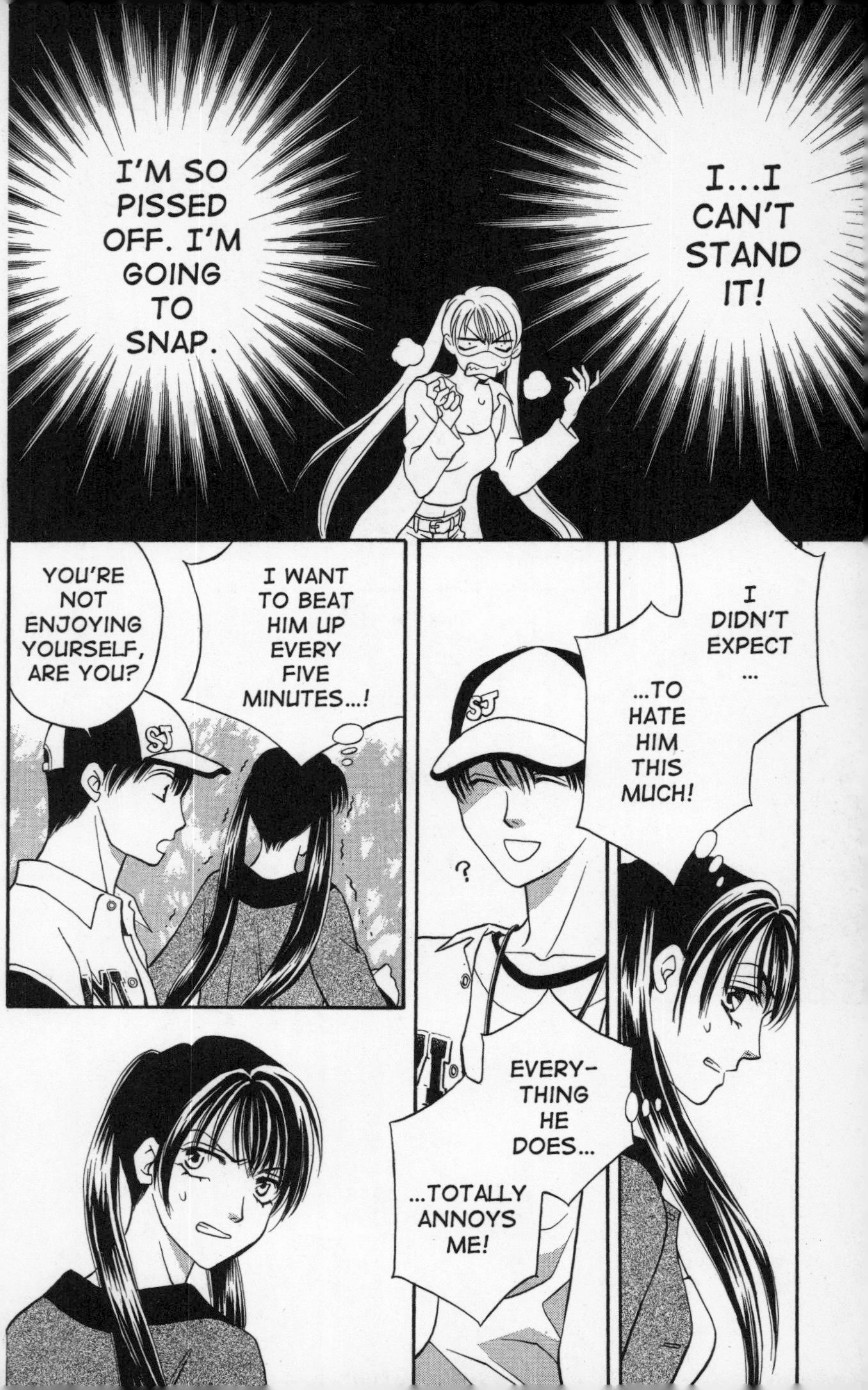
I...I CAN'T STAND IT!
I'M SO PISSED OFF. I'M GOING TO SNAP.
I DIDN'T EXPECT ...
...TO HATE HIM THIS MUCH!
?
EVERY-THING HE DOES...
...TOTALLY ANNOYS ME!
I WANT TO BEAT HIM UP EVERY FIVE MINUTES...!
YOU'RE NOT ENJOYING YOURSELF, ARE YOU?

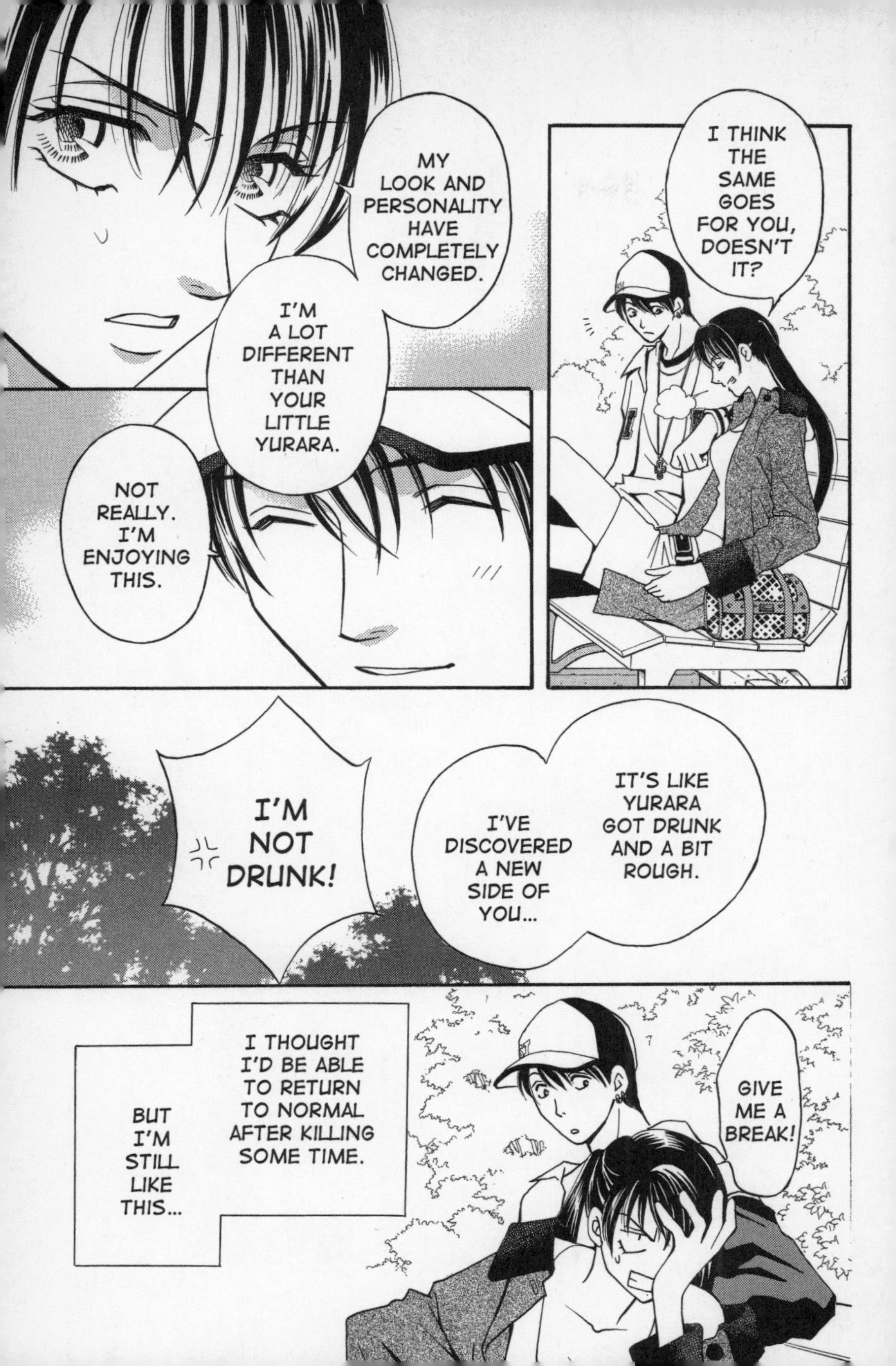

I THINK THE SAME GOES FOR YOU, DOESN'T IT?
MY LOOK AND PERSONALITY HAVE COMPLETELY CHANGED.
I'M A LOT DIFFERENT THAN YOUR LITTLE YURARA.
NOT REALLY. I'M ENJOYING THIS.
IT'S LIKE YURARA GOT DRUNK AND A BIT ROUGH.
I'VE DISCOVERED A NEW SIDE OF YOU...
I'M NOT DRUNK!
GIVE ME A BREAK!
I THOUGHT I'D BE ABLE TO RETURN TO NORMAL AFTER KILLING SOME TIME.
BUT I'M STILL LIKE THIS...

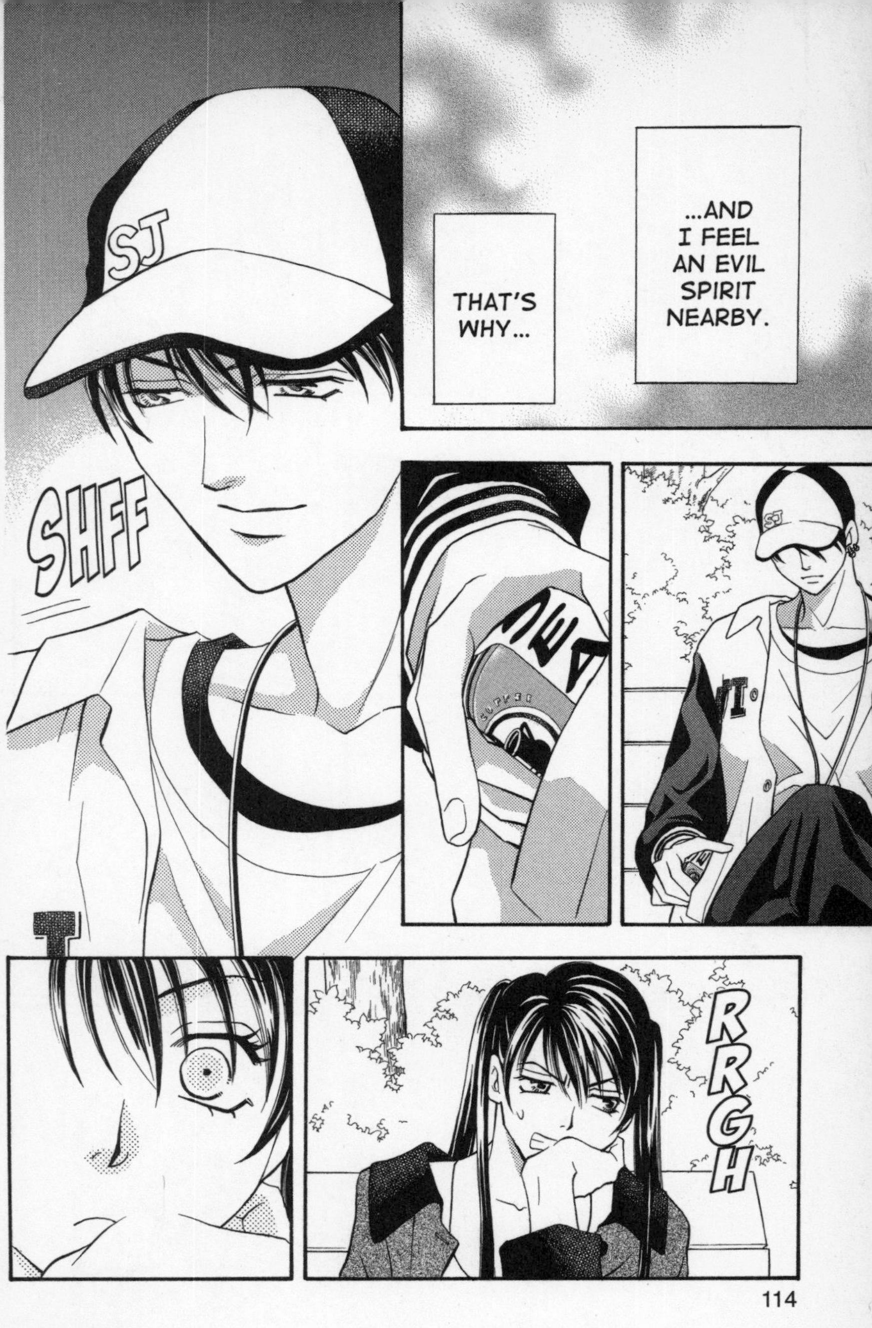

...AND I FEEL AN EVIL SPIRIT NEARBY.
THAT'S WHY...
SHFF
RRGH
T

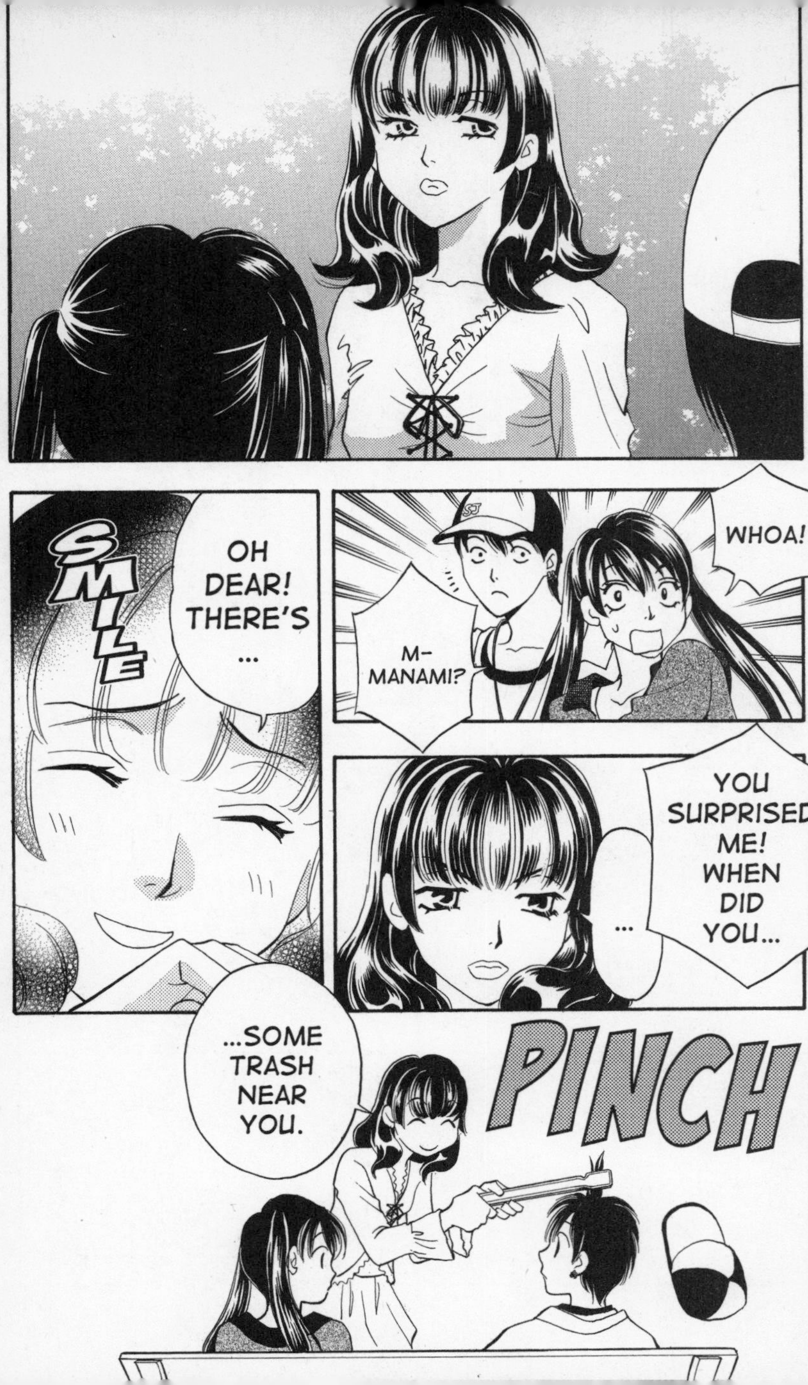
WHOA!
M-MANAMI?
YOU SURPRISED ME! WHEN DID YOU...
...
OH DEAR! THERE'S ...
SMILE
...SOME TRASH NEAR YOU.
PINCH

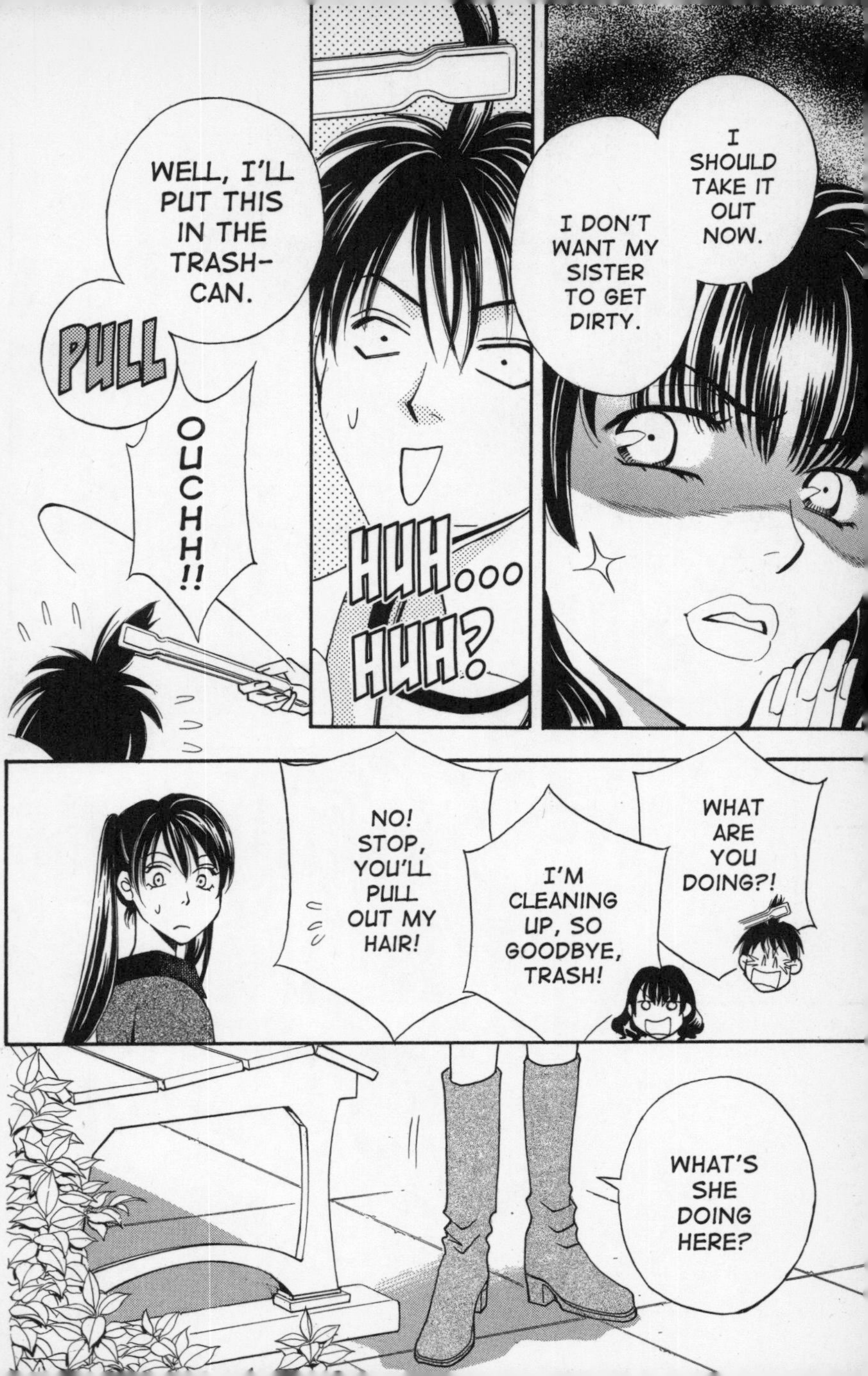
I SHOULD TAKE IT OUT NOW.
I DON'T WANT MY SISTER TO GET DIRTY.
HUH...
HUH?
WELL, I'LL PUT THIS IN THE TRASH-CAN.
PULL
OUCHH!!
WHAT ARE YOU DOING?!
I'M CLEANING UP, SO GOODBYE, TRASH!
NO! STOP, YOU'LL PULL OUT MY HAIR!
WHAT'S SHE DOING HERE?

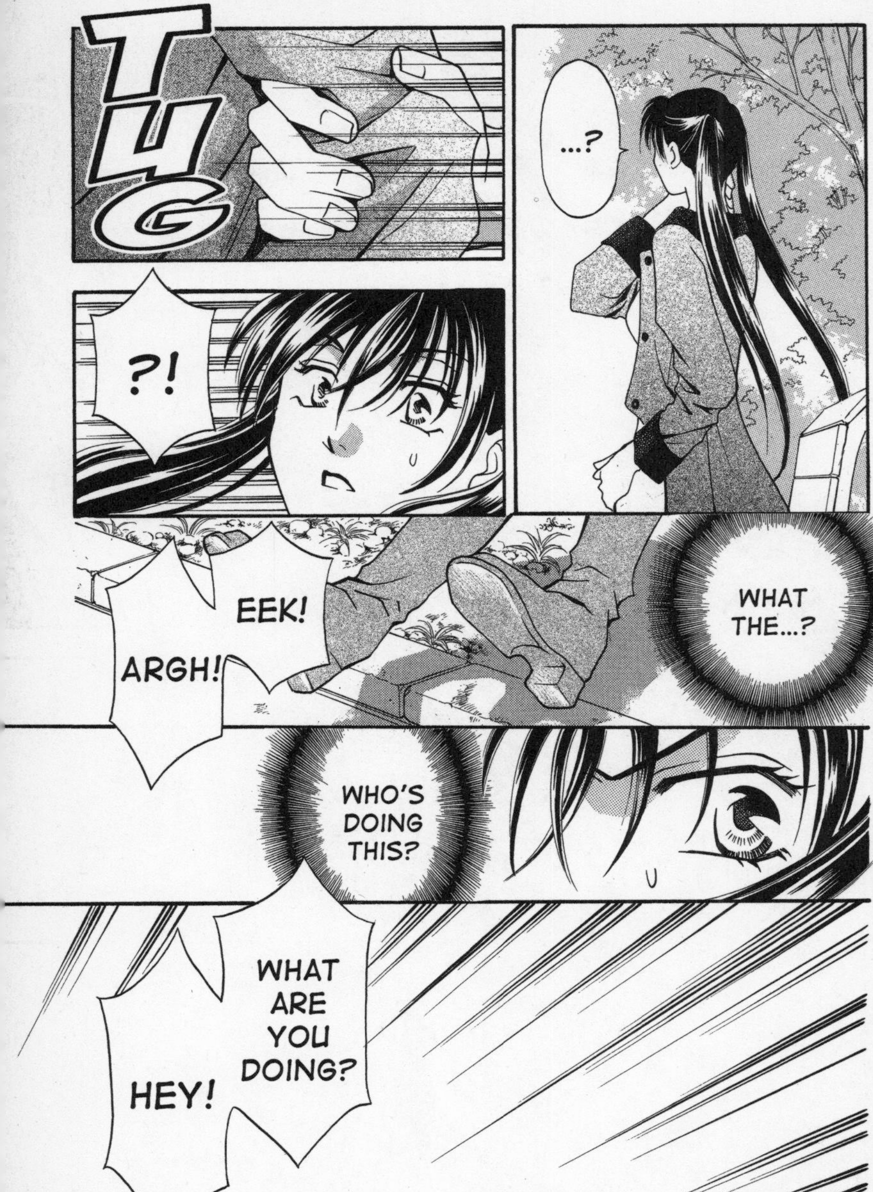
...?
TUG
?!
WHAT THE...?
EEK!
ARGH!
WHO'S DOING THIS?
WHAT ARE YOU DOING?
HEY!

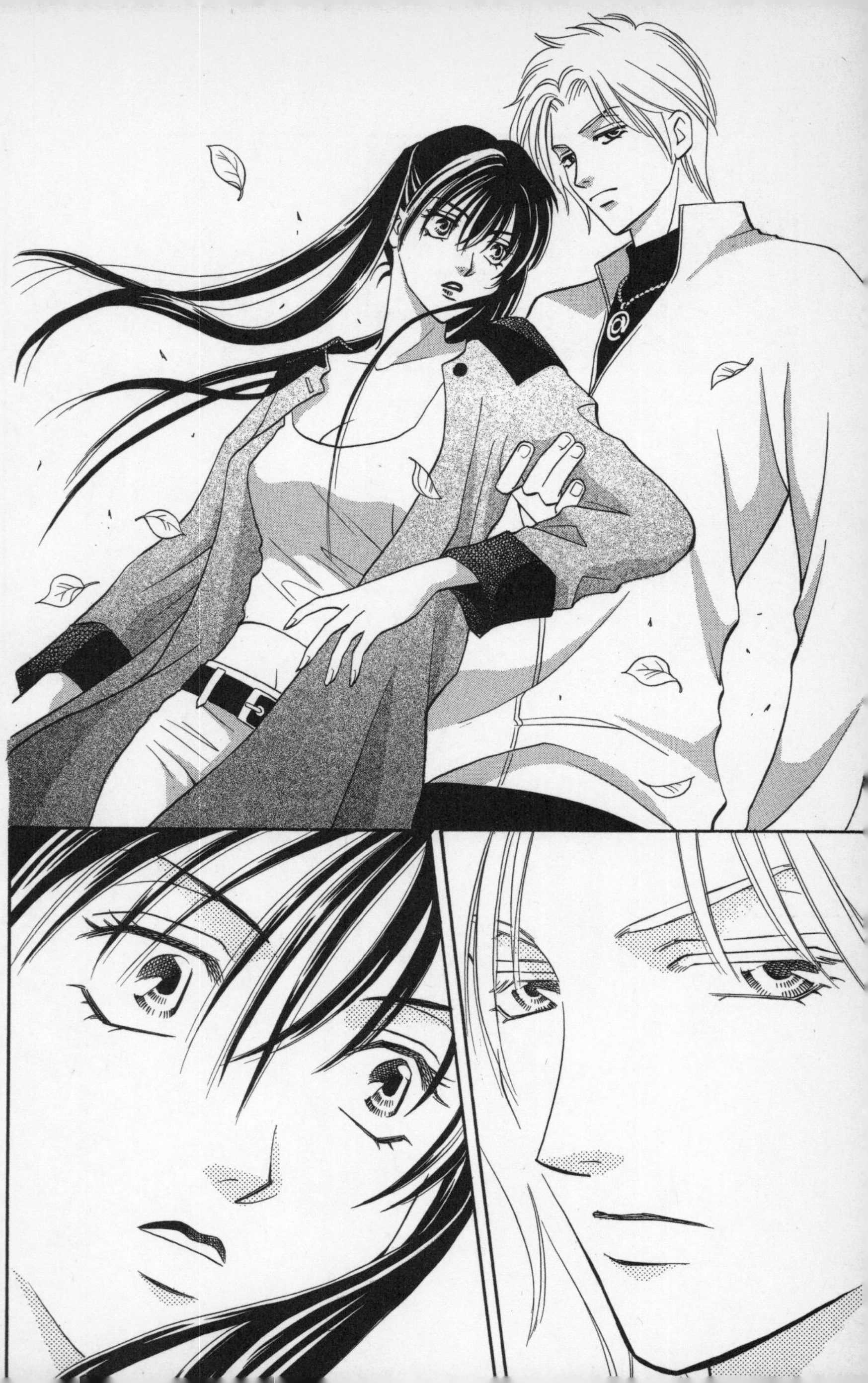

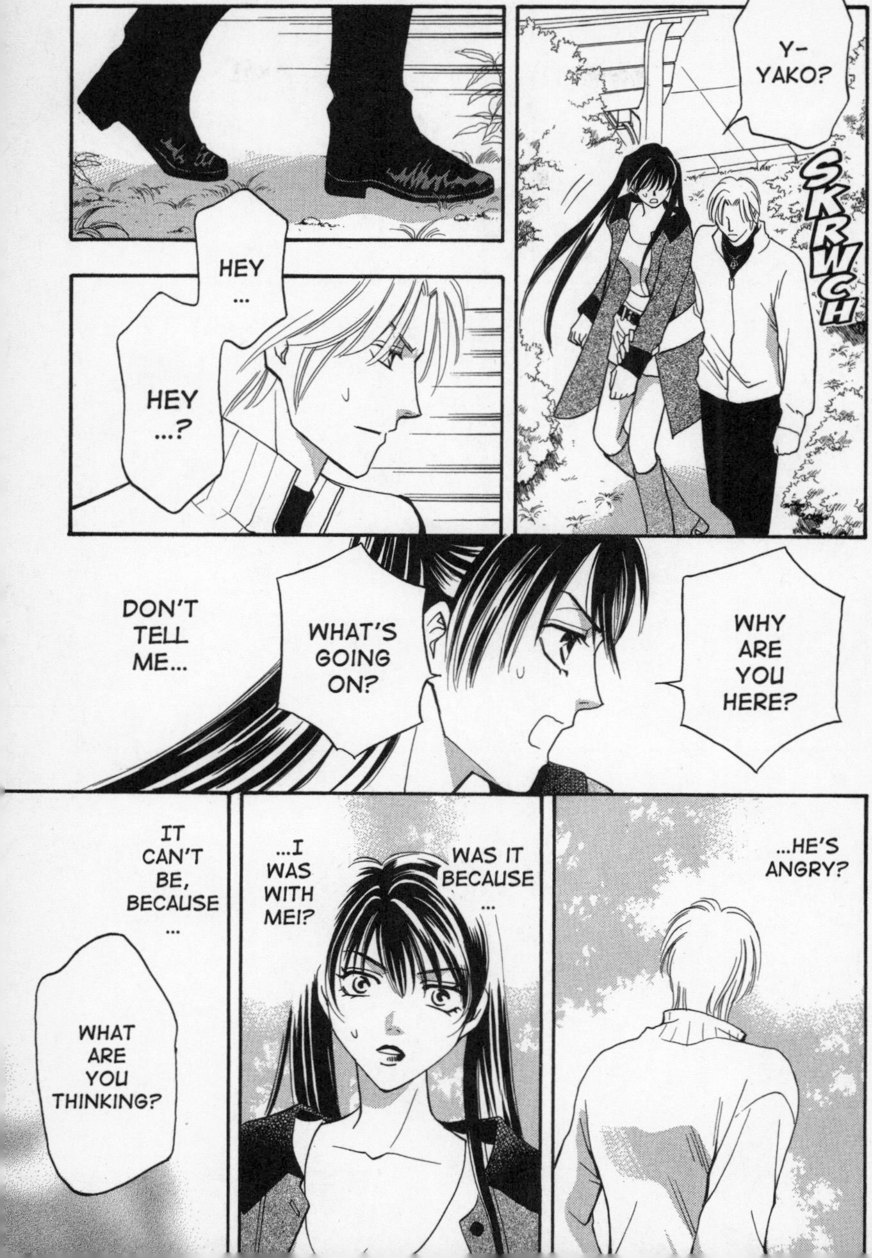
Y-YAKO?
SKRWCH
HEY ...
HEY ...?
WHY ARE YOU HERE?
WHAT'S GOING ON?
DON'T TELL ME...
...HE'S ANGRY?
WAS IT BECAUSE ...
...I WAS WITH MEI?
IT CAN'T BE, BECAUSE ...
WHAT ARE YOU THINKING?

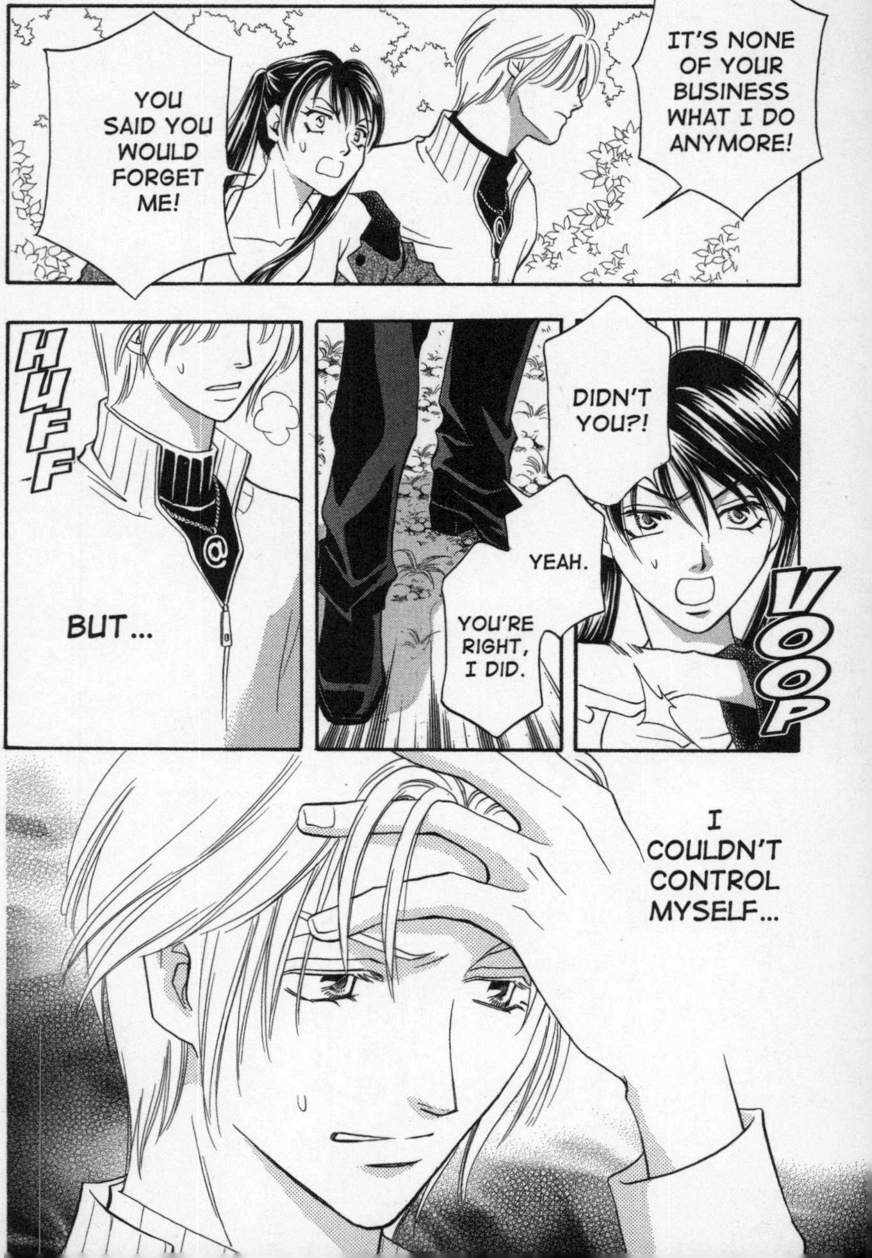
IT'S NONE OF YOUR BUSINESS WHAT I DO ANYMORE!
YOU SAID YOU WOULD FORGET ME!
DIDN'T YOU?!
VOOP
YEAH.
YOU'RE RIGHT, I DID.
HUFF
BUT...
I COULDN'T CONTROL MYSELF...

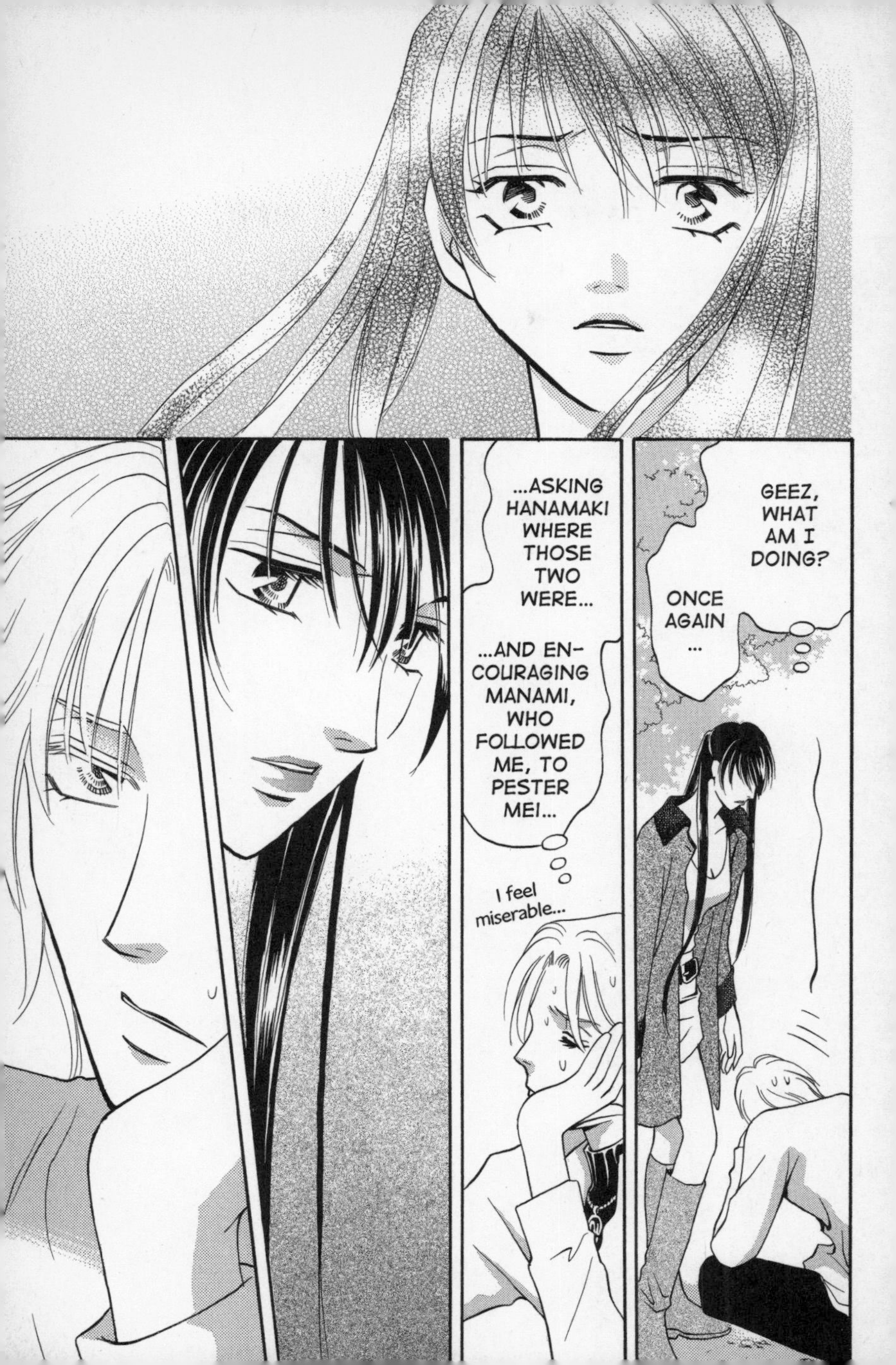
GEEZ, WHAT AM I DOING?
ONCE AGAIN ...
...ASKING HANAMAKI WHERE THOSE TWO WERE...
...AND EN-COURAGING MANAMI, WHO FOLLOWED ME, TO PESTER MEI...
I feel miserable...

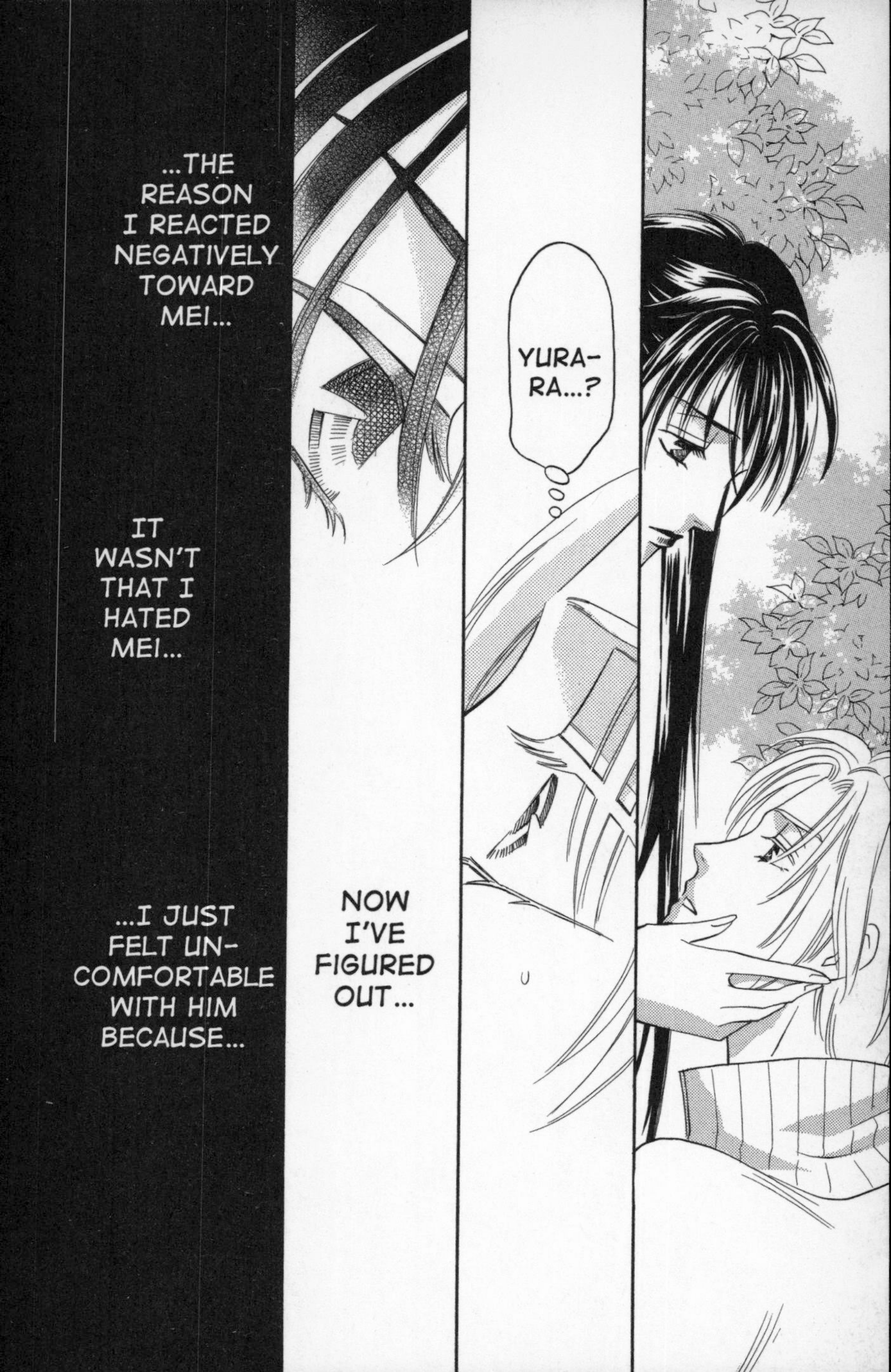
YURA-
RA...?
NOW
I'VE
FIGURED
OUT...
...THE
REASON
I REACTED
NEGATIVELY
TOWARD
MEI...
IT
WASN'T
THAT I
HATED
MEI...
...I JUST
FELT UN-
COMFORTABLE
WITH HIM
BECAUSE...

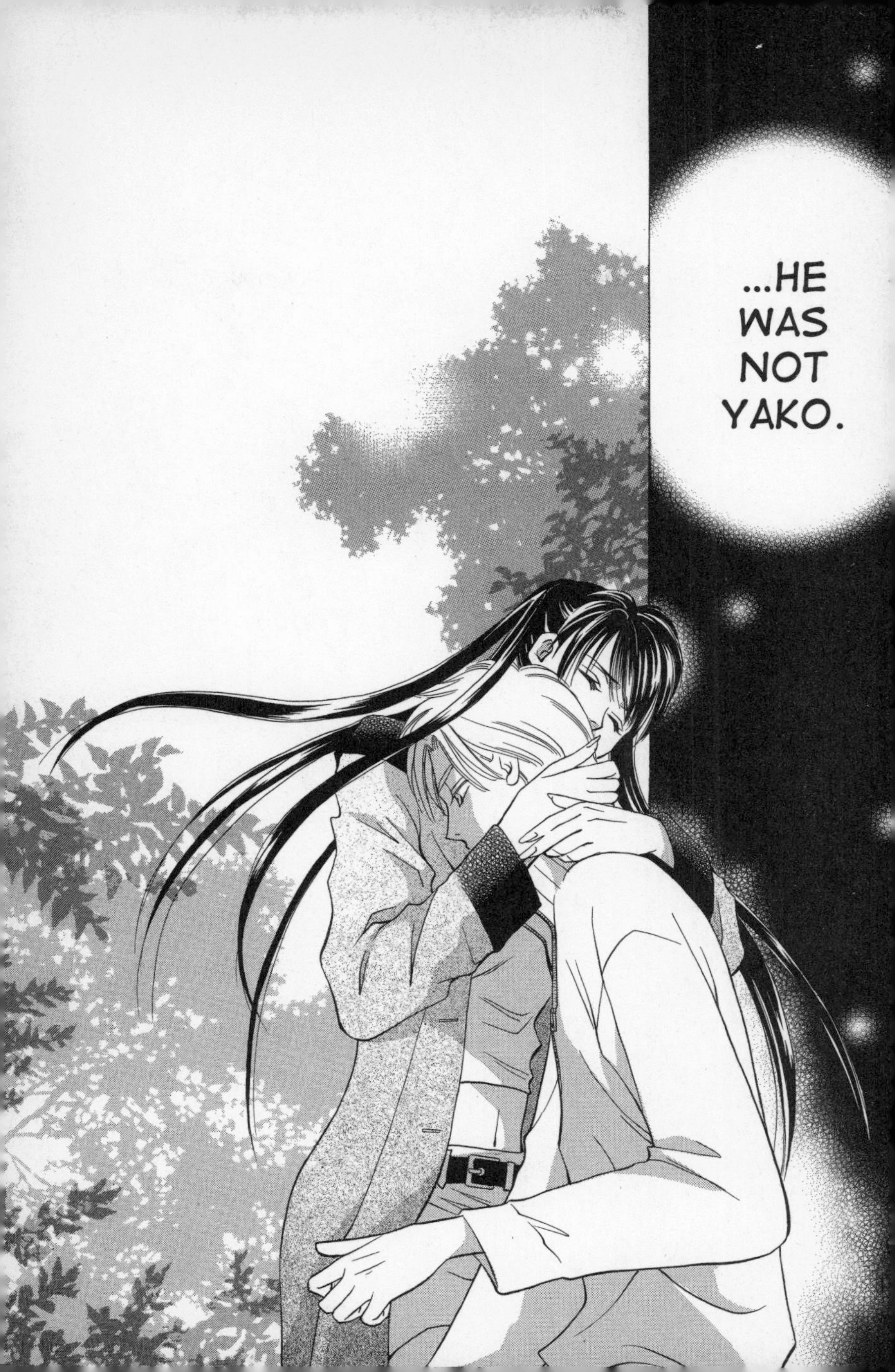
...HE WAS NOT YAKO.

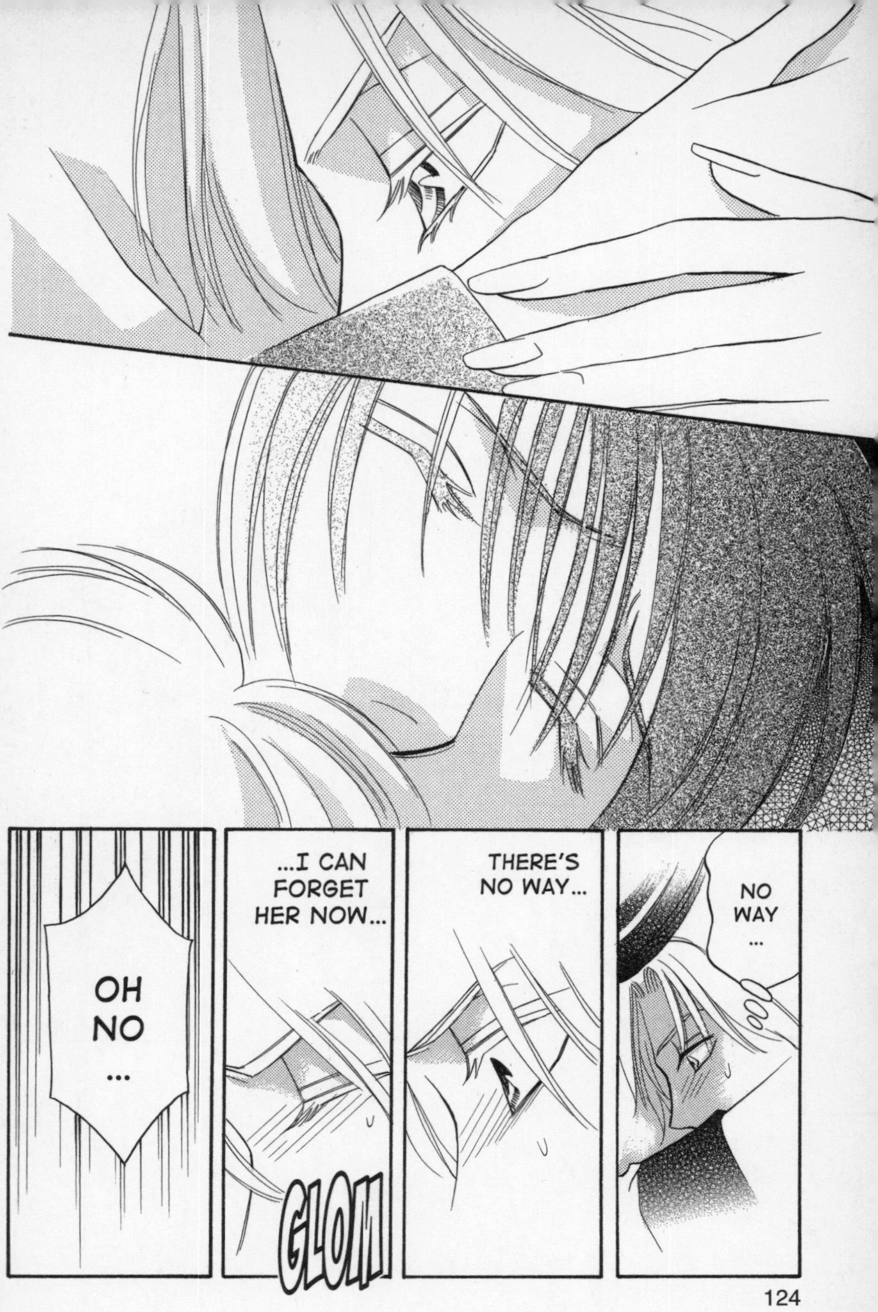
NO WAY ...
THERE'S NO WAY...
...I CAN FORGET HER NOW...
GLOM
OH NO ...

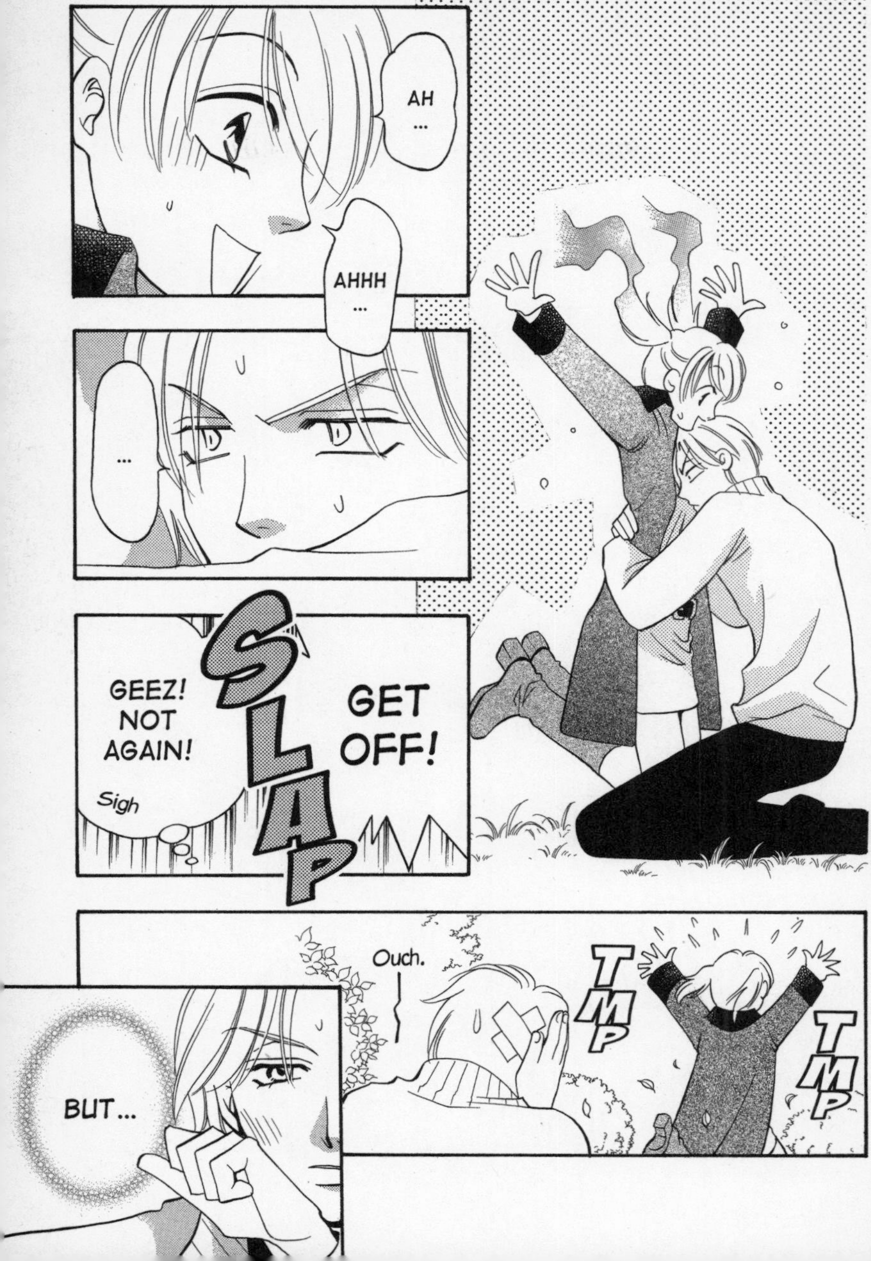
AH ...
AHHH ...
...
GET OFF!
SLAP
GEEZ! NOT AGAIN!
Sigh
TMP
TMP
Ouch.
BUT...

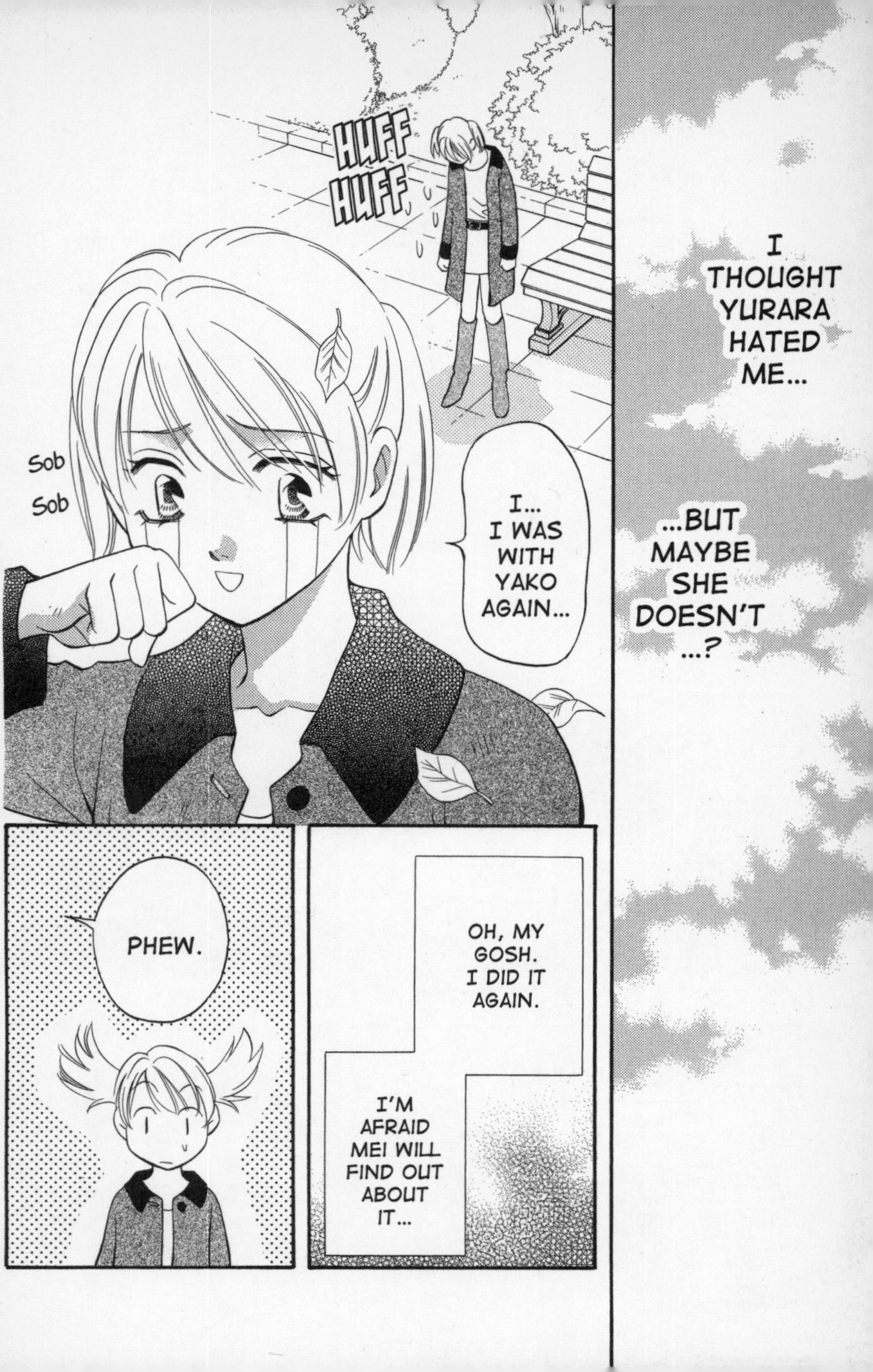
I THOUGHT YURARA HATED ME...
...BUT MAYBE SHE DOESN'T ...?
HUFF HUFF
I... I WAS WITH YAKO AGAIN...
Sob Sob
OH, MY GOSH. I DID IT AGAIN.
I'M AFRAID MEI WILL FIND OUT ABOUT IT...
PHEW.

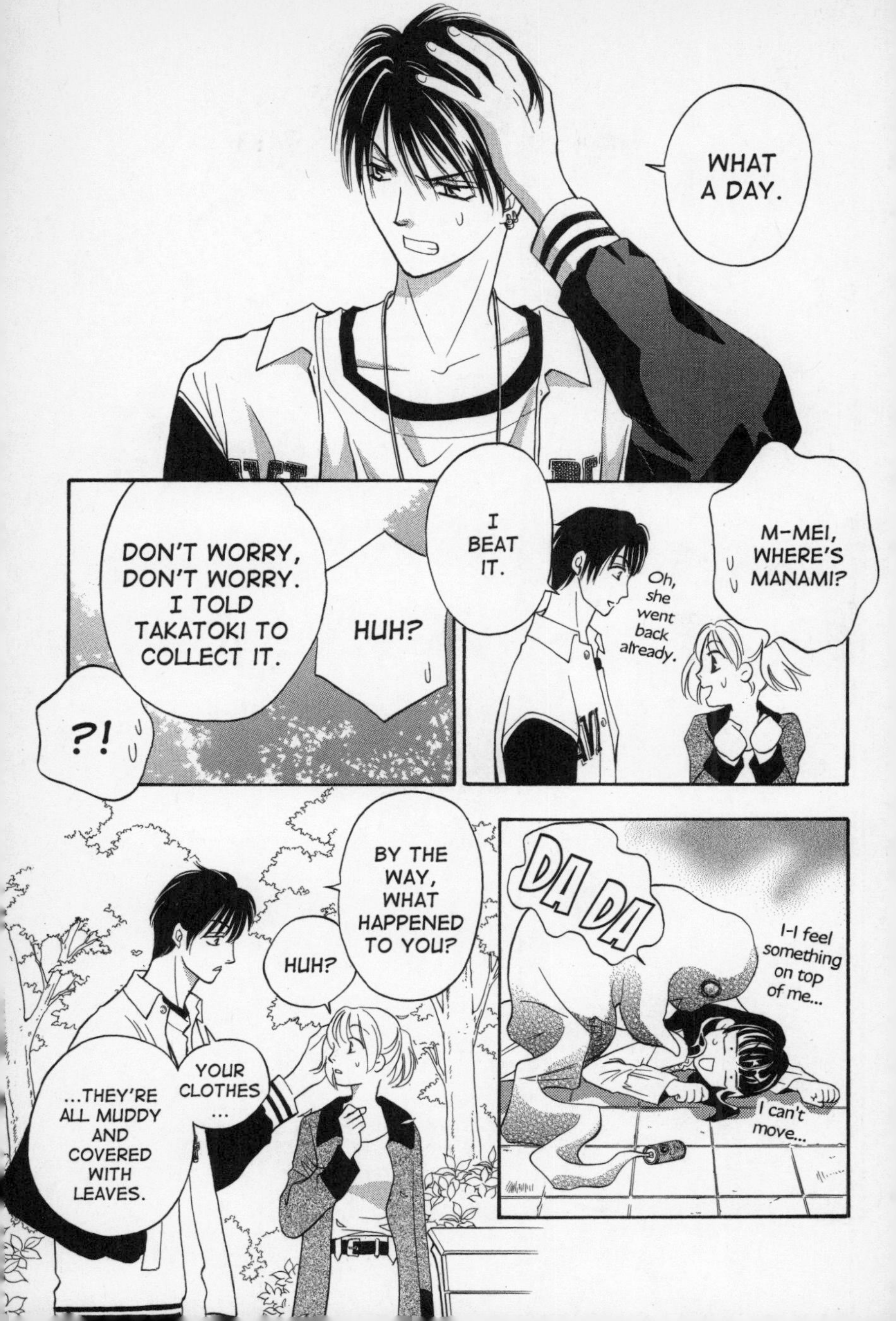
WHAT A DAY.
M-MEI, WHERE'S MANAMI?
Oh, she went back already.
I BEAT IT.
HUH?
DON'T WORRY, DON'T WORRY. I TOLD TAKATOKI TO COLLECT IT.
?!
DA DA
I-I feel something on top of me...
I can't move...
BY THE WAY, WHAT HAPPENED TO YOU?
HUH?
YOUR CLOTHES ...
...THEY'RE ALL MUDDY AND COVERED WITH LEAVES.

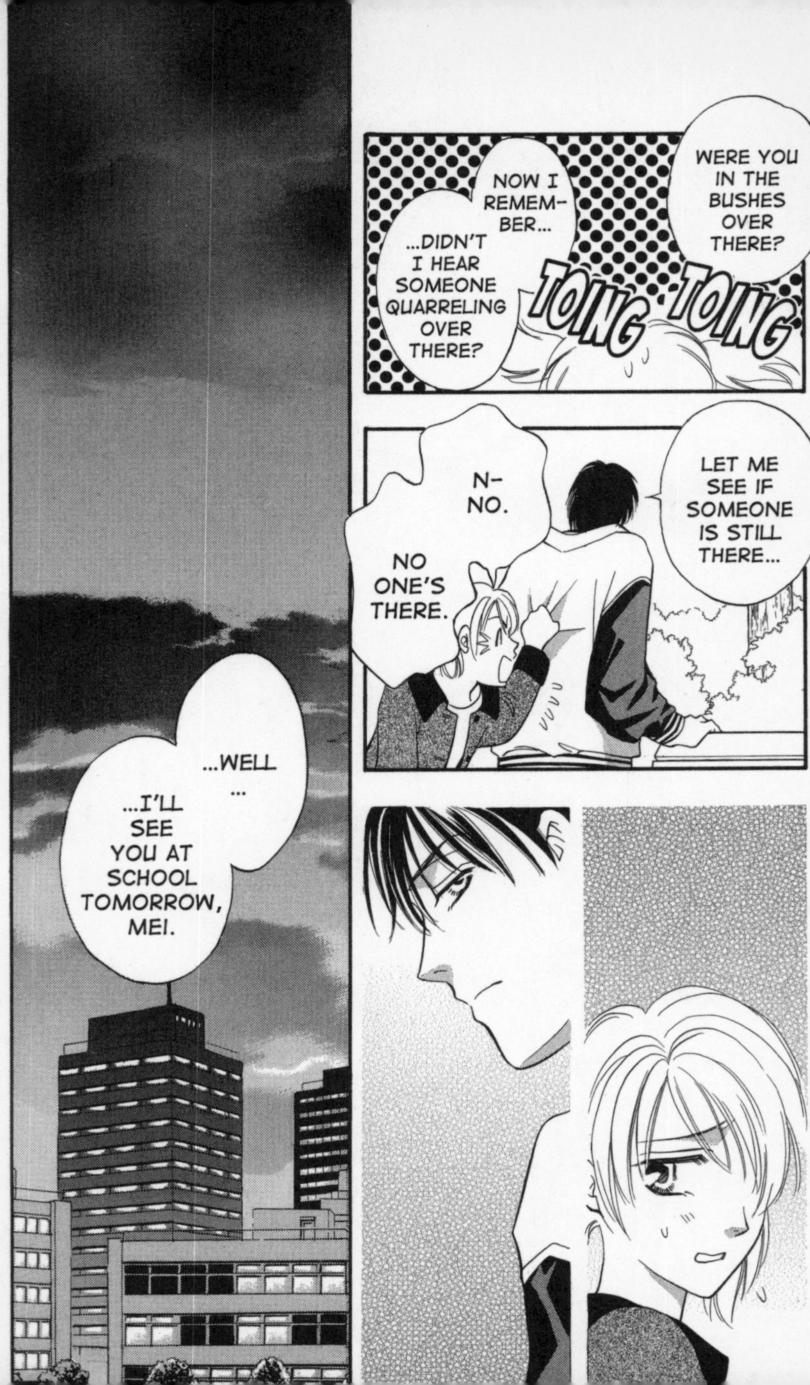
WERE YOU IN THE BUSHES OVER THERE?
NOW I REMEMBER...
...DIDN'T I HEAR SOMEONE QUARRELING OVER THERE?
TOING TOING
LET ME SEE IF SOMEONE IS STILL THERE...
N-NO.
NO ONE'S THERE.
...WELL ...
...I'LL SEE YOU AT SCHOOL TOMORROW, MEI.

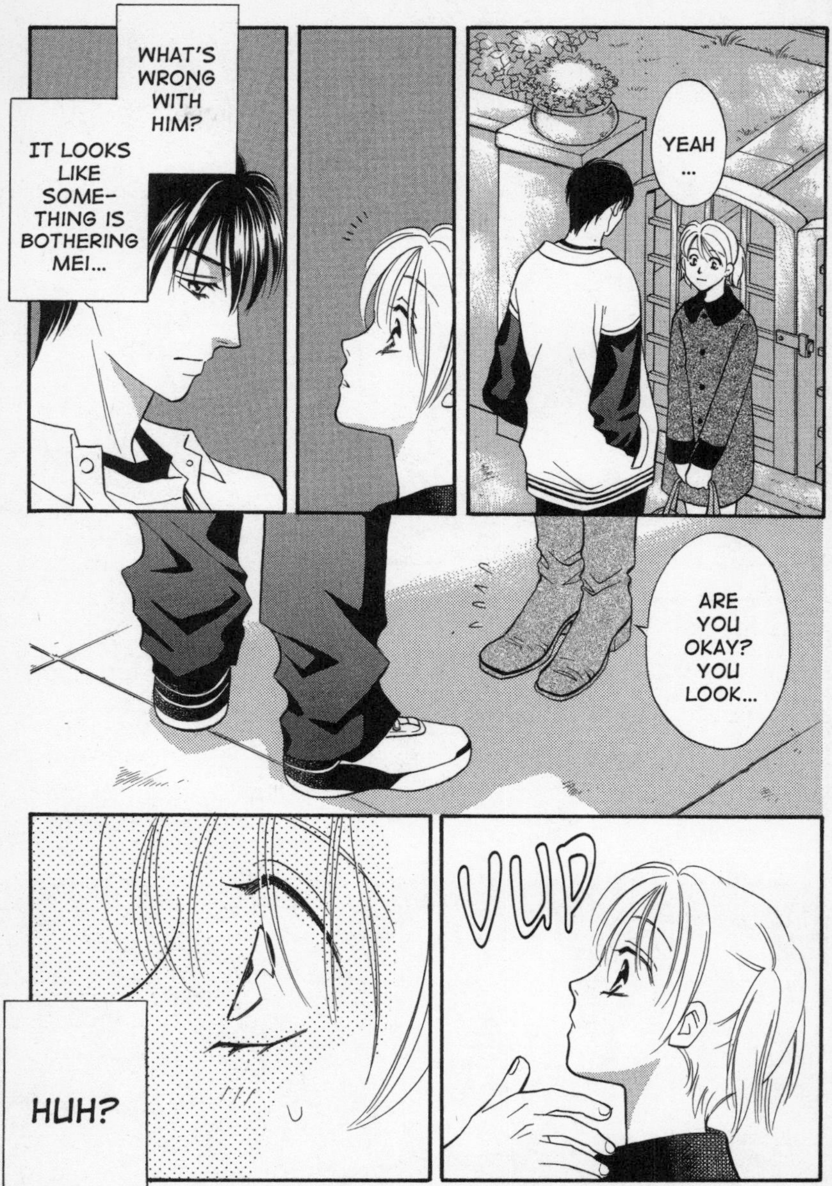
YEAH ...
WHAT'S WRONG WITH HIM?
IT LOOKS LIKE SOME-THING IS BOTHERING MEI...
ARE YOU OKAY? YOU LOOK...
VUP
HUH?

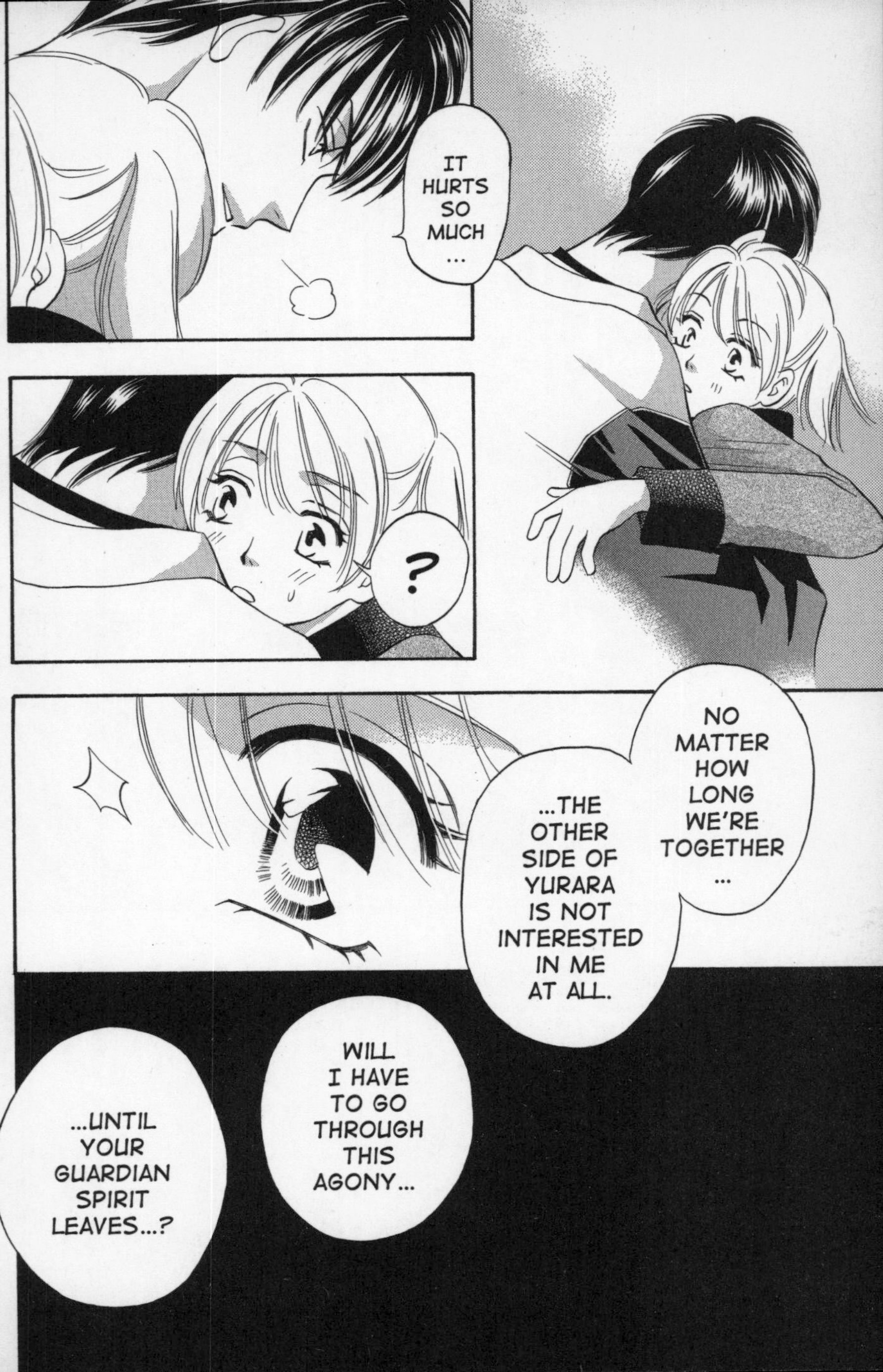
IT HURTS SO MUCH ...
?
NO MATTER HOW LONG WE'RE TOGETHER ...
...THE OTHER SIDE OF YURARA IS NOT INTERESTED IN ME AT ALL.
WILL I HAVE TO GO THROUGH THIS AGONY...
...UNTIL YOUR GUARDIAN SPIRIT LEAVES...?

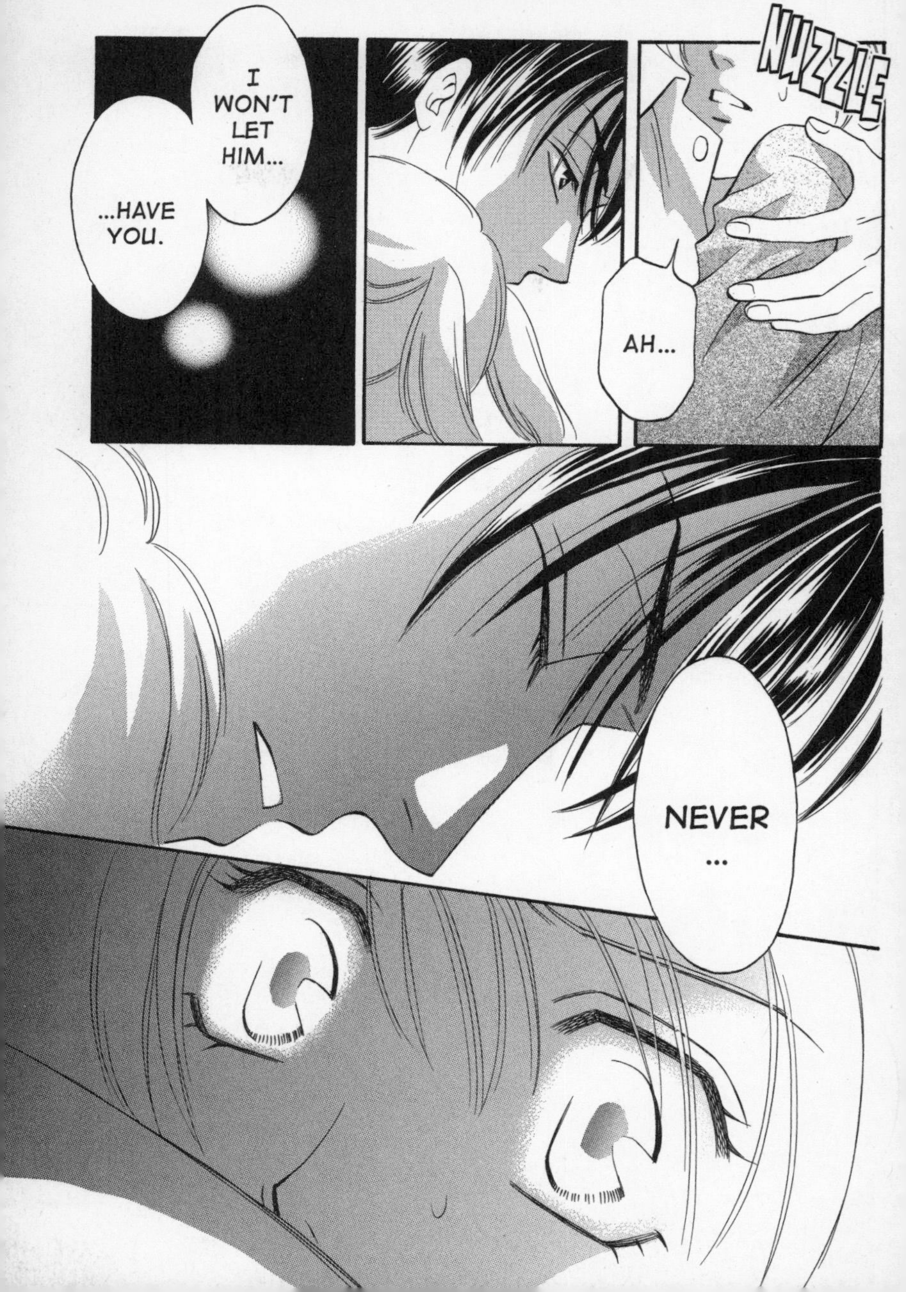
NUZZLE
AH...
I WON'T LET HIM...
...HAVE YOU.
NEVER ...

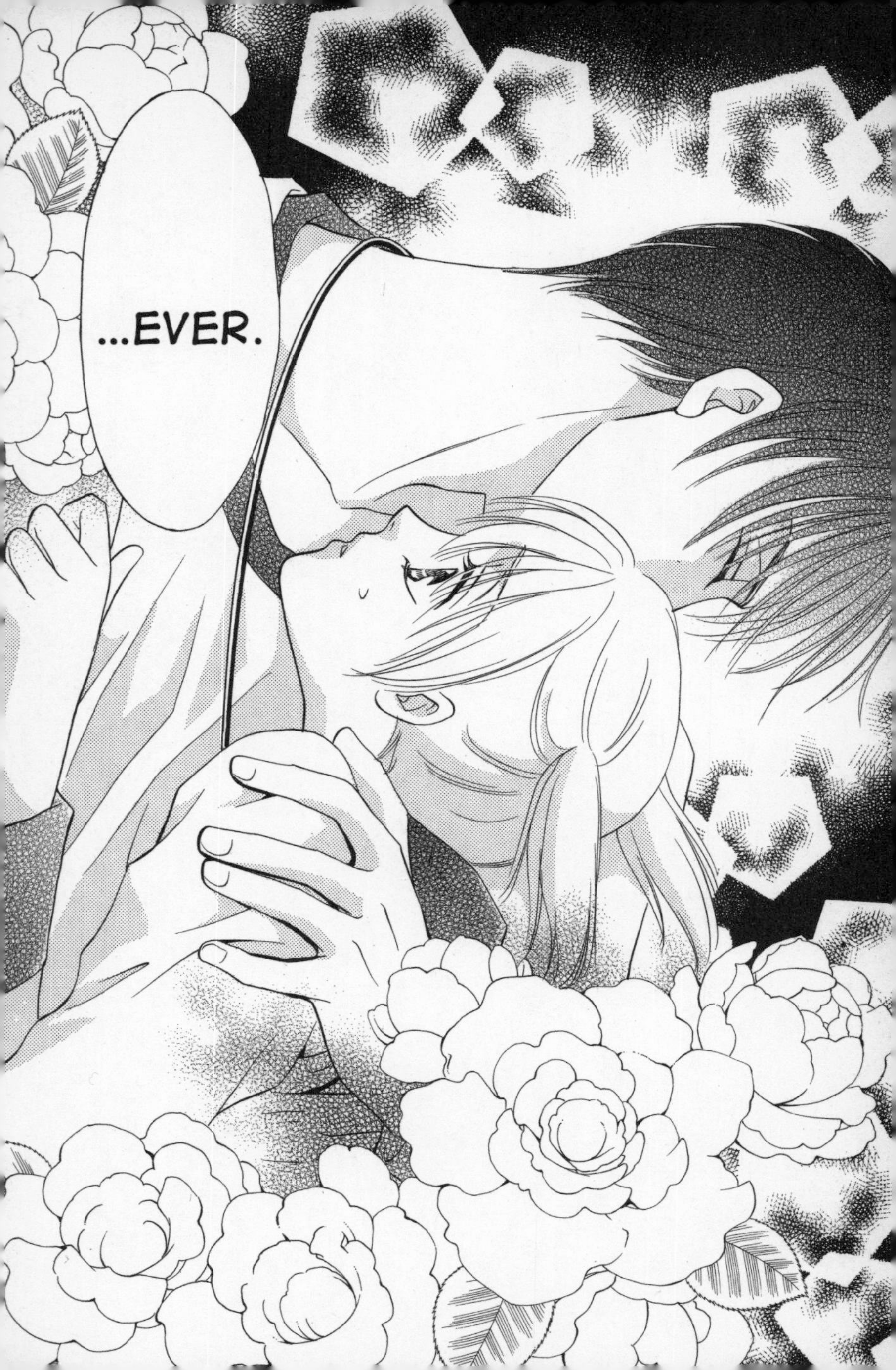
...EVER.

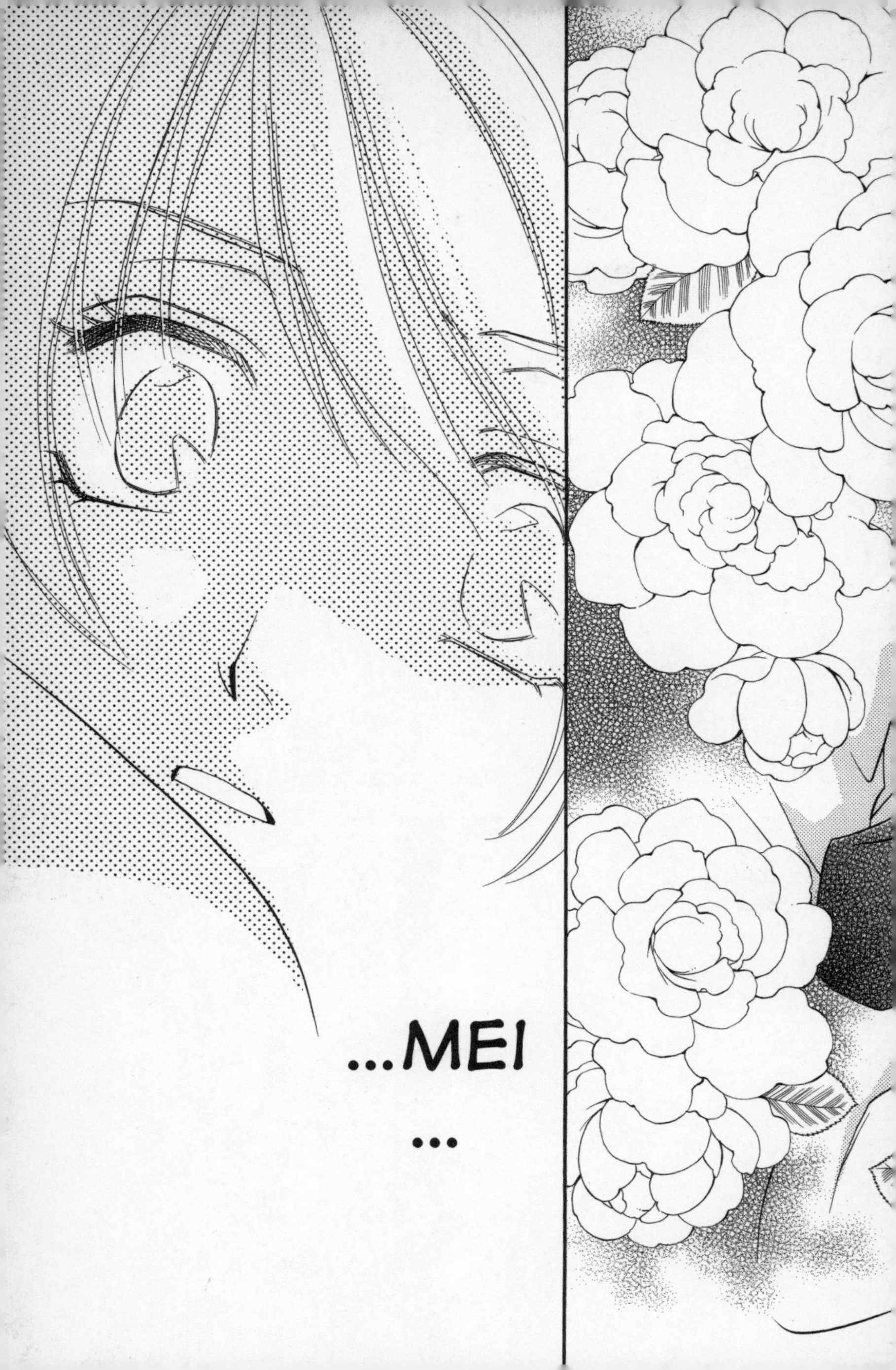
...MEI
...

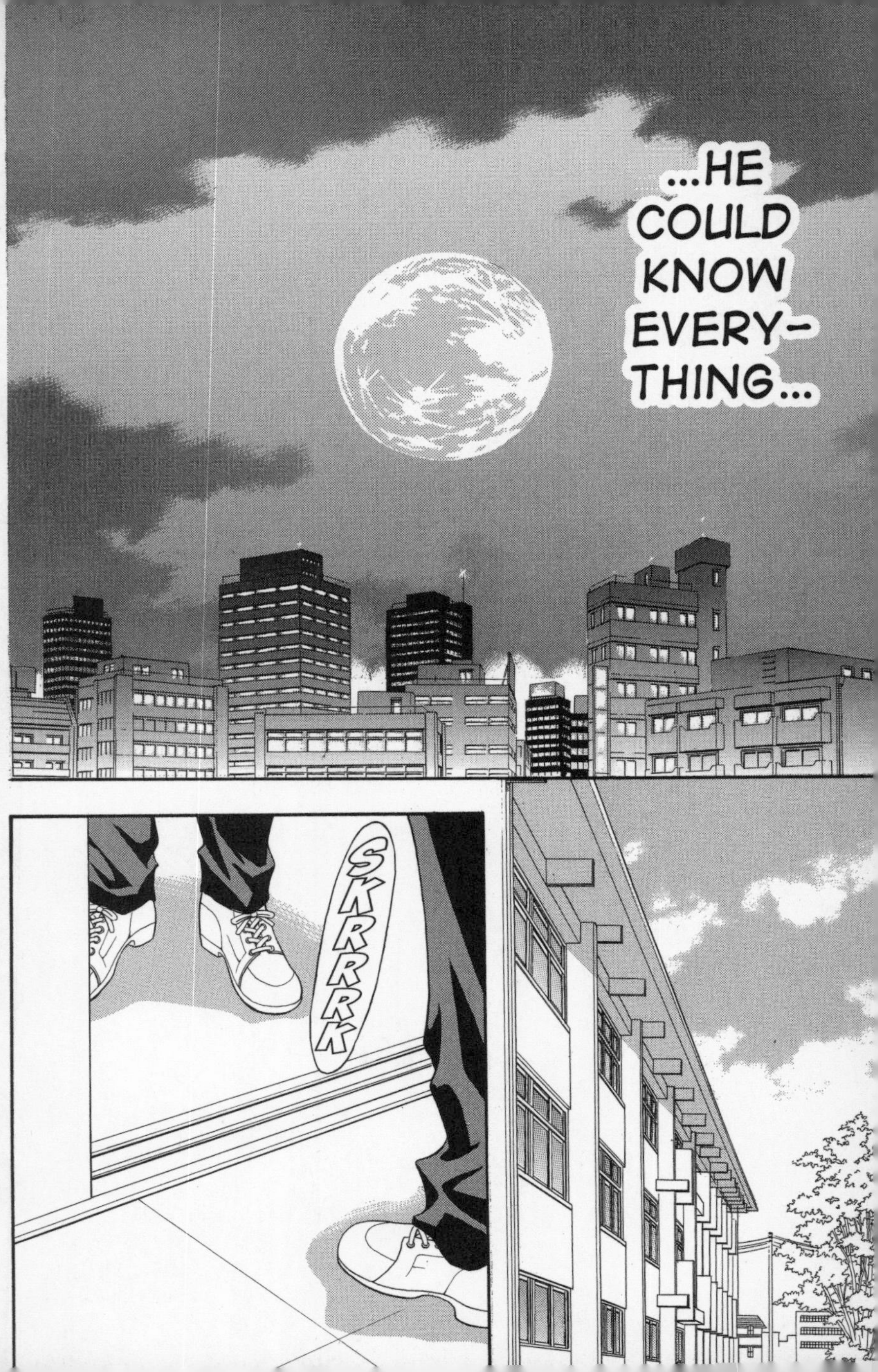
...HE COULD KNOW EVERY-THING...
SKRRRK

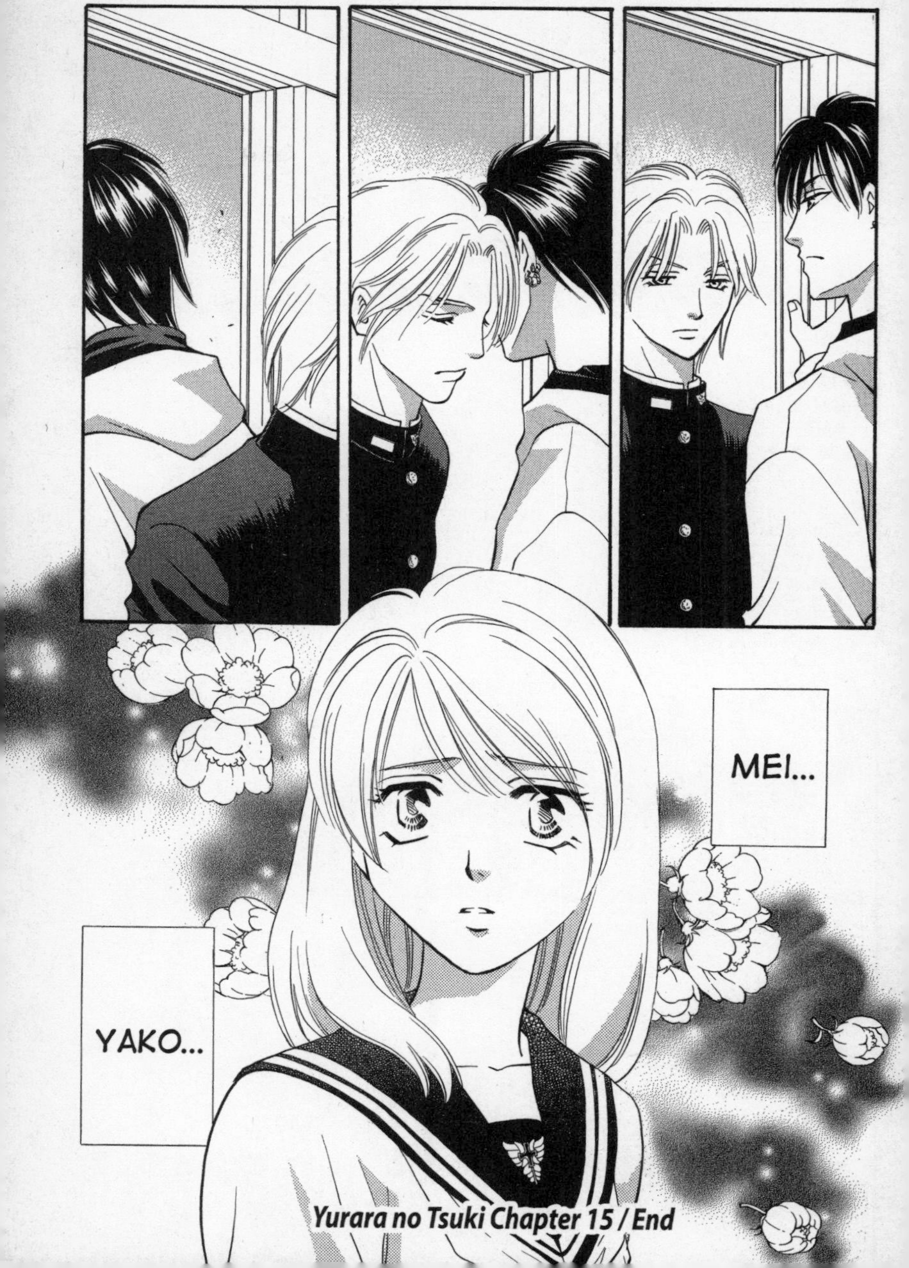
MEI...
YAKO...
Yurara no Tsuki Chapter 15 / End

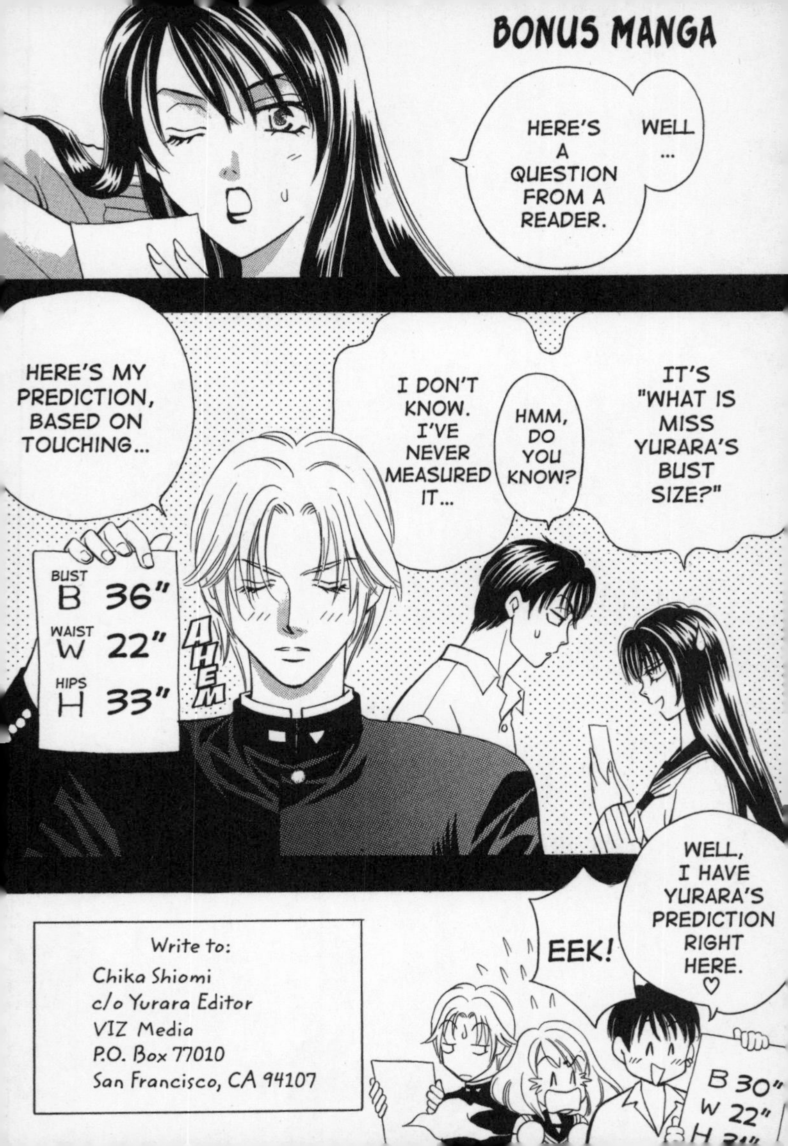
BONUS MANGA
WELL ...
HERE'S A QUESTION FROM A READER.
IT'S "WHAT IS MISS YURARA'S BUST SIZE?"
HMM, DO YOU KNOW?
I DON'T KNOW. I'VE NEVER MEASURED IT...
HERE'S MY PREDICTION, BASED ON TOUCHING...
BUST B 36" WAIST W 22" HIPS H 33"
AHEM
WELL, I HAVE YURARA'S PREDICTION RIGHT HERE. ♡
B 30" W 22"
EEK!
Write to:
Chika Shiomi
c/o Yurara Editor
VIZ Media
P.O. Box 77010
San Francisco, CA 94107

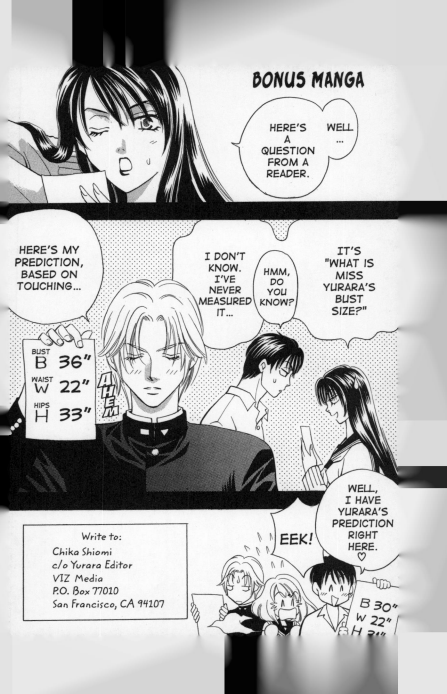

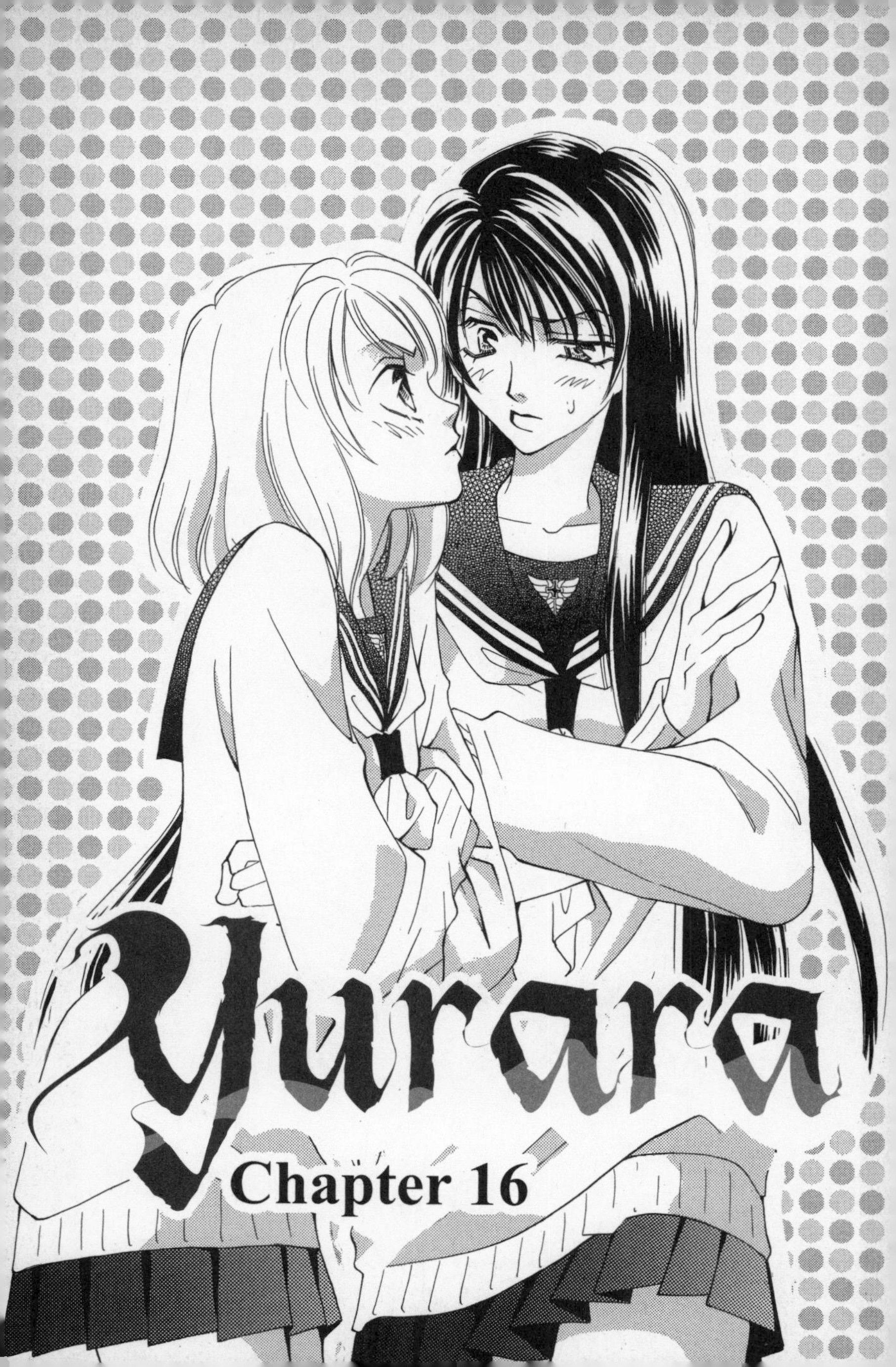
Yurara
Chapter 16

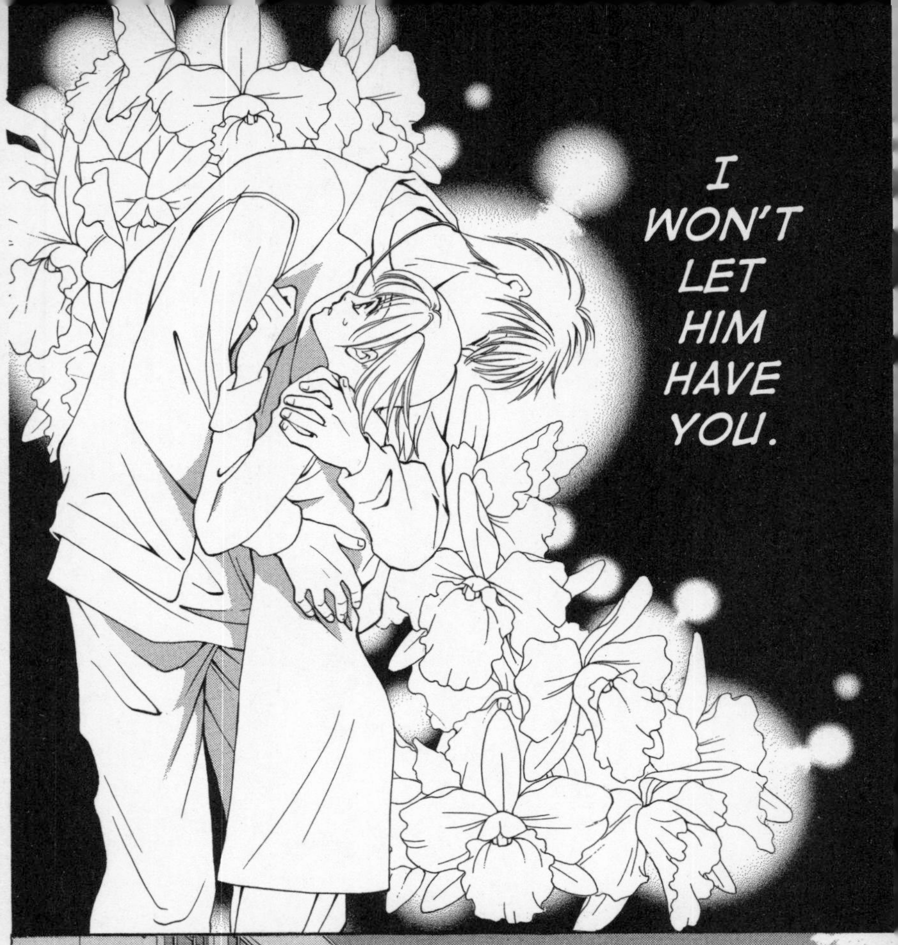
I WON'T LET HIM HAVE YOU.
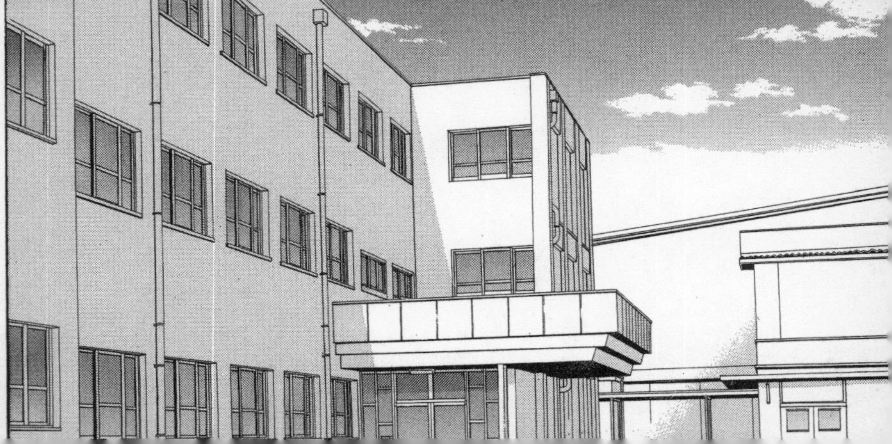

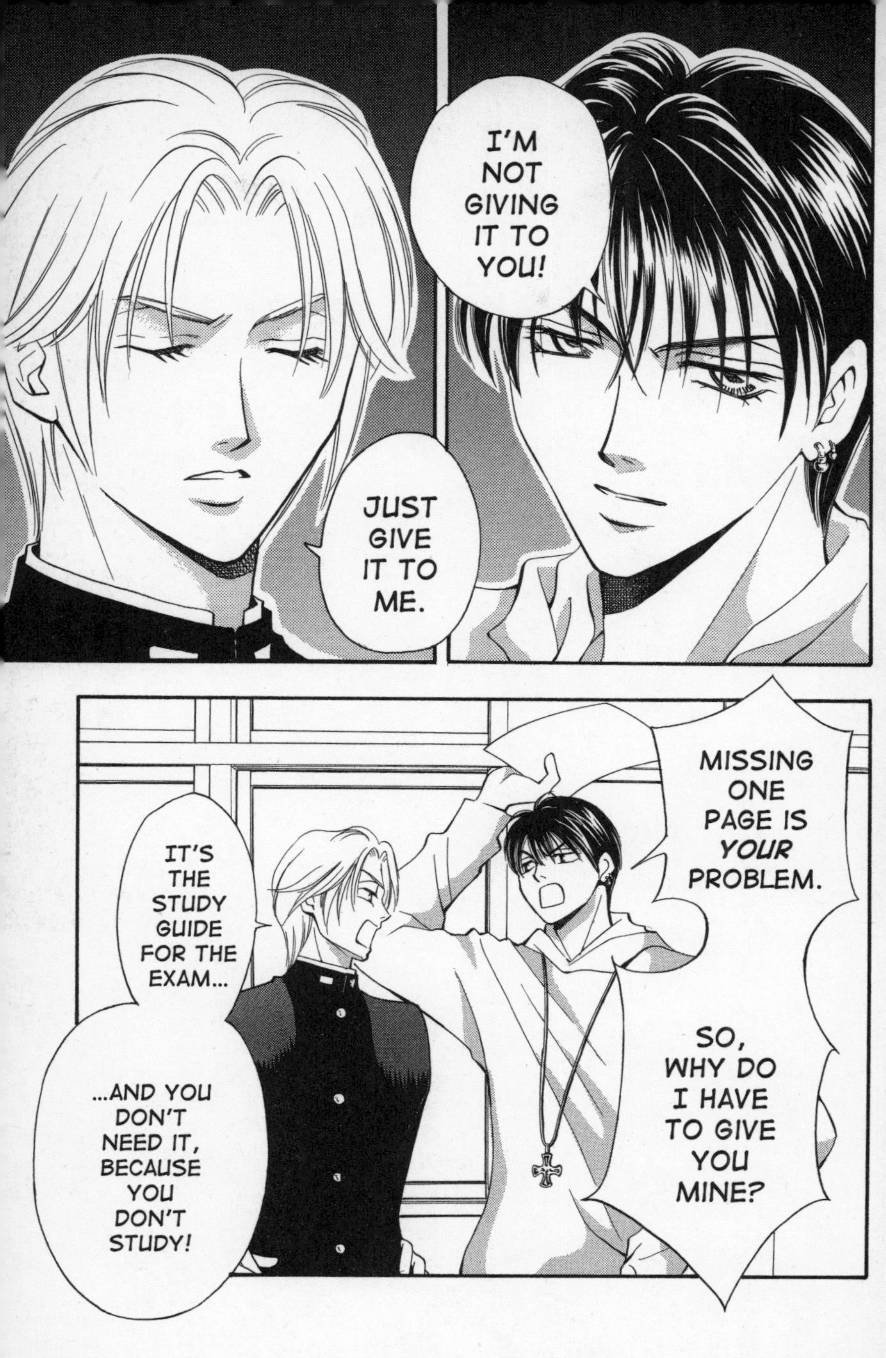
I'M NOT GIVING IT TO YOU!
JUST GIVE IT TO ME.
MISSING ONE PAGE IS *YOUR* PROBLEM.
SO, WHY DO I HAVE TO GIVE YOU MINE?
IT'S THE STUDY GUIDE FOR THE EXAM...
...AND YOU DON'T NEED IT, BECAUSE YOU DON'T STUDY!

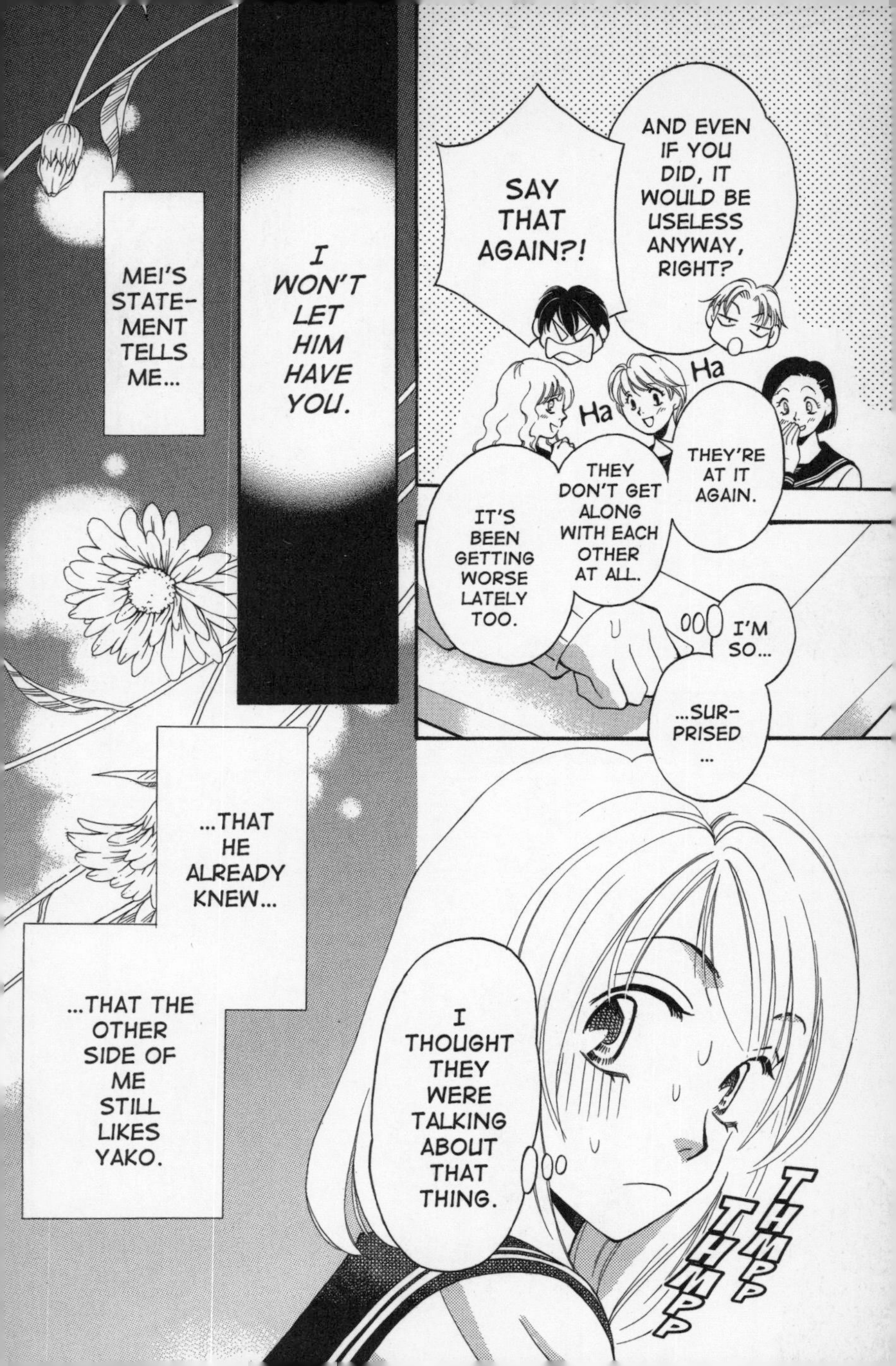
AND EVEN IF YOU DID, IT WOULD BE USELESS ANYWAY, RIGHT?
SAY THAT AGAIN?!
Ha
Ha
THEY'RE AT IT AGAIN.
THEY DON'T GET ALONG WITH EACH OTHER AT ALL.
IT'S BEEN GETTING WORSE LATELY TOO.
I'M SO...
...SUR-PRISED...
I THOUGHT THEY WERE TALKING ABOUT THAT THING.
THMPP
THMPP
I WON'T LET HIM HAVE YOU.
MEI'S STATE-MENT TELLS ME...
...THAT HE ALREADY KNEW...
...THAT THE OTHER SIDE OF ME STILL LIKES YAKO.

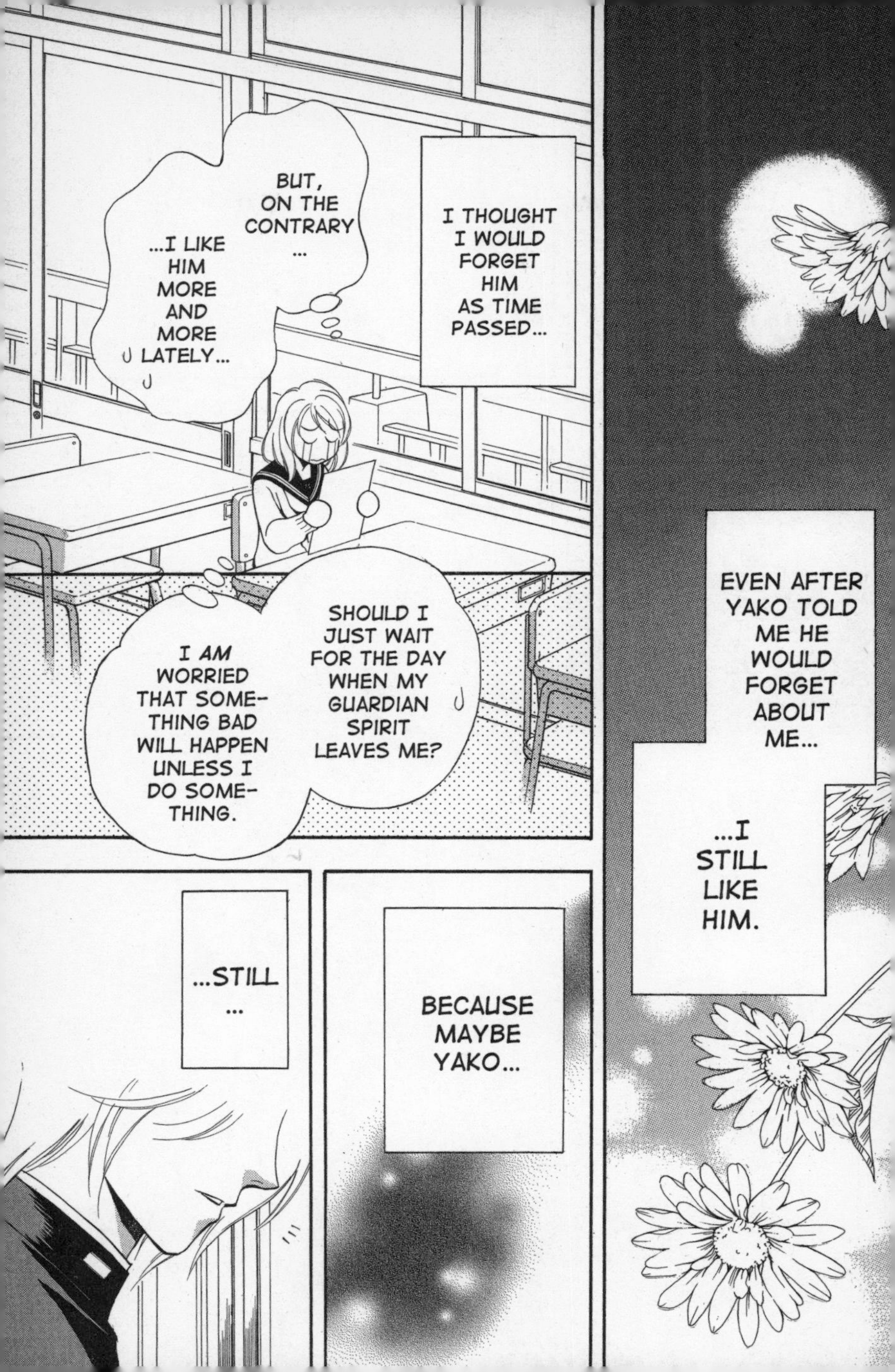
EVEN AFTER YAKO TOLD ME HE WOULD FORGET ABOUT ME...
...I STILL LIKE HIM.
I THOUGHT I WOULD FORGET HIM AS TIME PASSED...
BUT, ON THE CONTRARY...
...I LIKE HIM MORE AND MORE LATELY...
SHOULD I JUST WAIT FOR THE DAY WHEN MY GUARDIAN SPIRIT LEAVES ME?
I *AM* WORRIED THAT SOME-THING BAD WILL HAPPEN UNLESS I DO SOME-THING.
BECAUSE MAYBE YAKO...
...STILL ...

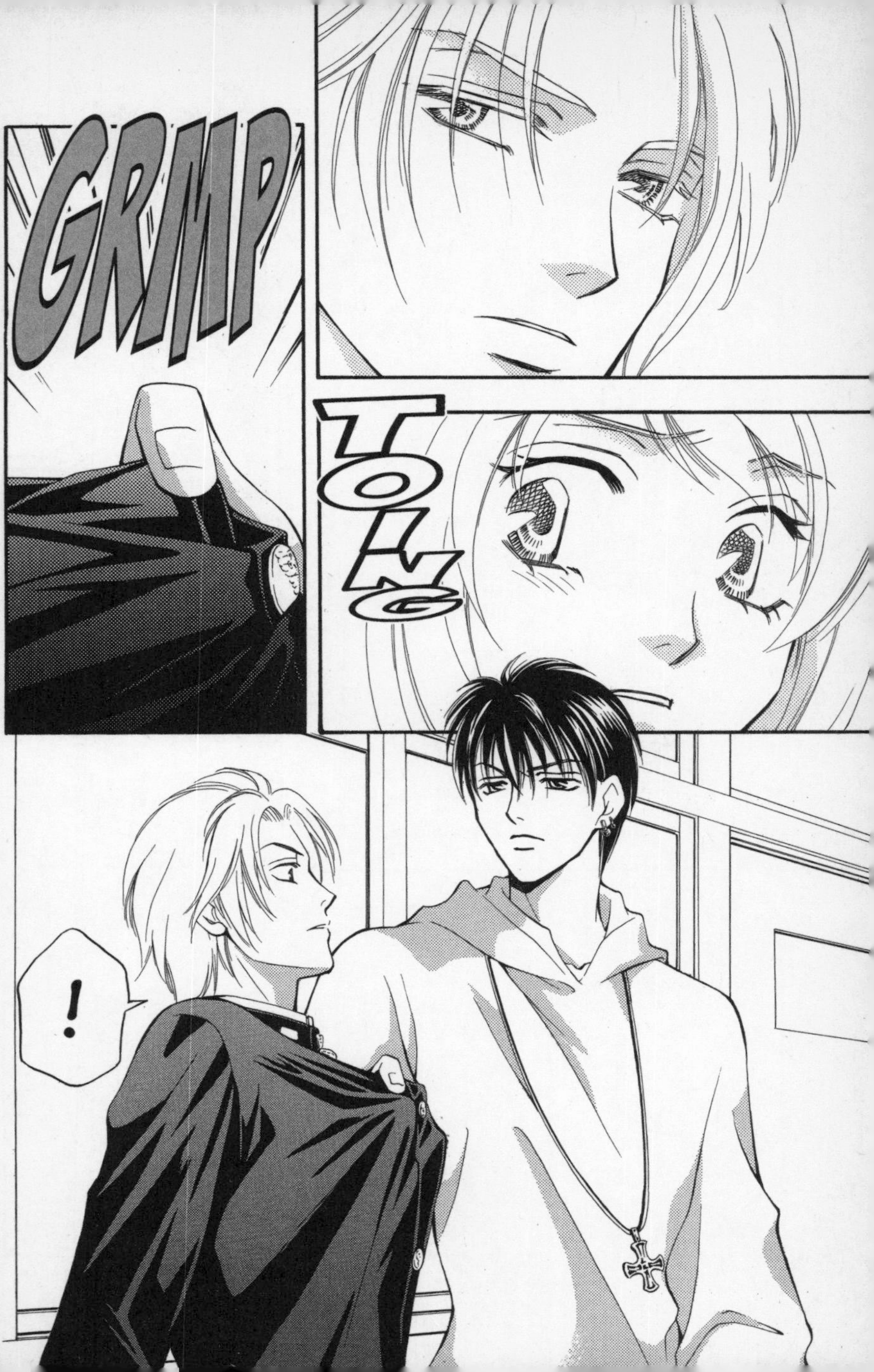
GRMP
YOING
!

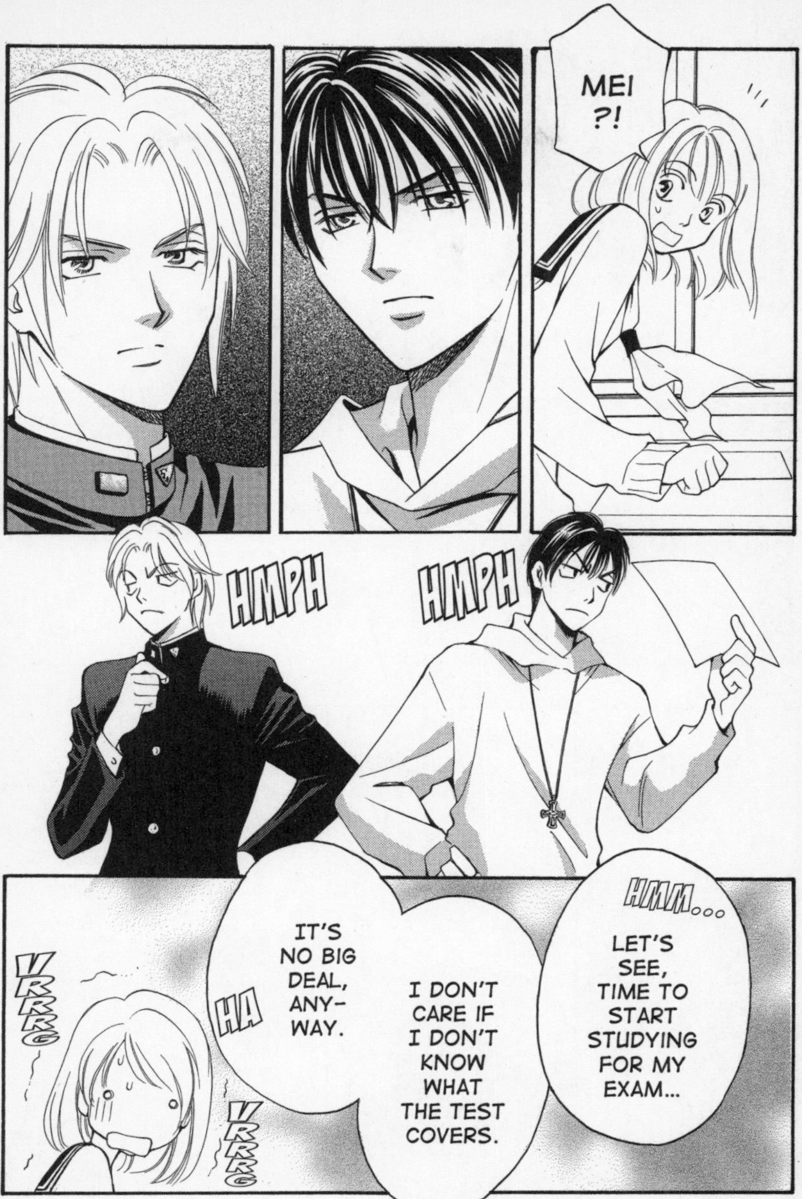
MEI ?!
HMPH
HMPH
HMM...
LET'S SEE, TIME TO START STUDYING FOR MY EXAM...
I DON'T CARE IF I DON'T KNOW WHAT THE TEST COVERS.
HA
IT'S NO BIG DEAL, ANY-WAY.
VRRRG
VRRRG

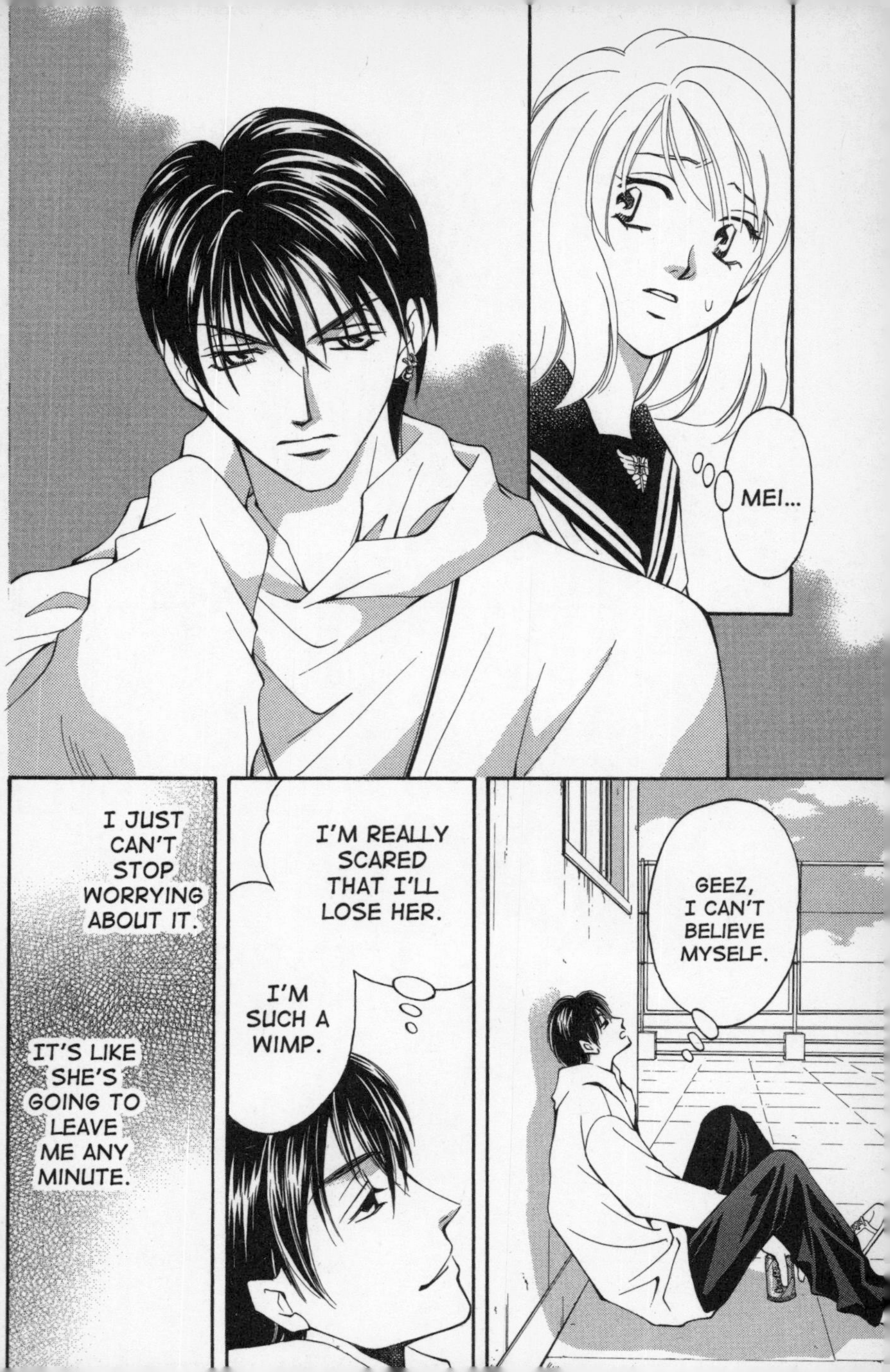
MEI...
GEEZ, I CAN'T BELIEVE MYSELF.
I'M REALLY SCARED THAT I'LL LOSE HER.
I'M SUCH A WIMP.
I JUST CAN'T STOP WORRYING ABOUT IT.
IT'S LIKE SHE'S GOING TO LEAVE ME ANY MINUTE.

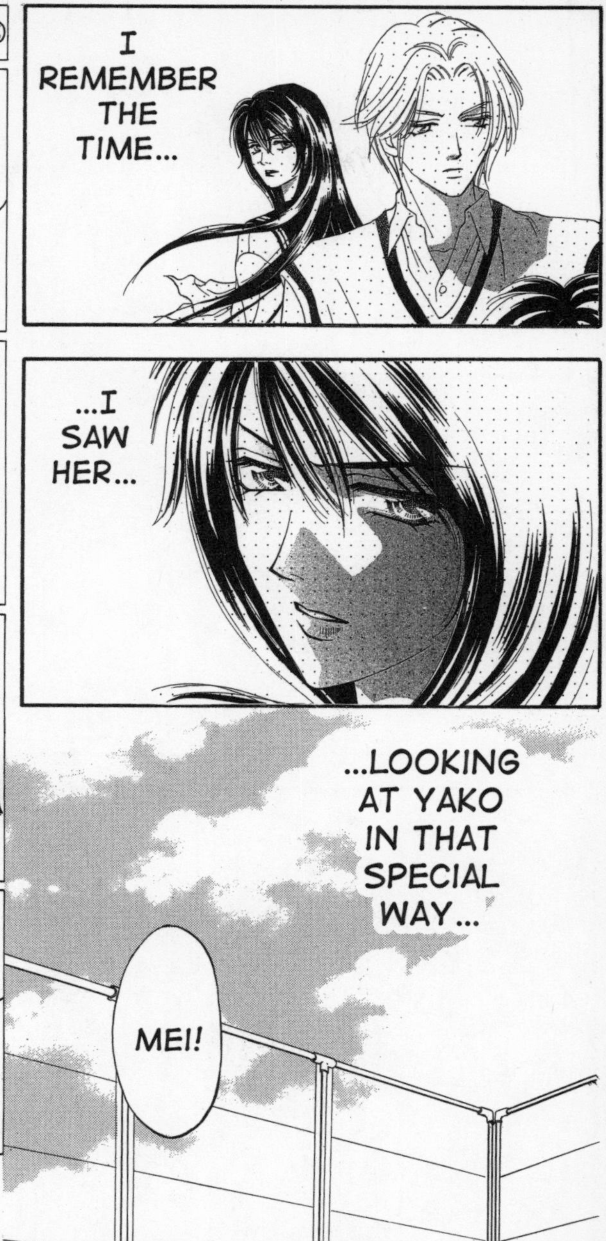
I REMEMBER THE TIME...
...I SAW HER...
...LOOKING AT YAKO IN THAT SPECIAL WAY...
MEI!

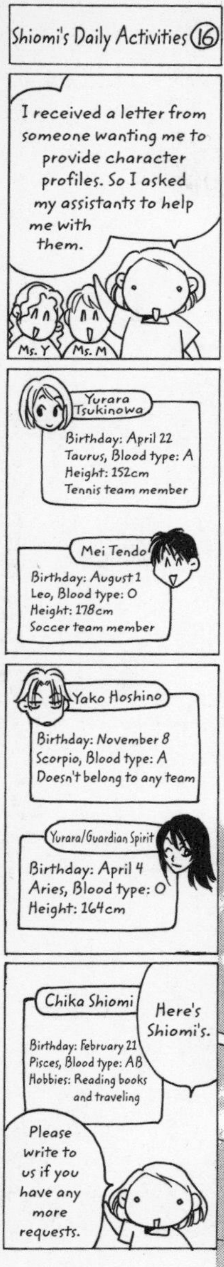
Shiomi's Daily Activities 16
I received a letter from someone wanting me to provide character profiles. So I asked my assistants to help me with them.
Ms. Y
Ms. M
Yurara Tsukinowa
Birthday: April 22
Taurus, Blood type: A
Height: 152cm
Tennis team member
Mei Tendo
Birthday: August 1
Leo, Blood type: O
Height: 178cm
Soccer team member
Yako Hoshino
Birthday: November 8
Scorpio, Blood type: A
Doesn't belong to any team
Yurara/Guardian Spirit
Birthday: April 4
Aries, Blood type: O
Height: 164cm
Chika Shiomi
Birthday: February 21
Pisces, Blood type: AB
Hobbies: Reading books and traveling
Here's Shiomi's.
Please write to us if you have any more requests.

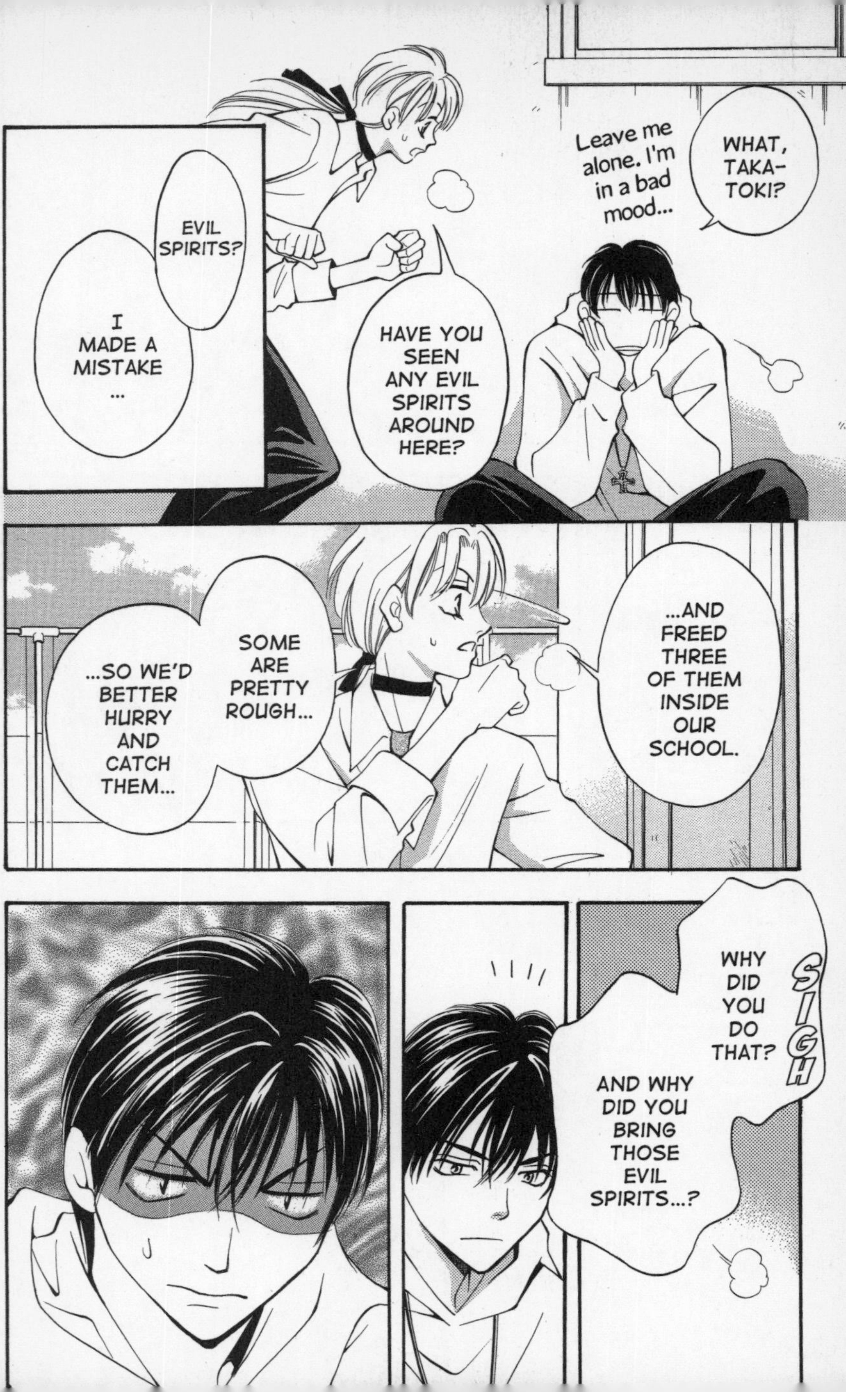
WHAT, TAKA-TOKI?
Leave me alone. I'm in a bad mood...
HAVE YOU SEEN ANY EVIL SPIRITS AROUND HERE?
EVIL SPIRITS?
I MADE A MISTAKE ...
...AND FREED THREE OF THEM INSIDE OUR SCHOOL.
SOME ARE PRETTY ROUGH...
...SO WE'D BETTER HURRY AND CATCH THEM...
SIGH
WHY DID YOU DO THAT?
AND WHY DID YOU BRING THOSE EVIL SPIRITS...?

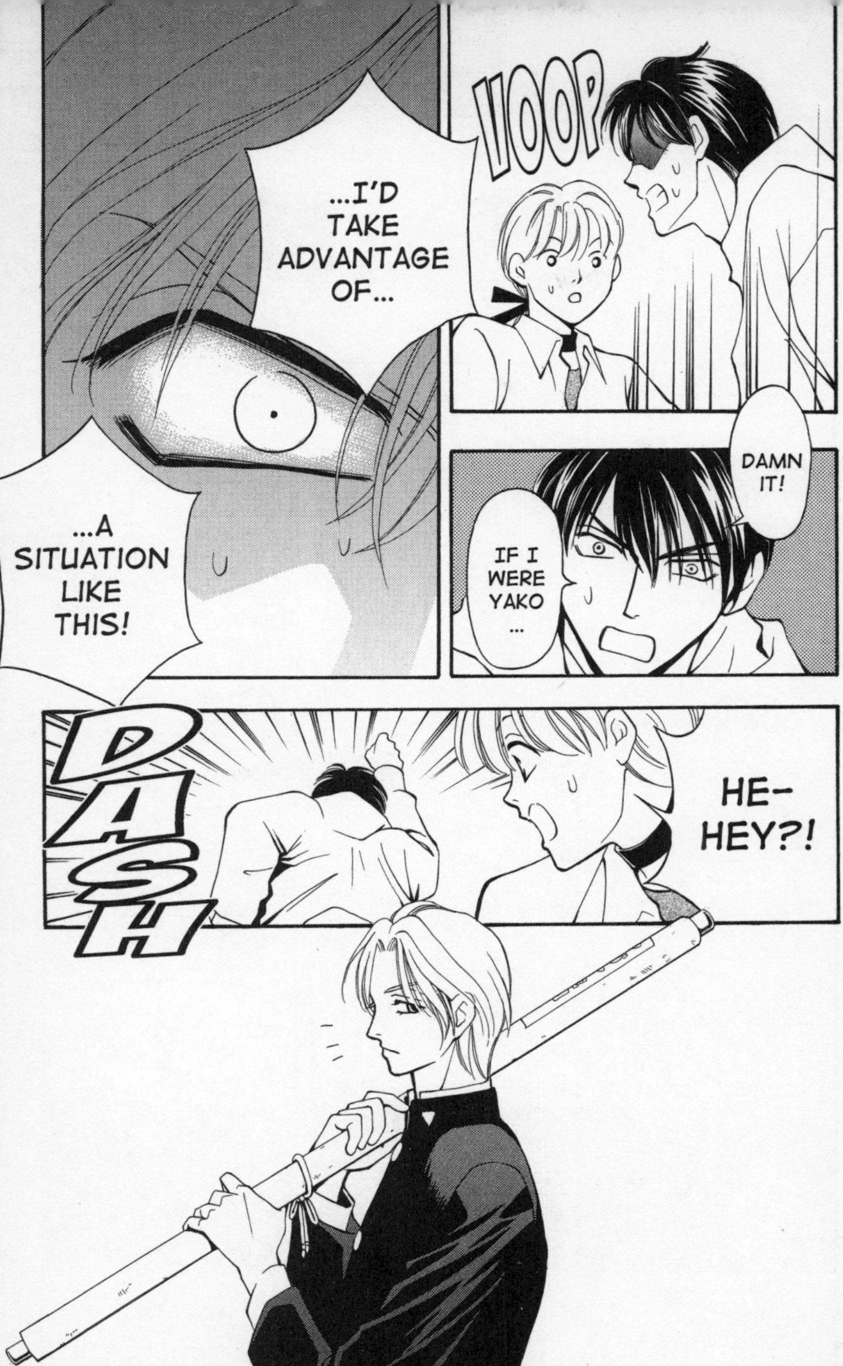
VOOP
DAMN IT!
IF I WERE YAKO ...
...I'D TAKE ADVANTAGE OF...
...A SITUATION LIKE THIS!
HE- HEY?!
DASH

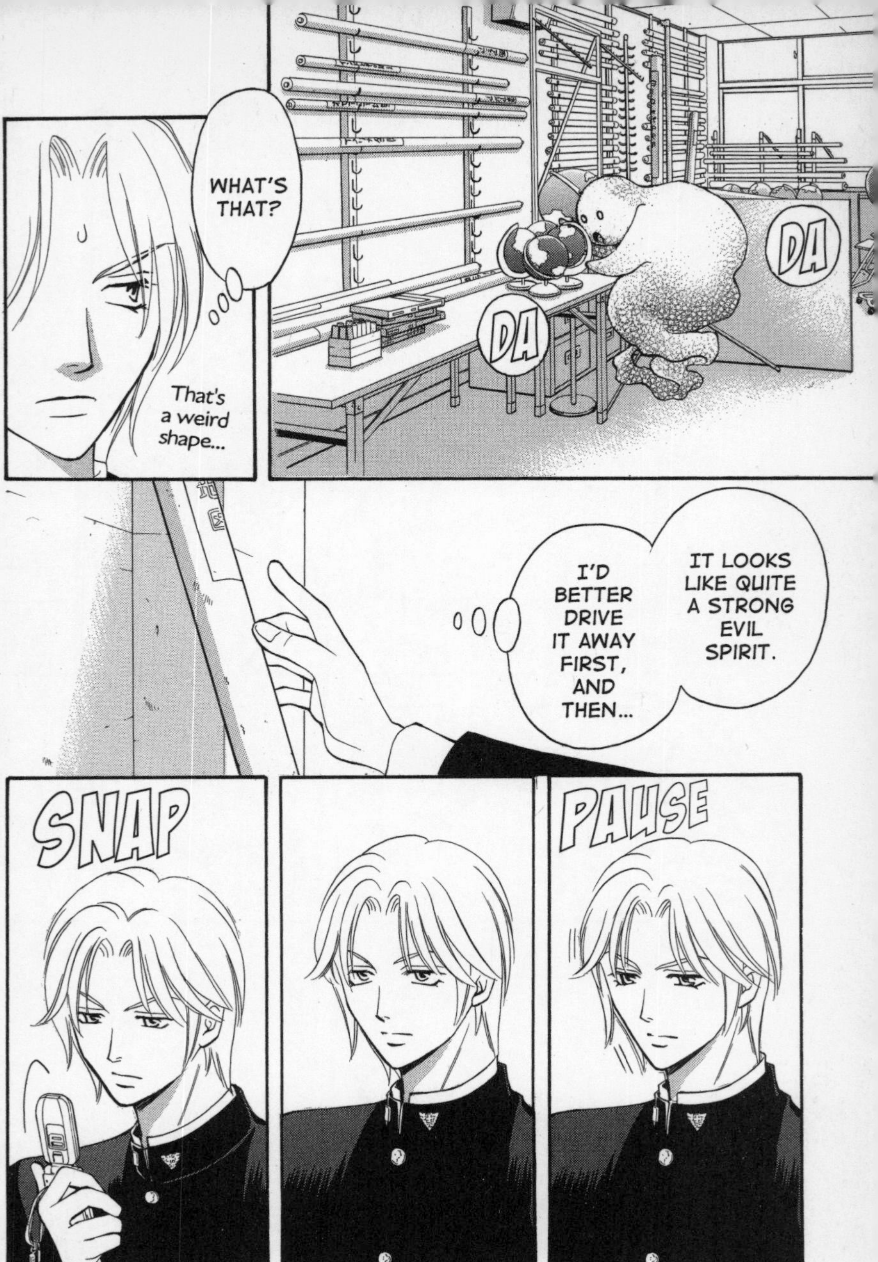
DA
DA
WHAT'S THAT?
That's a weird shape...
IT LOOKS LIKE QUITE A STRONG EVIL SPIRIT.
I'D BETTER DRIVE IT AWAY FIRST, AND THEN...
PAUSE
SNAP

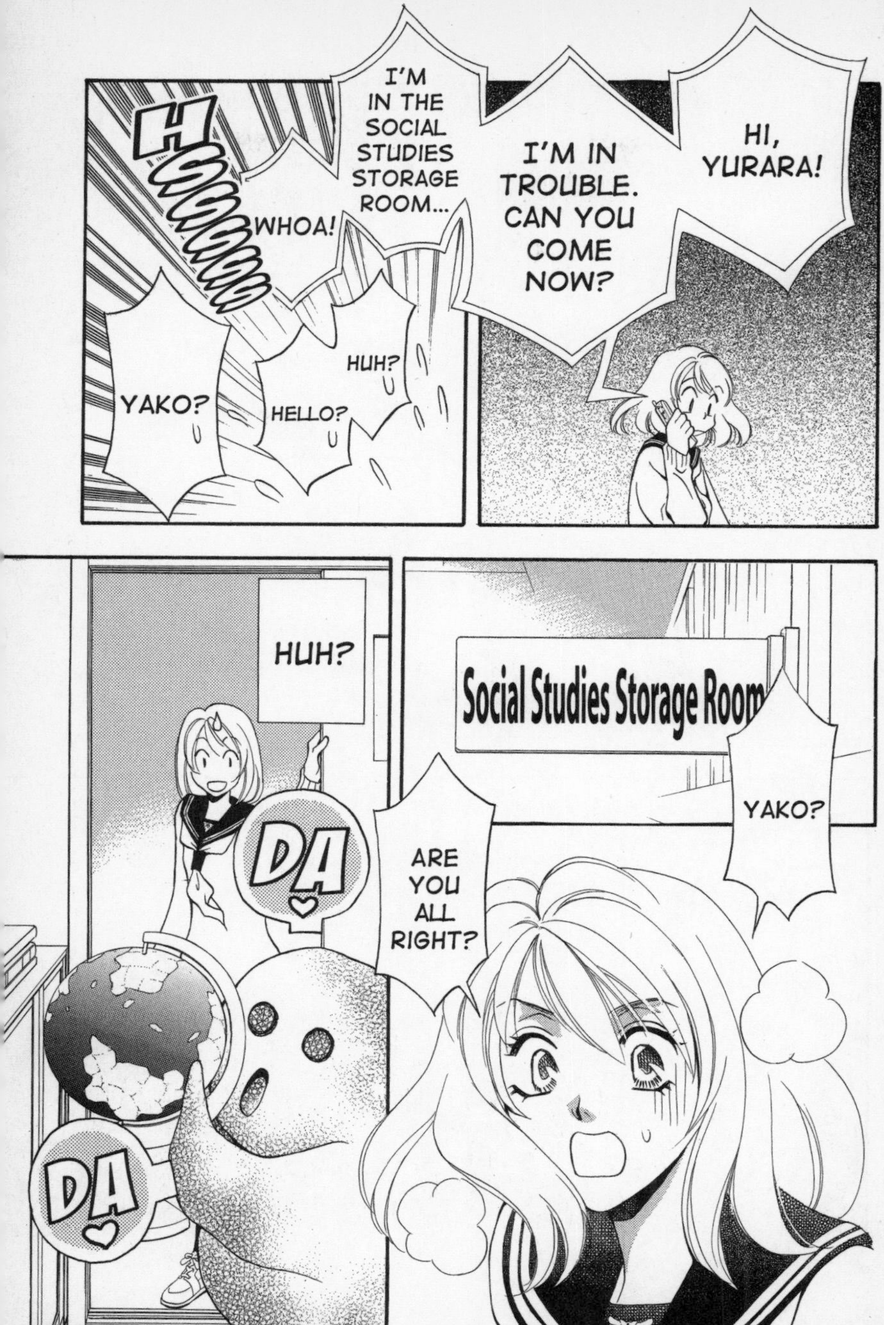
HI, YURARA!
I'M IN TROUBLE. CAN YOU COME NOW?
I'M IN THE SOCIAL STUDIES STORAGE ROOM...
WHOA!
HUH?
HELLO?
YAKO?
Social Studies Storage Room
YAKO?
ARE YOU ALL RIGHT?
HUH?
DA
DA

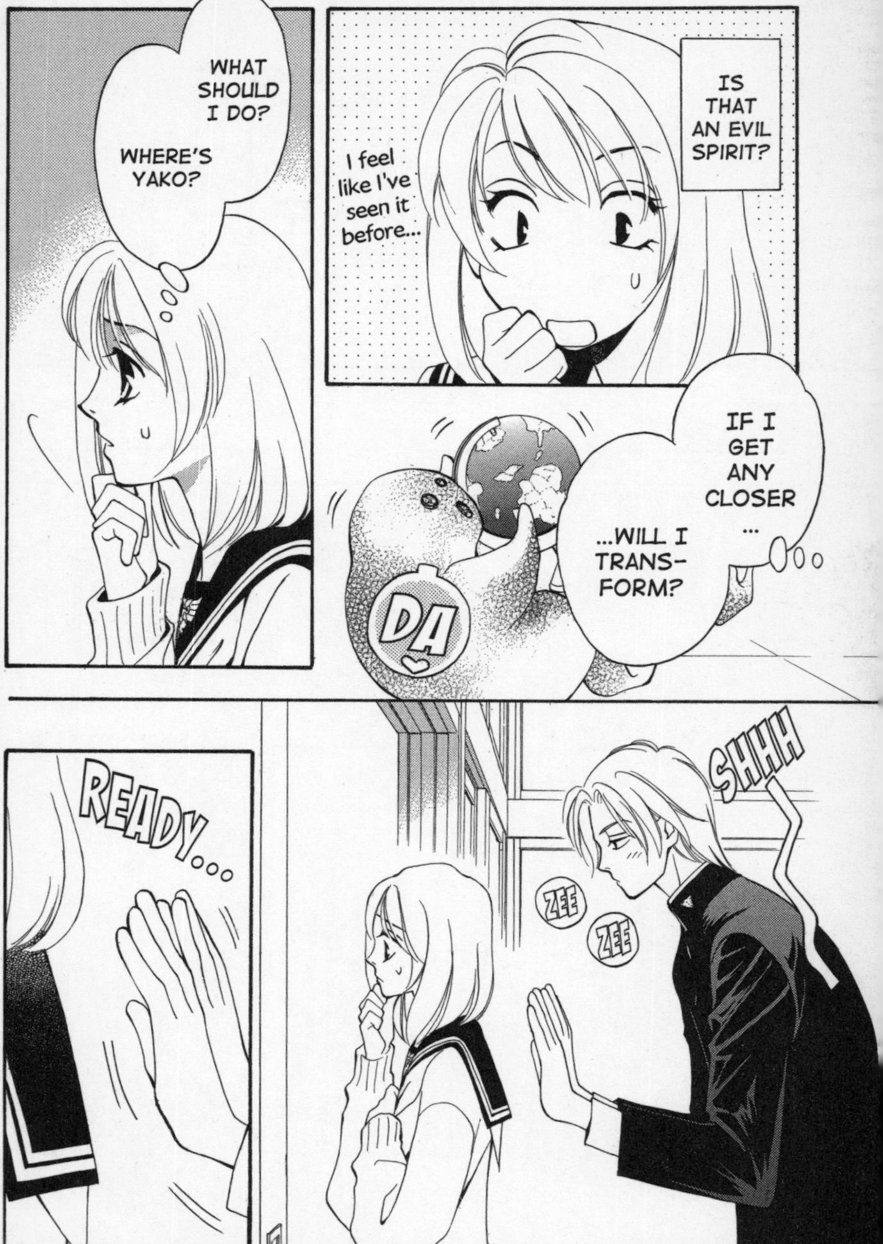
IS THAT AN EVIL SPIRIT?
I feel like I've seen it before...
IF I GET ANY CLOSER ...
...WILL I TRANSFORM?
DA
WHAT SHOULD I DO?
WHERE'S YAKO?
SHHH
ZEE
ZEE
READY...

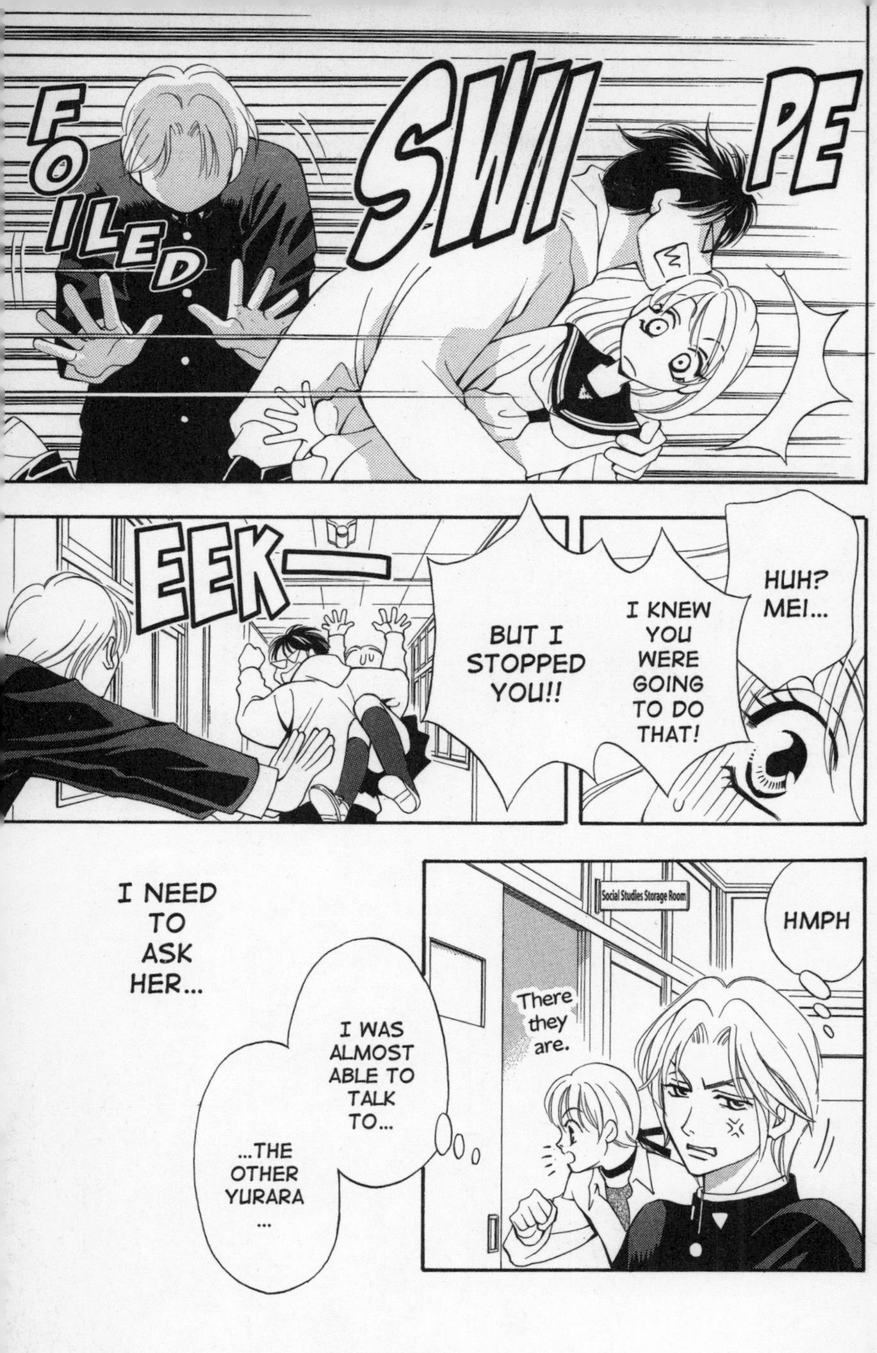
SWI PE
FOILED
HUH? MEI...
I KNEW YOU WERE GOING TO DO THAT!
BUT I STOPPED YOU!!
EEK—
HMPH
Social Studies Storage Room
There they are.
I WAS ALMOST ABLE TO TALK TO...
...THE OTHER YURARA ...
I NEED TO ASK HER...

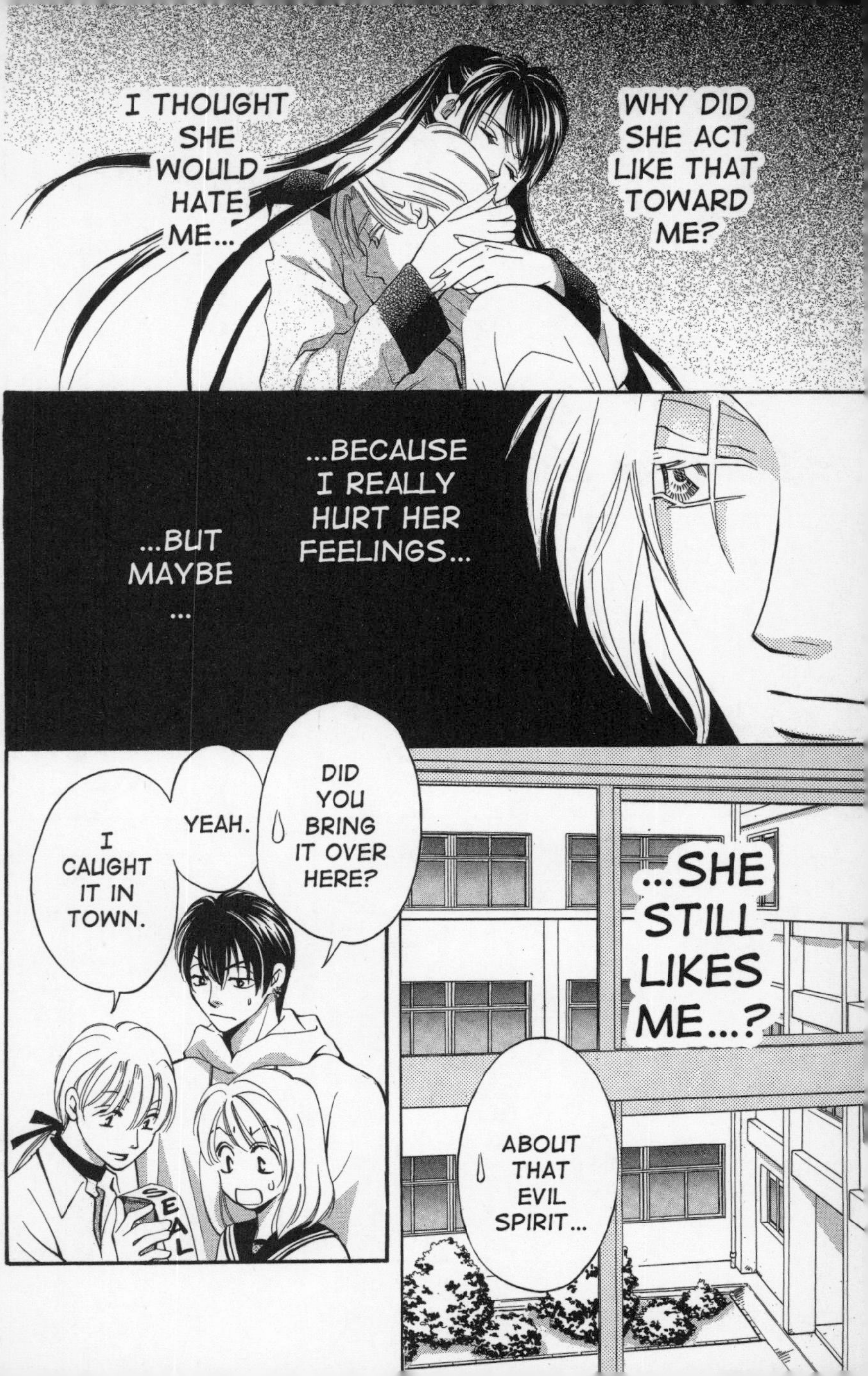
WHY DID SHE ACT LIKE THAT TOWARD ME?
I THOUGHT SHE WOULD HATE ME...
...BECAUSE I REALLY HURT HER FEELINGS...
...BUT MAYBE ...
...SHE STILL LIKES ME...?
ABOUT THAT EVIL SPIRIT...
DID YOU BRING IT OVER HERE?
YEAH.
I CAUGHT IT IN TOWN.
SEAL

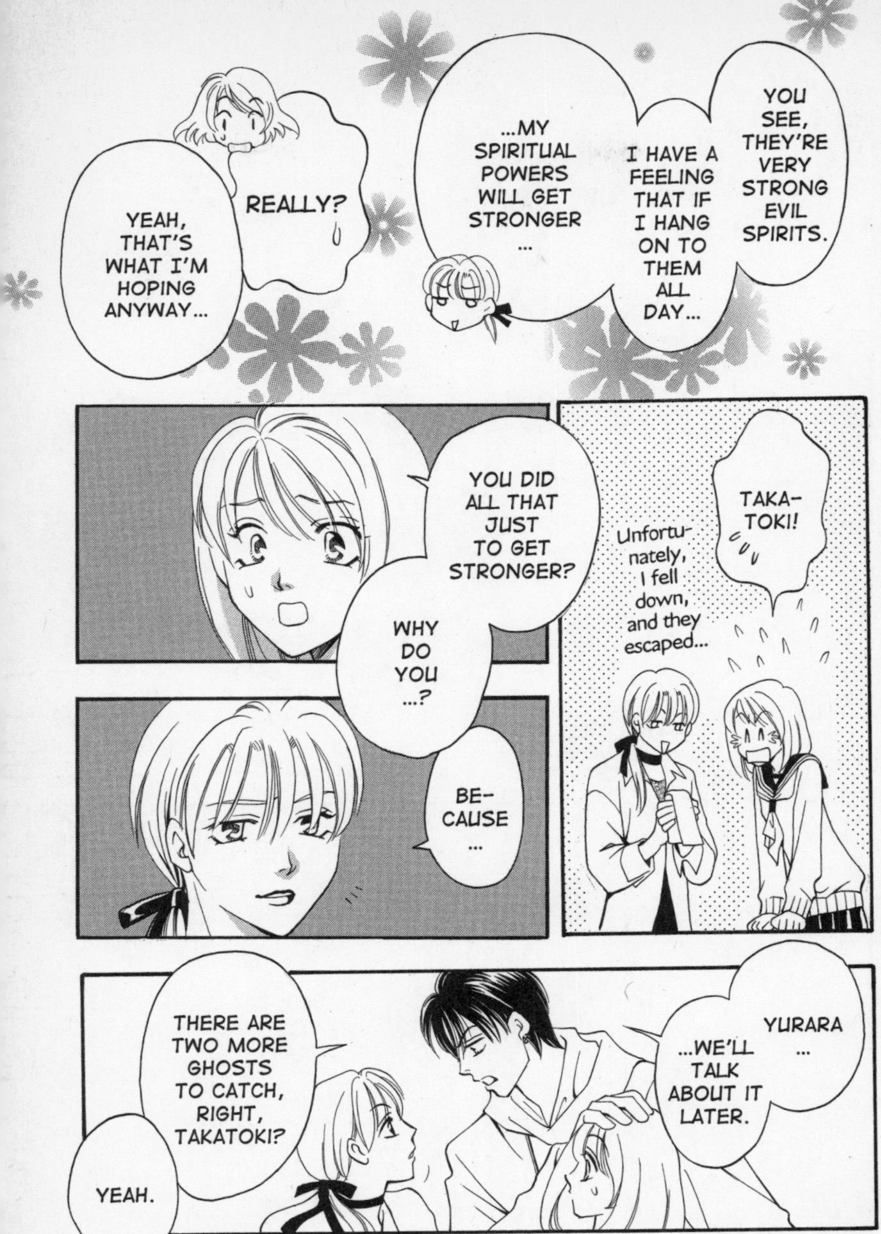
YOU SEE, THEY'RE VERY STRONG EVIL SPIRITS.
I HAVE A FEELING THAT IF I HANG ON TO THEM ALL DAY...
...MY SPIRITUAL POWERS WILL GET STRONGER ...
REALLY?
YEAH, THAT'S WHAT I'M HOPING ANYWAY...
TAKA-TOKI!
Unfortunately, I fell down, and they escaped...
YOU DID ALL THAT JUST TO GET STRONGER?
WHY DO YOU ...?
BE-CAUSE ...
YURARA ...
...WE'LL TALK ABOUT IT LATER.
THERE ARE TWO MORE GHOSTS TO CATCH, RIGHT, TAKATOKI?
YEAH.

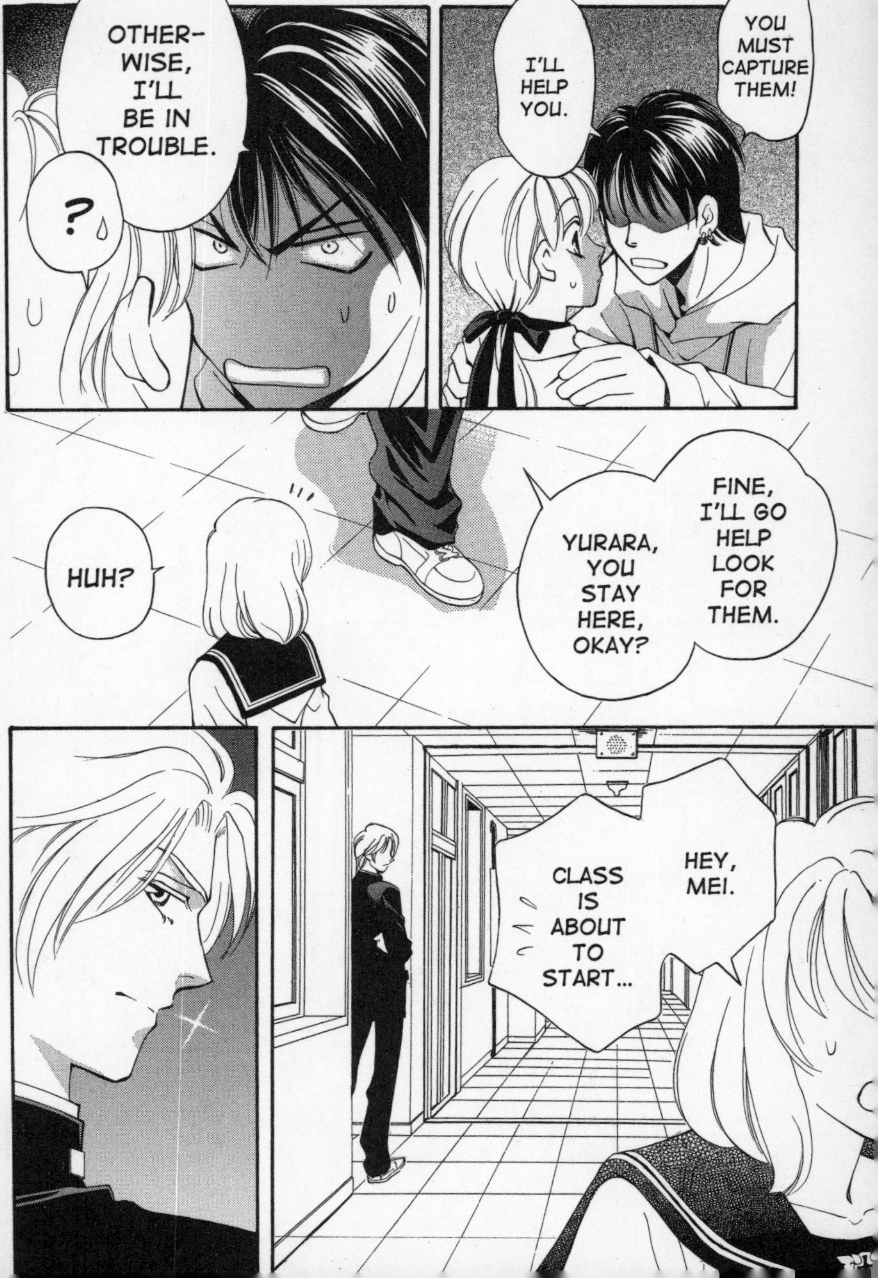
YOU MUST CAPTURE THEM!
I'LL HELP YOU.
OTHER-WISE, I'LL BE IN TROUBLE.
?
FINE, I'LL GO HELP LOOK FOR THEM.
YURARA, YOU STAY HERE, OKAY?
HUH?
HEY, MEI.
CLASS IS ABOUT TO START...

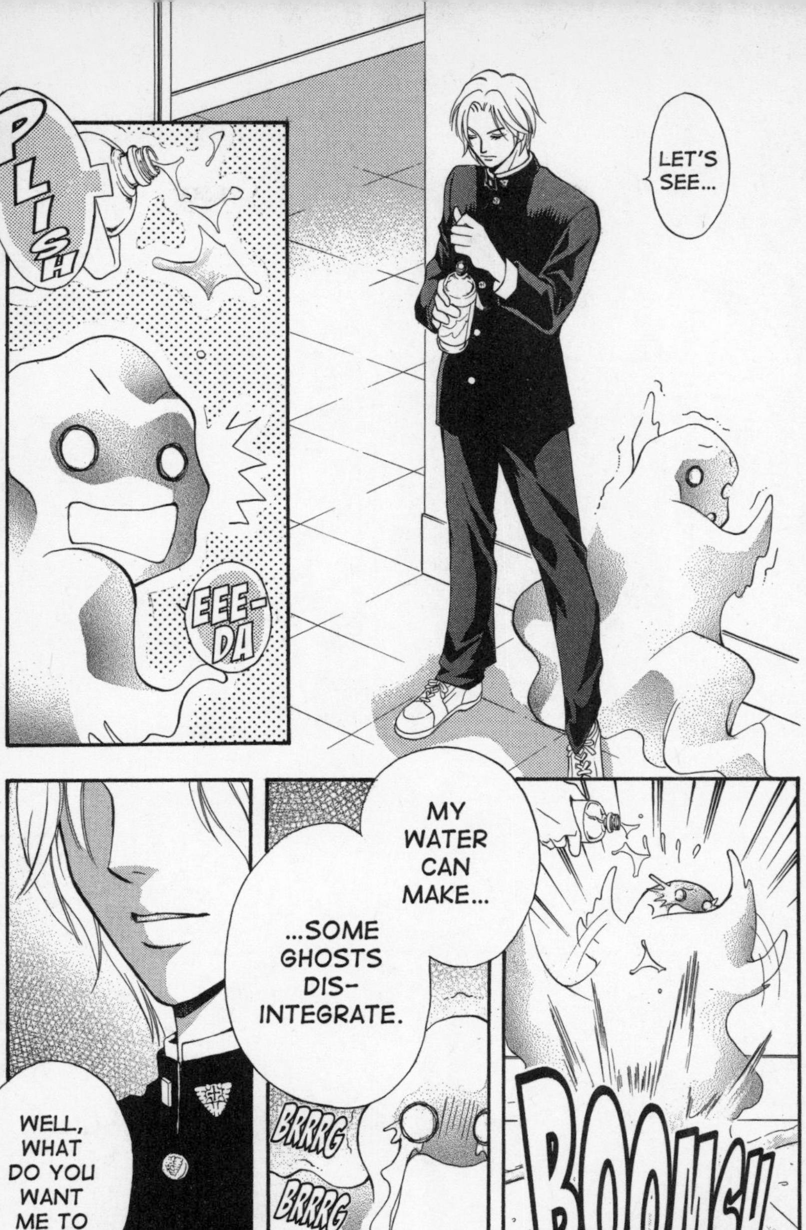
LET'S SEE...
PLISH
EEE-DA
BOOMSH
MY WATER CAN MAKE...
...SOME GHOSTS DIS-INTEGRATE.
BRRRG
BRRRG
WELL, WHAT DO YOU WANT ME TO DO?

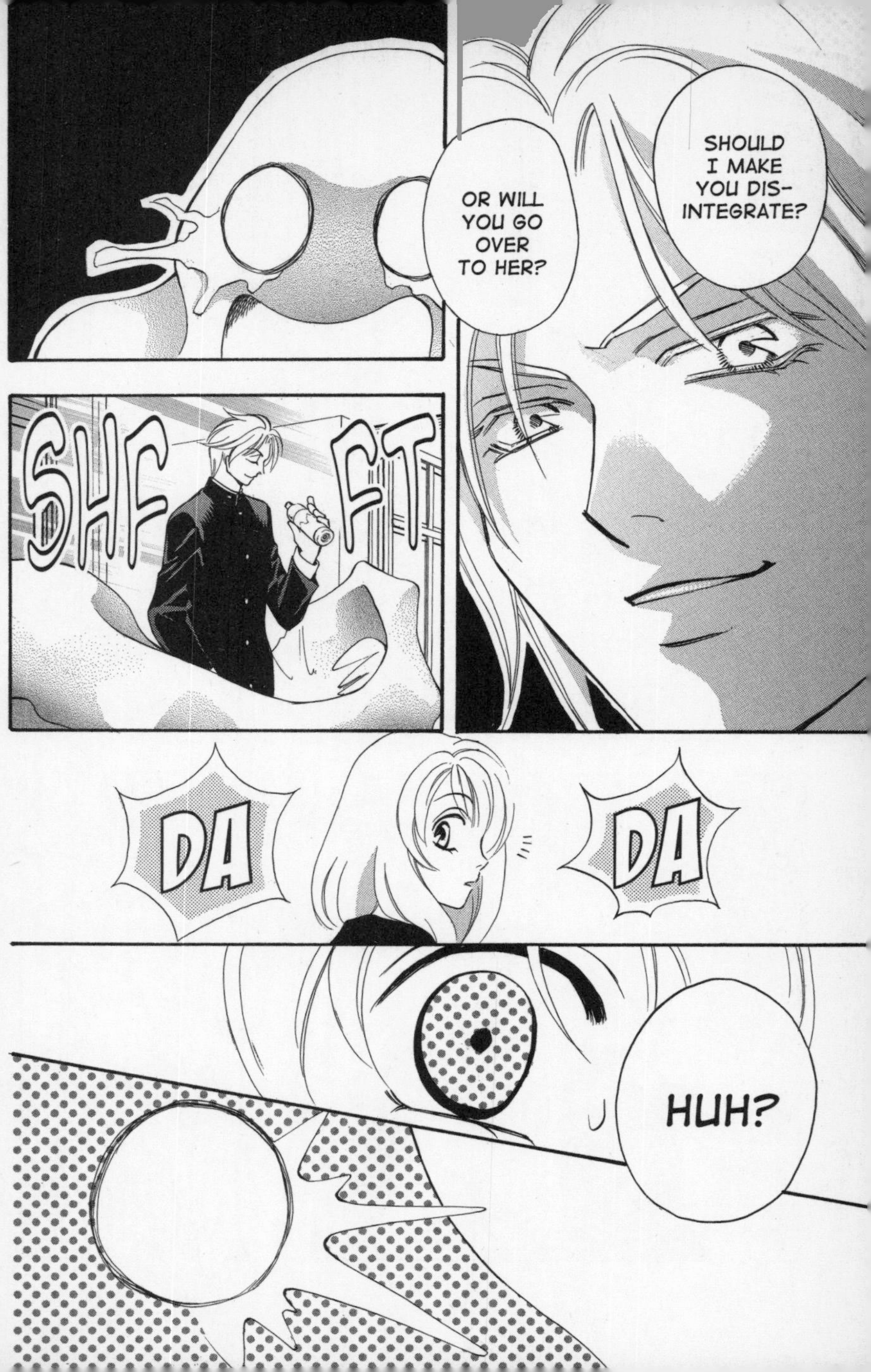
SHOULD I MAKE YOU DIS-INTEGRATE?
OR WILL YOU GO OVER TO HER?
SHF FT
DA
DA
HUH?

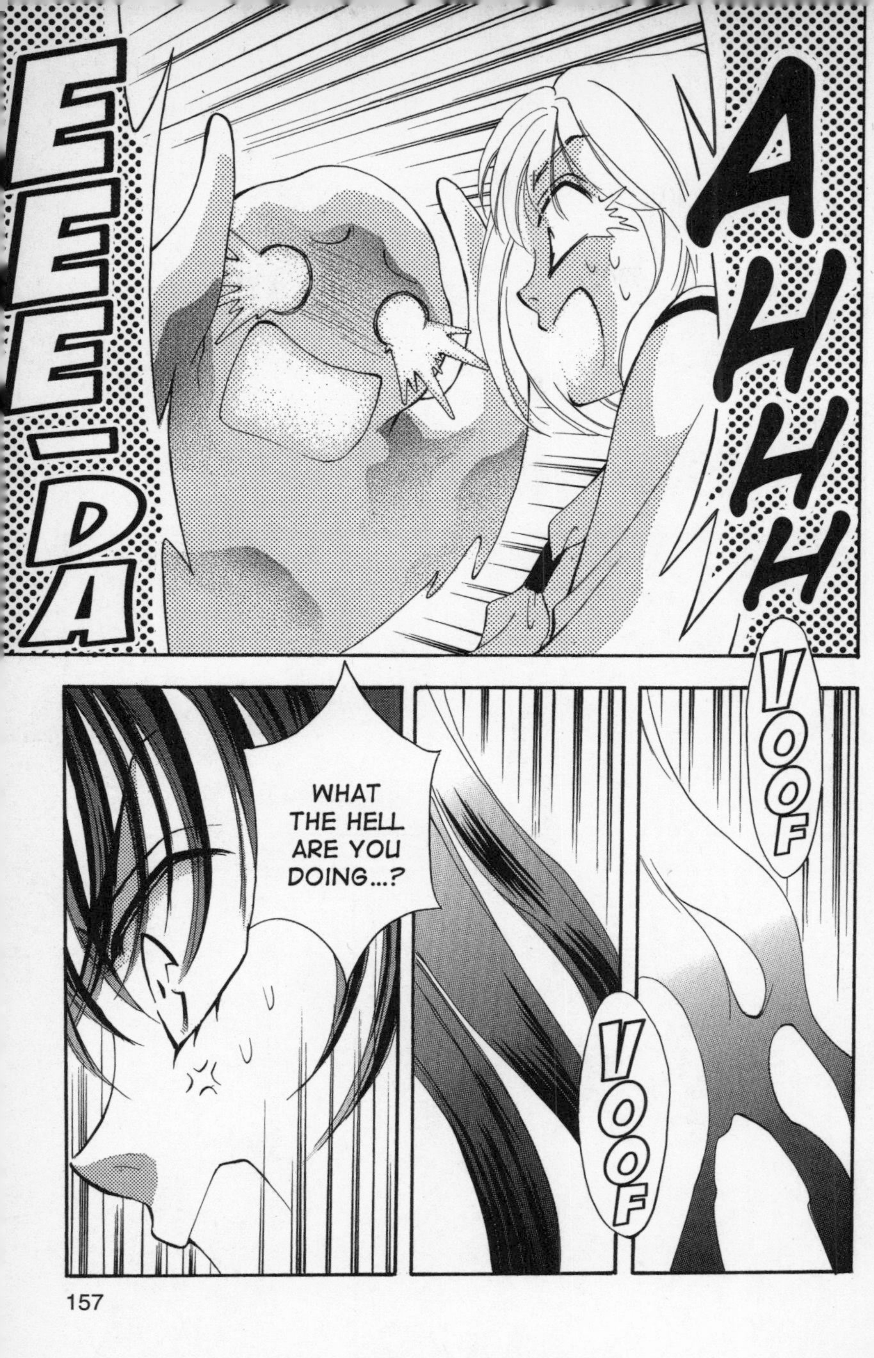
AHHHH
EEE-DA
VOOF
VOOF
WHAT THE HELL ARE YOU DOING...?

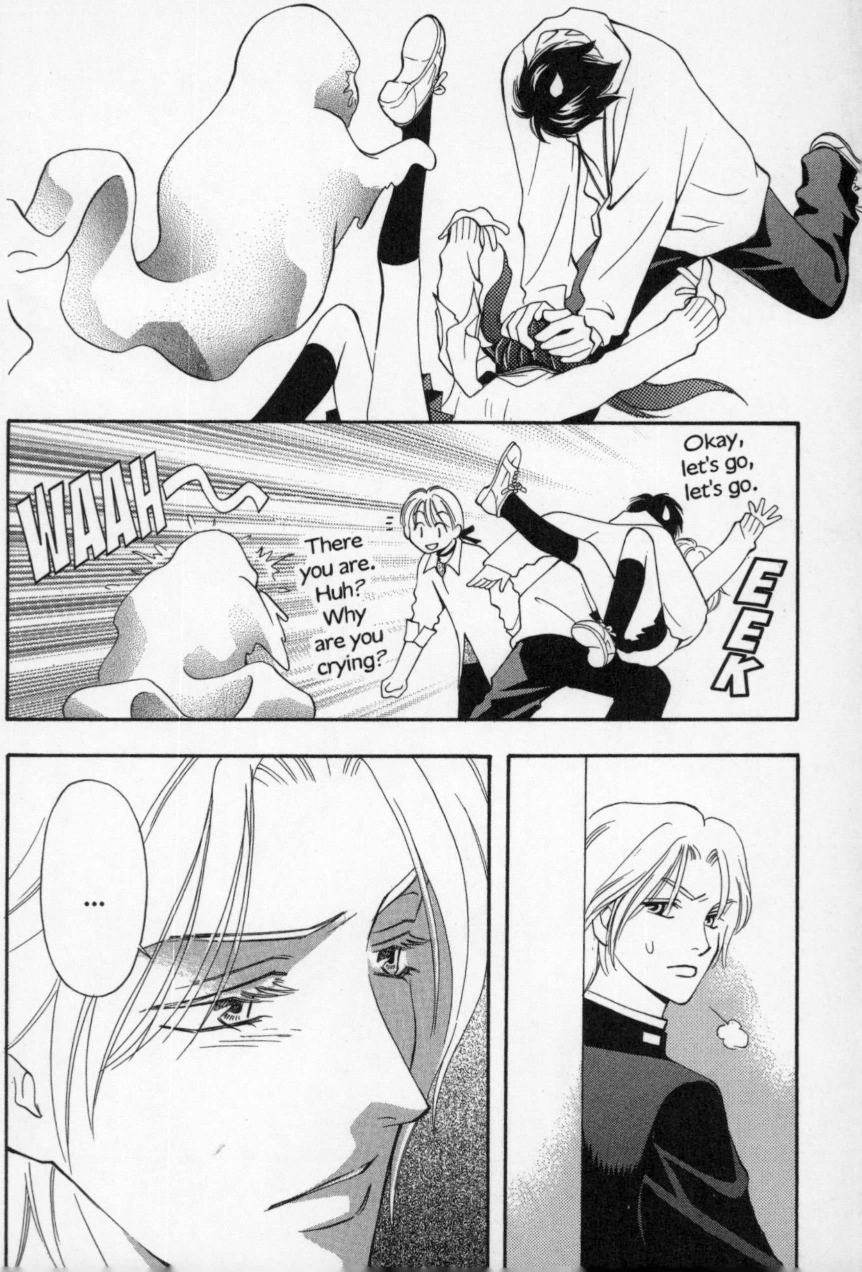
Okay, let's go, let's go.
EEEK
There you are. Huh? Why are you crying?
WAAH
...

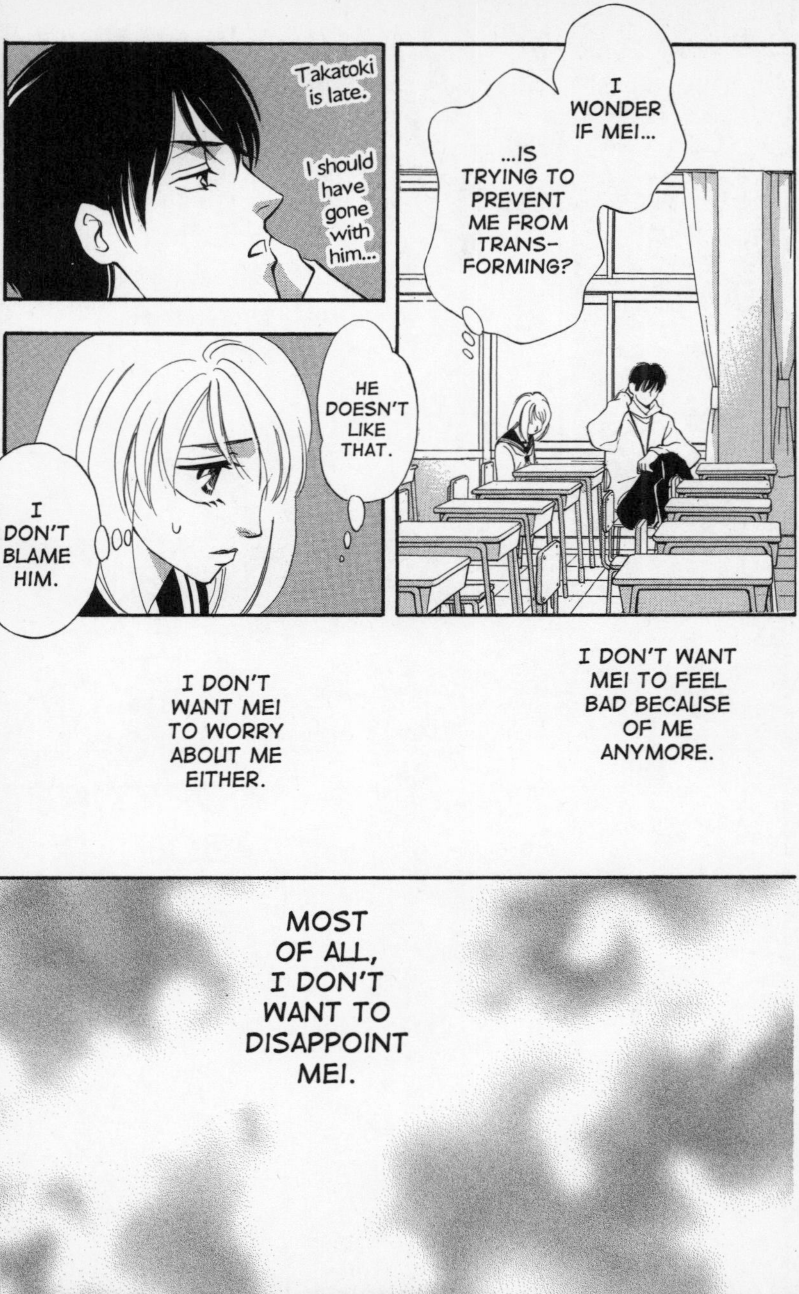
I WONDER IF MEI...
...IS TRYING TO PREVENT ME FROM TRANS-FORMING?
Takatoki is late.
I should have gone with him...
HE DOESN'T LIKE THAT.
I DON'T BLAME HIM.
I DON'T WANT MEI TO FEEL BAD BECAUSE OF ME ANYMORE.
I DON'T WANT MEI TO WORRY ABOUT ME EITHER.
MOST OF ALL, I DON'T WANT TO DISAPPOINT MEI.

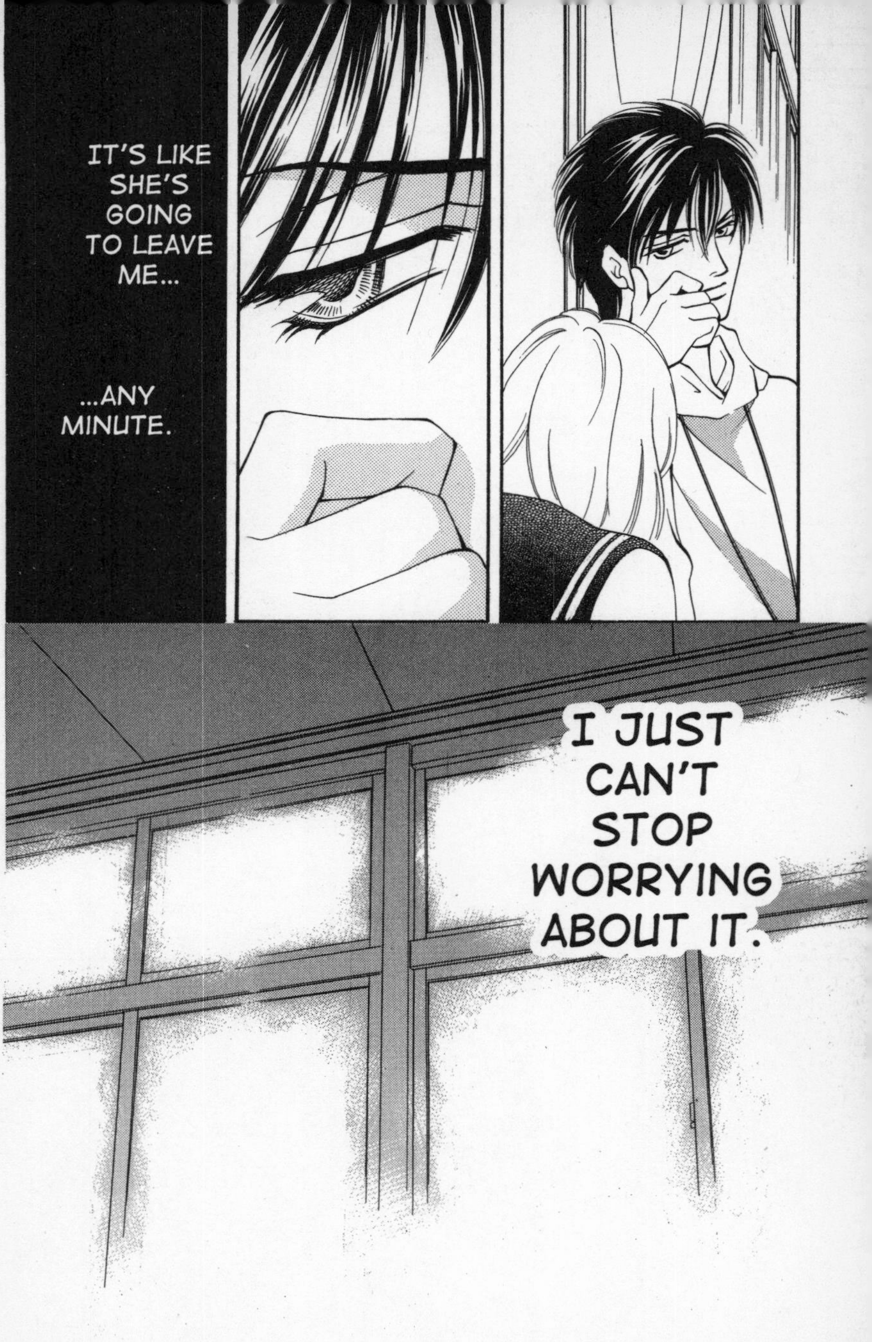
IT'S LIKE SHE'S GOING TO LEAVE ME...
...ANY MINUTE.
I JUST CAN'T STOP WORRYING ABOUT IT.

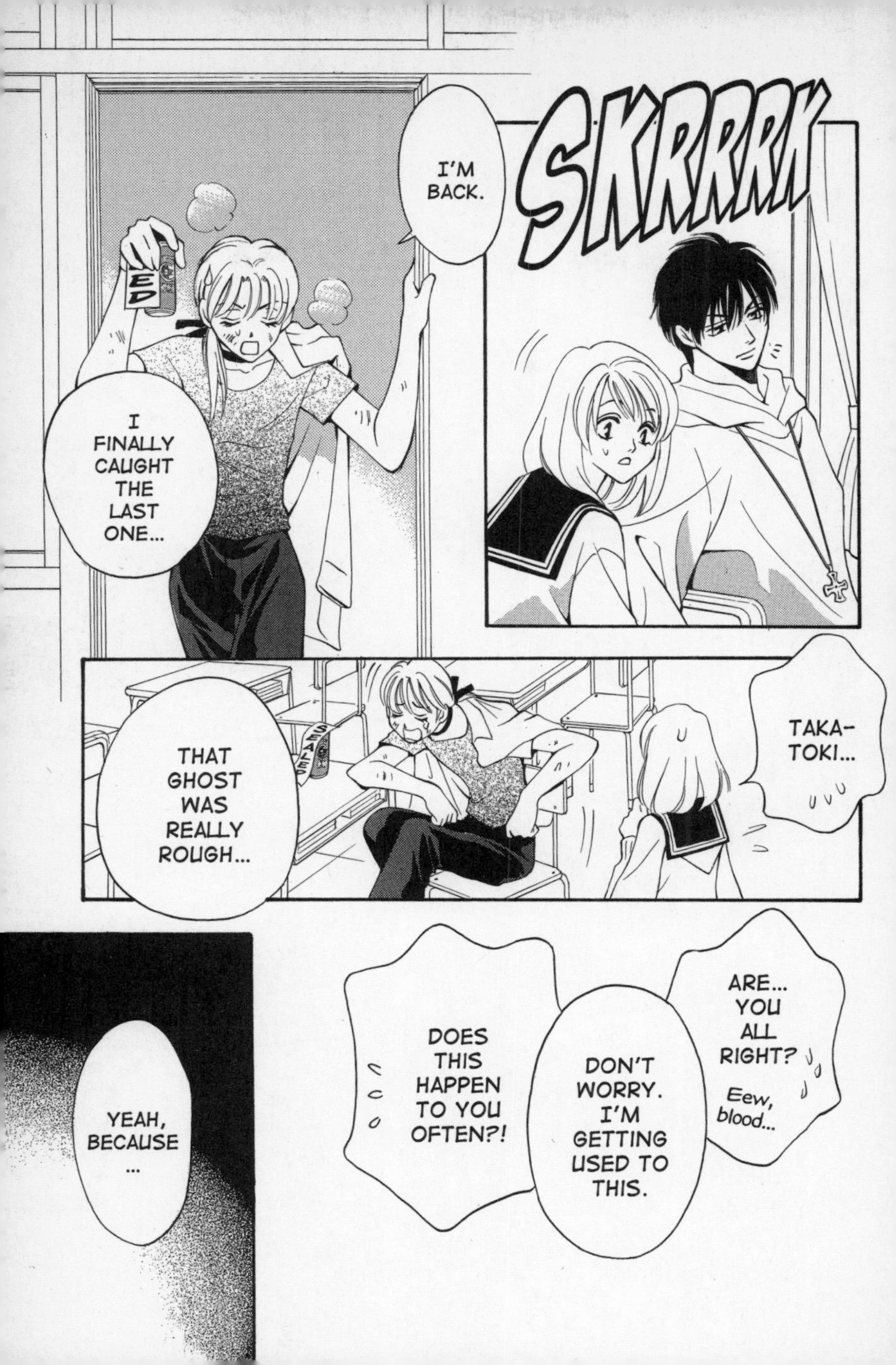
SKRRRK
I'M BACK.
I FINALLY CAUGHT THE LAST ONE...
TAKA-TOKI...
THAT GHOST WAS REALLY ROUGH...
SEALED
ARE... YOU ALL RIGHT?
Eew, blood...
DON'T WORRY. I'M GETTING USED TO THIS.
DOES THIS HAPPEN TO YOU OFTEN?!
YEAH, BECAUSE ...

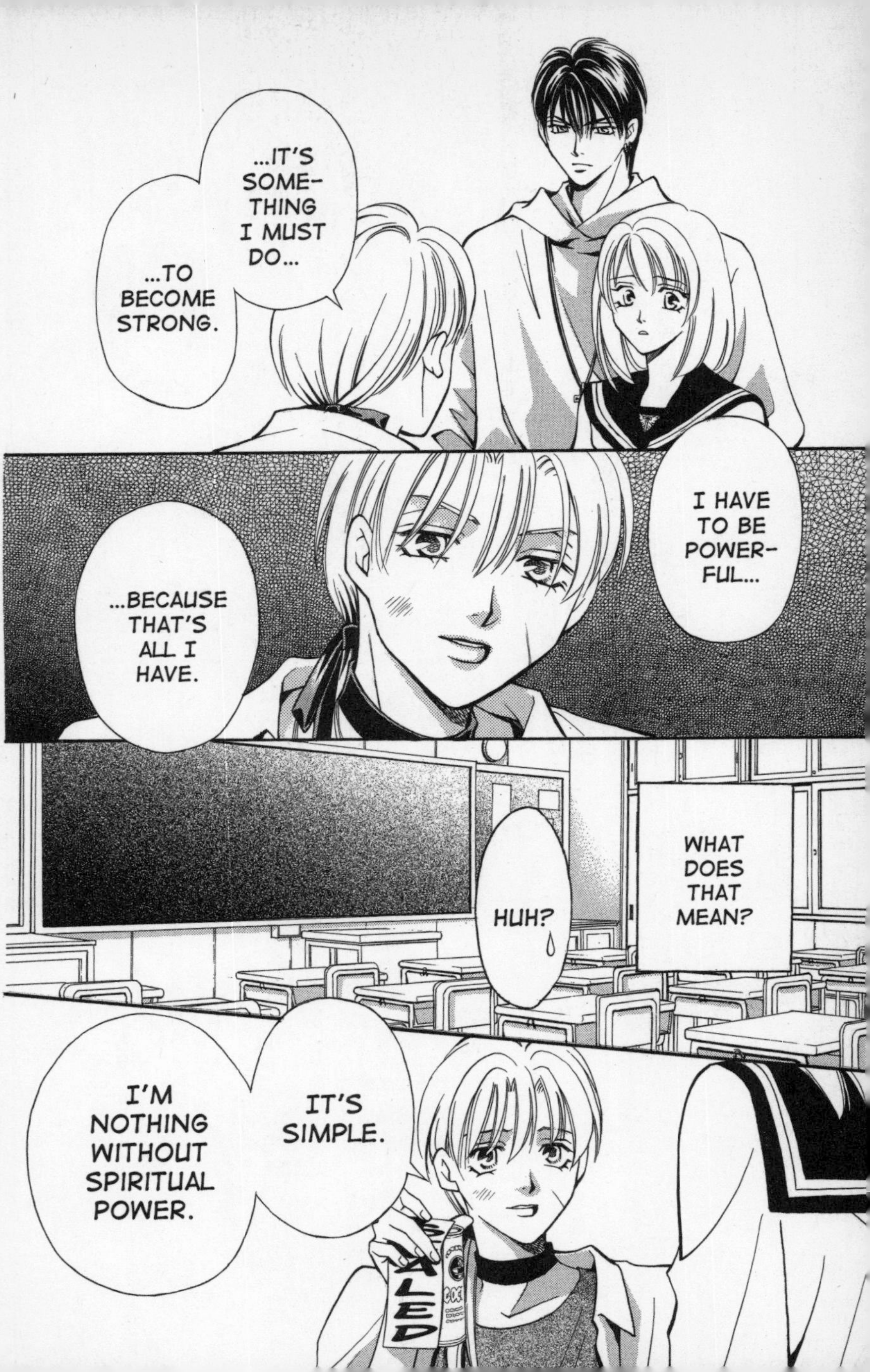
...IT'S SOMETHING I MUST DO...
...TO BECOME STRONG.
I HAVE TO BE POWERFUL...
...BECAUSE THAT'S ALL I HAVE.
WHAT DOES THAT MEAN?
HUH?
IT'S SIMPLE.
I'M NOTHING WITHOUT SPIRITUAL POWER.

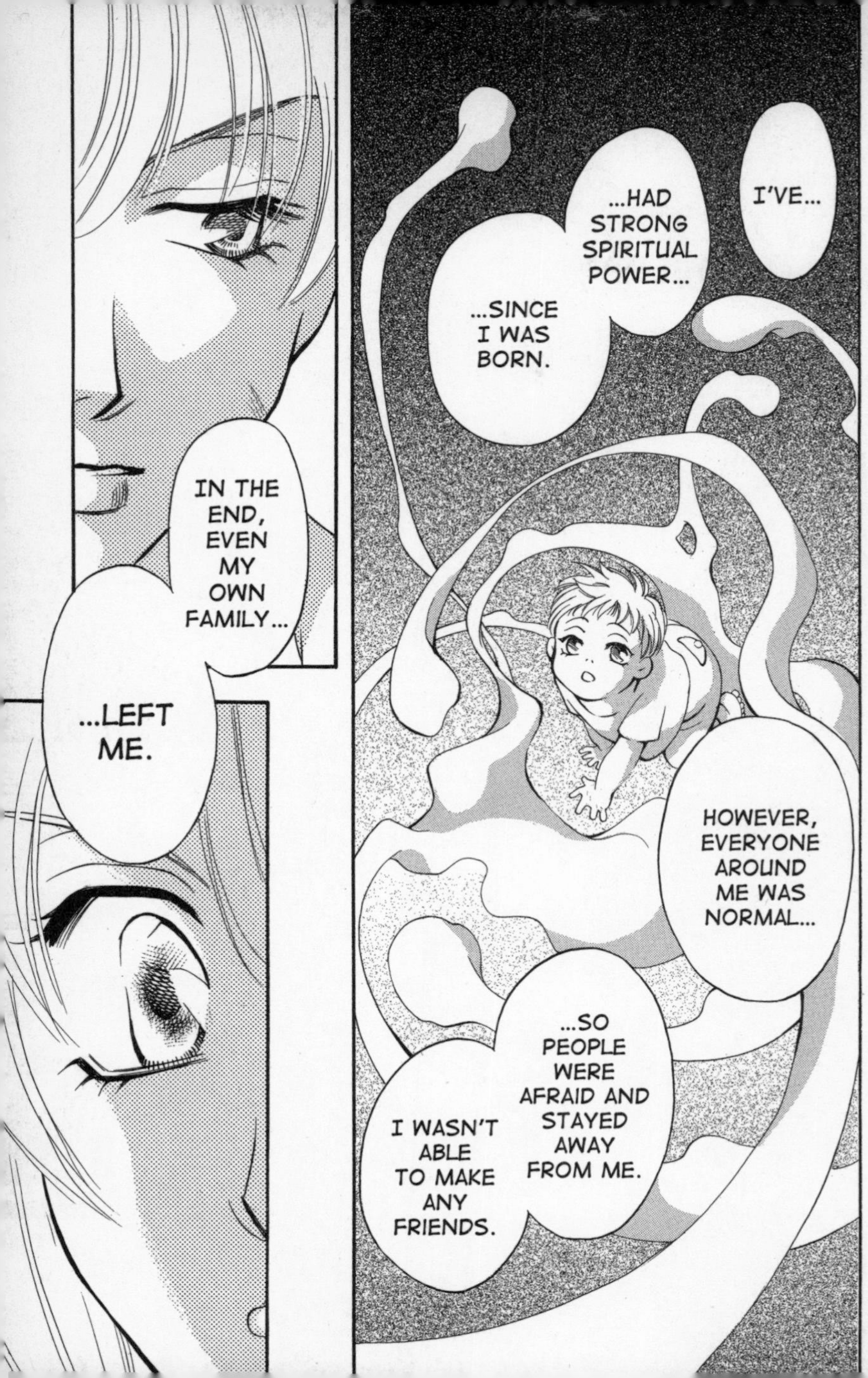
I'VE...
...HAD STRONG SPIRITUAL POWER...
...SINCE I WAS BORN.
HOWEVER, EVERYONE AROUND ME WAS NORMAL...
...SO PEOPLE WERE AFRAID AND STAYED AWAY FROM ME.
I WASN'T ABLE TO MAKE ANY FRIENDS.
IN THE END, EVEN MY OWN FAMILY...
...LEFT ME.

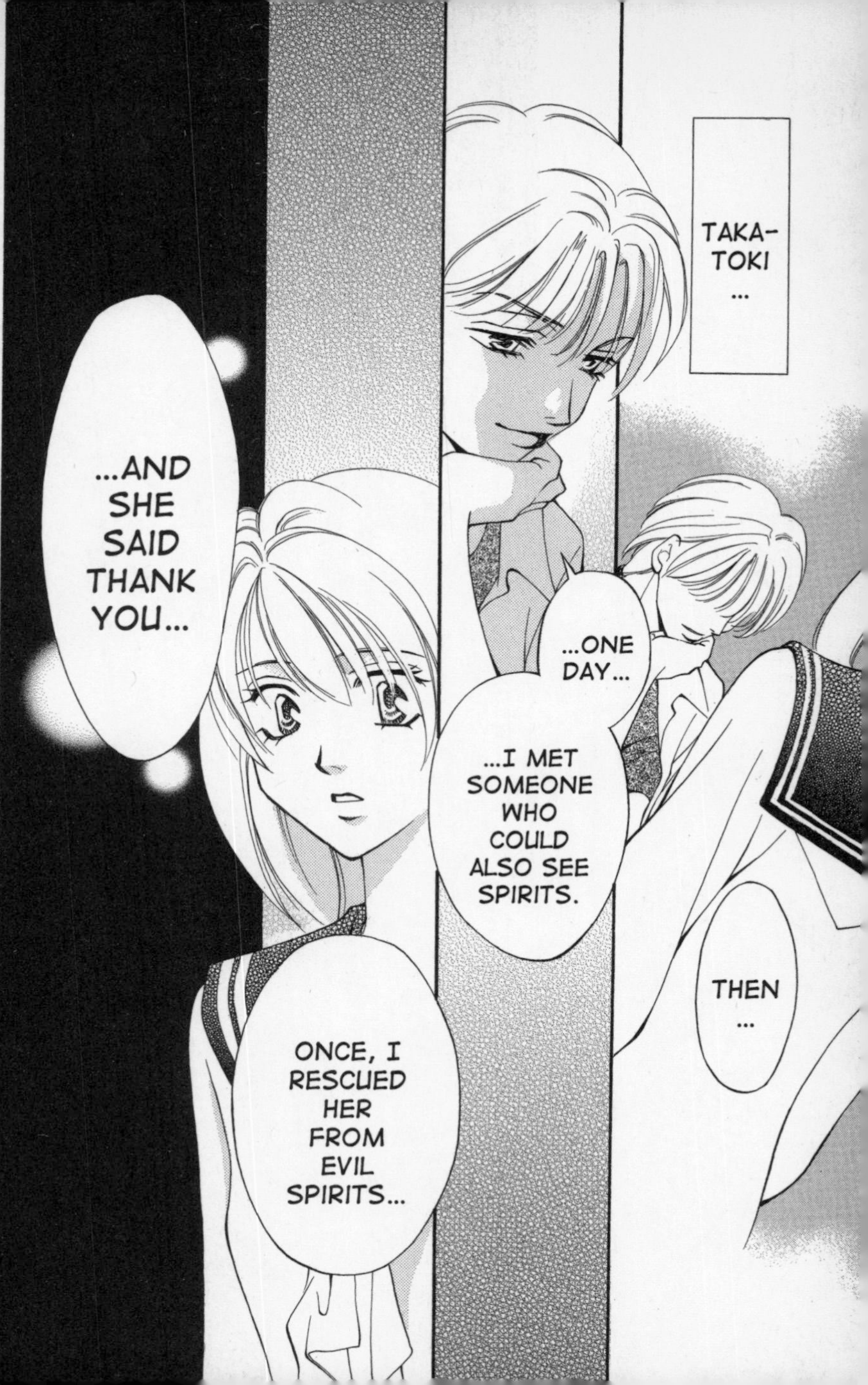
TAKA-TOKI ...
...ONE DAY...
...I MET SOMEONE WHO COULD ALSO SEE SPIRITS.
THEN ...
ONCE, I RESCUED HER FROM EVIL SPIRITS...
...AND SHE SAID THANK YOU...

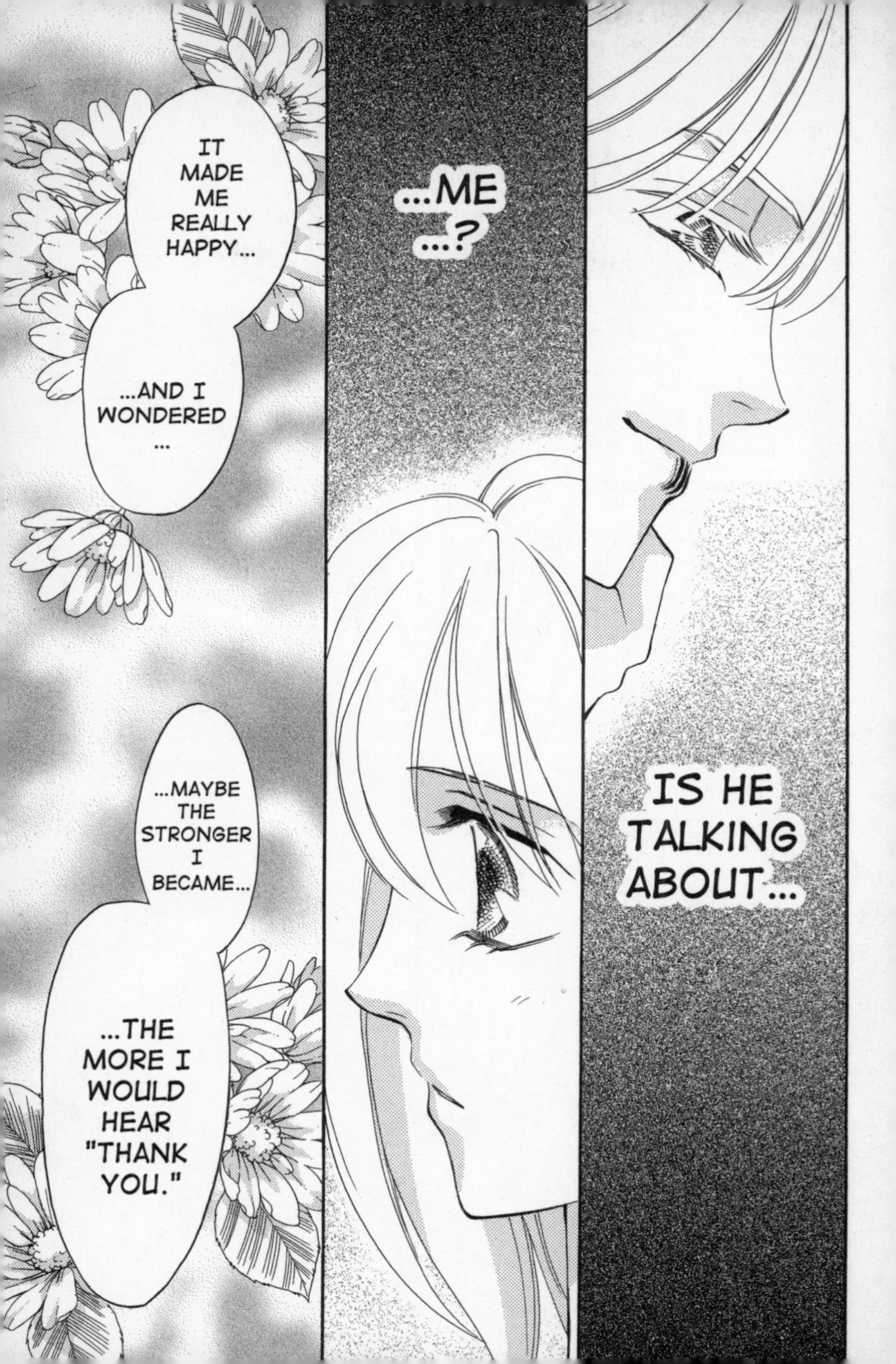
IS HE TALKING ABOUT...
...ME ...?
IT MADE ME REALLY HAPPY...
...AND I WONDERED ...
...MAYBE THE STRONGER I BECAME...
...THE MORE I WOULD HEAR "THANK YOU."

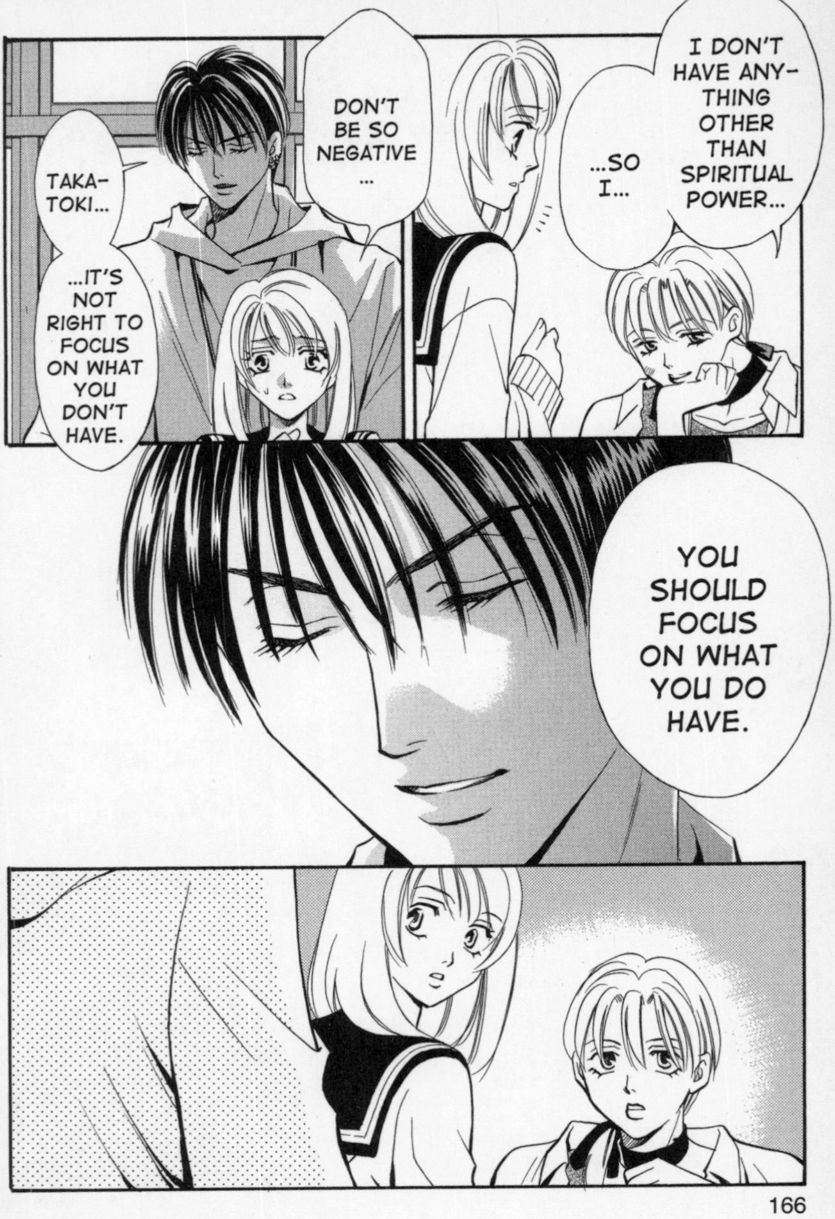
I DON'T HAVE ANY-THING OTHER THAN SPIRITUAL POWER...
...SO I...
DON'T BE SO NEGATIVE ...
TAKA-TOKI...
...IT'S NOT RIGHT TO FOCUS ON WHAT YOU DON'T HAVE.
YOU SHOULD FOCUS ON WHAT YOU DO HAVE.

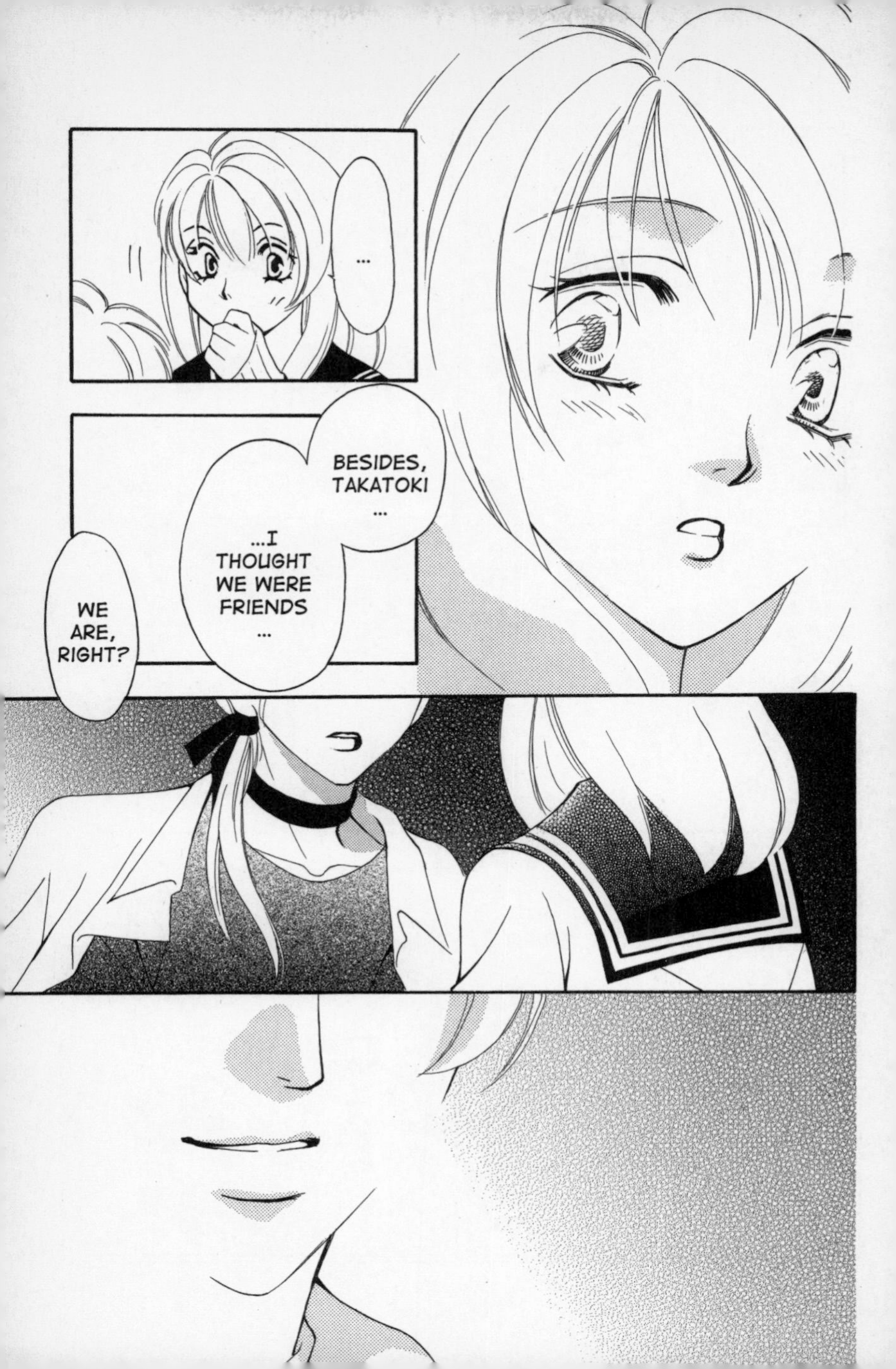
...
BESIDES, TAKATOKI ...
...I THOUGHT WE WERE FRIENDS ...
WE ARE, RIGHT?

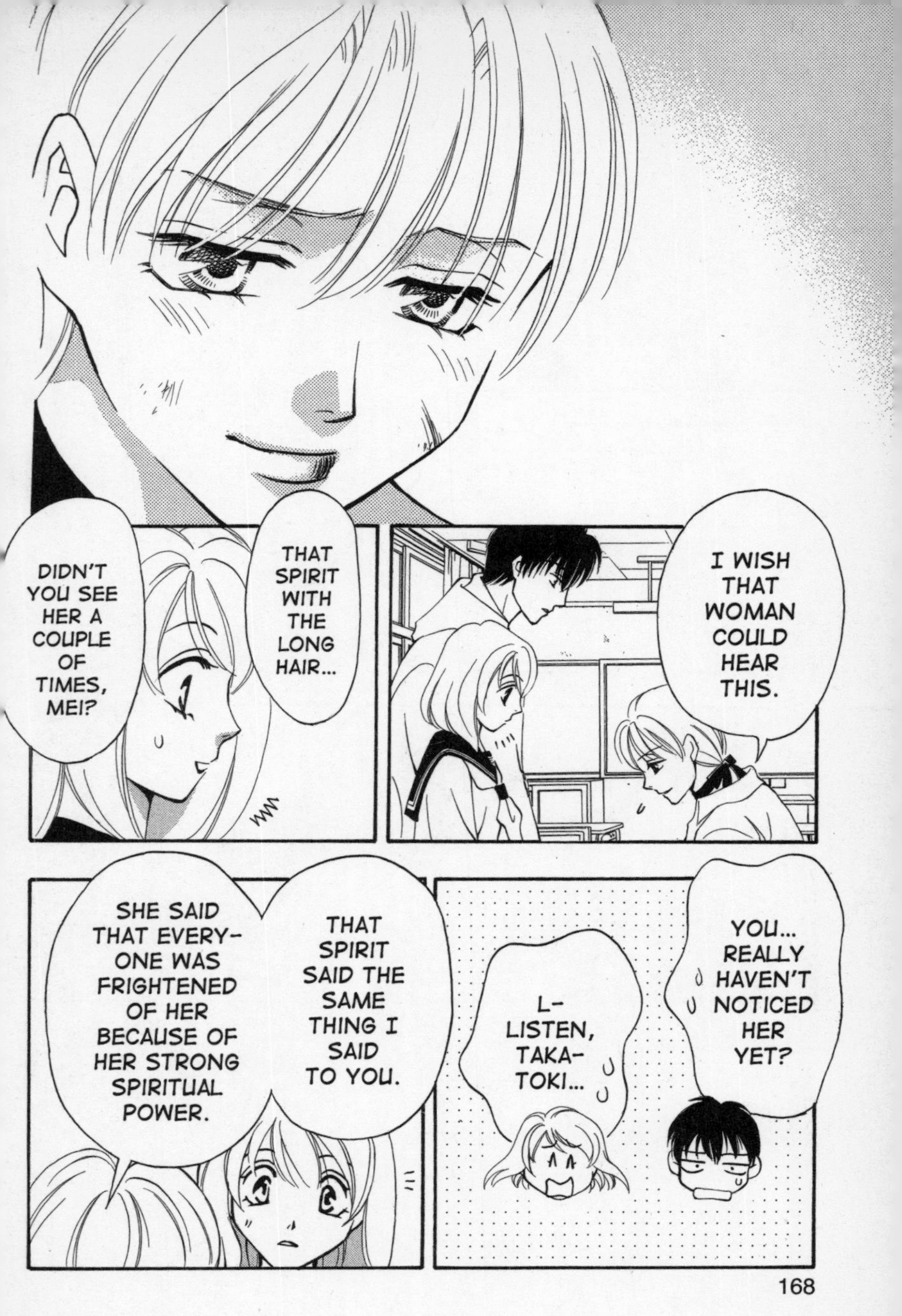
I WISH THAT WOMAN COULD HEAR THIS.
THAT SPIRIT WITH THE LONG HAIR...
DIDN'T YOU SEE HER A COUPLE OF TIMES, MEI?
YOU... REALLY HAVEN'T NOTICED HER YET?
L-LISTEN, TAKA-TOKI...
THAT SPIRIT SAID THE SAME THING I SAID TO YOU.
SHE SAID THAT EVERY-ONE WAS FRIGHTENED OF HER BECAUSE OF HER STRONG SPIRITUAL POWER.

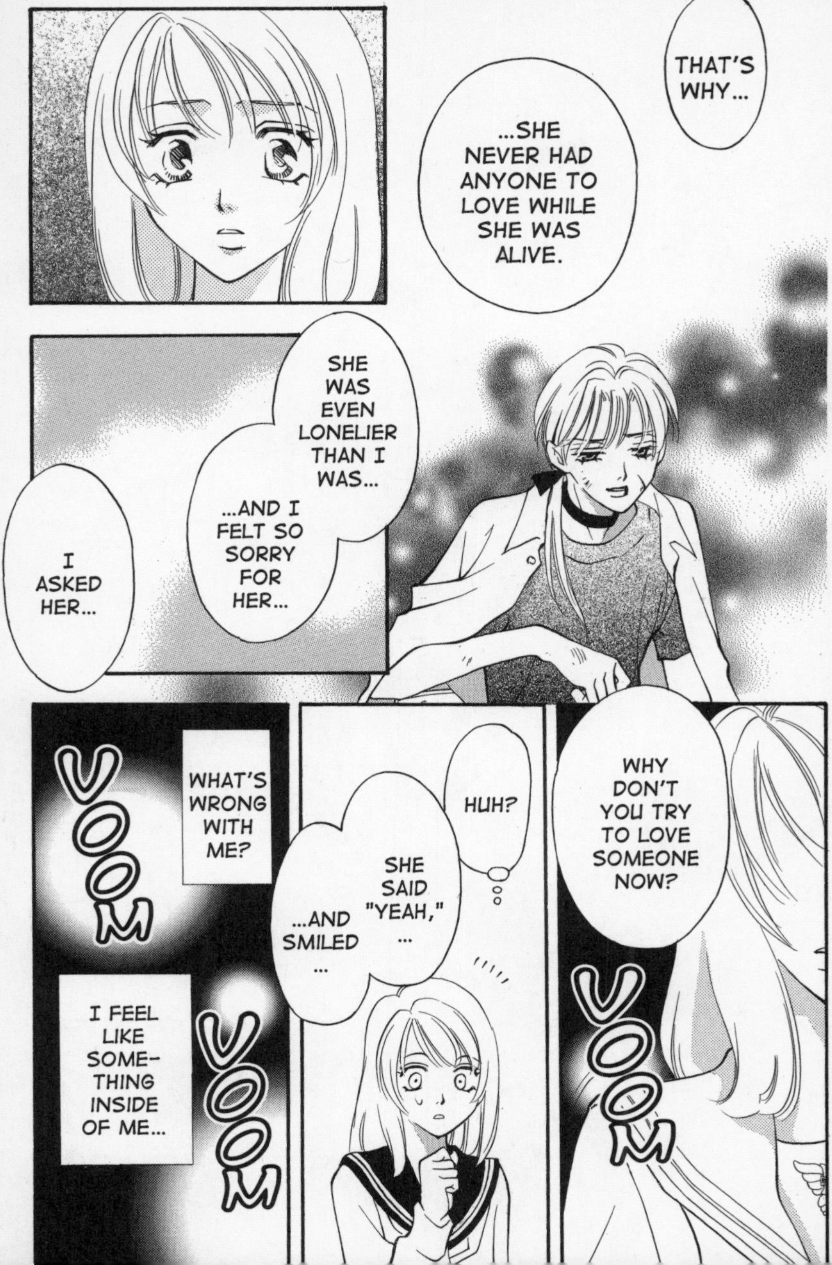
THAT'S WHY...
...SHE NEVER HAD ANYONE TO LOVE WHILE SHE WAS ALIVE.
SHE WAS EVEN LONELIER THAN I WAS...
...AND I FELT SO SORRY FOR HER...
I ASKED HER...
WHY DON'T YOU TRY TO LOVE SOMEONE NOW?
VOOM
HUH?
SHE SAID "YEAH," ...
...AND SMILED ...
WHAT'S WRONG WITH ME?
VOOM
I FEEL LIKE SOME-THING INSIDE OF ME...
VOOM

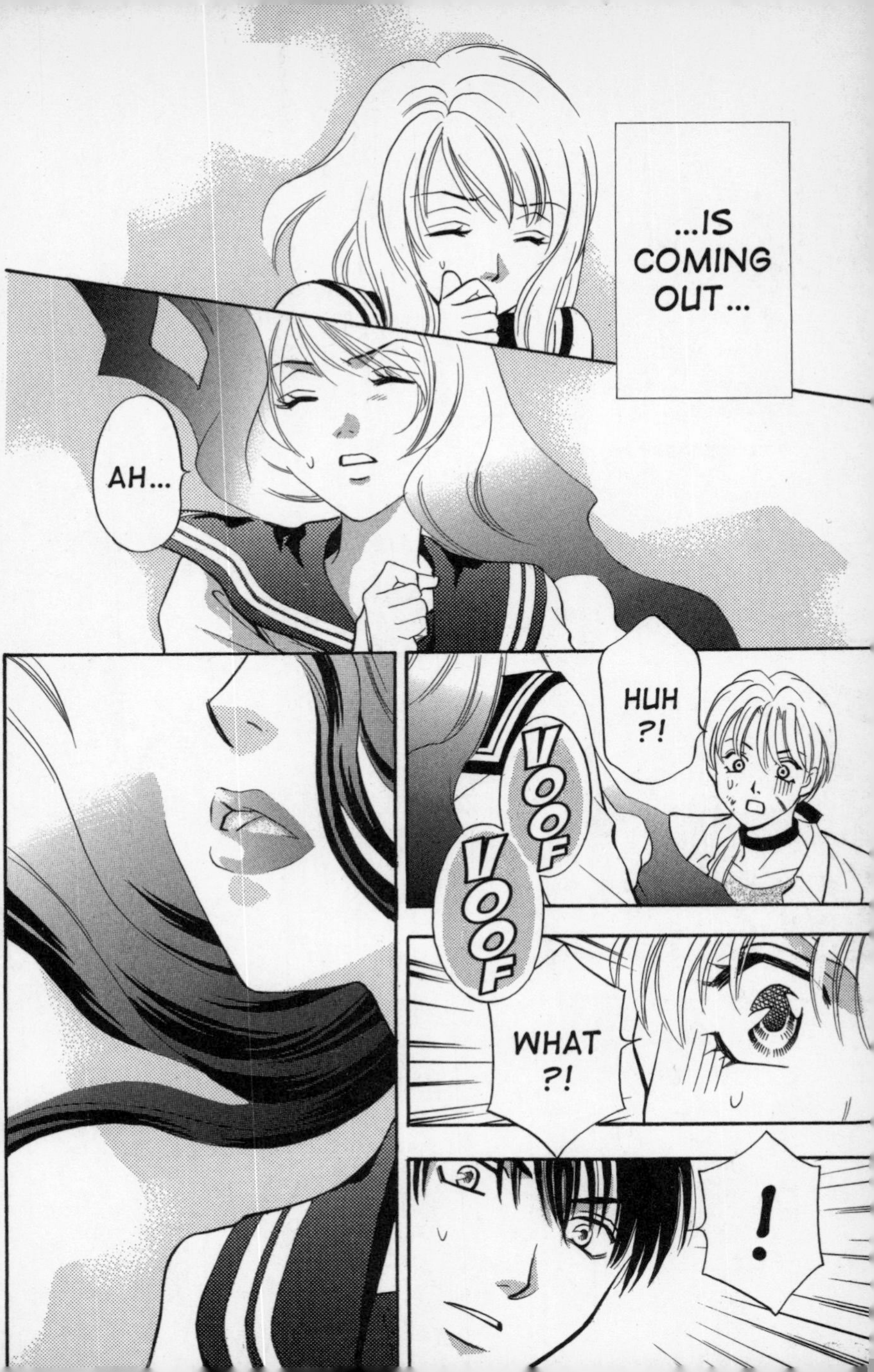
...IS COMING OUT...
AH...
HUH ?!
VOOF
VOOF
WHAT ?!
!

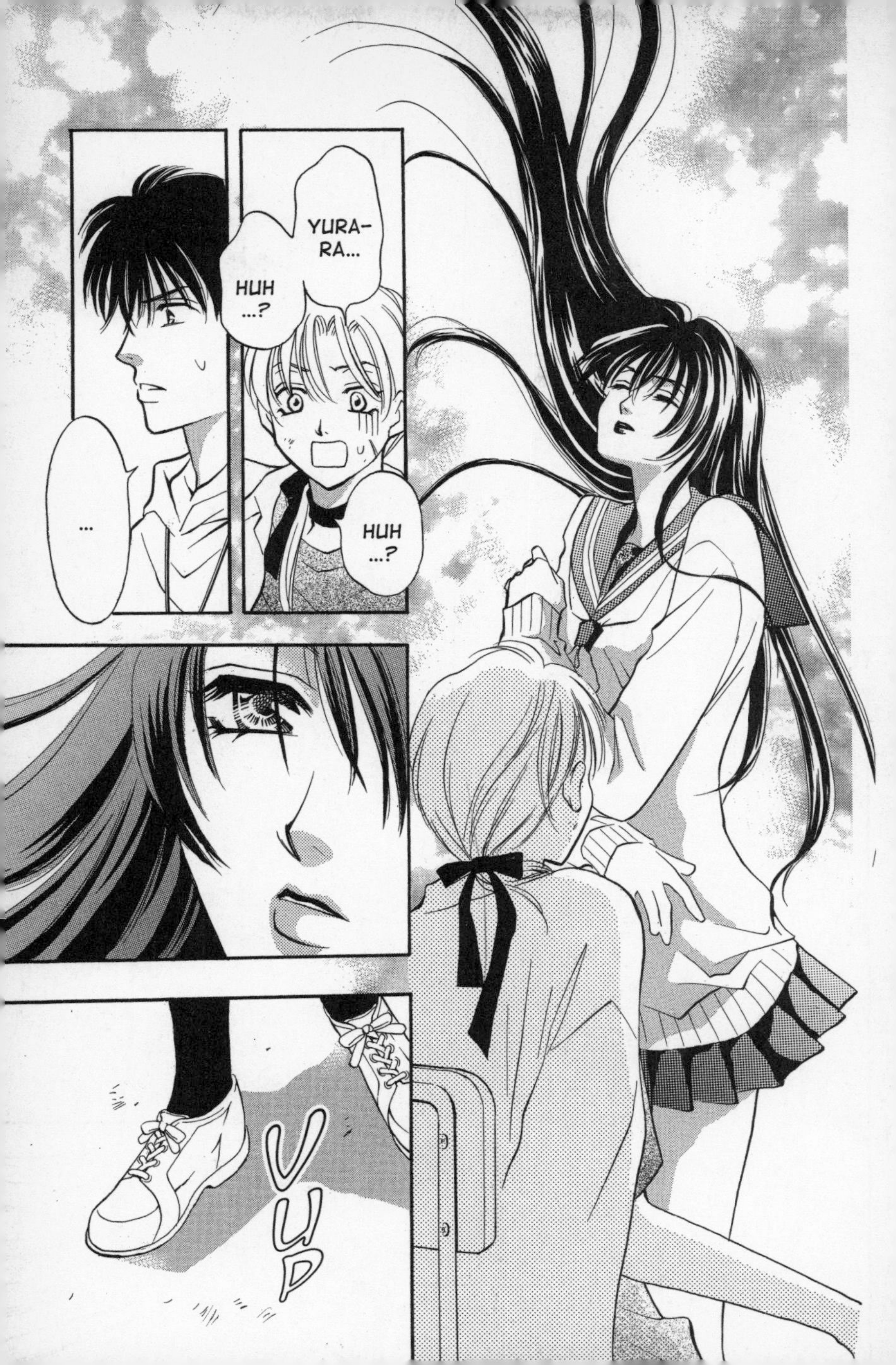
YURA-RA...
HUH ...?
HUH ...?
...
VUP

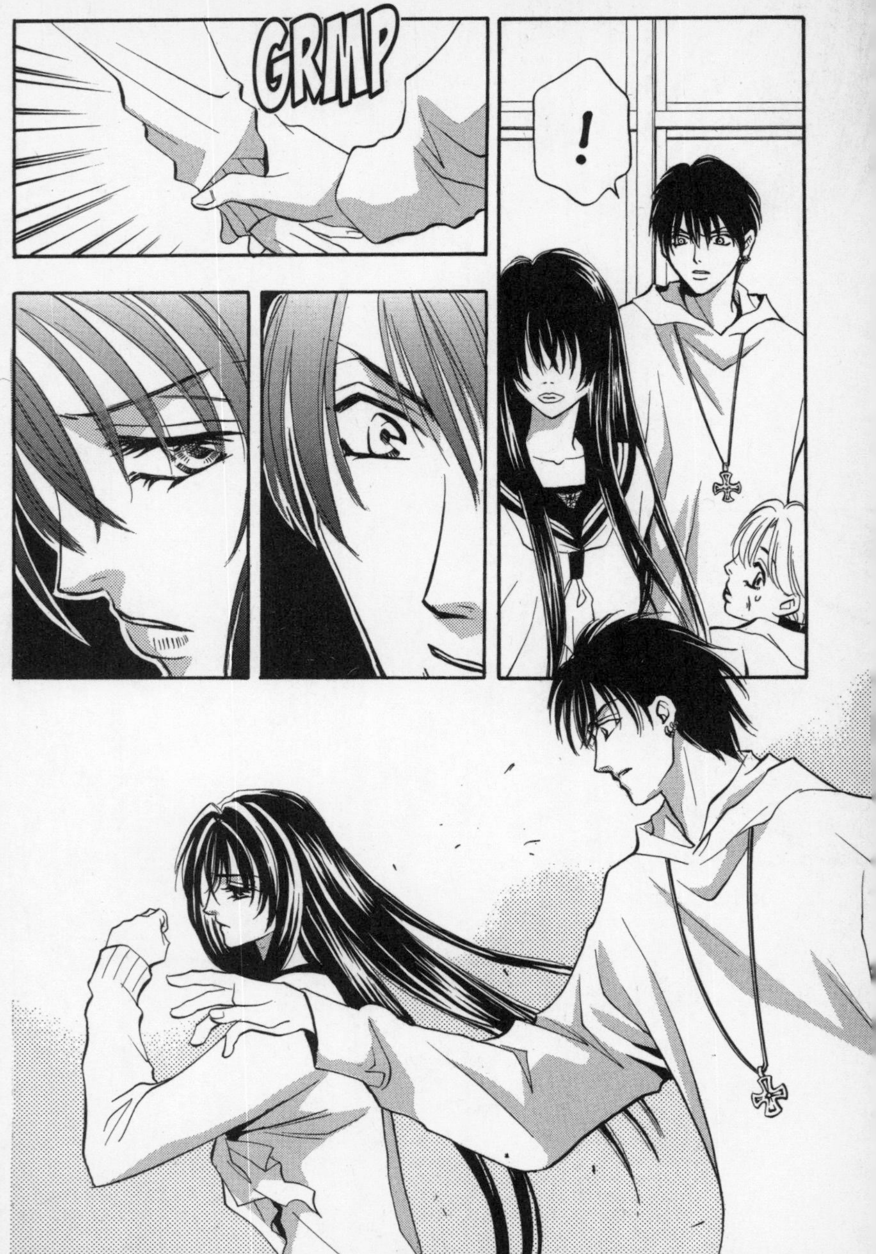
!
GRMP

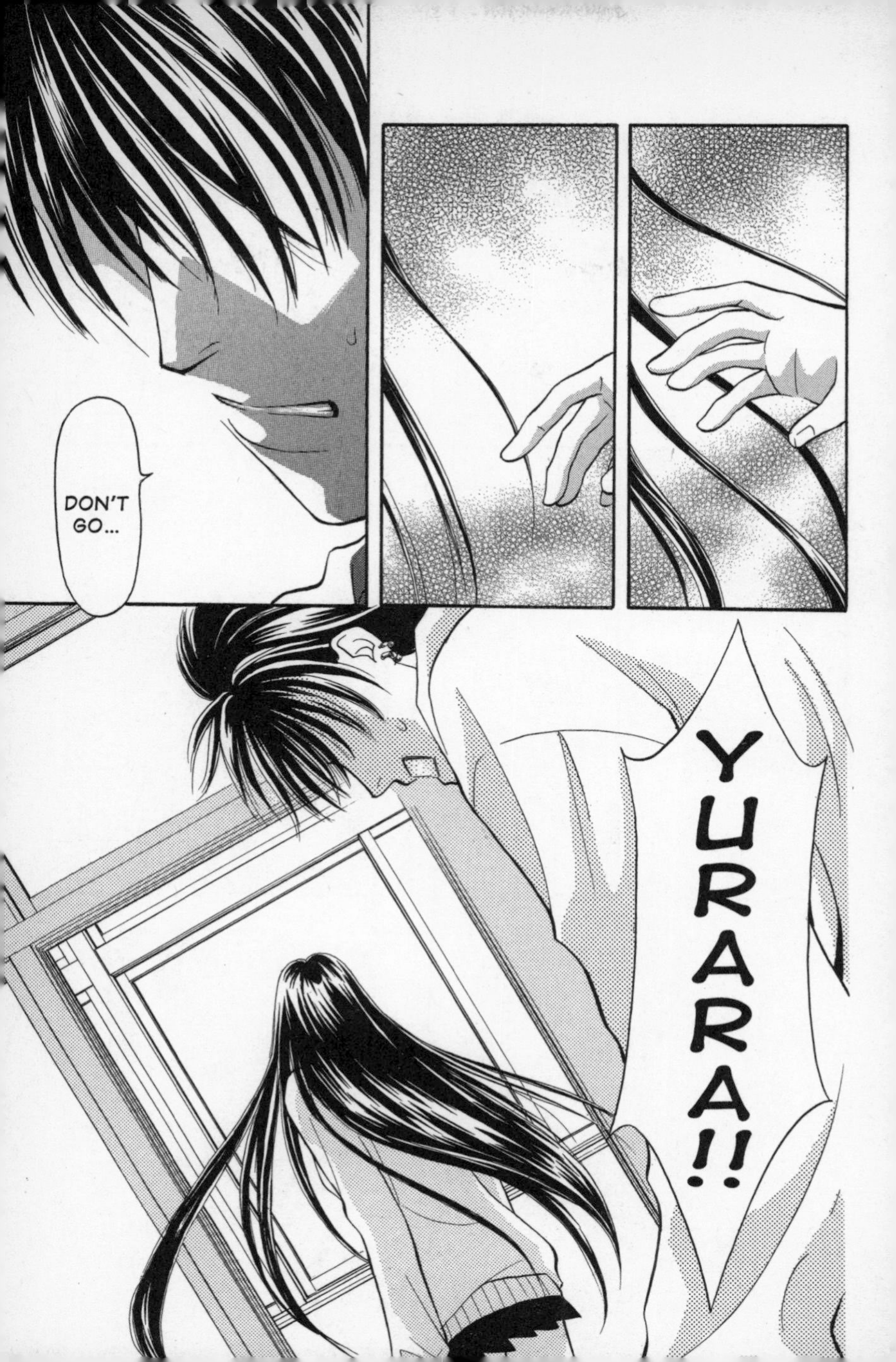
DON'T GO...
YURARA!!

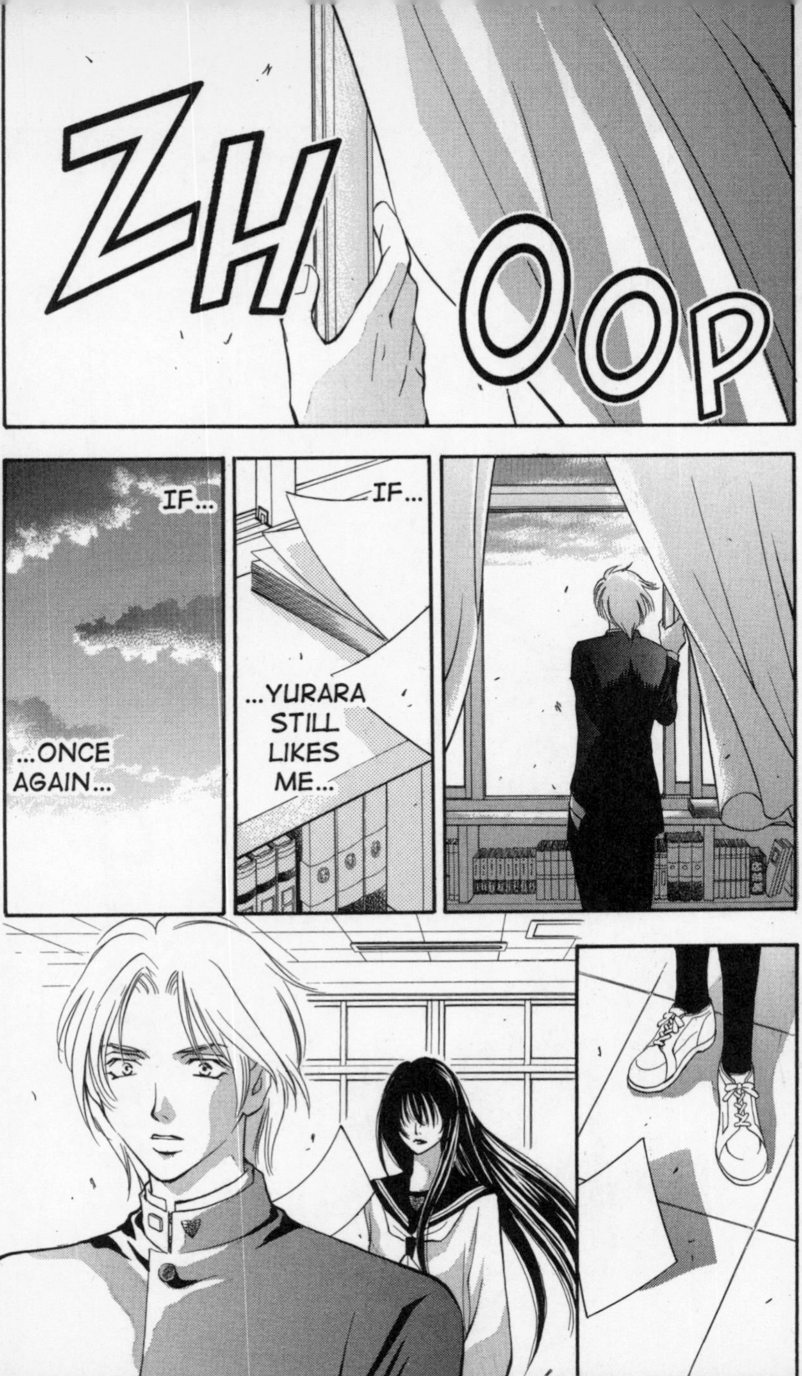
ZHOOP
IF...
...YURARA STILL LIKES ME...
IF...
...ONCE AGAIN...

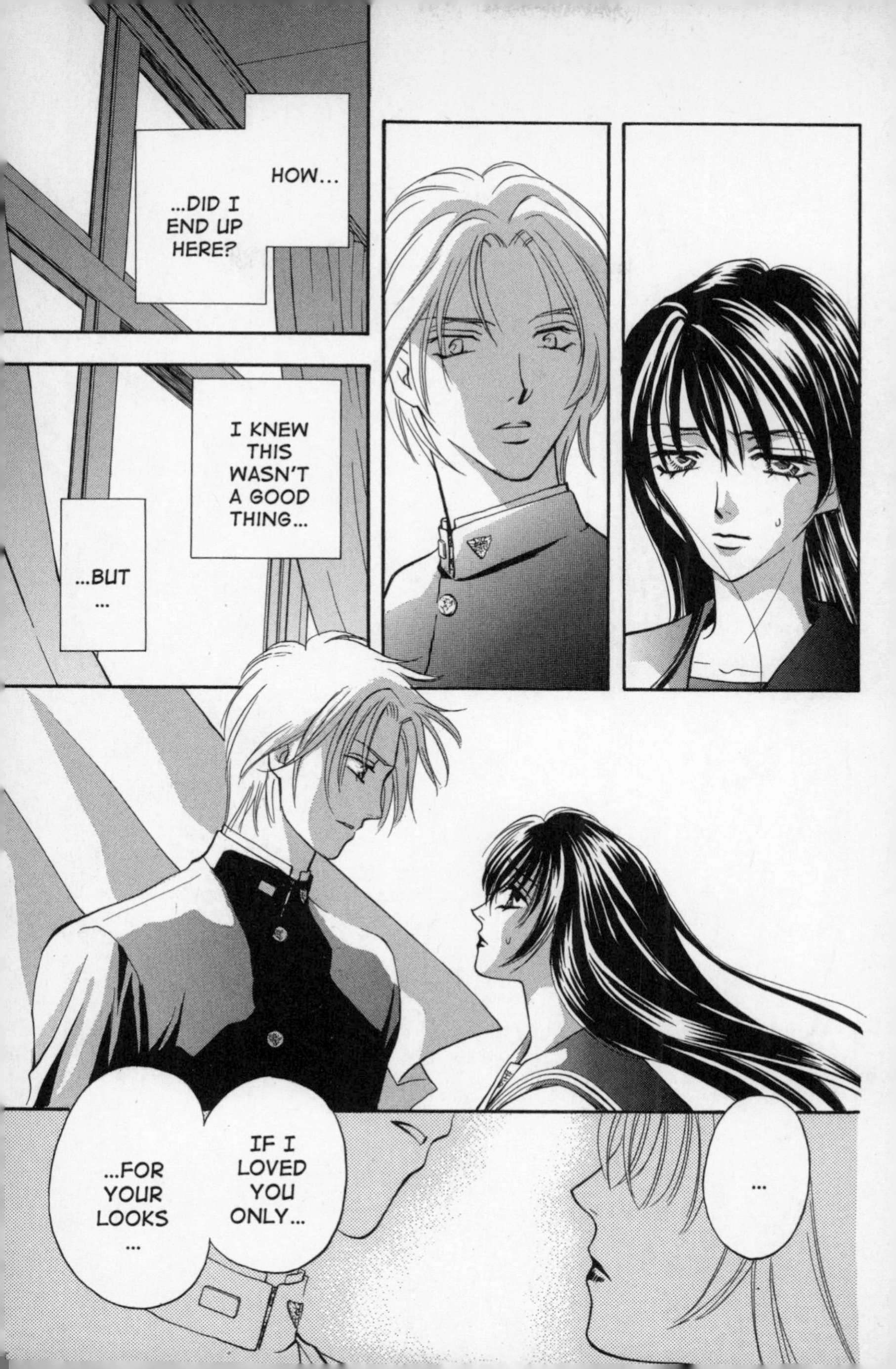
HOW...
...DID I END UP HERE?
I KNEW THIS WASN'T A GOOD THING...
...BUT ...
...
IF I LOVED YOU ONLY...
...FOR YOUR LOOKS ...

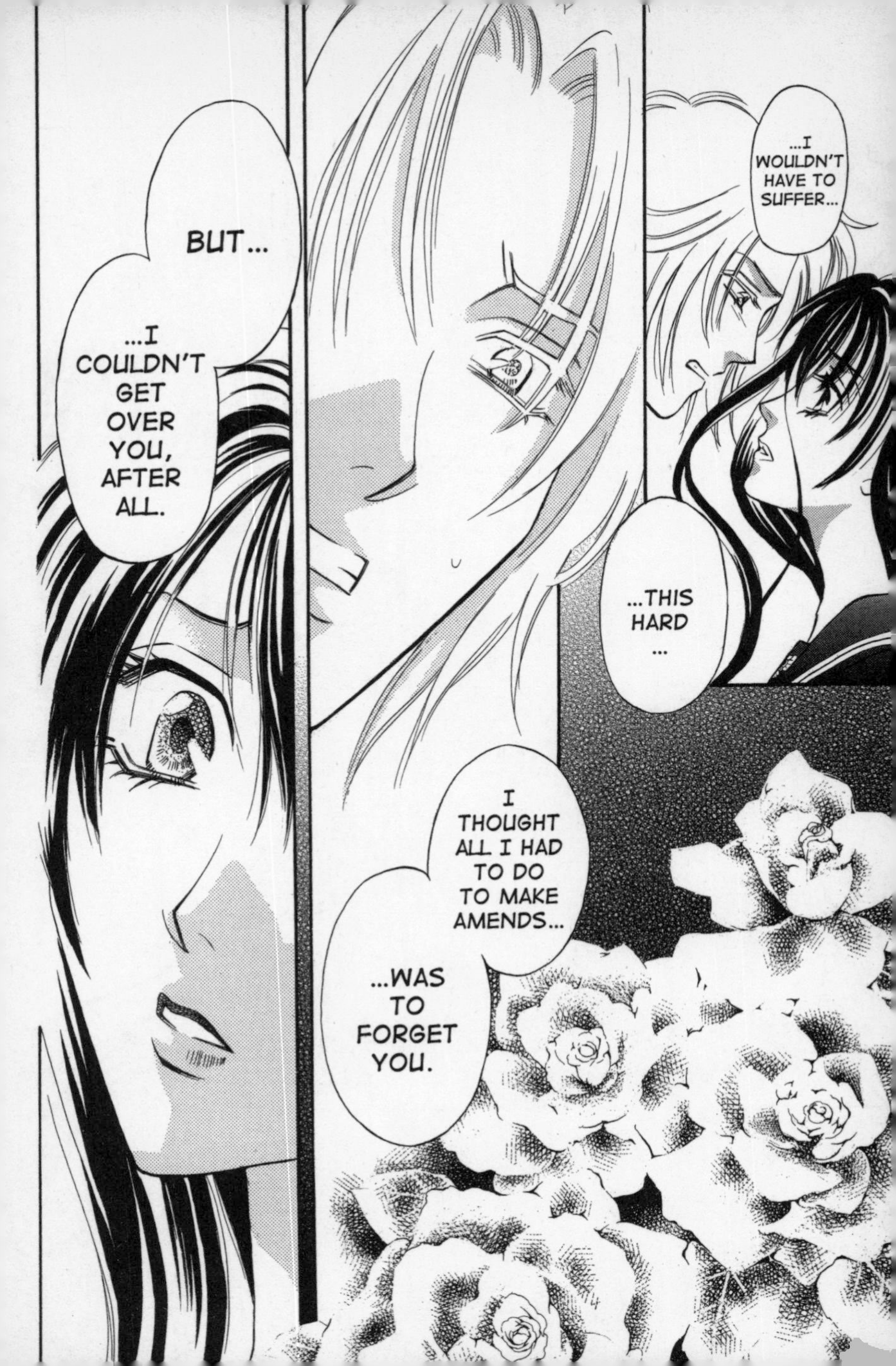
...I WOULDN'T HAVE TO SUFFER...
...THIS HARD ...
I THOUGHT ALL I HAD TO DO TO MAKE AMENDS...
...WAS TO FORGET YOU.
BUT...
...I COULDN'T GET OVER YOU, AFTER ALL.

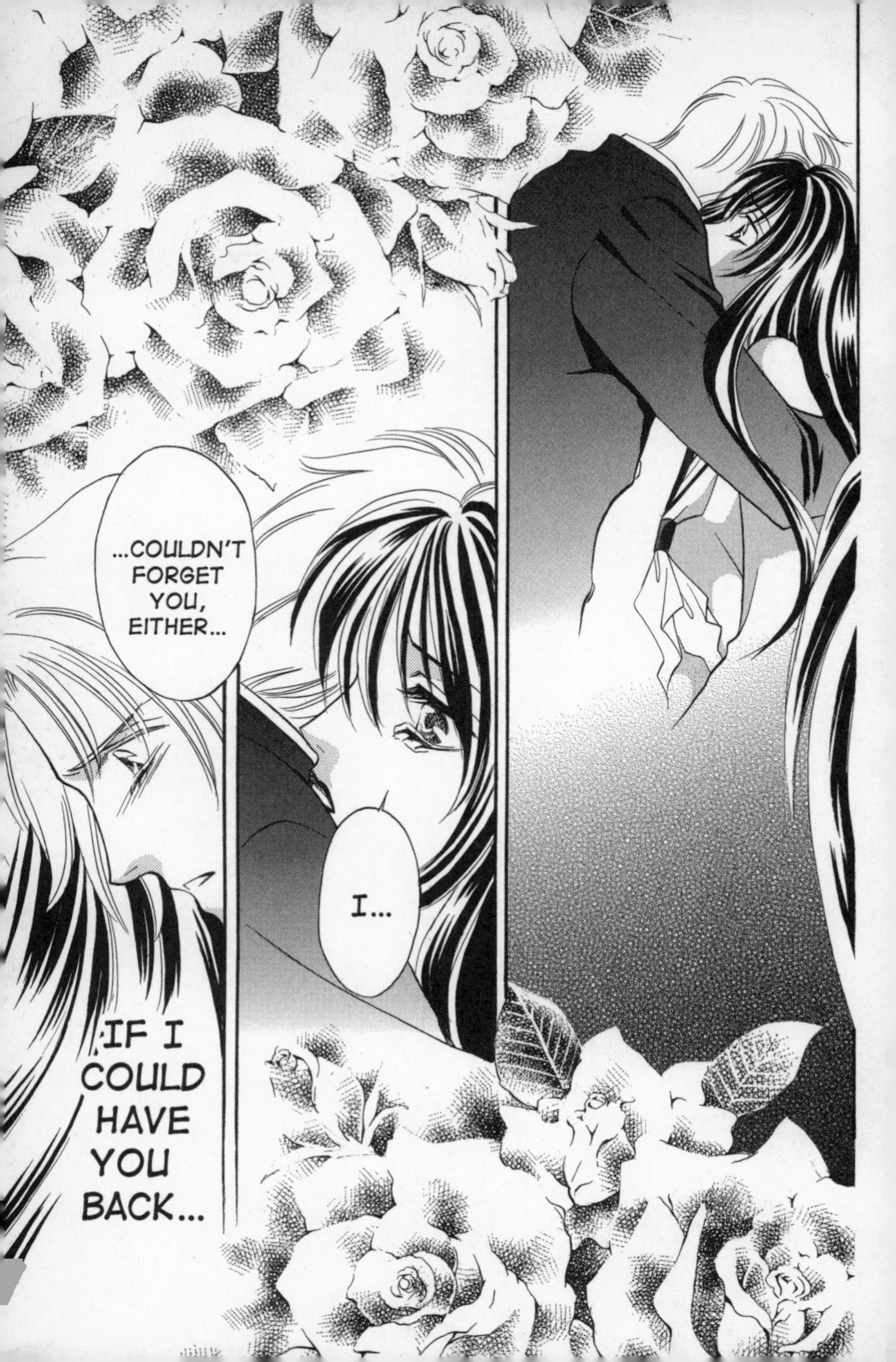
I...
...COULDN'T FORGET YOU, EITHER...
IF I COULD HAVE YOU BACK...

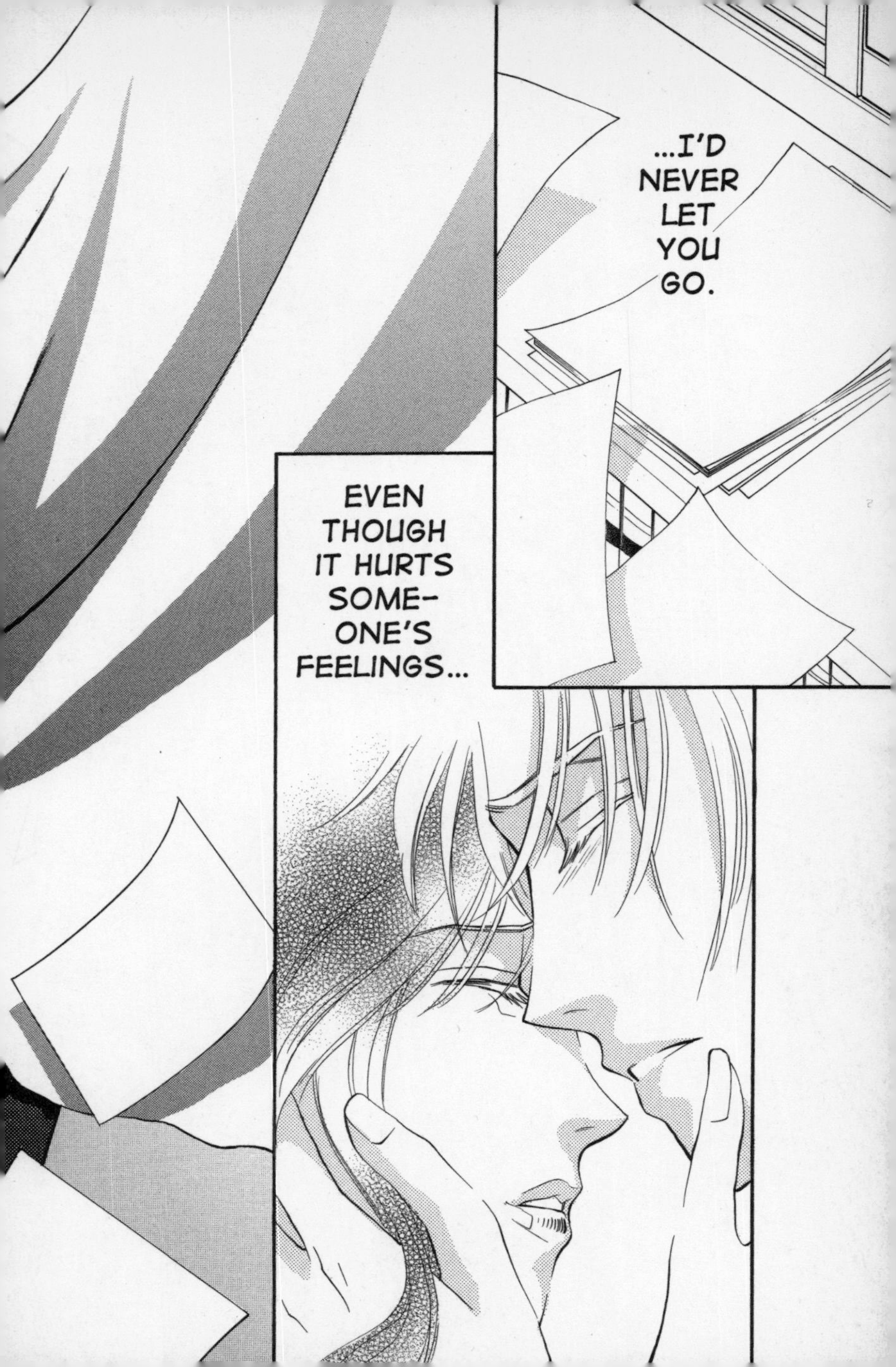
...I'D NEVER LET YOU GO.
EVEN THOUGH IT HURTS SOME-ONE'S FEELINGS...

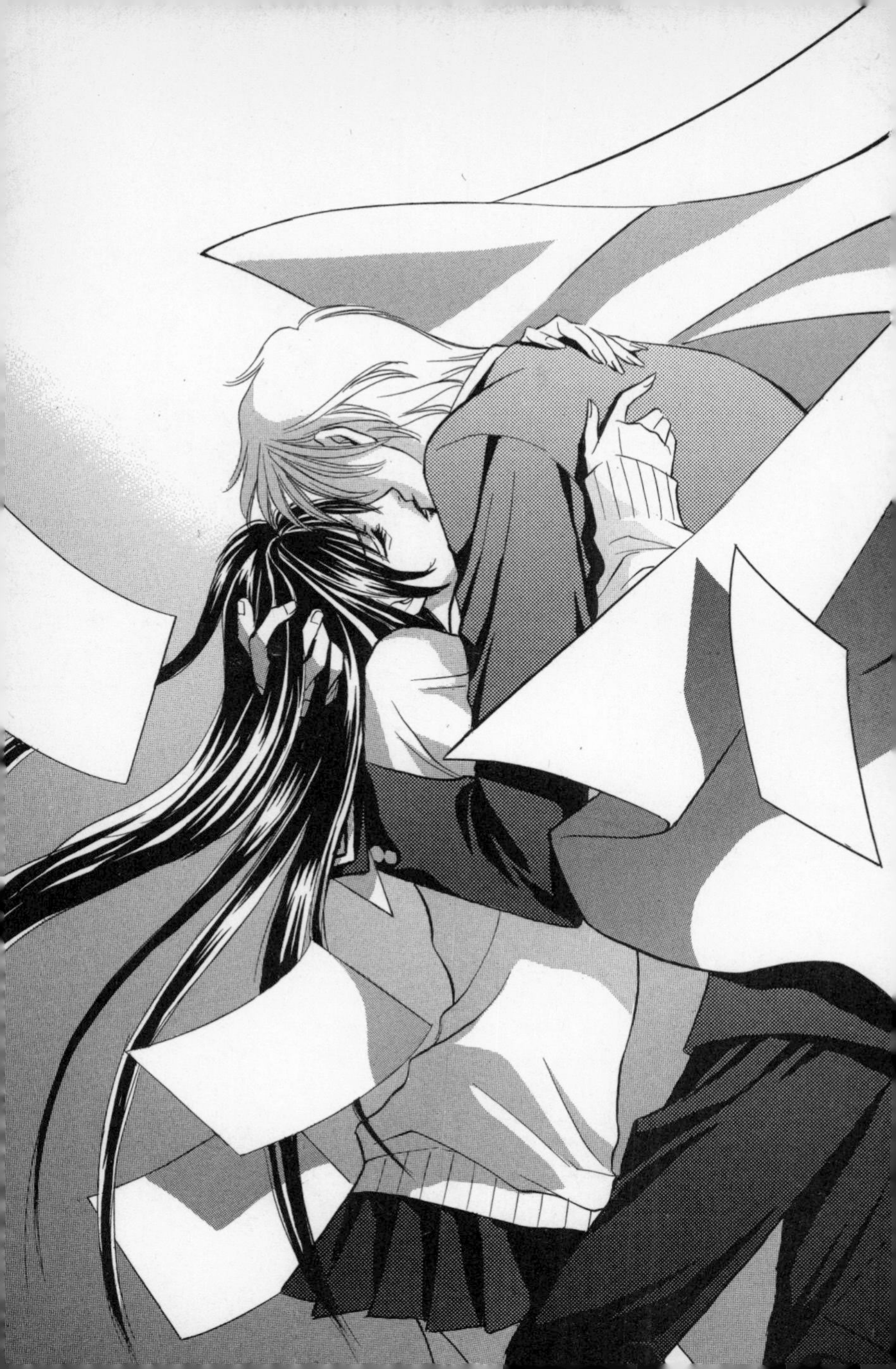

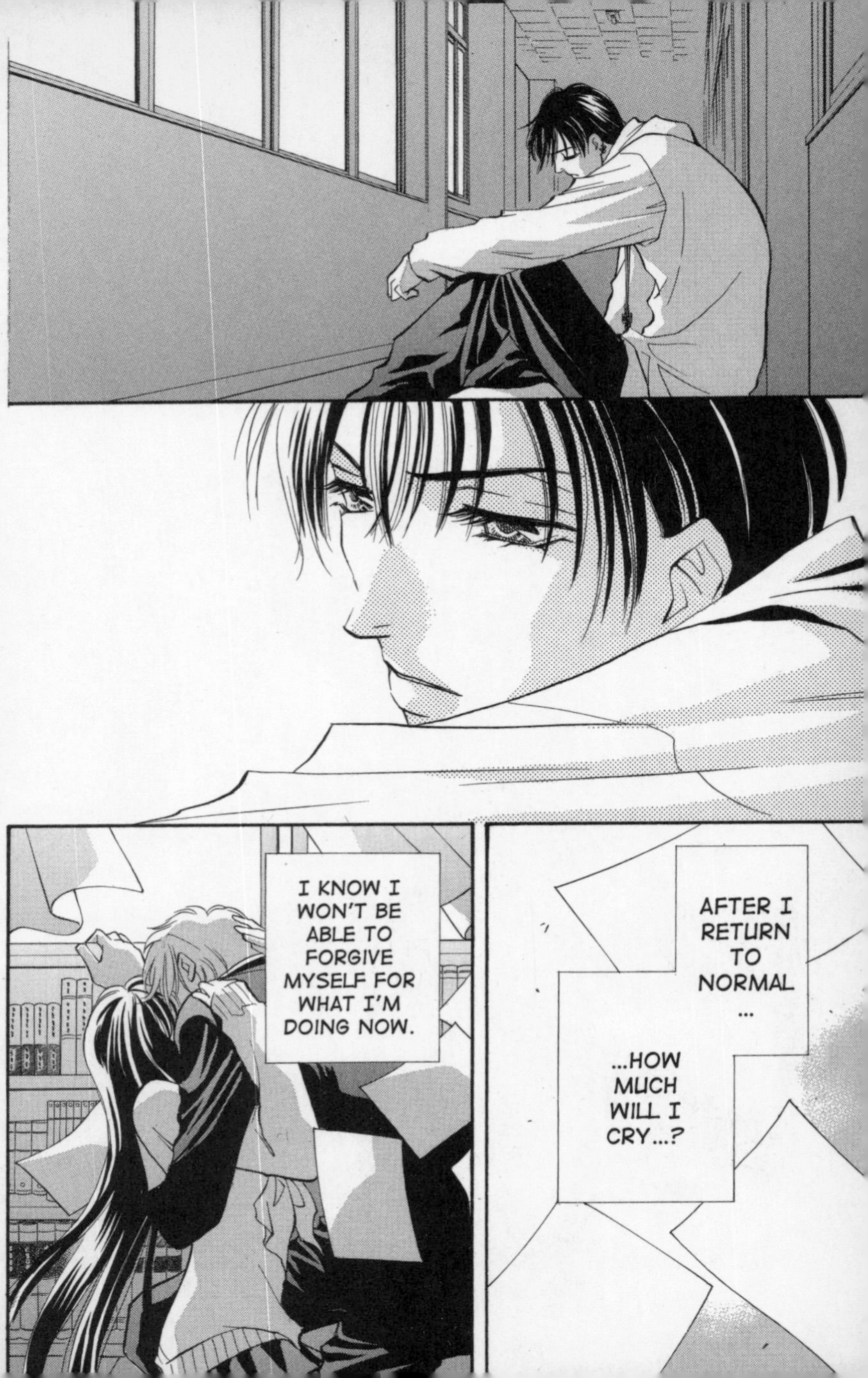
AFTER I RETURN TO NORMAL ...
...HOW MUCH WILL I CRY...?
I KNOW I WON'T BE ABLE TO FORGIVE MYSELF FOR WHAT I'M DOING NOW.

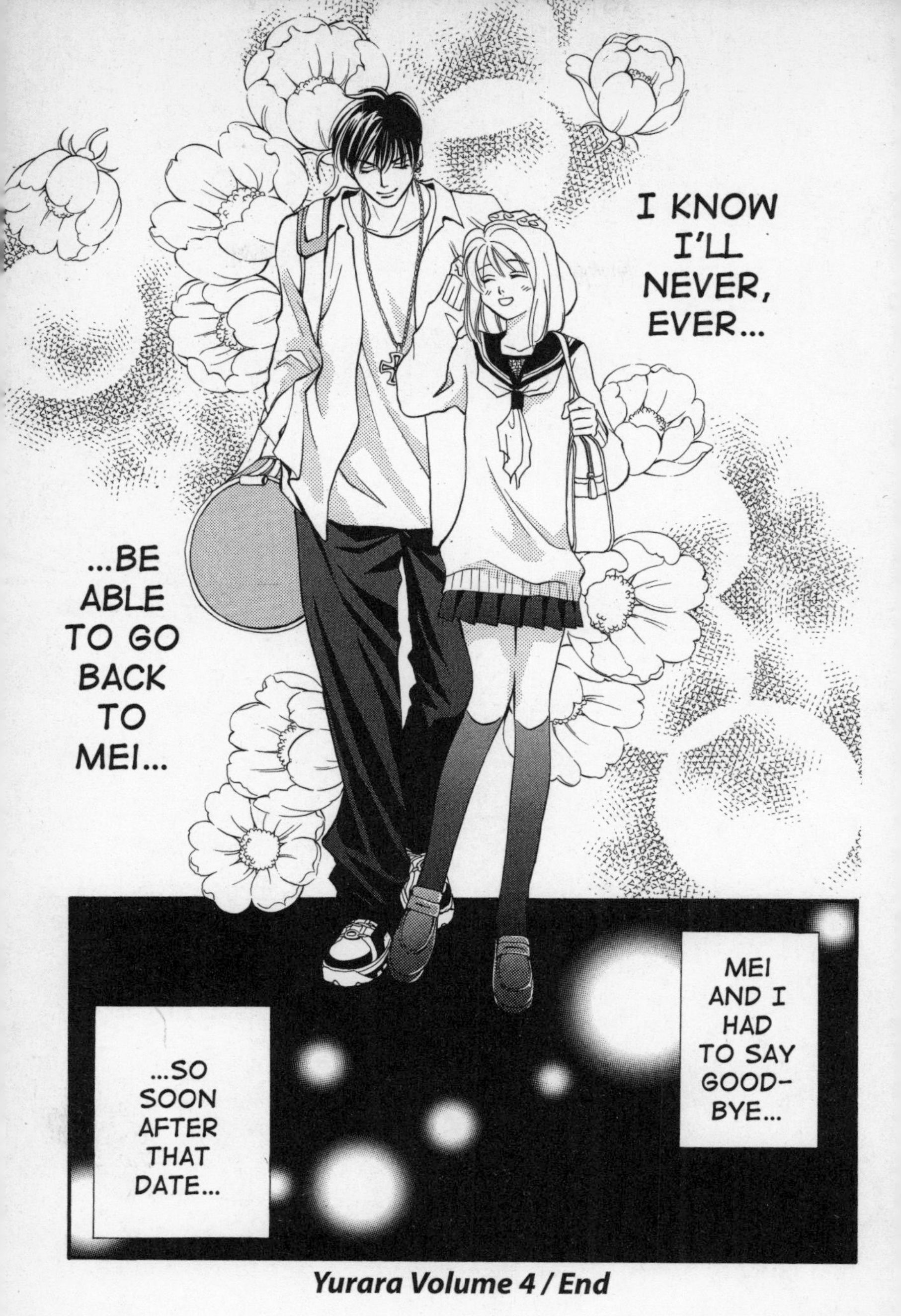
I KNOW I'LL NEVER, EVER...
...BE ABLE TO GO BACK TO MEI...
MEI AND I HAD TO SAY GOOD-BYE...
...SO SOON AFTER THAT DATE...

***Yurara* Volume 4 / End**

Chika Shiomi lives in the Aichi Prefecture
of Japan. She debuted with the manga
Todokeru Toki o Sugitemo (Even If the
Time for Deliverance Passes), and her work
is currently running in two magazines,
Bessatsu Hana to Yume and *Mystery Bonita*.
She loves reading manga, traveling, and
listening to music by Aerosmith, Hyde, and
Guns N' Roses. Her favorite artists include
Michelangelo, Hokusai, Bernini, and Gustav
Klimt.

Shojo Beat

Yurara

Vol. 4
The Shojo Beat Manga Edition

STORY & ART BY
CHIKA SHIOMI

English Adaptation/Heidi Vivolo
Translation/JN Productions
Touch-up Art & Lettering/Freeman Wong
Design/Izumi Hirayama
Editor/Mike Montesa

VP, Production/Alvin Lu
VP, Publishing Licensing/Rika Inouye
VP, Sales & Product Marketing/Gonzalo Ferreyra
VP, Creative/Linda Espinosa
Publisher/Hyoe Narita

Printed in Canada

Published by VIZ Media, LLC
P.O. Box 77064
San Francisco, CA 94107

Shojo Beat Manga Edition
10 9 8 7 6 5 4 3 2
First printing, March 2008
Second printing, February 2009

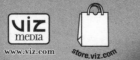

www.viz.com
store.viz.com